PAUL STEVEN

PAUL STEVEN

TPM IN PROCESS INDUSTRIES

TPM IN PROCESS INDUSTRIES

Edited by Tokutarō Suzuki

Originally published by the
Japan Institute of Plant Maintenance

Productivity Press
Portland, Oregon

Originally published as *Sōchi Kōgyō no TPM*, copyright © 1992 by Japan Institute of Plant Maintenance.

English translation copyright © 1994 by Productivity Press, a division of Productivity, Inc. Translated by John Loftus.

Productivity Press
P.O. Box 13390
Portland, OR 97213-0390
United States of America
Telephone: 503-235-0600
Telefax: 503-235-0909
E-mail: service@ppress.com

Cover design by Jay Cosnett
Typesetting and graphics by Caroline Kutil, Michele Saar, and Gayle Asmus
Printed and bound by Edwards Brothers in the United States of America

Library of Congress Cataloging-in-Publication Data

TPM in process industries / edited by Tokutarō Suzuki.
      p.   cm.
      Includes bibliographical references and index.
      ISBN 1-56327-036-6 :
      1. Plant maintenance—Management. 2. Total productive maintenance.
  I. Suzuki, Tokutarō.
  TS192.T72 1994
  658.2′02—dc20
                                           94-9749
                                           CIP

02 01 00 99 98 97   12 11 10 9 8 7 6 5 4

Contents

v

Publisher's Message

TPM improves business results dramatically and fosters safe, pleasant, and productive workplaces by optimizing the relationships between the people who work there and the equipment they rely on. In recent years, many process industries in Japan have profited from TPM, and more recently, divisions of American companies like Dupont, Exxon, and Kodak have been making TPM work in their specialized process environments. To be cost-effective, process plants must operate continuously for long periods. Accidents and breakdowns involving even one piece of equipment can shut down an entire plant and endanger life and the environment. Financial losses can be devastating. Process industries need a collaborative equipment management system like TPM that can guarantee safe, stable operation at low cost.

Over the years, it has been an abiding pleasure to watch the evolution and maturation of effective improvement strategies like TPM in Japan. We are indebted to the Japan Institute of Plant Maintenance for their continuing commitment to document the *processes* behind the excellent results achieved in TPM companies. Translating new materials as they become available, we invariably see new concepts and methods coming forward to fill gaps in earlier iterations.

TPM in Process Industries, edited by Tokutarō Suzuki, distills almost a decade of Japanese field experience tailoring the TPM methods and concepts developed in the fabrication and assembly industry to the process environment. Like the original *TPM Development Program, TPM in Process Industries* includes chapters on each of the fundamental TPM activities. However, since *TPM Development* was first published in Japan in 1982, many new concepts and refinements have been added to the basic program, in addition to the new focus on process environments. This book, published in Japan in 1992, includes chapters on relatively new topics, such as quality maintenance (QM) and safety programming. Moreover, the chapters on programs like planned maintenance and early management (MP design) are clearer and more comprehensive, and reflect 10 years' additional observation and application. Chapter 12 on measurement and management indicators will be particularly helpful for managers looking for ways to express TPM results more effectively.

Like many of its predecessors in our TPM series, this book answers questions readers have been asking since the basic text, *TPM Development Program*, was first published in English in 1989. For example, the types of losses encountered in process industries differ in striking ways from those found in fabrication and assembly industries. We have often received questions about categorizing, measuring, and evaluating loss in process environments. This book details for the first time how *overall plant effectiveness* (OPE) is calculated and reviews, with numerous examples, the philosophy and strategies for loss reduction in a process environment.

Other frequent questions concern the methods for promoting the most fundamental of TPM programs — cross-functional project team activity to reduce targeted equipment-related losses. In this book, these activities are referred to as "focused improvement" because in process industries, the priority for these intensive team activities is raising the effectiveness, not just of individual equipment items, but of an entire process or plant. Individual projects may be "focused" on bottleneck processes or on the need for process simplification, for example. A lengthy chapter by JIPM consultant Kōichi Nakazato explains how this activity can be effectively planned and coordinated on a plantwide scale — information that will be helpful to TPM managers in both process and discrete manufacturing environments.

Another important building block in TPM development is autonomous maintenance performed by the production department. The principal goals and activities of autonomous maintenance are the same in any manufacturing environment — to change people's understanding and work habits using equipment as instructional tools, while moving closer to optimal performance by restoring and controlling deterioration and correcting abnormalities. Process industries, however, have had to adapt certain aspects of autonomous maintenance planning and program focus. The key question in process environments is: how can operators effectively carry out the cleaning, inspection, lubrication, and improvement activities associated with autonomous maintenance when the number, variety, process complexity, and size of equipment and plant are so high compared to the number of operators? This book reveals how to overcome a low operator-to-equipment ratio with detailed practical suggestions for limiting the equipment to be included in the program, carefully planning and coordinating pilot activity and lateral deployment, and carrying out certain steps concurrently.

In American TPM implementations, autonomous maintenance is often limited to "task-transfer" — training and reallocating to operators PM work *required for equipment in its current state.* In the more progressive approach recommended in this book, activities focus first on understanding and improving conditions, then on defining and reallocating work. As equipment is restored and causes of deterioration are understood and controlled through maintainability improvements, the required work changes.

This is particularly important in view of many companies' long-range plans to minimize operating personnel and increase unattended operation. Short-term activities may involve operators in carrying out and improving the efficiency of periodic maintenance and repairs. The long-term focus of a mature TPM program, however, should be improving reliability and maintainability so that future operator responsibilities can conceivably consist only of inspection.

We are particularly grateful to the team of authors, all full-time consultants with the Japan Institute of Plant Maintenance, for their willingness to document and share their implementation experience. Their insights are based on many years' work with many different companies. We extend special thanks to Mr. Yoshiki Takahashi, Vice-president and Secretary General of JIPM, for granting permission to produce this English edition, and to John Loftus for his excellent translation.

Thanks also to the Productivity Press staff and freelancers who helped create this book: Julie Zinkus for copyediting and proofreading; Catchword, Inc. for proofreading and indexing; Karen Jones and Jennifer Albert for editorial management; Bill Stanton and Susan Swanson for design and production management; Caroline Kutil, Michele Saar, Gayle Asmus, and Harrison Typesetting, Inc. for typesetting and art preparation; Jay Cosnett for cover design.

Norman Bodek
Chairman, Productivity, Inc.

Connie Dyer
Director of TPM Research and Development
Productivity, Inc.

Preface

Over two decades have passed since the Japan Institute of Plant Maintenance (JIPM) began promoting TPM. Although TPM developed in the fabrication and assembly industries, it is now actively adopted in process industries. Japanese companies introducing TPM are currently split approximately fifty-fifty between the two types of industry.*

TPM was originally introduced by equipment users but is now being implemented increasingly by equipment manufacturers. It is also extending beyond production departments to encompass R & D, administrative and support departments, and sales. Interest in TPM is also growing rapidly around the world. People everywhere are beginning to realize that TPM is one of the keys to high productivity, excellent quality, low costs, and short lead times.

JIPM's original approach to implementing TPM was described at length in *TPM Development Program* (published in English in 1989 by Productivity Press). The program described in that book was slanted toward the fabrication and assembly industries, however, and had to be adapted to fit process industry needs. To reflect these adaptations and recent TPM developments in both types of industry, JIPM decided to prepare two new editions specifically tailored to each industry.

The implementation program described in the process-industry edition was compiled with process-industry characteristics in mind. The book identifies eight major losses common to all process industries in Chapter 2 and describes the thinking behind identifying and eliminating process and equipment failures. It also explains the application of P-M analysis in focused improvement projects, using actual process-industry examples in Chapter 3.

---

* Editor's note: In the United States, slightly over one-third of surveyed companies implementing TPM in 1990 were in process industries. Anecdotal evidence today suggests that this percentage is increasing.

Extensive TPM experience has amply demonstrated the effectiveness of the step-by-step approach. Chapter 4 details a step-by-step autonomous maintenance implementation process specially designed for application to process industries. Chapter 5 describes how a step-by-step approach can be used effectively for developing a planned maintenance system.

In this book's review of early equipment management (Chapter 6), maximum emphasis is placed on upstream stages with the aim of shortening commissioning periods and achieving instant, problem-free startup. Additional chapters also describe step-by-step programs for developing a quality maintenance system (a method of building quality into the product through the equipment) (Chapter 7), and for educating and training the high-caliber operators and maintenance technicians now needed in process industries (Chapter 8).

Interest in TPM in administrative and support departments is increasing rapidly in Japan, and Chapter 9 is devoted to this new area. Safety programming is also addressed for the first time in this process industry edition (Chapter 10), because eliminating accidents and pollution is an integral part of the eight TPM core activities described in this book. Chapter 11 explains the differences between TPM small-group activities and QC circle activities and suggests methods for energizing small groups as the driving force behind TPM.

The final chapter discusses the philosophy of goal-setting, details the types of performance indicators used in companies today, and gives examples of actual TPM benefits achieved.

Process industries are just beginning to apply TPM, and many companies are expected to introduce it in the future. On behalf of all the authors, I hope that this book may in some way help those companies introduce TPM smoothly and experience its undoubted benefits.

Tokutarō Suzuki
Vice Chairman, Japan Institute of Plant Maintenance
Director, TPM General Research Institute

Contributors

Supervising Editor:

Tokutarō Suzuki
　Vice Chairman, Japan Institute of Plant Maintenance (JIPM)
　Director, TPM General Research Institute

Authors:

Tokutarō Suzuki (as above) — Chapter 1

Ainosuke Miyoshi — Chapters 2 and 12
　Principal Consultant, Japan Institute of Plant Maintenance
　Director, TPM General Research Institute, Technical Center

Kōichi Nakazato — Chapters 3 and 4
　TPM Consultant, Japan Institute of Plant Maintenance
　Manager, TPM General Research Institute,
　Technical Center, Technical Division

Hisao Mizugaki — Chapter 5
　TPM Consultant, Japan Institute of Plant Maintenance
　TPM General Research Institute,
　Technical Center, Technical Division

Makoto Saitoh — Chapter 5
   TPM Consultant, Japan Institute of Plant Maintenance
   TPM General Research Institute,
   Technical Center, Technical Division

Hisamitsu Ishii — Chapters 6 and 8
   TPM Consultant, Japan Institute of Plant Maintenance
   TPM General Research Institute,
   Technical Center, Technical Division

Ikuo Setoyama — Chapters 7 and 10
   TPM Consultant, Japan Institute of Plant Maintenance
   TPM General Research Institute,
   Technical Center, Technical Division

Makoto Harada — Chapter 9
   TPM Consultant, Japan Institute of Plant Maintenance
   TPM General Research Institute,
   Technical Center, Technical Division

Akira Ichikawa — Chapter 11
   TPM Consultant, Japan Institute of Plant Maintenance
   TPM General Research Institute,
   Technical Center, Technical Division

TPM IN PROCESS INDUSTRIES

1
Overview of TPM
in Process Industries

Japan's process industries introduced preventive maintenance (PM) relatively early because production output and rate, quality, safety, and the environment depend almost entirely on the state of plant and equipment. The preventive and productive maintenance systems* introduced by Japanese process industries played a major role in improving product quality and productivity. They contributed significantly to overall progress in maintenance management and expertise in such areas as setting up specialized maintenance organizations, creating equipment management systems, improving equipment technology, and raising maintenance productivity.

ORIGIN AND DEVELOPMENT OF TPM

While the process industries focused on preventive and productive maintenance, the fabrication and assembly industries invested heavily in new equipment in an effort to become less labor intensive. The equipment used by these industries has become increasingly automated and sophisticated, and Japan is now the world leader in the use of industrial robots. This trend toward automation, combined with the trend toward just-in-time production, stimulated interest in improving maintenance management in the fabrication and

---

* Preventive maintenance was introduced to Japan from America in the 1950s, when Japanese process industries were beginning to get back on their feet after the war. *Productive maintenance*, developed in the 1960s, incorporates such disciplines as maintenance prevention design, reliability and maintainability engineering, and economic engineering to enhance the economic efficiency of equipment investment for the entire life of equipment.

assembly industries. This gave birth to a uniquely Japanese approach called *total productive maintenance (TPM)*, a form of productive maintenance involving all employees.

The Spread of TPM

TPM first took root in the automobile industry and rapidly became part of the corporate culture in companies such as Toyota, Nissan, and Mazda, and their suppliers and affiliates. It has also been introduced by other industries, such as consumer appliances, microelectronics, machine tools, plastics, film, and many others.

Having introduced preventive maintenance, the process industries then began to implement TPM. An increasing number of process plants have introduced TPM over the past few years in industries such as food, rubber, oil refining, chemicals, pharmaceuticals, gas, cement, papermaking, iron and steel, and printing.

Initially, corporate TPM activities were limited to departments directly involved with equipment, such as production. As Figure 1-1 shows, however, administrative and support departments, while actively supporting TPM in production, are now applying TPM to enhance the effectiveness of their own activities. TPM improvement methods and activities are also being adopted in product development and sales departments.

This last trend underlines the increasing tendency to consider production processes and equipment at the product development stage in an effort to simplify production, improve quality assurance, and enhance and reduce the startup period for new production. These issues are of particular concern in process industries today as product diversification continues and product life cycles shorten.

Interest in TPM outside Japan has also expanded in recent years. Many companies in the United States, Europe, Asia, and South America are planning to or are actively pursuing TPM.*

Why Is TPM So Popular?

There are three main reasons why TPM has spread so rapidly throughout Japanese industry and why companies outside Japan are becoming interested: It guarantees dramatic results, visibly transforms the workplace, and raises the level of knowledge and skill in production and maintenance workers.

---

* See the Appendix for a review of TPM implementation activities in the United States and other parts of the world.

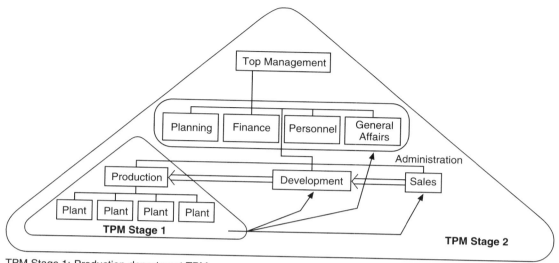

TPM Stage 1: Production-department TPM
TPM Stage 2: Companywide TPM embracing production, development, sales, and administration

Figure 1-1. From Production-Department TPM to Companywide TPM

Significant Tangible Results

Companies practicing TPM invariably achieve startling results, particularly in reducing equipment breakdowns, minimizing idling and minor stops (indispensable in unmanned plants), lessening quality defects and claims, boosting productivity, trimming labor and costs, shrinking inventory, cutting accidents, and promoting employee involvement (as shown by increased submission of improvement suggestions). (See Table 1-1.)

Transforming the Plant Environment

Through TPM, a filthy, rusty plant covered in oil and grease, leaking fluids, and spilt powders can be reborn as a pleasant, safe working environment. Customers and other visitors are impressed by these changes, and their confidence in the plant's products increases.

Transforming the Plant Workers

As TPM activities begin to yield concrete results (improving the working environment, minimizing breakdowns, improving quality, reducing change-over times, and so on), workers become motivated, involvement increases, and improvement suggestions proliferate. People begin to think of TPM as part of their job.

Table 1-1. Examples of TPM Results

Tangible Benefits

P . . . . Net productivity up by $1.5 - 2\times$

      • Number of sudden breakdowns down to $\frac{1}{10} - \frac{1}{250}$ of baseline

      • Overall plant effectiveness $1.5 - 2\times$

Q . . . . Process defect rate down 90%

      Customer claims down 75%

C . . . . Production costs down 30%

D . . . . Product and work-in-process inventories halved

S . . . . Shutdown accidents 0

      Pollution incidents 0

M . . . . Improvement suggestions up by $5 - 10\times$

Intangible Benefits

• Achieving full self-management — operators have ownership of the equipment, they look after it by themselves without direction.
• Eliminating breakdowns and defects and instilling confidence and a can-do attitude.
• Making previously dirty, grimy, and oily workplaces unrecognizably clean, bright and lively.
• Giving plant visitors a better image of the company and thereby winning more orders.

TPM helps operators understand their equipment and widens the range of maintenance and other tasks they can handle. It enables them to make new discoveries, acquire fresh knowledge, and enjoy new experiences. It strengthens motivation, engenders interest in and concern for equipment, and fosters the desire to maintain equipment in peak condition.

SPECIAL FEATURES OF PROCESS INDUSTRIES

Certain unique features and concerns distinguish process industries from the fabrication and assembly industries where TPM was born.

Diverse production systems. The term "process industry" covers a wide variety of industries including oil refining, petrochemicals, general chemicals, iron and steel, power generation, gas, papermaking, cement, food, pharmaceuticals, and textiles. Process plants in these industries employ a mixture of different production regimes, ranging from completely continuous integrated production to pure batch production. Also, the trend toward increased product diversification and high-variety, small-lot production has led in many cases to both process and fabrication/assembly production in the same plant.

Diverse equipment. In process industries, production processes consist of a combination of unit operations such as pulverization, dissolution, reaction, filtration, adsorption, concentration, crystallization, separation, molding, drying, cooling, and screening, together with the handling and transportation of various substances. Equipment includes static units such as columns, tanks, heat exchangers, kettles, and furnaces; rotating machinery such as pumps, compressors, motors, and turbines; and the piping, electrical, and instrumentation systems that connect them.

Use of static equipment. Static equipment is a particularly noteworthy feature of process industries. The special nature of such equipment requires TPM activities that focus on the relationship between process conditions and product quality and include techniques for diagnosing corrosion, cracking, burning, blocks, leaks, and so on.

Centralized control and few operators. Unlike in fabrication and assembly industries, control in process industries is centralized. Many process industries employ continuous, integrated production with centralized control of large equipment complexes. A wide range of equipment is often controlled by a handful of operators.

Diverse equipment-related problems. In addition to blocks, leaks, and other process problems, process industry equipment is often plagued by faults such as cracking, rupture, corrosion, seizure, fatigue, slack, parts falling off, wear, distortion, burning, short-circuiting, faulty insulation, wire breaks, misoperation, current leaks, and overheating. The most common problems, however, are corrosion, leaks, and blocks.

High energy consumption. Many processes in process industries, such as dissolution, reaction, crystallization, baking, and drying, are energy intensive and consume large amounts of electrical power, fuel, water, and so on.

Standby units and bypasses commonly used. To alleviate the effects of breakdowns, it is standard practice to install standby equipment, bypasses, and so on.

High accident and pollution risk. Some processes handle hazardous or poisonous substances and are operated at high temperatures and pressures, risking explosion and pollution of the plant and its surroundings. This makes strict plant management essential, as well as careful adherence to various statutory regulations.

Poor working environment. Intermediate and final products handled in process industries usually consist of bulk powders, liquids, or solids. While it is considered inevitable that the working environment will become dirty as a result of these being scattered, overflowing, leaking, and so on, such conditions frequently cause equipment problems.

Shutdown maintenance. Shutdown maintenance is a major feature of process industries. Carefully planned, systematically implemented shutdown maintenance is considered the most effective way of preventing breakdowns. However, since shutdown maintenance is time-consuming and labor-intensive, it is also expensive. Finding the most effective way of performing shutdown maintenance in view of its cost and the losses it incurs is therefore a perennial concern in process industries.

DEFINITION OF TPM

Because early TPM activities were targeted at production departments, TPM was originally defined by the Japan Institute of Plant Maintenance (JIPM) to include the following five strategies:

1. Maximize overall equipment effectiveness.
2. Establish a comprehensive PM system covering the life of the equipment.
3. Involve all departments that plan, use, and maintain equipment.
4. Involve all employees from top management to front-line workers.
5. Promote PM through motivation management, i.e. autonomous small-group activities.

Now, however, TPM is applied throughout many organizations — in many pre-production and product development departments as well as administrative and sales departments. To reflect this trend, JIPM introduced a new definition of TPM in 1989, with the following strategic components:

1. Build a corporate constitution that will maximize the effectiveness of production systems.
2. Using a shop-floor approach, build an organization that prevents every type of loss (by ensuring zero accidents, zero defects, and zero failures) for the life of the production system.

3. Involve all departments in implementing TPM, including development, sales, and administration.
4. Involve everyone — from top management to shop-floor workers.
5. Conduct zero-loss activity through overlapping small-group activities.

EQUIPMENT MANAGEMENT IN PROCESS INDUSTRIES

Equipment management in process industries has three aspects as Figure 1-2 shows. The first involves planning for the entire life cycle of equipment. The technology-cost tradeoff must be pursued throughout the engineering and maintenance phases — from the time a piece of equipment is first planned until it is finally replaced. The second aspect concerns the type of maintenance to be performed, that is, the approach (preventive, corrective, predictive, and so on) and its frequency (whether scheduled or unscheduled). To eliminate failures, companies must skillfully combine these different maintenance approaches.

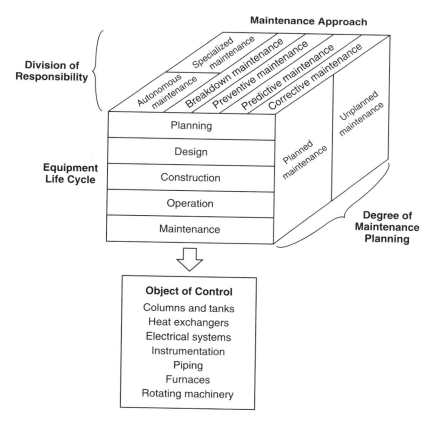

Figure 1-2. The Concept of Equipment Management

The third aspect involves allocating responsibility for maintenance, that is, deciding whether tasks will performed autonomously by production operations or by maintenance specialists. At present, maintenance and production departments tackle some maintenance tasks independently and some in collaboration. The boundary is likely to shift, however, as equipment becomes increasingly automated and requires less human intervention. The types of equipment being managed must also be considered. The combination of strategies adopted to achieve zero breakdowns, zero defects, and zero accidents will vary depending on the particular category of equipment, such as columns, tanks, heat exchangers, piping, rotating machinery, electrical systems, instrumentation, and furnaces.

TPM DEVELOPMENT

TPM is normally implemented in four phases (preparation, introduction, implementation, and consolidation), which can be broken down into twelve steps. (See Table 1-2.)

Preparation Phase (Steps 1–5)

It is vital to lay the foundation for a TPM program carefully and thoroughly. If planning is slipshod, repeated modifications and corrections will be needed during implementation. The preparation phase starts with top management's announcement of its decision to introduce TPM and is complete when the TPM development master plan has been formulated.

Step 1: Top Management Announces Its Decision to Introduce TPM

All employees must understand why their company is introducing TPM and be fully aware of its necessity. Rising raw and intermediate material costs, falling product prices, and other upheavals in the business environment are forcing industry to organize itself more effectively. Many companies are adopting TPM as a way of solving their complex internal problems and riding out the economic storm. Needless to say, top management must consider these points carefully before announcing its decision to introduce TPM.

When top management does make this commitment, however, it should declare the intention to see the TPM program through to the end. This informs all employees and interested outside parties that management understands the long-term value of TPM and will provide the physical and organizational support needed to solve the various problems that are likely to surface during implementation. Preparation for TPM begins formally when this announcement is made.

Table 1-2. The Twelve New TPM Development Program Steps

Step	Key Point
Preparation	
1. Formally announce decision to introduce TPM	Top management announcement at in-house meeting; publish in company magazine
2. Conduct TPM introductory education and publicity campaign	• Senior management: group training for specific management levels • General employees: slide shows
3. Create a TPM promotion organization	• Steering committee and specialist subcommittees • TPM Promotion Office
4. Establish basic TPM policy and goals	• Set baselines and targets • Forecast effects
5. Draft a master plan for implementing TPM	From preparation stage to application for PM Prize
Introduction	
6. Kick off TPM initiative	Invite customers, affiliates, and subcontractors
Implementation	
7. Build a corporate constitution designed to maximize production effectiveness	Pursue the ultimate in production effectiveness
7-1 Conduct focused improvement activities	Project-team activities and workplace small-group activities
7-2 Establish and deploy autonomous maintenance program	Proceed step-by-step, with audits and pass certificates at each step
7-3 Implement planned maintenance program	• Corrective maintenance • Shutdown maintenance • Predictive maintenance
7-4 Conduct operation and maintenance skills training	Group education for group leaders who then pass on their training to members
8. Build an early management system for new products and equipment	Develop products that are easy to use and equipment that is easy to use
9. Build a quality maintenance system	Establish, maintain, and control conditions for zero defects
10. Build an effective administration and support system	• Increase production-support effectiveness • Improve and streamline administrative functions and office environments
11. Develop a system for managing health, safety, and the environment	Assure an accident-free, pollution-free environment
Consolidation	
12. Sustain full TPM implementation and raise levels	• Apply for PM Prize • Aim for even higher targets

Step 2: TPM Introductory Education

Before a TPM program can be implemented it must be understood. To achieve this, some people attend outside seminars, and an in-house training program is planned and implemented.

Step 3: Create a TPM Promotion Organization

TPM is promoted through a structure of overlapping small groups. As Figure 1-3 shows, in this system leaders of small groups at each organizational level are members of small groups at the next higher level. Top management itself also constitutes a small group. This system is extremely effective for deploying top management policy and goals throughout an organization.

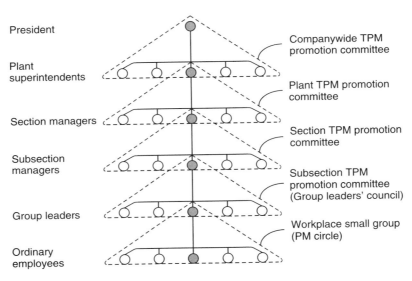

Figure 1-3. Overlapping Small-Group Activities

Establish a TPM promotion office responsible for developing and promoting effective TPM promotion strategies. To be effective, the office should be run by a permanent, full-time staff, assisted by various committees and subcommittees. Its functions include preparing the TPM master plan and coordinating its promotion, devising ways to keep the various TPM activities on track, spearheading focused campaigns, disseminating information, and arranging publicity. The promotion office plays an especially important role in managing the implementation of autonomous maintenance and focused improvement activities (see Chapters 3 and 4).

Step 4: Establish Basic TPM Policy and Goals

A company's basic TPM policy must be an integral part of its overall business policy and should indicate the goals and directions of the activities to be carried out. (See Figure 1-4.) TPM goals should relate to the company's long- and mid-range business goals and should only be decided after thorough consultation among everyone involved, including top management. The TPM program lasts for the length of time required to attain these goals.

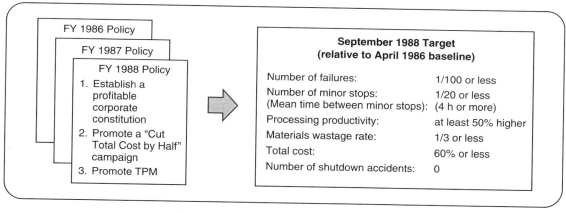

Basic TPM Policy

- With everyone's participation, to aim for zero breakdowns and zero defects and seek to maximize overall equipment effectiveness
- To create well-engineered equipment and use it to build in quality
- To develop equipment-competent personnel and have them exercise their full potential
- To create lively, energetic workplaces

Annual Policy and Companywide TPM Goals

FY 1986 Policy
FY 1987 Policy
FY 1988 Policy
1. Establish a profitable corporate constitution
2. Promote a "Cut Total Cost by Half" campaign
3. Promote TPM

September 1988 Target (relative to April 1986 baseline)	
Number of failures:	1/100 or less
Number of minor stops:	1/20 or less
(Mean time between minor stops):	(4 h or more)
Processing productivity:	at least 50% higher
Materials wastage rate:	1/3 or less
Total cost:	60% or less
Number of shutdown accidents:	0

Figure 1-4. Example of Basic TPM Policy and Goals (Kansai NEC)

Express goals numerically as far as possible. To set goals, start by establishing clear baselines. These should provide a snapshot of the existing situation and be expressed partly quantitatively and partly qualitatively. Setting a goal means aiming for a desirable level of attainment above a particular baseline. Deciding how far above the baseline to set the goal is always the most difficult question. Goals should be very challenging, but also achievable. See Chapter 12 for more on establishing goals and progress indicators.

Step 5: Draft a TPM Master Plan

To formulate a master plan for implementation, first decide what activities must be pursued to achieve the TPM goals. This is an important step, because it makes people think about the most efficient ways of bridging the gaps between baselines and goals.

The eight core TPM activities are:

- Focused improvement
- Autonomous maintenance
- Planned maintenance
- Education and training
- Early management
- Quality maintenance
- Administrative and support department activities
- Safety and environmental management

Other important activities include:

- Diagnostics and predictive maintenance
- Equipment management
- Product development and equipment design and construction

These activities need budgets and must be properly supervised. A schedule should be drawn up for each activity and integrated in the master plan.

Introduction Phase — Step 6: Kick Off TPM Initiatives

Once the master plan has been approved, the TPM kick-off can take place. The kick-off should be designed to cultivate an atmosphere that raises morale and inspires dedication. In Japan, it is often a companywide meeting to which client companies, affiliates and subcontractors are invited. At the meeting, top management reconfirm their commitment to implementing TPM and report on the plans developed and the work accomplished during the preparation phase.

Implementation Phase (Steps 7–11)

During the implementation phase, selected activities designed to achieve the targets shown in the master plan are carried out. The order and timing of the activities in Steps 7–11 should be tailored to suit the particular characteristics of the company, division, or plant. Some activities may be carried out concurrently. The fundamental TPM activities are summarized below.

Consolidation Phase — Step 12: Sustain Levels and Refine

In Japan, the first stage of a TPM program ends when a company wins a PM Prize. However, the company's TPM activities must not stop there. Embed them firmly in the corporate culture and continue to make them more effective.

A company grows by continually pursuing higher and higher goals — goals that reflect a vision of what the company believes it ought to become. Businesses are struggling to map out their development plans for the fast-approaching twenty-first century. Their TPM programs must be able to support them in this.

Recently, more companies are realizing the importance of locking into place the improvements their initial TPM program brings. Such companies are introducing a further stage to their activities with the aim of winning the Special PM Prize.

FUNDAMENTAL TPM DEVELOPMENT ACTIVITIES

Companies must select and implement activities that will achieve the goals of TPM effectively and efficiently. Although different companies may choose slightly different activities, the eight described below are the most common. They have been shown to yield excellent results when properly pursued, and they are the foundation and support of any successful TPM development program.

Step 7-1: Focused Improvement

Focused improvement is an improvement activity performed by cross-functional project teams composed of people such as production engineers, maintenance personnel, and operators. These activities are designed to minimize targeted losses that have been carefully measured and evaluated.

In addition to the seven major losses experienced in fabrication and assembly industries, process industries sustain three additional types of loss: people-related losses such as work and misoperation losses; raw-materials losses such as yield, unit-consumption, and recycling losses; and management losses such as shutdown maintenance and energy losses. (Chapter 2, *Maximizing Production Effectiveness*, provides a detailed review of the approach to identifying, measuring, and attacking the various individual losses that occur in process industries.)

In process industries, focused improvement activity is directed at a specific object such as a process, a flow system, an item of equipment, or an operating procedure. For example, process design must be an integral part of product development and improvement. A focused improvement project can address vital, related issues such as establishing criteria for selecting processes and their conditions, discovering deficiencies in process conditions, and finding and closing gaps between actual and ideal process conditions.

The trend toward unattended operation is well advanced in process industries and will probably be taken even further in the future. For this reason, ideas for stabilizing processes and eliminating equipment breakdowns, idling, and minor stops are also important topics for focused improvement.

When the focus is strictly on equipment, project teams follow a similar approach to that developed in fabrication and assembly industries. They document and analyze the major equipment-related losses, then study the equipment carefully to identify the process conditions it is required to provide and to ensure that it can fulfill them.

Whether the focus is on the process, work flow, equipment, or operating procedures, however, focused improvement activity is founded on effective use of cause analysis methods, such as why-why analysis and P-M analysis.

Chapter 3, *Focused Improvement*, provides a detailed review of the planning and management of focused improvement team activities, the methods used, strategies for specific losses, and case examples.

Step 7-2: Autonomous Maintenance

Autonomous maintenance, detailed at length in Chapter 4, is one of the most distinctive activities in TPM. After preventive maintenance was introduced into Japan from America, operation and maintenance were formally separated. As operators lost ownership of their equipment, they gradually lost their sense of responsibility for maintaining it.

The autonomous maintenance practiced in TPM reverses this tendency. Operators become involved in routine maintenance and improvement activities that halt accelerated deterioration, control contamination, and help prevent equipment problems. Because process plants employ a small number of operators in relation to the number and size of equipment units, strategies for achieving autonomous maintenance goals must be adapted somewhat from the traditional approach followed in fabrication and assembly industries. When tailoring autonomous maintenance to individual process environments, planning teams must:

- Consider how autonomous maintenance steps can be conducted most effectively on different types of equipment

- Investigate the relative importance of different equipment items and determine appropriate maintenance approaches
- Prioritize maintenance tasks
- Allocate responsibilities appropriately between production and specialized maintenance personnel

Autonomous maintenance activities are typically implemented in steps and are only effective if the progression from one step to the next is strictly controlled. To manage this, appoint official auditing groups and lay down pass/fail standards. A plant's top management should give final approval for groups to graduate from one step and move on to the next.

Why is close control so important? Initial cleaning (Step 1), for example, involves much more than merely cleaning and tidying the equipment and adjacent areas. If team efforts are not focused on identifying and treating problems found in the course of thorough cleaning, the goals of eliminating and controlling deterioration cannot be achieved.

Similarly, depending on the plant's location, salt spray, rain, snow, and so on, may corrode the equipment and erode its foundations. Products such as powders, liquids, solids, gases, and so on can also cause accelerated deterioration of equipment, through scattering, leaking, blocks, and so forth. How such deterioration is treated will depend in part on the environment, the equipment, or form of the product. However, if Step 2 of an autonomous maintenance program (action against contamination sources and inaccessible places) is not properly implemented, the program will slip right back to Step 1 or even further. Step-by-step auditing of team activities to keep them properly focused is essential for successful implementation of autonomous maintenance. For a detailed discussion of autonomous maintenance activities adapted for process industry environments, see Chapter 4, *Autonomous Maintenance*.

Step 7-3: Planned Maintenance

Planned or scheduled maintenance, detailed in Chapter 5, embraces three forms of maintenance: breakdown, preventive, and predictive. Like other TPM activities, building a planned-maintenance system should done systematically, one step at a time.

The purpose of performing predictive and preventive maintenance is to eliminate breakdowns, but even when systematic maintenance practices are carried out, unexpected failures still occur. Such failures reveal inadequacies in the timing and content of maintenance plans and highlight ineffective recurrence-prevention measures. In TPM, planned maintenance activities emphasize monitoring mean times between failures (MTBF) and using that analysis to specify the intervals for tasks in annual, monthly, and weekly maintenance calendars.

A classic example of planned maintenance activity is shutdown maintenance.* To make them more effective, companies are preparing for shutdowns earlier and earlier. Their goal is to lay out reliable plans before the job begins. Because the tasks performed during shutdown maintenance follow a set pattern, it is helpful to base the work plan on a work breakdown structure (WBS) diagram. This diagram facilitates accurate estimation of the tasks to be performed during shutdown maintenance, along with their sizes. It can be used to gauge the staff and materials needed for the job and to monitor the budget and the achievement of the objectives. (See pp. 186–188 for more about the WBS diagram.)

Step 7-4: Training

A company's workforce is a priceless asset, and all companies must train their employees systematically. Process-industry workers are becoming scarcer, increasingly elite, and more multiskilled, so training must be an integral part of a career development system. Visualize the type of people you want your training programs to produce. In other words, identify the specific knowledge, skills, and management abilities you want them to have and then design training that will achieve your vision. (See Chapter 8 for models of successful program design.)

Training must also be tailored to serve the individual's needs. Assess each person to measure his or her grasp of the required knowledge and skills and pinpoint weaknesses, then use the results to make the general training more effective. Workers and their supervisors should discuss the results of this assessment annually and use them to set the next year's targets and plan the next phase.

Also set firm schedules for achieving program targets. Decide the kind of people you want to have in how many years' time, then draw up comprehensive plans for on-the-job and off-the-job training (including seminars and courses) designed to achieve this.

---

* Thanks to a change in the law, shutdown maintenance of large plants in Japan can now be performed once every two years instead of annually, depending on the type and state of the equipment, and provided that an examination has been passed and official authorization received. Implementing a TPM program is of great assistance in obtaining this authorization.

Step 8: Early Management

Early management, addressed in Chapter 6, includes both early product management and early equipment management. The purpose of these activities is to achieve — quickly and economically — products that are easy to make and equipment that is easy to use. This section highlights early equipment management.

Early equipment management concerns equipment users, engineering companies, and equipment manufacturers, and addresses the following areas:

- Equipment investment planning
- Process design
- Equipment design, fabrication, and construction
- Test operation
- Startup management.

All activities from the initial design of a piece of equipment to its installation and test operation can be viewed as a single, giant project. The project starts with process design, basic plant design, and detailed design and unfolds to include procurement, fabrication, construction, and test operation. In planning such a project, the project team determines the plant and equipment's required technical levels (functions and performance) together with its availability levels (reliability, maintainability, etc.), and then establishes budgets and schedules to achieve them.

In designing a plant, various designs are performed: functional design, reliability and maintainability design, safety design, and economy design. Establishing maintenance prevention (MP) specifications and performing MP design, in particular, help ensure that the plant and equipment are reliable and easily maintained. Several design reviews should be performed in the course of designing, fabricating, and constructing a plant.

After completing these activities, teams install the equipment, perform test operation, and initiate the startup management phase. Startup management is an activity designed to achieve as quickly as possible the conditions for its own termination, that is, conditions that enable the plant to start producing stable-quality product with zero failures. In TPM this efficient approach to stable, full-scale production is known as "vertical startup."

For an overview of TPM early management activities for equipment and product design, as well as startup management, see Chapter 6.

Step 9: Quality Maintenance

Quality maintenance (QM) is a method for building in quality and preventing quality defects through the process and through the equipment. In quality maintenance, variability in a product quality characteristic is controlled by controlling the condition of equipment components that affect it.

Quality characteristics are mainly influenced by the four production inputs: equipment, materials, people's actions (skills), and methods used. The first step in quality maintenance is to clarify the relationships between these factors and a product's quality characteristics by analyzing quality defects. In process industries, the effect of equipment on quality characteristics is particularly important.

In process industries, the process determines the type of equipment needed. Therefore, teams should focus first on the process, then on the equipment. In other words, first clarify the relationships between product quality and process conditions and ascertain the precise process conditions required for producing perfect product.

Equipment is a means of implementing a process. Therefore, applying a QM approach in equipment design, teams begin by identifying the components that will affect the product's quality characteristics. These are called "quality components." Next, they pinpoint the quality component conditions required to maintain the quality characteristics.

Quality maintenance used in this way assures quality at the very beginning of the production process. (See Chapter 7 for a detailed review of the quality maintenance methodology and examples of its application.)

Step 10: TPM in Administrative and Support Departments

Administrative and support departments play an important role in backing up production activities. The quality and timeliness of the information supplied by administrative and support departments has a major impact on these activities.

TPM activities performed by administrative and support departments must not only support TPM in the workplace; they should also strengthen the functions of the departments themselves by improving their own organization and culture. Compared with production, however, it is not as easy for administrative and support departments to measure the effects of their activities. A TPM program in such a department must aim to create an "information factory" and apply process analysis to streamline the information flow. Think of administrative and support departments as process plants whose principal tasks are to collect, process, and distribute information. This understanding makes it easier to promote and measure autonomous maintenance, focused improvement, and other TPM activities in an office environment.

Autonomous maintenance in administrative departments aims for efficient, trouble-free work execution from two angles: administrative function and administrative environment. Implemented step by step, the first set of activities reduce costs and boost efficiency by improving administrative processes. The second set of activities removes obstacles to effective work hidden in the physical and psychological environment.

Focused improvement of administrative tasks aims to improve their efficiency and speed and reduce the number of staff required. To achieve this, automate office tasks and install electronic data-processing systems such as local-area networks. At the same time, increase administrative efficiency to support the planning and decision-making of executives and managers. See Chapter 9 for a more detailed review of TPM activities in office environments.

Step 11: Safety and Environmental Management

Assuring safety and preventing adverse environmental impacts are important issues in process industries. Operability studies combined with accident prevention training and near-miss analysis are effective ways of addressing these concerns. Safety is promoted systematically as part of TPM activities. As with all TPM activities, safety activities are implemented step by step.

Certain issues are of particular importance in the process environment. For example, it is particularly important to incorporate fail-safe mechanisms — that is, to design equipment that will remain safe even when people do not take the proper precautions. Assuring safety during shutdown maintenance is also important. In process industries, shutdown maintenance requires considerable assistance from outside subcontractors, as do operations such as cleaning. This makes it doubly important to ensure safety during such operations. Check the skills and qualifications of subcontract workers well in advance whenever possible. Take every practicable step to assure safety, including giving rigorous safety training and carefully supervising the work itself. See Chapter 10 for examples of safety training programs and activities.

Step 12: Sustaining TPM Implementation and Raising Levels

There are several keys to maintaining TPM levels once they are achieved. Building strong teams at every level and staffing a promotion organization helps integrate TPM in daily work, for example. Following the systematic, step-by-step approach recommended for TPM activities helps lock in results. Emphasizing a continuous-improvement approach through the CAPD cycle, continually revising goals upward, and setting new challenges, like the PM Special Prize, are also helpful. None of these approaches will be effective without the support of careful, continuous, and concrete measurement. Start with clear baselines and document improvement results regularly and in detail. Use management indicators that show everyone (at every level) what concrete progress is being made and motivate their continued involvement. See Chapter 12, *Measuring TPM Effectiveness*, for a detailed summary of key management indicators to use for charting and encouraging progress in TPM activities.

2
Maximizing Production Effectiveness

In process industries, products are manufactured in plants (equipment complexes) that consist of units such as columns, tanks, heat exchangers, pumps, compressors, and furnaces, all of which are connected by piping, instrumentation systems, and so on. As a result of this integration, it is more important to maximize the overall effectiveness of a plant than to focus exclusively on the efficiency of the individual equipment items.

PRODUCTION EFFECTIVENESS IN PROCESS INDUSTRIES

The effectiveness of a plant's production depends on the effectiveness with which it uses equipment, materials, people, and methods. Raising production effectiveness in process industries, therefore, starts with the vital issues of maximizing overall plant effectiveness (equipment), raw material and fuel efficiency (materials), work efficiency (people), and management efficiency (methods). This is done by examining the inputs to the production process (equipment, materials, people, and methods) and identifying and eliminating the losses associated with each to maximize the outputs (productivity, quality, cost, delivery, safety and environment, and morale).

Performance Losses

Production in process industries is usually either fully continuous or a basically continuous batch type. Shutdown maintenance, which closes down an entire plant once or twice a year, distinguishes both types of production. Periodically shutting process plants down has always been regarded as necessary for maintaining performance and assuring safety. With regard to raising a plant's production effectiveness, however, the time spent in shutdown is considered a loss. To maximize the effectiveness of the plant, therefore, entails increasing the number of days the plant operates without a break and speeding up and improving its shutdown maintenance program.

Process plants suffer from process failures and problems as well as individual equipment failures. Contamination, leaks, and blocks affect equipment both inside and out. Actual properties of the substances being handled, corrosion, or scattered powder can cause problems that necessitate plant shutdown. Such losses are in a separate category from the usual type of equipment breakdown.

In a large equipment complex such as a processing plant, it is not very useful to compare the design performance (the standard) and the actual performance of individual equipment units. It is more meaningful to use the overall process performance (the production rate) as a yardstick. Production drops that occur during plant startup, shutdown, or changeover are considered *normal production losses*; those that result from plant defects and abnormalities are *abnormal production losses*. Reducing these two types of performance losses improves the plant's overall production effectiveness.

Defect and Reprocessing Losses

Defect losses are a separate category of loss from the performance losses noted above. Losses in this category include quality defect and reprocessing losses, major impediments to raising production effectiveness.

Quality defect losses include losses due to downgrading product, as well as rejectable product and scrap. These obviously must be reduced to improve production effectiveness.

Reprocessing losses arise when rejectable product is recycled through a previous process, as often happens in chemical plants. Reprocessing generates enormous losses, including time losses, physical losses, and energy losses. It is important to minimize them.

OVERALL PLANT EFFECTIVENESS

Process industries must maximize the effectiveness of their equipment complex or plant by extracting its best possible functions and performance. Overall effectiveness is raised by painstakingly eliminating everything that tends to lower it. In other words, maximizing plant effectiveness involves bringing the plant to peak operating conditions and then keeping it there by eliminating or at least minimizing any factors such as failures, defects, or problems that might diminish its performance.

The Eight Major Plant Losses

The following eight plant losses are the major losses that prevent any plant from achieving its maximum effectiveness:

1. Shutdown
2. Production adjustment
3. Equipment failure
4. Process failure
5. Normal production loss
6. Abnormal production loss
7. Quality defects
8. Reprocessing

1. Shutdown Loss

Shutdown loss is time lost when production stops for planned annual shutdown maintenance or periodic servicing.

Process industries usually operate continuously throughout the year or employ a batch style of production that is basically continuous. Most plants in such industries follow a periodic maintenance system in which the entire plant shuts down completely once or twice a year for maintenance. Periodic inspections are usually performed during shutdown maintenance, and may be required by law or voluntary. In either case, maintenance personnel measure deterioration and try to reverse it while the plant is shut down. Shutdown periods are therefore essential for maintaining a plant's performance and assuring its security and safety.

Maximizing a plant's production effectiveness, however, requires treating shutdown periods as losses and minimizing them. The plant's continuous operation can be extended by curtailing its shutdown periods and improving the efficiency of shutdown maintenance work.

Shutdown losses also arise as a result of periodic servicing required while the plant is operating. For example, part of a plant may be shut down for repair work based on a monthly maintenance plan. Such jobs must also be carefully planned to make them more efficient.

2. Production Adjustment Loss

Production adjustment loss is time lost when changes in supply and demand require adjustment in production plans. They would never arise if all the product that a plant manufactures could be sold according to plan. If the demand for a product falls because market needs change, however, the plant that produces the product may have to close down temporarily. Production adjustments are governed by production plans based on factors such as demand and inventory and are, to some extent, unavoidable for producers. A company can minimize adjustment losses, however, if it maintains a strong lead in quality, cost, and delivery and continually stimulates demand by improving its product lineup and developing new products. This will naturally increase the plant's overall effectiveness.

3. Equipment Failure Loss

Equipment failure loss is time lost when a plant stops because equipment suddenly loses its specified functions.

Two types of equipment-related loss can be distinguished: function-failure loss and function-reduction loss. *Function-failure loss* is a time loss that occurs when rotating machinery or static equipment suddenly loses its specified functions and stops the plant. This type of loss is considered an equipment failure loss.

Function-reduction loss, on the other hand, is a physical loss such as defects or reduced yield that occurs while a plant is operating, when various factors cause equipment to underperform.

4. Process Failure Losses

Process failure loss is time lost when a plant shuts down as a result of factors external to the equipment, such as operating errors or changes in the physical or chemical properties of the substances being processed.

In process industries, plants shut down frequently as a result of problems other than equipment failure. Such problems may result from misoperation or raw materials. They may also result from valves sticking because they are clogged by material being processed, blockages tripping safety devices, leaks and spills causing electrical measuring equipment to malfunction, and loads changing as a result of variations in the physical properties of the substances being handled.

These problems may originate either in the properties of the materials being processed or in phenomena such as corrosion, erosion, or powder scatter. Process failures will decrease only when their sources are stamped out. As already mentioned, such problems should be distinguished and dealt with separately from sudden equipment failures. Process industries achieve the zero-breakdown goal only if they pay sufficient attention to eradicating problems related to process failures.

5. Normal Production Losses

Normal production losses are rate losses that occur during normal production at plant startup, shutdown, and changeover.

A plant's standard production rate cannot be achieved during the warmup period when the plant is started up or maintained during the cooldown period when it is shut down, or during changeover periods when production switches from one product to another. Drops in production that occur at these times should be treated as losses.

The time a plant takes to warm up after shutdown maintenance (from the time it first starts up until acceptable product emerges) is lost time. This loss can be minimized by introducing systematic "vertical startup" procedures (immediate, trouble-free startup). The same applies to the cooldown period when the plant is shut down. Also, reducing internal setup and using external setup techniques to prepare in advance can minimize changeover losses.

6. Abnormal Production Losses

Abnormal production losses are rate losses that occur when a plant performs inadequately as a result of malfunctions and other abnormal conditions that interfere with performance.

The overall capacity of a plant is expressed by the standard production rate (t/h). When a plant must run at a rate lower than its standard production rate, the difference between the standard and actual production rates is the abnormal production loss.

7. Quality Defect Losses

Quality defect losses include time lost in producing rejectable product, physical loss in scrap, and financial losses due to product downgrading.

Quality defects can have many causes. Some may arise when production conditions are set incorrectly due to instrument malfunction or operating errors; others arise from external factors such as failures, problems with raw materials, or contamination.

8. Reprocessing Losses

Reprocessing losses are recycling losses that occur when rejected material must be returned to a previous process to make it acceptable.

In the past, people concentrated on the condition of the final product, and tended to overlook losses in intermediate processes such as production-rate losses and energy lost from recycling. In process industries, however, we need to re-examine the notion that recycling is permissible simply because it can make rejectable product acceptable. We must bear in mind that recycling is a significant loss and wastes time, materials, and energy.*

Table 2-1. The Eight Major Plant Losses — Definitions and Examples

Loss	Definition	Units	Example
1. Shutdown loss	Time lost when production stops for planned annual shutdown maintenance or periodic servicing	Days	Shutdown work, periodic servicing, statutory inspections, autonomous inspections, general repair work, etc.
2. Production adjustment loss	Time lost when changes in supply and demand require adjustments to production plans	Days	Production-adjustment shutdown, inventory-reduction shutdown, etc.
3. Equipment failure loss	Time lost when equipment suddenly loses its specified functions	Hours	Failed pumps, burned-out motors, damaged bearings, broken shafts, etc.
4. Process failure loss	Time lost in shut down due to external factors such as changes in chemical or physical properties of materials being processed, operating errors, defective raw materials, etc.	Hours	Leaks, spills, blocks, corrosion, erosion, dust scatter, misoperation
5. Normal production loss	Rate and time losses at plant startup, shutdown, or changeover	Rate decrease, hours	Production rate reductions during warmup period after startup, cooldown period before shutdown, and product changeover
6. Abnormal production loss	Rate loss occuring when plant underperforms due to malfunctions and abnormalities	Rate decrease	Low-load operation, low-speed operation, and operation at below standard production rate
7. Quality defect loss	Losses due to producing rejectable product, physical loss of rejected product, financial losses due to product downgrading	Hours, tons, dollars	Physical and time losses due to making product that fails to meet quality standards
8. Reprocessing loss	Recycling losses due to passing material back through the process	Hours, tons, dollars	Recycling nonconforming product from the final process to the starting process to make it acceptable

---

* In certain industries or with certain products, reprocessing or reworking is impossible. In plants where this applies, what would have been reprocessing losses are treated as quality losses, and the eight major plant losses are reduced to seven.

Table 2-1 defines the eight major plant losses and provides examples, and Figure 2-1 shows the relationship between these losses and the production rate.

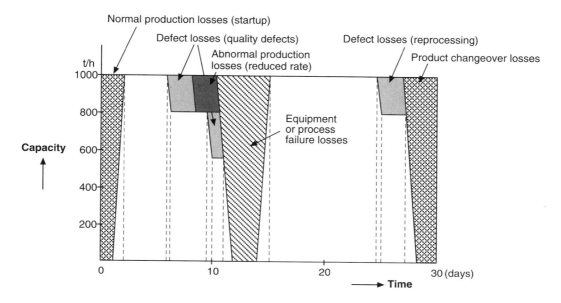

Figure 2-1. Production and the Eight Major Losses

The Structure of Losses

To distinguish and quantify losses that impede effectiveness, it is helpful to identify the structure of losses that occur in a plant. Figure 2-2 outlines the structure of the eight major plant losses and provides the formula for calculating overall plant effectiveness. This loss structure was devised by considering the eight losses from the aspect of time.

Calendar Time

Calendar time is the number of hours on the calendar:

$$365 \times 24 = 8{,}760 \text{ hours in a year}$$
$$30 \times 24 = 720 \text{ hours in a 30-day month.}$$

Working Time

Working time is the actual number of hours that a plant is expected to operate in a year or month. To calculate working time, subtract from the calendar

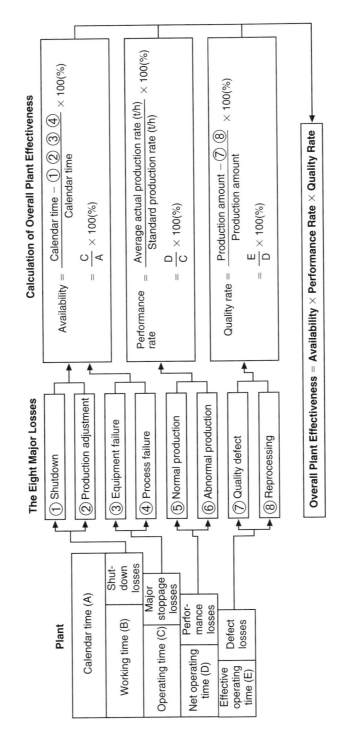

Figure 2-2. Overall Plant Effectiveness and the Structure of Losses

time the time lost as a result of closing the plant for production adjustment or for periodic servicing such as shutdown maintenance.

Operating Time

Operating time is the time during which a plant actually operates. To calculate operating time, subtract from the working time the time a plant loses when it shuts down as a result of equipment and process failures.

Net Operating Time

Net operating time is the time during which a plant is producing at the standard production rate. To calculate net operating time, subtract performance time losses from the operating time. Performance time losses consist of normal production losses (production rate reductions due to startup, shutdown, and changeover) and abnormal production losses (production rate reductions due to abnormalities).

Valuable Operating Time

Valuable operating time is the net time during which the plant actually produces acceptable product. To calculate valuable operating time, add the time wasted reprocessing and producing rejectable product, then subtract the result from the net operating time.

Availability

Availability is the operating time expressed as a percentage of the calendar time. To calculate availability, subtract from calendar time the time lost during shutdown (for planned maintenance and production adjustments) and the time lost in major stoppages (equipment and process failures). Then, divide the result by calendar time and multiply by 100.

$$\text{Availability} = \frac{\text{Calendar time} - (\text{shutdown loss} + \text{major stoppage loss})}{\text{Calendar time}} \times 100(\%)$$

Shutdown losses = shutdown maintenance loss + production adjustment loss

Major stoppage loss = equipment failure loss + process failure loss

Performance Rate

A plant's *performance rate* expresses the actual production rate as a percentage of the standard production rate.

The *standard production rate* is equivalent to a plant's design capacity and is the intrinsic capacity of a particular plant. It can be expressed as production (in tons) per hour (t/h), or per day (t/day). The actual production rate is expressed as an average. To calculate it, divide the actual production (t) by the operating time.

$$\text{Performance rate} = \frac{\text{Average actual production rate (t/h)}}{\text{Standard production rate (t/h)}} \times 100(\%)$$

$$= \frac{(D)}{(C)} \times 100(\%)$$

$$\text{Average actual production rate} = \frac{\text{Actual production rate (t/h)}}{\text{Operating time}}$$

Quality Rate

The *quality rate* expresses the amount of acceptable product (total production less downgraded product, scrap, and reprocessed product as a percentage of total production. The quality rate is equivalent to the straight-through rate in a fabrication/assembly plant.

$$\text{Quality rate} = \frac{\text{Production quantity (t)} - \text{(quality defect loss + reprocessing loss) (t)}}{\text{Production quantity (t)}}$$

$$= \frac{(E)}{(D)} \times 100(\%)$$

Overall Plant Effectiveness

Overall plant effectiveness is the product of the availability, performance rate, and quality rate. It is a comprehensive indicator of a plant's condition that takes into account operating time, performance, and quality. It can be used to judge the effectiveness with which a plant is being used to add value.

Figure 2-3 shows the relationship between monthly production and losses in a particular plant. The overall plant effectiveness is calculated based on this figure.

Calendar time: 24 hrs × 30 days

Operating time: 24 hrs × 27 days

$$\therefore \text{ A. Availability} = \frac{24 \times 27}{24 \times 30} \times 100 = 90\%$$

Actual production volume:

    1. (500 t/day × 1 day) + (1,000 t/day × 6 days)
       + (800 t/day × 5 days) + 400 t/day × 1 day = 10,900 t

    2. (500 t/day × 1 day + 1,000 t/day × 12 days)
       + (500 t/day × 1 day) = 13,000 t

Total: 10,900 + 13,000 = 23,900 t

$$\therefore \text{ Actual production rate: } \frac{23,900}{27} = 885 \text{ t/day}$$

$$\text{B. Performance rate} = \frac{885}{1,000} \times 88.5\%$$

If 100 t of rejectable product are produced,

$$\text{C. Quality rate} = \frac{23,800 \text{ t}}{23,900 \text{ t}} \times 100 = 99.6\%$$

$$\text{D. Overall plant effectiveness} = (A) \times (B) \times (C) \times 100$$
$$= (0.9 \times 0.885 \times 0.966) \times 100$$
$$= 79.3\%$$

The plant's overall effectiveness in this example is 79.3 percent. Its performance rate and availability obviously need to be improved.

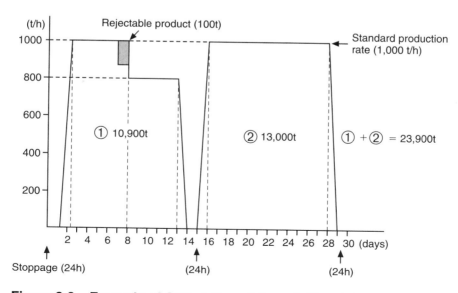

Figure 2-3. Example of Calculation of Overall Plant Effectiveness

MAXIMIZING THE EFFECTIVENESS OF PRODUCTION INPUTS

As explained earlier, to maximize production effectiveness in process industries a company must painstakingly increase the effectiveness with which it uses its production inputs (equipment, materials, people, and methods). Equipment has already been discussed, so this section concentrates on maximizing the efficiency of materials (including energy), people (work), and methods (management), using case examples.

Reducing Raw Material and Energy Losses

The proportion of production costs accounted for by raw materials and energy is far higher in process industries than in fabrication and assembly industries. It is therefore vital to eliminate losses in these areas.

Production Costs and Unit Consumption

As Figure 2-4 shows, production costs usually consist of fixed and variable elements.

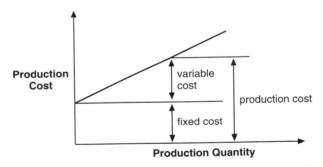

Figure 2-4.   The Structure of Production Costs

Variable costs include the costs of raw materials, subsidiary materials, packaging materials, fuel, steam, electrical power, water, compressed air, and so on. Monitoring and controlling unit consumption (consumption per unit of product) can reduce variable costs and lower production costs.

$$\text{Production unit consumption} = \frac{\text{Variable-cost item used}}{\text{Amount of product}} \text{ or } \frac{\text{Variable-cost item used}}{\text{Raw materials processing cost}}$$

Some examples of various types of production unit consumption are given below.

- Unit consumption of subsidiary materials $= \dfrac{\text{Subsidiary materials used}}{\text{Amount of product}}$ (kg/t)

- Unit consumption of fuel $= \dfrac{\text{Fuel used}}{\text{Amount of product}}$ (kℓ/t)

- Unit consumption of electrical power $= \dfrac{\text{Electrical power used}}{\text{Amount of product}}$ (kWh/t)

- Unit consumption of packaging materials $= \dfrac{\text{Packaging materials used}}{\text{Amount of product}}$ (rolls/t)

Control of Unit Consumption by Production

Production unit consumption generally tends to decrease as production increases. As Figure 2-5 shows, the fixed-cost element of consumption decreases in inverse proportion to production. Direct comparison of unit consumption figures at different daily production amounts is therefore inappropriate.

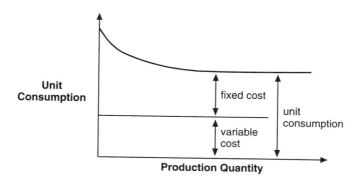

Figure 2-5. Unit Consumption by Production Quantity

Instead, compare unit consumption figures at the same production amount by preparing a suitable graph for each type of production unit consumption. For example, if the standard production rate of a plant is 1,000 t/day, we can calculate its unit consumption at production rates of 1,000 t, 950 t, 900 t, 850 t, etc. from past results, and use a graph of unit consumption versus production to monitor the unit consumption. To control unit consumption even more accurately use the graph to derive a quadratic equation.

Control of Unit Consumption by Season

Seasonal temperature changes affect some elements of production unit consumption, such as fuel, steam, electrical power, and water, so it is difficult to compare them directly over the whole year. For example, as Figure 2-6 shows, unit consumption of fuel and steam usually decreases in summer and increases in winter, while unit consumption of electricity and water often increases in summer because of increased use of air-conditioning and cooling systems. Therefore it is important to collect monthly data on actual unit consumption and establish separate seasonal unit-consumption indices for the periods from March to September and September to March. This improves the accuracy with which unit consumption can be controlled.

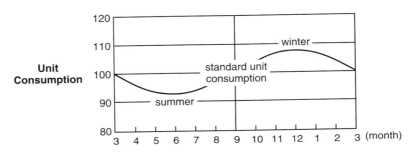

Figure 2-6. Unit Consumption by Season

Control of Unit Consumption by Product

In process industries, the same plant often produces several different products. If a product changes, then unit consumption also changes.

For example, compare the production of 300-micron particles with that of 500-micron or 900-micron particles. The unit consumption increases with the particle size as a result of increasing the use of steam for concentration, screening out the larger amount of undersized product, and so on. As Figure 2-7 indicates, to control unit consumption, measure its value at different product ratios and establish indices for these.

Reducing Raw Material Losses

At a certain gasworks that produces foundry coke from coal, a lot of coal was falling off the conveyors that carried it from the coal yard to the coke ovens. The improvement team drew a map that showed where the coal was falling off and made detailed measurements of the amount of coal falling off and from which parts of what equipment. The improvement team then inaugurated a *Zero Coal Spill* campaign in an effort to eliminate the problem. As a result, the company was able to decrease the amount of coal spilled by a factor of 7, from 35 t/month to 5 t/month.

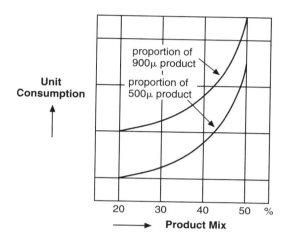

Figure 2-7. Unit Consumption by Product

Preventing Raw Material Losses and Saving Energy

At a paper mill, an improvement team drastically reduced the amount of raw materials discharged with the waste water by improving the raw-material blending process. This reduced raw-material losses by 400 t/year. The improvement in the process also made two large pumps redundant, which reduced energy losses and saved the company $150,000 per year in electricity charges.

Process Simplification

Companies often expand or modify older plants when they introduce new products or alter processes to improve existing products. Frequently, they simply add new equipment and leave old, redundant equipment in place. Static units, machinery, piping, and wiring become more and more complicated, often producing raw material losses and energy losses.

An improvement team at the paper mill mentioned earlier, initiated a plantwide process simplification campaign to eliminate unnecessary equipment. They eliminated 160 pumps, 61 holding tanks, and 18 km of piping, with a total weight of 4,000 t. They dispensed with 63 rotating machines, which saved 2,600 kW of electricity. The plant also reduced staffing requirements drastically by centralizing and simplifying processes.

Clearing out unnecessary equipment freed up 6,800 m^2 of space, making the workplace brighter and less cluttered. Now, leaks, rusting, vibration, and other abnormalities are much easier to detect and the plant's maintainability, operability, and safety are much improved.

Reducing Maintenance Materials

To cope with unexpected breakdowns and emergency repairs, plants typically try to keep sufficient maintenance materials and parts in stock so that the right item will always be available for use at exactly the right time. These materials, however, are often overstocked (from the standpoint of the plant as a whole) when individual workplaces maintain their own stores and issue their own purchase orders. Keeping maintenance materials in a single central storage facility often systematically reduces inventories and storage costs. It is therefore best to classify spares into two categories: permanent stores, stocked at minimum levels in a central location, and nonpermanent stores (standby units, reserves, general consumable parts, and tools) stored as needed in individual workplaces.

The key to reducing maintenance parts and materials inventories is to minimize the quantity of permanent stores. A satisfactory goal is to reduce the number of different items by 30 percent and their total quantity and value by 50 percent.

Reducing Work Losses

Work losses include wasteful human labor necessitated by a plant's poor operating condition. A plant that develops abnormalities or faults generates extra work, such as inspecting and reporting on the faulty equipment and making appropriate adjustments. Taking emergency action and following up on process failures characteristic of process plants (leaks, spills, blocks, and so on) require many work-hours. All this extra work is a loss and must be eliminated.

Reducing Cleaning Losses

At the gasworks mentioned earlier, an improvement team launched a drive to eliminate coke-dust spills during Step 2 of the plant's autonomous maintenance program. (Step 2 introduces countermeasures against contamination sources and inaccessible areas.) Campaign activities consisted of localizing coke-dust spills from the conveyors and taking action to deal with the sources. As a result, the plant reduced the amount of spilled coke dust by a factor of 6 — from 12 t/day to 2 t/day — and annually saved $67,000 in cleaning fees. Their *Zero Coal Spill* campaign mentioned earlier also drastically reduced the amount paid to cleaning companies.

New Control Systems for Personnel Reduction

In order to reform its plant operation and reduce the number of operators, a certain chemical works updated its measuring equipment and modernized and centralized its control rooms. The introduction of the new control system allowed operators to become computer-literate and to control a wider range of equipment. As a result, the plant was able to reassign 40 shift workers.

Process Centralization and Simplification

The paper mill mentioned earlier instituted a campaign to streamline the entire plant. Teams reorganized the flow of materials through the plant to eliminate unnecessary equipment and centralize and simplify the various processes. As a result, the plant succeeded in cutting its workforce by a total of 60.

Reducing Management Losses

Management losses are losses that arise from poor management systems or poor operation of those systems.

Management losses include frequent changeovers caused by modifications to production plans, and distribution losses that arise from poor transportation and handling of materials within a plant. It is important to minimize such losses.

Reducing Distribution Losses

The chemical plant mentioned earlier stored raw materials for textiles in a distant warehouse and issued them in accordance with raw-materials utilization plans prepared by the production department. Cutting the level of raw materials stocked and delivering them directly to the production department greatly reduced in-plant transportation costs. Effective use of the resulting space in the warehouse enabled the company to reduce outside storage rental costs and annually saved the company $720,000.

Reducing Administrative Losses

Reducing administrative losses and improving administrative skills through the use of better information processing systems can raise administrative efficiency.

At the chemical plant mentioned earlier, reorganization of offices reduced the number of files by half and reduced the number of documents in circulation by a quarter. The introduction of automated office equipment also cut the administrative workload, while the preparation of administrative procedure manuals improved the efficiency of routine administrative tasks. In addition, cross-training administrative personnel freed 12 people for other duties. Introducing a system for sharing desks yielded extra space, greatly improved communication among office workers, and created a more effective work environment.

Reducing Testing and Analysis Losses

Chemical plants perform many types of testing and analysis, including raw-material acceptance tests, between-process sampling tests, and product analyses. These tasks are important for quality control and delivery control, but many are performed manually and efficiently. The gasworks mentioned earlier improved the efficiency of its testing and analysis work and strengthened its quality management system by introducing automated testing and analysis procedures. Newly developed automatic equipment and procedures, including on-line analysis, enabled the company to reduce testing and analysis losses and increase the number of measurements made. As a result, they were able to reduce their staff by 30 percent.

CONTINUOUS IMPROVEMENT

The philosophy behind improving production effectiveness in process industries is fundamentally the same as in fabrication and assembly industries. There are differences between these two types of industry, however. Process industries are distinguished by their large-scale equipment, continuous 24-hour operation, handling of many different materials, a high likelihood of corrosion, and many problems with leaks, spills, and scattered powder.

Nevertheless, process industries must apply the same basic philosophy and approach to continuous improvement. Like fabrication and assembly industries process industries must prevent accelerated deterioration, reverse any untreated deterioration, eliminate all slight abnormalities, and get the whole plant functioning optimally.

The following discussion of continuous improvement philosophy and approaches focuses on problems characteristic of process industries.

Process Failure

Process failure refers to anything that creates a process or quality abnormality that necessitates shutting a plant down. Its source may lie inside or outside the equipment. Physical properties of materials being handled, leaks due to corrosion or cracking, blocks, contamination, scattered powder — all may cause process failures. The number of process failures will not decrease unless the plant eliminates the sources of such problems.

Countermeasures for Leaks from Corrosion and Cracking

Problems in machinery and piping, such as stress corrosion cracking or erosion by process fluids, can arise as a result of painting defects or deterioration in the materials from which the equipment is made. While it is vital to perform thorough daily checks, it is also important, as part of a specialized maintenance program, to follow strict acceptance procedures for new plants. Taking great care from the design stage onward helps to quickly spot and correct materials or installation defects.

Countermeasures for Blocks

Blocks usually occur as a result of scaling, foreign matter, moisture absorption, and so on, but abnormal reactions such as polymerization can also block pipes, depending on the properties of the materials passing through them. Hammer marks are frequently seen on hoppers and pipes, but merely beating the equipment cannot stop blocks. While the moisture content of the materials is often a key factor in their formation, blocks have been eliminated in many cases for example, by improving the shapes of hoppers, the angles of their sides, or their lining materials.

Block Prevention Systems

The gasworks mentioned earlier constructed a system for monitoring columns, heat exchangers, and pipes so they could predict and prevent blocks. Blocks frequently occur as a result of tar sludge and naphthalene that collect in the piping and heat exchangers through which unrefined gas passes, or high-carbon compounds that collect in tar-extraction equipment. To cope with this, the company developed diagnostic techniques for predicting blocks. They measured pressure drops, temperature distribution, and thermal conductivity and also applied radiation and laser-reflection techniques.

To prevent blocks, new cleaning fluids were developed and internal cleaning systems that operate without opening the equipment were installed. Ultrasonic cleaning gear was also developed.

Anti-Contamination Measures

Contamination refers to any foreign matter, reactant, or corrosive substance that either adheres to machinery or piping or is scattered around inside a plant. This kind of problem does not go away unless the sources of the contamination are discovered and eliminated.

Contamination sources include leaking seals in pumps and other rotating machinery and corroded, cracked, or perforated piping. The best way of detecting them is to launch a comprehensive program of autonomous maintenance. It is difficult, however, to eliminate such sources completely through autonomous maintenance alone, and the plant needs the support of a specialized maintenance staff.

Preventing Powder Scatter

Scattered powder is usually a big headache for many processes in plants that handle these materials. It is particularly prevalent in large-scale conveying gear such as bucket elevators and conveyor belts, pulverizing machines such as impeller breakers, weighing gear, and drying equipment such as rotary kilns. Until such problems are solved, the autonomous maintenance program cannot make progress.

A good starting point is to enclose the open sections of conveying equipment. Connecting sections and hoppers on conveyor belts cause particular problems, but it is possible to reduce the amount of powder scattered over the surroundings by localizing the sources with devices such as dust-tight curtains.

In pulverizers, common contamination sources include inspection doors, shaft seals, and collecting ducts. To locate all dust sources, it is important to inspect the pulverizer thoroughly, both internally and externally, then enclose or seal off the dust sources. Increasing the equipment's dust-collecting capacity or localizing the dust collection may also be effective.

Drying equipment also has many dust sources. In such large equipment, there is a limit to what can be done through autonomous maintenance alone.

Before starting autonomous maintenance activities, it is helpful to attack the problem through project activities that specialized groups implement or through focused improvement sessions.*

Preventing Operating Errors

Operator error sometimes cause process failures. Such errors can easily arise as a result of forgetfulness, confusion, inattention, ignorance, or poor teamwork. Process industries must therefore develop process-competent, as well as equipment-competent operators. Creating and implementing a system of general inspection of processes can teach operators to understand equipment processes intimately. As part of this program, develop good manuals with which to train them to operate, regulate, and adjust their plants properly. Doing so will improve the safety and stability of processes.

For operators to become equipment-competent, general equipment inspection must be part of an autonomous maintenance program as in fabrication and assembly industries.**

The Philosophy of Zero Equipment Failures

TPM specifies six zero-breakdown measures, all of which must be performed to thoroughly eliminate equipment failures in general machinery.

- Establish basic conditions
- Comply with conditions of use
- Reverse deterioration
- Abolish environments causing accelerated deterioration
- Correct design weaknesses
- Improve skills

These six activities cannot be effective if a plant rushes into them all at once. It is more effective to split them into four phases or stages and implement these systematically and in order. In this way, steady progress can be made toward achieving zero breakdowns. The four phases, which are integral to the building of an autonomous maintenance and planned maintenance systems, have the following main themes:***

---

*   For further discussion of measures to control contamination and scattering, see generally, Chapter 3, and Chapter 4, pp. 111–112.
** For further discussion of the general equipment and process inspection program, see Chapter 4, pp. 119–129.
*** For further discussion of the four-phase zero-failures program, see Chapter 3, pp. 66–75.

1. Reduce variation in failure intervals
2. Lengthen equipment lifetimes
3. Periodically reverse deterioration
4. Predict equipment lifetimes

Promoting Measures Against Equipment Failures and Damage

A distinguishing feature of process industries is the large variety of equipment employed. The most practical approach to maintaining and improving this equipment is to divide it into categories such as rotating machinery, columns and tanks, heat exchangers, piping, electrical instrumentation systems, and so on.

Rotating Machinery

Process plants use large numbers of rotating machines, such as pumps, fans, stirrers, separators, and compressors. The basic philosophy and approach to continuous improvement of such equipment is the same as that for general equipment as described in the previous subsection. Vibration measurement methods are commonly used as diagnostic techniques.

Columns and Tanks

By the time a plant has been operating for 10 years, it is likely that factors such as rainwater have corroded equipment exteriors. Advanced erosion and corrosion are particularly common in externally lagged equipment such as piping and fractionating columns in places where the waterproofing is defective. The many techniques for diagnosing, measuring, and repairing the damage that this kind of external corrosion causes are in the province of specialized maintenance departments.

Piping and Valves

Piping carried on racks is often located at a dangerous height, so dealing with it is a job for specialized maintenance personnel. An autonomous maintenance program, however, must include daily checks for abnormalities such as leaking, blocked, corroded, or vibrating ground-level piping and leaking or faulty valves. Various countermeasures for tackling such problems exist, but it is best to implement them under the supervision of a specialized maintenance department.

Also, since outside piping rusts and corrodes particularly rapidly, personnel sometimes paint the pipes unsystematically as a stopgap measure. This is a poor practice that should be abandoned. Before painting anything, it is important first to locate all defects such as leaks, blocks, deformation, and damaged areas, then repair or correct these. Painting is appropriate *only* after eliminating abnormal conditions and preparing surfaces properly.

Electrical Equipment

For safety reasons, only qualified maintenance personnel usually deal with electrical equipment. Electrical breakdowns and problems are actually quite frequent, however, so it is important to start an improvement program in this area after operators have been trained in safety and general inspection of electrical equipment.

Detection switches, such as limit switches, photoelectric switches, and proximity switches are particularly trouble-prone and problems often occur. Trouble also often occurs in control equipment as a result of burnout and other damage to electromagnetic relays. Problems in detection and control equipment can be reduced considerably by establishing basic equipment conditions (e.g., cleaning, lubricating, and tightening), observing proper conditions of use, and restoring deterioration.

Instrumentation

Abnormalities in measuring instruments, such as inaccuracy and jamming, are often caused by defects in the instruments themselves, internal contamination, ingress of foreign matter, corrosion, blocked strainers, and so on. Including them as items for daily checking in an autonomous maintenance program can eliminate such problems.

Promoting Countermeasures for Quality Defects

We have long been exhorted to "build in quality through the process" or "build in quality through the equipment." This is, in fact, the goal of quality maintenance.

In a nutshell, to forestall quality problems that originate in equipment or processing conditions quality maintenance teams integrate quality assurance and equipment management activities, identify the relationships between quality characteristics and processing and equipment conditions, and then establish and maintain processing and equipment conditions that do not create defects. They accomplish this by clarifying the cause-and-effect system that gives rise to defects and the range of process and equipment conditions that must be maintained for the cause-and-effect system to yield defect-free products.

The basic prerequisite for successful quality maintenance is a base of equipment-competent and process-competent operators developed through a program of autonomous maintenance and skills training. Trained operators can then maintain and control the specified conditions and, consequently, achieve zero defects.*

To establish conditions that do not create defects, plants must abandon the old approach in which personnel detected and corrected defective conditions only when equipment was inspected. Instead, personnel should measure over time changes in inspection items that affect quality and take corrective action before these items deviate from acceptable ranges. In essence, plants must switch from a reactive control system based on checking effects to a proactive one based on checking causes.

REFERENCES

Imagawa and Konishi. *Plant Failure Analysis and Measurement/Diagnostic Technology.* (seminar text in Japanese) Tokyo: Japan Institute of Plant Maintenance, n.d.

Japan Institute of Plant Maintenance, ed., *TPM Promotion in Process Industries — Symposium.* (proceedings in Japanese) Tokyo: Japan Institute of Plant Maintenance, 1989.

——. *1989 National Equipment Management Symposium.* (proceedings in Japanese) Tokyo: Japan Institute of Plant Maintenance, 1989.

——. *1989 Digest of PM Prize Winners, Acceptance Reports.* (proceedings in Japanese) Tokyo: Japan Institute of Plant Maintenance, 1989.

——. *TPM Development Programs in Process Industries.* (seminar text in Japanese) Tokyo: Japan Institute of Plant Maintenance, 1989.

——. *TPM Glossary.* (in Japanese) Tokyo: Japan Institute of Plant Maintenance, 1985.

——. *TPM for Managers.* (course text in Japanese) Tokyo: Japan Institute of Plant Maintenance, n.d.

——. *TPM Development Program.* Tokyo: Japan Institute of Plant Maintenance, 1983. (English edition, Portland, Ore.: Productivity Press, 1989.)

Tokutarō Suzuki. *New Directions in TPM.* Tokyo: Japan Institute of Plant Maintenance, 1989. (English edition, Portland, Ore.: Productivity Press, 1992.)

---

* For a detailed description of a quality maintenance program, see Chapter 7, p. 235 et seq.

3
Focused Improvement

Like all activities designed to revitalize organizations, TPM's goal is to improve corporate business results and create cheerful and productive workplaces. An important feature of TPM is its potential impact on the bottom line. Hearing others talk about "profiting through TPM," however, some people conclude that it is an easy way to make money for their company. This passive attitude cannot yield significant results. Only by adopting a proactive approach and putting in the time and effort required to make a TPM program profitable can a company realize TPM's benefits such as a 1.5-fold increase in productivity or a 10-fold increase in return on investment.

Focused improvement* activity is a priority in any TPM development program and is at the top of the list of the eight fundamentals of TPM development. It is one of the major activities in the TPM master plan, and its implementation begins simultaneously with the TPM kick-off.

WHAT IS FOCUSED IMPROVEMENT?

Focused improvement includes all activities that maximize the overall effectiveness of equipment, processes, and plants through uncompromising elimination of losses and improvement of performance.

Many people ask about the difference between focused improvement and the daily continuous improvement activities they may already be practicing. The basic point to remember about focused improvement is that if a company

---

* Focused improvement is analogous to the TPM activity known as "equipment improvement activity" in fabrication and assembly industries, but somewhat broader in scope. See S. Nakajima, *TPM Development Program* (Portland, Ore.: Productivity Press, 1989).

45

is already making all possible improvements in the course of routine work and small-group activities, focused improvement is unnecessary. Day-to-day improvements, however, do not, in practice, go as smoothly as they should. People claim they are too busy, that improvements are too difficult to make, or there is not enough money. As a result, difficult problems remain unsolved, and loss and waste continue to build up, making the possibility of improvement seem even more remote.

Focused Improvement is Implemented Systematically

The following procedure is extremely effective for breaking out of the vicious cycle that prevents improvements and locking them firmly into place:

- Select a topic
- Form a project team
- Register the topic
- Implement the improvement
- Evaluate the results

An improvement carried out in accordance with this procedure is a *focused improvement* as distinguished from the general, day-to-day continuous improvement. It is characterized by project teams that include engineering, maintenance, production, and other specialized staff and by a carefully planned and monitored approach.

Focused Improvement Should Not Displace Small-Group Improvement Activity

Managers and staff must be careful not to become so engrossed in focused improvement that they neglect to support small-group activities at the line and shopfloor level, since this may have the opposite effect and actually damage the overall TPM program. It is, therefore, vital to give people a sense of achievement by actively encouraging the improvement aspect of the autonomous maintenance program and carefully nurturing ideas that evolve there. This kind of activity permeates the organization with great energy and enthusiasm.

Focused Improvement Emphasizes Overall Plant Effectiveness

It is important, finally, to understand that focused improvement activity in process industries is not directed solely at individual equipment items, rather teams should give priority to raising the effectiveness of the whole process or plant.

LOSSES AND THE SIX MAJOR RESULTS

Focused improvement aims to eliminate all kinds of losses. Identifying and quantifying those losses are therefore important issues.

The traditional method of identifying losses, analyzes results statistically to identify problems, then searches back to find their causes. The method adopted in TPM emphasizes a hands-on, practical approach and examines production inputs as causes *directly*. It examines the four main inputs to the production process (equipment, materials, people, and methods), and treats any deficiencies in these inputs as losses.

Achieving profitable TPM in process industries can be difficult if improvement teams limit their approach to that used in fabrication and assembly industries (i.e., maximizing overall *equipment* effectiveness by eliminating the seven major losses). Consider the unique features of process industries:

- Production is continuous.
- The process as a whole is more important than individual equipment items.
- The properties of the materials being processed change in complex ways.
- The process consumes large amounts of energy.
- Operators must control a wide range of equipment.

Process industry companies must often add to or take away from the basic seven losses to emphasize the problems that characterize their own environments. For example, Table 3-1 lists ten major losses and associated improvement topics used in one particular process plant.

The Six Major Results

Assessing the results achieved through focused improvement requires teams to evaluate the six production outputs (PQCDSM) as quantitatively as possible. Table 3-2 gives an example of how these major results or indicators can be further broken down. Improvement teams commonly use indicators like those shown in this table to evaluate the results of focused improvement projects as they are completed. If a topic is particularly large or complex, the results may be easier to understand if the indicators are broken down even further. For example, improvement in labor productivity can be measured in terms of:

- reduction in manual work time (work hours)
- reduction in checking and lubricating time
- reduction in adjustment time
- reduction in preparation and setup time

Likewise, improvement in equipment productivity can be measured in terms of:

- reduction in sudden breakdowns
- reduction in process failures
- reduction in idling, minor stops, and minor adjustments
- reduction in warmup and cooldown times
- increase in availability
- increase in performance rate

Evaluating the results of focused improvement in this manner and making them visual locks gains into place. Activities are less likely to decline when graphs and charts that show the problems the team tackled and the results achieved over time are shared publicly on special focused improvement activity boards.

Table 3-1. Major Losses and Associated Improvement Topics

Loss	Improvement Topic
1. Equipment failure loss	Eliminate failures by improving construction of main-shaft bearings in product separators
2. Process failure loss	Reduce manual work by preventing clogging of pH meter electrodes in decolorizers
3. Idling and minor stoppage loss	Increase production capacity by reducing malfunction of unloaders in separators
4. Speed loss	Increase performance rate by improving attachment of stirrers in crystallizers
5. Process defect loss	Prevent contamination with foreign matter by improving lubrication of intermediate bearings in screw-type product conveyors
6. Startup and yield loss	Reduce normal production losses by improving remelting work during startup
7. Energy loss	Reduce steam consumption by concentrating liquid feed to crystallization process
8. Quality defect loss	Eliminate customer complaints by preventing product adhesion resulting from moisture absorption by kraft-paper product sacks
9. Leakage and spillage loss	Increase product yield by improving lower bearing takeup in bucket elevators
10. Manual work loss	Reduce number of workers by automating acceptance of subsidiary materials

Table 3-2. Sample Indicators for Evaluating Production Outputs

P (Production)	Q (Quality)
1. Increased labor productivity	1. Reduced process defect rate
2. Increased equipment productivity	2. Reduced customer complaints
3. Increased value-added productivity	3. Reduced scrap rate
4. Increased product yield	4. Reduced cost of quality-defect countermeasures
5. Increased plant operating rate	5. Reduced reprocessing costs
6. Reduced number of workers	
C (Cost)	**D (Delivery)**
1. Reduced maintenance labor hours	1. Reduced late deliveries
2. Reduced maintenance costs	2. Reduced product inventories
3. Reduced resource costs (decreased unit consumption)	3. Increased inventory turnover rate
4. Energy saving (decreased unit consumption)	4. Reduced spare-parts inventories
S (Safety)	**M (Morale)**
1. Reduced number of shutdown accidents	1. Increased number of improvement suggestions
2. Reduced number of other accidents	2. Increased frequency of small-group activities
3. Elimination of pollution incidents	3. Increased number of one-point lesson sheets
4. Degree of improvement on statutory environmental requirements	4. Increased number of irregularities detected

FOCUSED IMPROVEMENT IN PRACTICE

Proper mental and physical preparation is essential before starting any focused improvement project. Improvement teams should prepare in the following ways:

- Understand fully the philosophy of focused improvement.
- Understand fully the significance of losses and the rationale behind improving overall effectiveness.
- Understand the production process well, including its basic theoretical principles.
- Gather data on failures, trouble, and losses, and plot these over time.
- Clarify the basic conditions necessary to assure proper functioning of equipment and define clearly what factors contribute to its optimal state.
- Understand the necessary techniques for analyzing and reducing failures and losses.
- Observe the workplace closely to discover what is actually happening.

Adopt a Macro Approach

As already stated, it is more important in process industries to identify deficiencies in the process as a whole than in individual equipment items. The goal is to improve the plant's overall effectiveness. For example, to increase the production capacity of a process, investigate the entire process and clearly identify the subprocesses and equipment that create bottlenecks. This is a more effective first step than rushing to improve equipment that fails frequently or cutting back unreasonably (and perhaps unnecessarily) on startup procedures or shutdown maintenance periods.

Figure 3-1 shows an example of process capacity analysis (PCA) intended to increase the standard production rate by 10 percent, that is, from 400 tons/day to 440 tons/day.

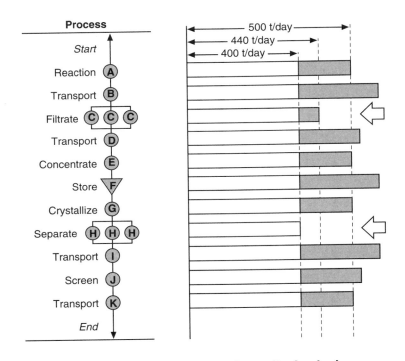

Figure 3-1. Example of Process Capacity Analysis

In this case, the improvement team first studied the subprocess that caused the bottleneck (the separation process), and identified an improvement topic. They calculated that raising the rotation rate by 5 percent, and thereby increasing the centrifugal force, would decrease the cycle time by 10 percent. As a result of focused improvements, mainly to the electrical control system, they raised process capacity by 10 percent.

Later, when a further increase in demand was forecast, the overall production capacity required rose to 500 tons/day. The filtration process and the separation process now became the bottlenecks. Improving the precoating of the filters in the filtration process decreased the washing frequency and increased throughput as a result of the longer filtration cycle. In the separation process, analysis of past failure results revealed that breakdowns and minor stops due to main-shaft breakage and unloader malfunction had lowered the operating rate by at least 10 percent. Installing noncontact sensors and improving the construction of the main-shaft bearings completely eliminated these failures and enabled the overall production capacity target to be achieved.

Starting in this way with a macro approach and gradually proceeding to a more and more detailed analysis can steadily raise the overall capacity of a process and lead to excellent results.

Be "Zero-Oriented"

A major feature of TPM is its "zero-orientation," which encourages teams systematically to reduce all kinds of losses to zero. The key to zero losses is to identify and establish optimal conditions as part of an autonomous maintenance program. To succeed with this approach, emphasize the following points:

- Meticulously detect, expose, and eliminate all minor flaws.
- Establish and maintain basic equipment conditions (cleaning, lubricating, tightening), then identify and establish optimal or ideal conditions.
- Exhaustively correct every deficiency identified, regardless of its apparent relative importance.

Simplify Equipment

Fearing lost production due to breakdowns and other problems, process industries have adopted the costly habit of installing standby units, buffer tanks, bypass pipes, and other redundant items. Very often, equipment that has been idle for years is simply left to rot. An inadequate maintenance prevention (MP) program also frequently leads to equipment duplication and unnecessarily high capacity.

Developing a positive program of equipment and process simplification can eliminate many of these types of losses and yield the following results:

- Minimizing the equipment maintained reduces daily checking and lubricating work.
- Minimizing the equipment maintained also reduces the number of shutdown maintenance work-hours and lowers repair costs.
- As less electrical power and steam are used, unit consumption decreases.
- Streamlining complex piping and equipment layouts reduces the number of operating errors.

Raise the Level of Engineering Technology

Focused improvement in process plants often requires a high level of engineering technology. In addition to improving the level of proprietary technology relating to a company's products, it is also necessary to raise standards of chemical engineering, thermodynamics, hydrodynamics, metallurgy, new materials, instrumentation engineering, control engineering, engineering economics, and so on. While these disciplines cannot be mastered overnight, an energetic TPM focused improvement program helps raise levels in these areas by exposing gaps in knowledge.

THE STEP-BY-STEP APPROACH TO FOCUSED IMPROVEMENT

It is easier and more effective to conduct improvement activities step by step, documenting progress visually as you proceed. This approach has the following advantages:

- Everyone can see what is happening and take an active interest in the focused improvement program.
- Plans for individual topics and teams are developed separately but integrated with plantwide goals to maximize results.
- The focused improvement committee can more easily monitor progress and control the schedule.
- Holding presentations and audits on completion of each step makes it easier to consolidate gains and sustain enthusiasm.

Table 3-3 shows the complete step-by-step procedure, from Step 0 (select improvement topic) to Step 7 (consolidate gains).

Step 0: Select an Improvement Topic and Form a Project Team

When starting a focused improvement project, first select a topic, assess its difficulty, and then register the topic.

Table 3-3. Step-by-Step Procedure for Focused Improvement

Activity/Step	Detailed Outline
Step 0: Select improvement topic	1. Select and register topic 2. Form project team 3. Plan activities
Step 1: Understand situation	1. Identify bottleneck processes 2. Measure failures, defects, and other losses 3. Use baselines to set targets
Step 2: Expose and eliminate abnormalities	1. Painstakingly expose all abnormalities 2. Restore deterioration and correct minor flaws 3. Establish basic equipment conditions
Step 3: Analyze causes	1. Stratify and analyze losses 2. Apply analytical techniques (P-M analysis, FTA, etc.) 3. Employ specific technology, fabricate prototypes, conduct experiments
Step 4: Plan improvement	1. Draft improvement proposals and prepare drawings 2. Compare cost-effectiveness of alternate proposals and compile budget 3. Consider possible harmful effects and disadvantages
Step 5: Implement improvement	1. Carry out improvement plan 2. Practice early management (perform test operation and formal acceptance) 3. Provide instruction on improved equipment, operating methods, etc.
Step 6: Check results	1. Evaluate results with time as improvement project proceeds 2. Check whether targets have been achieved 3. If not, begin again from Step 3 (analyze causes)
Step 7: Consolidate gains	1. Draw up control standards to sustain results 2. Formulate work standards and manuals 3. Feed information back to maintenance prevention program

Selecting the Topic

Although sections and subsections in a plant select their own topics, the themes must still harmonize with plant goals as a whole and with company policy. They also should deal with processes or equipment giving rise to major losses such as recurrent quality defects, costly customer claims, high subcontracting fees, extensive rework, or serious powder spills and liquid leaks. Start with topics that will yield the greatest loss reductions.

Remember also that the easiest way to achieve acceptance of a focused improvement program is to start in the areas that produce the biggest headaches in daily production. This will require managers to visit the production area to gain a clearer understanding of the difficulties their people confront from day to day. If this is not a regular practice in your company, now is the time to adopt it.

Decide on an Improvement Type

The next step is to classify the improvement topic by type (profit-seeking or autonomous-maintenance-backup). In process industries, with large-scale contamination sources, it is extremely important to adopt the correct approach for each of these two types of improvement.

It is relatively easy to budget for a profit-seeking improvement, because the return on investment is easily calculated, it produces highly-visible results, and the capital payback period is clear. The autonomous-maintenance-backup improvement, on the other hand, addresses contamination sources and inaccessible places and is, therefore, less spectacular in effects. Its direct financial benefit is small compared with its cost and it takes longer to pay for itself, which makes it harder to justify economically.

If, however, the plant uses a smaller return as an excuse for putting off this type of improvement, the autonomous maintenance program will not get beyond the cleaning stage. This can easily kill people's enthusiasm and stop the program in its tracks. The working environment will remain dark, dirty, and smelly, and younger employees will shun it. Leaking powders and liquids are major causes of accelerated deterioration, so give high priority to the autonomous-maintenance-backup improvement.

The two types of improvement require different approaches to budgeting. Table 3-4 shows an approach to devising and budgeting a focused improvement system for both types of improvement. A fixed budgeting framework makes cash available on an ad hoc basis for profit-seeking improvements. Funds for autonomous-maintenance-backup improvements are appropriated in lump sums every accounting year or half-year.

Assess Difficulty

After categorizing an improvement topic, the next step is to assess its difficulty against preset criteria and decide who is to implement it. Table 3-5 is an example of a ranking system, but each industry and workplace must develop criteria to suit its own characteristics.

Based on this assessment, decide who will be responsible for implementing the improvement project. Ideally, all improvements should be carried out by people in the course of their daily work or as part of autonomous maintenance

Table 3-4. Focused Improvement System

Type of Focused Improvement	Improvement Topic	Degree of Difficulty	Responsibility
Profit-seeking, i.e., ad hoc budget appropriation	All-out elimination of losses	Rank A Rank B Rank C	Project team Maintenance department Autonomous maintenance teams
Autonomous maintenance backup, i.e., lump-sum budget appropriation	Contamination-source countermeasures Inaccessible-place countermeasures	Rank A Rank B Rank C	Project team Maintenance department Autonomous maintenance teams

activities. This avoids contention about who is responsible for what. When tackling difficult topics, however, form teams with a good cross-section of members, including people from production, maintenance, design, engineering, quality control, and so on. For certain topics, some teams will be more effective if they also include operators and equipment manufacturers' representatives.

Table 3-5. Sample Criteria for Assessing Difficulty

Rank	Assessment Criterion
A	1. Losses and problems affecting many departments 2. Major sources of spills and leaks left unchecked for many years 3. Serious, urgent problems causing late deliveries, significant customer claims, etc. 4. Complex problems requiring a high level of engineering technology 5. Improvements predicted to cost $40,000 or more
B	1. Losses and problems restricted to a single department; medium-severity contamination sources 2. Correcting equipment weaknesses such as structural strength, construction, materials, etc. 3. Improvements requiring an intermediate level of engineering technology and forecast to cost between $8,000 and $40,000
C	1. Losses that operators can eliminate with guidance and assistance 2. Improving inaccessible places hampering routine operation, inspection, and lubrication 3. Eliminating contamination sources without major equipment modifications

While Table 3-4 shows the equipment maintenance department as responsible for B-ranked improvement projects, this is not an unbreakable rule. For example, the quality control or quality assurance department can take charge of improvements concerned with quality losses, while the production or engineering department can handle those dealing with adding value or simplifying processes.

Register the Topic

After selecting a topic and forming the group responsible for implementing it, the group must register the topic. To ensure that focused improvement projects have sufficient impetus, a focused improvement committee or office should handle tasks such as coordinating topics, securing budgets, monitoring progress, arranging audits, and maintaining improvements by standardizing.

To clarify where responsibility for projects lies, indicate whether the improvement will be carried out by a project team or a regular department, or as part of autonomous maintenance activity. Figure 3-2 is an example of a topic registration form.

TOPIC REGISTRATION FORM

To: *Chairman, Focused Improvement Committee*   **From:** *No.1 Production Section, Production Department*

Date: *20 December 1989*   **Prepared by:** *W. Batchelor*

Topic: *Countermeasures against foreign matter*   **Responsible:** *Project team*
in product conveyor system

Type of Loss: *Quality loss*   **Members:** *Wilson*
                                                                       Majewski
Planned Duration: *January 1990 to March 1990*   *Klein*

Leader: *Sperber*

Scheduled Meetings: *1:00 - 3:00 pm every Friday*

Figure 3-2.   Sample Topic Registration Form

Plan the Activity

Plan the activities to take three to six months to complete all the steps. If a project lasts too long, it can easily get bogged down and produce disappointing results.

Step 1: Understand the Situation

Use process capacity analysis to identify the major losses and bottlenecks in the overall process. When identifying losses, pay attention to energy losses and other losses peculiar to your process plant in addition to the eight major losses. Set targets that are as high as possible without being completely unreachable.

Step 2: Expose and Eliminate Abnormalities*

Past experience shows that most losses originate either in deterioration or in failure to establish and maintain the basic conditions that assure proper functioning of equipment (e.g., cleaning, lubrication, routine checking, tightening bolts). Before applying any complex analytical techniques, scrupulously eliminate all minor flaws and effects of deterioration. Similarly, ensure that careful housekeeping procedures (cleaning, lubricating, and tightening) are followed to establish basic conditions. During this step, gradually construct a picture of the optimal conditions for equipment and processes. This will help identify a direction and specific targets for improvement.

Step 3: Analyze Causes

Use devices such as high-speed video cameras to analyze rapid movements or record lengthy observations. Base analysis of causes firmly on the actual workplace and equipment. In analyzing causes, use all appropriate techniques. For matters that involve specific engineering technology, enlist the aid of equipment manufacturers (but do not become overly dependent on them).

Step 4: Plan Improvement

During the drafting and development of proposals, formulate several alternatives. Never dismiss any ideas at this stage. For the best results, do not limit participation to one or two members of the engineering staff or pass on the responsibility to manufacturers or other experts. The higher a person's technical qualifications, the more likely he or she is to make an arbitrary decision and avoid changing it even if it is subsequently found to be wrong.

Guard carefully against improvements that create fresh problems. For example, increasing the capacity of a process may cause it to produce defective product, while raising product quality to an unnecessarily high level may lead to excessive energy consumption. When planning improvements, carefully consider the possible use of new materials.

---

* If you are already correcting abnormal conditions satisfactorily in the first three steps of the autonomous maintenance program, proceed to Step 3 (analyze causes).

Step 5: Implement Improvement

It is crucial that everyone in the workplace understands and accepts the improvements being implemented. Improvements carried out in a top-down, coercive manner will never be properly supported. Particularly when improving work methods, be sure to consult with and inform those in the workplace fully at every stage.

When a plant has more than one of the same type of machine or unit, start by implementing the improvement on one unit, then extend the improvement to the others after checking the results. (This procedure is known in TPM as "lateral deployment.")

Step 6: Check Results

If you do not meet a target, it is especially important to persevere and be flexible — do not stay tied down to the original plan. Monitor the results from the implementation stage on and detail the improvements that were most effective, together with the reasons why. Displaying this kind of information on focused improvement activity boards throughout the company helps ensure that every area benefits from the teams' experience.

The focused improvement committee or office should devise a suitable chart for listing all the improvement projects, monitoring their progress, and ensuring that the gains made at each step are locked firmly into place. Table 3-6 shows one example.

Table 3-6. Sample of Focused Improvement Schedule Control Chart

Focused Improvement Schedule Control Chart	Step 1: ⊢━━┥ Understand situation			Step 2: ⊢═══┥ Expose and eliminate abnormalities					Step 3: ⊢●●●┥ Analyze causes		
	Step 4: ⊢⚡⚡⚡┥ Plan improvement			Step 5: ⊢━━┥ Implement			Step 6: ⊢ – – ┥ Check results		Step 7: ⊢☆☆┥ Consolidate gains		
Topic Title	**Loss**	**Resp.**	**Present Value**	**Target Value**		**Schedule (months)**					**Results Eval.**		
						1	2	3	4	5	A	B	C
1. Prevent foreign matter in product conveyor system	Quality	Project team	Sludge 80	Sludge 10	Plan	⊢━┿●●┿⚡⚡⚡┥━┼━⊢☆☆┥							
					Actual								
2. Improve construction of product separator main-shaft bearing	Failure	Mainte-nance	2/year: 50 h	0	Plan	⊢━┿●┿⚡⚡┥━┼━⊢☆┥							
					Actual								
3.					Plan								
					Actual								

Step 7: Consolidate Gains

Improvements based on restoring deterioration or establishing basic conditions can easily lose ground. It is important to lock them into place by means of periodic checking and maintenance standards. After improving work methods, it is important to standardize them to prevent people from slipping back into old habits.

Similarly, perform an audit on completion of each step and take appropriate action to ensure that the gains made up to that step are maintained. An audit requires team members to reflect on their progress and consider possible next steps carefully before rushing ahead.

ANALYTICAL TECHNIQUES FOR IMPROVEMENT

TPM aims for the ultimate—zero losses and zero breakdowns—so it never excludes any method that helps achieve those ends. Although this book addresses focused improvement in the process industry, it is fine to use techniques commonly used in other industries where they are appropriate to the improvement topic.

Focused improvements go more smoothly if responsible team members learn basic analytical techniques in advance by reading books or attending seminars. Some analytical methods useful in focused improvement include:

- P-M analysis (phenomena are analyzed in terms of their physical principles)
- Know-why analysis (also called "why-why analysis")
- Fault-tree analysis (FTA)
- Failure mode and effect analysis (FMEA)
- Industrial engineering (IE)
- Value analysis (VA)
- Just-in-time production (JIT) (Toyota production system)
- The original seven QC tools and the seven new QC tools (also called the seven management tools)

Analytical techniques are tools for pinpointing all the causes of failures, quality defects, and so on from among large numbers of complex, interrelated phenomena. As mentioned before, they may end up requiring a high level of specific engineering technology. However, make sure teams routinely base any analysis on information gathered at the site of the problem, according to the "three actualities" — the actual location, the actual object, and the actual phenomenon.

Table 3-7 shows how some of the most common analytical techniques are applied. One technique (P-M analysis) is described in more detail below.

Table 3-7. Common Analytical Techniques

Technique	P-M Analysis	Operability Studies	FMEA	Fault Tree Analysis	Event Tree Analysis
Analytical principle	Deductive	Deductive/inductive	Inductive	Deductive	Inductive
Analytical result	Qualitative	Qualitative	Qualitative/quantitative	Quantitative	Quantitative

Upper level (accidents, explosions)

Intermediate level (flow rate, pressure changes)

Lower level (valve, pump failure)

Abnormal phenomenon

P-M Analysis: Chronic loss → Minor flaw

Operability Studies: (Influences, effects) ← Intermediate phenomenon → (Causes, counter-measures)

FMEA: (Influences) ← Effect ← Element failure → Failure mode

Fault Tree Analysis: Top event → Causes

Event Tree Analysis: Trigger phenomenon — Successful / Unsuccessful → Minor accident, Medium-scale accident, Major accident

P-M ANALYSIS

P-M analysis is a technique for analyzing phenomena like failures or process defects in terms of their physical principles and elucidating the mechanisms behind those phenomena in relation to the four production inputs (equipment, materials, people, and methods). It is a suitable technique for tackling chronic losses. (See Figure 3-3.)

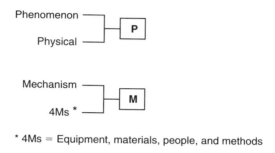

* 4Ms = Equipment, materials, people, and methods

Figure 3-3. P-M Analysis

Characteristics of P-M Analysis and Cautions on Its Use

P-M analysis is especially suited for addressing losses that arise from a variety of complex, interrelated causes, intractable problems that resist repeated attempts at solution by other methods; and chronic problems that promise to be time-consuming in their solution. For this reason, improvement teams often use P-M analysis when they seek the ultimate improvement — to reduce a defect rate from 0.5 percent to zero, for example.

When the occurrence rate of losses and failures is as high a level as 5 or 10 percent, teams should first reduce the level using conventional methods such as restoring all signs of deterioration, establishing basic conditions, and applying why-why analysis. P-M analysis is appropriate only when these methods no longer yield results. (See Figure 3-4.)

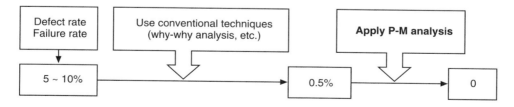

Figure 3-4. Correct Application of P-M Analysis

The P-M Analysis Steps

The following eight steps outline improvement activity using P-M analysis. Success lies in performing close, on-the-spot observations of the actual phenomena and analyzing them in terms of physical laws and principles.

Step 1: Clarify Phenomena

Stratify the phenomena according to type. To understand a phenomenon precisely, study how it manifests, where and when it occurs — at the site. Do not guess or theorize. Distinguish carefully the different types of phenomena and variations in occurrences on different pieces of equipment.

Step 2: Investigate Physical Principles Involved

Analyze the problem in terms of the physical laws and principles that govern it. Describe *how* the problem occurs — the mechanics of its generation. Do not describe it in terms of possible causes. For example, the piston rod in an air cylinder may stop halfway for several reasons. A physical analysis describes what actually occurs in physical terms: resistance received by the rod is greater than its advancing force.

Step 3: Identify Conditions Producing the Problem

Pinpoint all the conditions that consistently give rise to the problem. What conditions must be present for the problem to manifest? In the air cylinder example, there are two conditions that might cause the problem: (1) The driving force of the rod is low. (2) Resistance received by the rod is high.

Step 4: Consider Production Inputs

Investigate the relationships between conditions established in the previous step and production inputs (equipment, materials, people, and methods). Systematically list all the factors that might be involved in producing those conditions. For example, if the driving force of the rod is low, air may not be reaching the piston. In that case the air pressure may be low, the air hose may be malfunctioning, there may be clogging or a leak in the joint, or there may be air leaks inside the cylinder caused by any number of possible abnormalities in the packing, gasket, O-ring, bushing, and so on. All these potential factors should be enumerated and investigated.

Step 5: Determine Optimal Conditions

Based on actual objects, drawings, and standards, determine the optimal condition for each causal factor. Ideally, what conditions, if present, will prevent this problem from occurring? For example, are standard values for process conditions identified? Do practices exist that will ensure they are followed?

Step 6: Investigate Measurement Methods

Determine the most reliable ways of measuring the gaps between the causal conditions and their ideal values.

Step 7: Identify Deficiencies

List all factors that deviate from the optimal and any incidental minor flaws or abnormalities. Using the methods identified in the previous step, survey the relevant processes and mechanisms and identify all deviating conditions.

Step 8: Formulate and Implement an Improvement Plan

Draw up and implement a plan for correcting each deficiency and controlling or eliminating its recurrence.

Key Points in Performing P-M Analysis

Steps 1 through 4 represent the first stage of a P-M analysis. In performing Steps 3 and 4, it is essential to observe the actual plant and equipment *at the site*. Preparing a three-dimensional structural drawing is extremely helpful for performing analytical work while the plant is still on stream.

Chronic losses are often caused by factors that have been consistently overlooked. To get at these hidden roots of problems, P-M analysis is specifically intended to expose every possible contributing factor. Do not exclude any factor when considering the relationships between the conditions that give rise to the problem and the production inputs. Be careful not to throw cold water on anyone's opinions. If you omit factors at this stage, the improvement plan will be incomplete and the problem may not be eradicated.

The key to the second stage of the P-M analysis is determining the optimal conditions or standards and checking how these deviate from the actual situation. For example, you cannot take the correct action if you do not know the optimal values of physical properties (viscosity, concentration, pH, grain size, and moisture content) and the standard values of the factors that influence them (temperature, pressure, degree of vacuum, flow speed, flow rate, and so on). The same naturally applies to performance, precision, capacity, and other attributes of machinery, static units, catalysts, and so forth.

Selecting measuring instruments and techniques for checking discrepancies between actual conditions and standards is also important and requires considerable investigation and preparation. Some topics may require the use of reconstruction test apparatus or other devices not available within the company, and you may then have to consider leasing the equipment or commissioning outside agencies to perform the work.

FAILURE-LOSS REDUCTION PROGRAM

To achieve zero failures, it is essential to uncover all hidden defects in equipment conditions. The six measures described below are designed to deal with these defects once they have been exposed.

The Six Zero-Breakdown Measures

1. Eliminate accelerated deterioration by establishing basic equipment conditions (cleaning, lubricating, and tightening). The most basic activity is to establish and maintain the minimum conditions required to keep equipment running—that is, to keep it clean, well-lubricated, and securely tightened. Failures are far less likely in equipment that is uncontaminated and well-oiled and has no loose parts.

2. Eliminate accelerated deterioration by complying with conditions of use. Equipment is designed for use under certain conditions, and these must be adhered to. For example, pumps are designed to handle materials with certain properties at certain pressures, viscosities, temperatures, and so on. Operating them under different conditions is bound to cause accelerated deterioration, greatly shorten their lifetimes, and result in unexpected failures.

The same applies to catalysts. Using them under conditions for which they were not designed produces abnormal changes in the products being treated, adversely affect the rest of the production process, and leads to process failures (blocks and so forth) and quality failures.

It is particularly important in process industries to operate all machinery, static equipment, catalysts, and so on in accordance with their specifications to minimize the possibility of major accidents.

3. Restore equipment to its optimal condition by restoring deterioration. Equipment deterioration is of two types: accelerated and natural. *Accelerated deterioration* is an artificial cause of failure that arises when basic equipment conditions are not maintained or when conditions of use are not heeded. It often proceeds rapidly. *Natural deterioration* is a gradual form of deterioration due to such factors as wear, corrosion, and changes in the properties of materials. It can result in a succession of failures, starting from the weakest part of the equipment. For example, if the sleeve is worn, a leaking pump gland will not be fixed however many times the packing is replaced. Replacing the sleeve will also not help if the shaft is worn, since this rapidly causes uneven wear of the sleeve. Furthermore, uneven wear of the shaft and sleeve is inevitable unless excessive play due to deterioration in the bearing itself is prevented.

The quickest way to achieve zero failures is thus to examine every part of the equipment, measure its degree of deterioration accurately, and adopt a balanced approach to restoring deterioration. The firefighting approach (dealing with problems as they arise, without ever addressing root causes) is no good at all. To achieve zero failure, you must detect and predict deterioration accurately — through shutdown maintenance and predictive maintenance — as part of a planned maintenance system. Chapter 5 addresses this aspect of failure-loss reduction in detail.

4. Restore processes to their optimal condition by abolishing environments that cause accelerated deterioration. In many process plants, it is impossible to read oil-level gauges or check for loose bolts because spilled powders and leaking fluids contaminate them. V-belts and chains are covered with dust, and motors are caked with dirt and grime. An environment like this is a perfect breeding ground for accelerated deterioration. Autonomous maintenance activities are helpful here, but focused improvement projects aimed at eliminating major contamination sources are even more important. It is vital to clean up and control environments that encourage accelerated deterioration. Otherwise, it will not be possible to maintain basic equipment conditions and observe proper conditions of use.

5. Lengthen equipment lifetimes by correcting design weaknesses. Operating equipment under stressful conditions, such as high rotation speeds, high loads, and frequent stops and starts (for example, in suspended-type centrifuges) results in failures due to shaft breakage, bearing damage, and so on. Observing the correct load, cycle time, and other conditions of use is not enough to address these kinds of problems and failures. In such cases, it may be necessary to change the material or dimensions of the shaft or the construction of the bearings. The only way to achieve zero breakdowns without correcting design weaknesses such as insufficient strength, inadequate materials, or structural defects is to shorten the interval between periodic services, which can result in extravagant maintenance bills.

6. Eliminate unexpected failures by improving operating and maintenance skills. Even when equipment is extremely reliable, unexpected breakdowns may still occur as a result of operating errors and repair errors. Production departments must cultivate operators' abilities to detect abnormalities at an early stage by asking them to maintain basic conditions and inspect using their five senses. Improving their inspection and operating skills will also eliminate operating errors. Meanwhile, maintenance departments must support operators' autonomous maintenance activities, create a periodic inspection and servicing system that avoids omissions and duplications, and enable maintenance technicians to master the most advanced maintenance skills in their role as "equipment doctors." Human sensitivity — the ability to recognize when something is amiss — is vital in both production and maintenance personnel. The goal of zero failures cannot be achieved if people fail to sharpen this faculty.

Figure 3-5 (pp. 68–69) outlines the rationale behind the six zero-breakdown measures and shows the distinct roles of the operating and maintenance departments.

Four Phases to Zero Breakdowns

As Figure 3-5 shows, the six zero-breakdown measures discussed above entail a tremendous amount of work. Trying to speed up a failure reduction program by putting all six countermeasures into effect simultaneously is counterproductive. Implementing a planned maintenance system before establishing basic conditions — when equipment is still dirty, nuts and bolts are loose or missing, and lubrication devices are not working properly — frequently leads to failures before the next major service is due. To prevent these would require making the service interval unreasonably short, and the whole point of the planned maintenance program would be lost.

Rushing into predictive maintenance is equally risky. Many companies purchase diagnostic equipment and software that monitors conditions, while neglecting basic maintenance activities. It is impossible, however, to predict optimal service intervals in an environment where accelerated deterioration and operating errors are unchecked.

The most effective way of achieving the zero-breakdown target is to implement the six measures in the following four phases. (See Table 3-8.)

Table 3-8. Zero Breakdowns in Four Phases

Phase 1 Stabilize Failure Intervals	Phase 2 Lengthen Equipment Life	Phase 3 Periodically Restore Deterioration	Phase 4 Predict Equipment Life
1. Establish basic conditions by cleaning, lubricating, and tightening 2. Expose abnormalities and restore deterioration 3. Clarify operating conditions and comply with conditions of use 4. Abolish environments causing accelerated deterioration (eliminate or control major contamination sources) 5. Establish daily checking and lubricating standards 6. Introduce extensive visual controls	1. Evaluate equipment to select PM items (prioritize maintenance tasks) 2. Rank failures according to seriousness 3. Prevent major break-downs from recurring 4. Correct equipment design weaknesses 5. Eliminate unexpected failures by preventing operating and repair errors 6. Upgrade adjustment and setting skills	1. Build a periodic maintenance system • Perform periodic servicing • Perform periodic inspection • Establish work standards • Control spares • Control data • Computerize maintenance information processing 2. Recognize process abnormality signs and detect abnormalities early 3. Deal with abnormalities correctly	1. Build a predictive maintenance system • Train equipment diagnosticians • Introduce equipment diagnostic techniques • Perform condition monitoring 2. Consolidate improvement activities • Perform sophisticated failure analysis using specific engineering techniques • Extend equipment life by developing new materials and technology

Phase 1: Reduce Variation in Failure Intervals

Restore deterioration. This activity restores equipment in a deteriorated state to its original condition, thereby reducing variation in failure intervals. As Figure 3-6 shows, equipment subject to accelerated deterioration fails often even when an extremely short replacement period is set, as indicated by the shaded portion under the curve. You must reduce the dispersion to decrease the failure frequency.

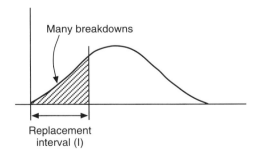

Figure 3-6. Reducing Variation in Failure Intervals (Phase 1)

| THE SIX ZERO-BREAKDOWN MEASURES |

(1) **Establish Basic Conditions**	(2) **Comply with Conditions of Use**	(3) **Restore Deterioration**	
		Detect and Predict Deterioration	**Restore and Prevent Deterioration**

1. Cleaning – Eliminate causes of accelerated deterioration
2. Tightening – Check nuts and bolts and prevent loosening
3. Lubrication
  • Lubricate where needed and replace dirty lubricants
  • Improve lubrication systems
  • Standardize lubricant types
4. Prepare cleaning, checking, and lubricating standards
	1. Set operating and handling conditions – set values for pressure, degree of vacuum, temperature, concentration, viscosity, moisture content, grain size, etc.
	2. Standardize operation and handling methods – prepare manuals and provide OJT
	3. Standardize adjustment/ setting tasks
	  • List adjustment points
	  • Improve adjustment methods
	4. Standardize process startup and shutdown procedures
		1. Check processes using the five senses and identify areas of deterioration
		2. Check equipment using the five senses and identify deteriorated parts
		3. Prepare periodic patrol checking standards
		4. Prepare periodic inspection and replacement standards
		5. Set and standardize replacement and restoration times, e.g.:
		  • Filter washing times
		  • Cycle times for catalysts, etc.
		  • Sieve screen cleaning times
		6. Devise techniques for recognizing signs of process abnormality
		7. Formulate condition monitoring standards – specify measurements and improve measuring equipment
			1. Evaluate and prioritize equipment (select PM equipment)
			2. Prepare equipment logs
			  • Control equipment records
			  • Optimize service intervals
			3. Standardize periodic overhaul inspection procedures
			  • Prepare annual maintenance calendar
			  • Computerize information processing
			4. Standardize disassembly, assembly, and replacement tasks
			5. Improve work methods for inspection, replacement, and repair
			6. Tighten control of maintenance materials and spares
			  • Standardize and centralize
			  • Draw up inventory control standards
			7. Tighten control of drawings and data – share and centralize data; improve retrieval techniques

Production Department
1. Daily checking and lubricating 2. Operation and manipulation 3. Early detection of abnormalities 4. Adjustment and setting 5. Minor improvements to contamination sources and inaccessible places

Figure 3-5. The Six Zero-Breakdown Measures

Abolish Environments (4) Causing Accelerated Deterioration	**(5) Correct Design Weaknesses**	**(6) Improve Operating and Maintenance Skills**	
		Ensure Correct Operation and Manipulation	**Ensure Error-free Repairs**

1. Countermeasures for major contamination sources • Expose contamination sources • Perform general inspection of powder scatter locations • Perform general inspection of powder collection and disposal equipment • Reduce sources of powder spills, liquid leaks, and gas leaks • Remove accumulated materials from buildings and structures 2. Countermeasures against important inaccessible places • Identify hard-to-check and hard-to-measure points • Identify areas of poor layout • Improve inaccessible places 3. Support autonomous-maintenance improvements in contamination sources and inaccessible places	1. Eliminate weaknesses inherent in equipment as a result of design or fabrication defects • Dimensions, strength • Materials • Equipment construction, parts construction • Shape (chute gradients, etc.) • Corrosion resistance • Wear resistance 2. Improve resistance to environmental conditions • Improve anti-corrosion painting • Investigate new corrosion-resistant materials • Consider new lining materials 3. Improve bottleneck processes – introduce measures to prevent overloading 4. Adopt measures to prevent recurrence of major failures	1. Prevent operating and handling errors • Prepare manuals detailing changes in physical properties and operating conditions • Display correct adjustment values on equipment • Introduce more visual controls • Mark pipes with flow direction and contents • Indicate whether valves are open or shut • Provide clear displays on measuring instruments • Indicate rotation directions • Employ error-proofing and tagging 2. Prevent errors in dealing with abnormalities • Standardize procedures for handling abnormalities • Standardize prediction techniques 3. Ensure safe working • Install safety interlocks • Indicate whether switches are on or off • Provide accident prevention training and sharpen individual danger awareness	1. Prevent repair errors • Analyze recurrent failures • Improve repair methods • Standardize materials selection • Standardize parts and spares • Formulate work standards • Draw up work order standards 2. Prevent acceptance errors • Strengthen supervisory skills • Formulate acceptance standards • Establish an operation and maintenance acceptance system 3. Prevent test-operation errors • Standardize test-operation procedures • Prepare checklists

Maintenance Department

1. Periodic checking and inspection
2. Periodic servicing
3. Improvement of major contamination sources and inaccessible places
4. Equipment improvement
5. Recurrence prevention and failure analysis
6. Test operation and acceptance

Deterioration is often left unchecked, even when people are aware of it and understand that it will lead to breakdowns. The plant lacks money, they claim, and no labor resources or time for shutdown. The result of this shortsighted attitude is frequent breakdowns that waste large amounts of time and money, the very reason why these resources were lacking in the first place. Phase 1 is designed to break out of this vicious cycle.

Prevent accelerated deterioration. The next task is to extend equipment life and continue to reduce the variation in failure intervals by preventing further accelerated deterioration. As Figure 3-7 shows, lengthening equipment life by controlling deterioration greatly reduces the number of failures, even when you extend the replacement interval from (I) to (II).

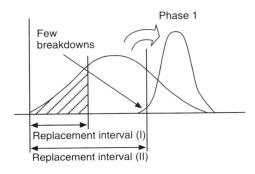

Figure 3-7. Lengthening Lifetimes (Phase 1)

Preventing accelerated deterioration requires the following actions:

Establish basic conditions. Begin by getting equipment into excellent running order through basic housekeeping. This corresponds to the first step in the autonomous maintenance program (initial cleaning).

Comply with conditions of use. Conditions of use are usually followed when equipment is new but forgotten after a few years of operation. Ignoring conditions of use, however, builds up stresses and strains that can lead to a major breakdown. It is important to clarify the conditions of use. Then ensure compliance by standardizing the conditions and using appropriate workplace displays (visual controls) to remind people of them.

Eliminate accelerated deterioration. Major sources of contamination such as powder scatter and liquid leaks create dire situations that promote deterioration and make checking and complying with conditions impossible. Autonomous maintenance activities and minor improvement projects cannot cope with such situations. Tackle them by means of thoroughgoing focused improvements implemented by project teams composed of managers and technical staff.

Prepare user-friendly daily inspection and lubrication standards. To maintain the optimal equipment and process conditions, prepare cleaning, checking, and lubrication standards that are easy to carry out. Use extensive visual controls to make observing these standards part of everyone's daily work.

Phase-1 activities are the foundations of equipment maintenance and equipment management. Unless these foundations are solid, constructing a planned or predictive maintenance system on them is like building a house on sand.

Phase 2: Lengthen Equipment Lifetime

Correct design and fabrication weaknesses. Once you eliminate accelerated deterioration, equipment will only suffer from natural deterioration. Equipment has an inherent life span because it deteriorates naturally; as the balance of deterioration shifts from accelerated to natural, the dispersion in failure intervals decreases and equipment life lengthens. Like people, however, some items of equipment live longer than others. A piece of equipment with a short inherent life must have something wrong with its design or fabrication. Phase 2 activities correct design and fabrication weaknesses and strengthen the equipment's innate constitution by improving its dimensions, strengths, materials, shape, construction, and so on.

Prevent major breakdowns from recurring. Correcting design and fabrication weakness in one unit of equipment can prevent the recurrence of major breakdowns in other equipment units. Every failure is a valuable learning aid that teaches you about weaknesses. Past experience demonstrates that countermeasures based on the results of extensive failure analysis are extremely effective in lengthening equipment life.

Phase-2 activities are generally lumped together under the title *corrective maintenance*. As Figure 3-8 shows, they can greatly lengthen equipment life spans and extend the replacement interval to (III) in the figure.

Prevent operating and repair errors. One obstacle to extending equipment life is the unexpected failure that occurs as a result of operating or repair errors. This irksome problem cannot be solved by maintaining optimal conditions or correcting design weaknesses, no matter how much effort is exerted in these areas. Also, the fact that human error is involved makes these failures difficult to solve quickly. The only way to deal with them is through comprehensive, sustained training in operating and maintenance skills and the use of visual controls and error-proofing (poka-yoke) measures.

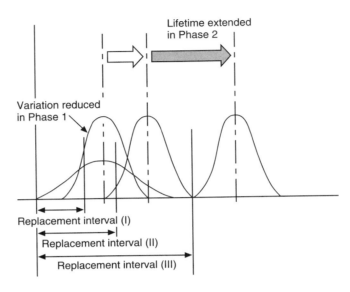

Figure 3-8.   Lengthening Lifetimes (Phase 2)

Phase 3: Periodically Restore Deterioration

Perform periodic servicing and inspection. To preserve and extend the lengthened equipment life achieved in Phases 1 and 2, establish a system of planned or preventive maintenance. The key is determining optimal servicing and inspection intervals. Those that are too long result in recurrent break-downs; those that are too short waste the maintenance budget. To determine the appropriate intervals, it is vital to accurately forecast the longer equipment life spans that result from the Phase 2 improvements.

As Figure 3-9 illustrates, failures do not occur if you select the correct replacement interval. The interval can be quite long as in (III), provided that you effectively extend equipment life in Phases 1 and 2.

Finally, as part of keeping a maintenance calendar for equipment units or components, continually re-evaluate and establish the most economical inspection and service intervals as you repeatedly inspect and service the equipment. One way to extend a service interval is to perform a simple diagnostic check a few months before a scheduled service.

Establish maintenance work and inspection standards. A planned main-tenance system will be more reliable if maintenance teams develop and follow standards for streamlining periodic servicing and inspection while constantly improving maintenance work and inspection methods.

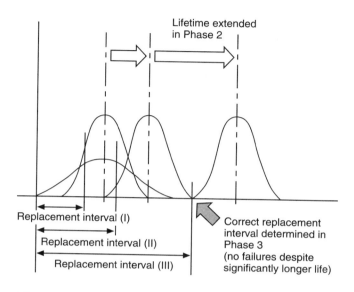

Figure 3-9. Periodically Reversing Deterioration (Phase 3)

Control spare parts and maintenance materials. To perform planned maintenance effectively with a small team of maintenance personnel, just-in-time control of spare parts and maintenance materials is essential.

Recognize signs of process abnormality. While preventive maintenance is a reliable form of maintenance, it is not a cure-all for maintaining zero break-downs in process plants, which are becoming more complex all the time. Pro-duction and maintenance departments must work together to develop finely-tuned diagnostic skills. Operators, who are most intimately in touch with the process, must develop the ability to recognize signs of internal abnormality by sharpening their sensitivity and honing their "five-senses" checking skills.

Phase 4: Predict Equipment Life from Its Conditions

Completing the first three phases, greatly reduces the number of failures as a result of developing the planned maintenance system and operators' keener sensitivity to abnormalities. No matter how carefully you calculate a service interval, however, it is still no more than an educated guess. To be on the safe side, maintenance personnel usually set service intervals shorter than neces-sary. If you try to guarantee trouble-free operation of all equipment through planned maintenance, however, you will inevitably overmaintain it, because not all equipment fails between services.

On the other hand, operators' abilities to recognize danger signals are limited. In Phase 4, therefore, instruments are used to assess equipment condition and accumulate data, and then to predict equipment lifetimes from trends in this data.

Figure 3-10 shows the relationship between the four phases.

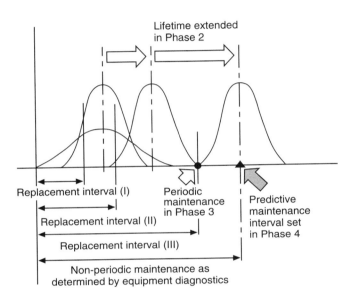

Figure 3-10. Predicting Lifetimes (Phase 4)

Suppose the replacement interval for a piece of equipment is set at (III) in Phase 3 and that planned maintenance is to take place at point ●. Even though no breakdowns will occur, the distribution of equipment life shows that some operating time is still available. To enjoy continued trouble-free operation and yet lengthen the maintenance interval to avoid overmaintenance, you must use equipment diagnostics to predict point ▲. This is why predictive maintenance is regarded as the ideal, and potentially most profitable, type of maintenance.

Recently, astonishing advances have been made in diagnostic equipment and data-processing software, and these can now be applied in a considerable range of fields. Before employing them, however, first decide what equipment to monitor, where to install the equipment, and what to predict by means of what data. If equipment is purchased without preparing for its introduction, it may end up gathering dust on a shelf. Remember, also, that people can monitor many types of equipment satisfactorily using only their five senses. Companies frequently develop their own measuring instruments to extend the limits of what they have discovered to be humanly possible. Try to introduce the form of condition monitoring best suited to your own particular equipment and processes.

The Relationship Between the Four Phases and Focused Improvement

Table 3-9 shows the relationship between the four phases and the various TPM activities. It illustrates how the four phases form the basis for operators' seven-step autonomous maintenance program and for the six-step program for building a planned maintenance system carried out by the maintenance department. Adding focused improvement projects creates a trinity of activities that, when properly performed, guarantees zero breakdowns.

An Example of Design Weakness Improvement

This example, detailed in Figure 3-11, illustrates how an improvement to correct a design weakness was developed at a sugar refinery.

The equipment is a suspended-type centrifugal separator that separates sugar crystals from syrup in 500-kg batches at 1,350 rpm. The main shaft has an upper bearing only, while its lower end is free. Before improvement, the operation of the shaft was unstable and it often bent or broke.

Deterioration was restored and basic conditions established through the autonomous maintenance program. An improvement team also took various measures to eliminate idling and minor stoppages on the crystal unloader, improving the movement detectors, for example. Even so, shaft failures continued to delay production and replacing the damaged shafts was extremely costly and time-consuming.

The team discovered that the problem actually lay in the construction of the main shaft bearing. No further shaft failures occurred after the bearing was improved. This improvement was also standardized and laterally deployed to similar equipment with the same weakness.

PERFORMANCE-LOSS IMPROVEMENT PROGRAM

As mentioned earlier, performance losses consist of normal and abnormal production losses. These two losses are addressed by different types of improvement activity.

Table 3-9. The Relationship Between the Four Zero-Breakdown Phases and TPM Activities

7 Autonomous Maintenance Steps	Reduce Variation in Failure Intervals	Lengthen Equipment Lifetimes	Periodically Restore Deterioration	Predict Equipment Lifetimes
1. Perform initial cleaning	Restore deterioration and establish basic conditions			
2. Control contamination sources and improve accessibility	Abolish conditions causing accelerated deterioration			
3. Establish cleaning and checking standards	Maintain optimal conditions			
4. Perform general equipment inspection	Develop equipment-competent operators (prevent operating errors)			
5. Perform general process inspection		Develop process-competent operators (able to operate, adjust, and handle abnormalities correctly)		
6. Systematize autonomous maintenance			Systematize, remove or discard unnecessary items, efficiently arrange what remains	
7. Practice full self-management				Consolidate improvement activities

	Reduce Variation in Failure Intervals	Lengthen Equipment Lifetimes	Periodically Restore Deterioration	Predict Equipment Lifetimes
6 Specialized Maintenance Steps				
1. Evaluate and understand current equipment conditions	Prepare equipment logs, evaluate equipment			
2. Reverse deterioration and correct weaknesses	Support autonomous maintenance, prevent recurrence of abnormalities, conduct improvement projects			
3. Build an information management system		Create data-management systems to monitor failures, equipment, and budgets		
4. Build a periodic maintenance system			Improve efficiency of PM, inspection planning, SDM	
5. Build a predictive maintenance system				Introduce equipment diagnostic techniques and PdM
6. Evaluate planned maintenance				Evaluate planned maintenance system / Assess equipment R/M
Focused Improvement Projects	Eliminate accelerated deterioration by controlling major contamination sources / Improve maintainability by enhancing accessibility	Correct design and fabrication weaknesses	Employ sophisticated failure analysis techniques	Develop new materials and technology

Note: PM = periodic maintenance; SDM = shutdown maintenance; PdM = predictive maintenance; R/M = reliability and maintainability

Topic

Improvement of Product Separator Main-Shaft Bearing

Rationale

The lower separator shaft often bends during operation. Not only does this destabilize the process; it is also expensive to repair and therefore increases maintenance costs

Assessment and Analysis

Assessment of Situation

1. The 110-mm-diameter shaft, supporting a 500 kg basket of massecuite frequently suffers bending failure from lateral deflection when the shaft rotates at 1,200 rpm. Since 1977, when the units were installed, there have been two such failures on average per year
2. Repair costs:
   $17,000/unit × 2 = $34,000/year

Analysis of Causes

1. In the old B'-type bearing, the center of the spherical part is distant from the rubber buffer, which thus sustains a large force as the shaft deflects
2. The rubber buffer is smaller than in other models
3. The rubber buffer thus absorbs distortion poorly; when packed with massecuite, from which the syrup is hard to extract, the basket vibrates more strongly and becomes unbalanced, striking the monitor casing. This imparts severe shock, causing the shaft to bend

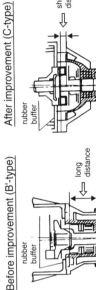

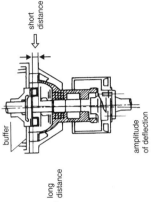

Improvement

Improved bearings were installed in two No.5-line separators, where syrup extraction is poor and which easily became unbalanced, and operating tests were performed

1. C-type bearings with a short distance between the center of the spherical part and the rubber buffer were selected
2. The buffer was enlarged with the aim of increasing its distortion-absorbing capacity

Before improvement (B'-type)

After improvement (C-type)

Results

No similar failures since October 1978, when improvements were implemented.

Amount invested: $36,000/unit × 2 units = $72,000

Repair costs saved: $17,000/unit × 2 units x 3.5 years = $119,000

Future Topics

Although a satisfactory result was obtained with the separators on the No.5 line, parts compatibility with nine similar separators on other lines was lost. We will replace the bearings on those separators with compatible C-type bearings as they wear out

Figure 3-11. Example of Design Weakness Correction

Normal production losses can be reduced by increasing production during plant shutdown and during startup before and after shutdown maintenance. In process industries, it often takes many hours or even several days for a plant to achieve normal production after it starts up. There are three main reasons for this:

- Operators must check control-system settings during operation, so the plant starts up well below the standard production rate and gradually increases.
- Even after raw materials are fed into the process, it takes a long time for them to pass through the various subprocesses and emerge as final product.
- Before it produces acceptable product, the system must be purged of foreign matter introduced during shutdown maintenance work and cleared of decomposed residues that collect while the plant is shut down. This is accomplished by flushing with the materials to be processed or with other materials.

To reduce normal production losses during startup, therefore, requires the plant to improve the efficiency of raw-material input and minimize the time it takes to reach the standard production rate. The same applies to shutdown: Maintenance personnel can decrease shutdown time by increasing the efficiency of storing work-in-process and by devising better ways of dealing with residues.

Reducing abnormal production losses requires a different approach — teams must search out and eliminate the causes of process failures. A process that operates at the standard production rate does not suffer any losses provided it is stable. In practice, however, equipment failures occur often, and process failures are also extremely common as a result of adhesion, blocks, spills, adjustment, and other similar problems. While these may not shut a process down completely, they may force it to operate at low load and give its operators all sorts of headaches trying to maintain the standard production rate.

At one plant, maintenance patrols were sent out regularly to inspect the equipment and maintain safety but were unable to fulfill this role because their portable transceivers constantly cracked with messages like "The dust collector outlet's blocked — go and give it a good thump"; "Go and do something about the bucket elevator — the inlet's clogged up and the current is rising"; and "The damper on the silo outlet isn't working properly — go and take a look at it right away." As a result, the plant was trapped in a vicious cycle: Abnormalities were not detected in time; accelerated deterioration remained unchecked.

Breakdowns were frequent, which forced the plant to operate at low load. To reduce abnormal production losses teams must eliminate adhesion, blocks, leaks, spills, overflowing, and other causes of process failure.

Eliminating Normal Production Losses

Imagine a process that takes two days to start up. The first step toward improvement is to understand thoroughly the current situation by working out and illustrating graphically what happens from the time the plant starts up to the time it takes to reach the standard production rate. If the team sets a target of reducing the startup time by half a day (twelve hours), for example, they must then formulate the ideal procedure for achieving the standard production rate in 36 hours and use process capacity analysis to determine which subprocesses are causing bottlenecks, as illustrated in Figure 3-1. The team must then reduce the startup time by improving the equipment or work methods used in those bottleneck processes. Some examples of such improvements are:

- Improving piping layouts to simplify internal cleaning
- Improving the methods by which in-process materials (intermediates) become products
- Improving recycling methods or equipment for dealing with residues left within the system
- Eliminating intuitive adjustments in control systems by developing standard settings and providing backup systems for detecting deviations from the set values.

Reducing Abnormal Production Losses

To improve a plant's performance rate, either consistently maintain the standard production rate by reducing abnormal production losses or alter the process so that it produces at a higher-than-standard rate. This requires equipment or methods improvements to prevent adhesion, clogging, blocking, overflowing, and other problems. Measures to prevent clogging and blocking, for example, include altering the inclination of equipment such as chutes, silos, and ducts, or improving their internal linings, and introducing or improving strainers, shakers, pneumatic hammers, and so on. Adhesion can be prevented by introducing improved cleaning methods or using materials with better anti-scaling properties, for example.

Table 3-10 shows an example of a process where a team identified ten major process losses and improved the "effective operating rate" (identical to the performance rate).

Table 3-10. Improvement in MSG Production Process Operating Rate

						ASSESSMENT					
Process/ Subprocess	Effective operating rate (%)	Loss breakdown (%)									
		Produc- tion adjust.	Failure	Setup/ adjust.	Minor stops	Idling	Capacity	Defect	Startup	Other- process	Oper- ation
Decolorizing/filtration	48	25	0	5	0	8	5	1	3	5	0
Concentration	55	20	3	10	0	0	8	0	0	4	0
Crystallization	55	20	2	3	0	0	15	0	0	5	0
Separation/drying	45	25	5	10	0	0	13	1	0	1	0

CAUSE ANALYSIS

~~~~~~

		PREPARATION AND IMPLEMENTATION OF IMPROVEMENT PLAN		
Equipment	Operating loss		Improvements	
	Before	After	Item	Details
Concentrator (A)	33.5%	28.6%	• Reduction of setup/ adjustment losses	• Improved scaling removal • Altered operating conditions designed to prevent scaling
Concentrator (B)	20.2	10.3	• Alleviated load • Improved concentrator	• Increased concentration in previous process • New material with better anti-scaling properties
Separator	26.7	2.8	• Process improvement • Separator operating conditions	• Improved crystallization yielding better crystals • Higher rotation speed
Filter (A)	75.0	64.0	• Minimization of setup/adjustment • Reduction of failure losses	• Reduced cycle time • Improved drive unit
Filter (B)	60.0	12.9	• Suppressed progressive capacity loss	• Improved filter-medium washing method and frequency • Improved filter-medium separability

Confirmation of Results: Top-management audit after improvement
Consolidation: Rewrite standards

Source: 1986 National Plant Management Symposium.

This example is taken from the monosodium glutamate production process at Ajinomoto's Kyūshū plant. The team's use of know-why analysis to
improve various operation and production conditions and methods and reduce
failures is noteworthy. Improvements included the following:

- Preventing scaling by devising better washing methods
- Employing more suitable operating conditions
- Introducing improved materials
- Achieving consistently higher filtration capacities by improving filter-
  media washing methods and separating properties
- Boosting separator capacities by increasing their rotation rates

DEFECT-LOSS REDUCTION PROGRAM

As described earlier, defect losses in process industries consist of losses
due to quality defects and reprocessing. Losses from quality defects arise when
product is scrapped because of contamination by foreign matter or problems
with concentration, viscosity, moisture content, grain size, purity, color, and so
on that occur within the process.

Foreign matter may include extraneous objects such as insects, but usually
consists of rust, metal particles, solidified process substances, and other materials that originate in the plant and equipment itself. Problems with properties such as concentration, moisture content, purity, and color occur when the
process operates under conditions that deviate from their preset values. It is
therefore essential to clarify the relationships between equipment and quality
and between operating conditions and quality before trying to effect any
improvements. A quality maintenance program is indispensable for this. Chapter 7 describes the philosophy and practice of quality maintenance and its analytical tools in detail.

Quality defects that consist of incorrect concentration, moisture content,
purity, color, and so on often arise when actual process operating conditions
deviate from the standard. Operators therefore play a very important role in
preventing these. They must have a clear understanding of the materials being
processed and be able to set up and adjust their processes correctly. It is therefore essential to develop process-competent operators in Step 5 of the autonomous maintenance program described in Chapter 4 on pp. 124–129.

Countermeasures Against Reprocessing Losses

Process industries often turn rejectable product produced in one process into acceptable product by recycling it to a previous process. Most plants make no distinction between reprocessed and product right the first time through when they calculate the quality rate. These results are extremely misleading. Reprocessing squanders an enormous amount of energy, makes it difficult to maintain the standard production rate, and lowers the yield. Take a long, hard look at the size of the losses it generates. When managers claim proudly that their plant produces no scrap product, it probably means that a considerable amount of reprocessing is taking place.

To reduce reprocessing losses, begin by taking them seriously — by calculating and assessing the extent of the loss. Then developing a comprehensive program of quality maintenance to ensure that the process never produces any rejectable product. This approach is a much better than continuing to reprocess while vainly searching for ways to reduce its cost. It is important to accurately estimate how much money reprocessing wastes. The costs can be expressed, for example, as the cost per ton of recycling the output of each subprocess.

PROCESS SIMPLIFICATION PROGRAM

When considering improvements in process industries, always remember the payoff of simplification in terms of increased efficiency. Simplification has many direct advantages as well as various useful spin-off benefits:

- Since materials no longer flow through unnecessarily long runs of piping and equipment, process failure losses decrease and yields improve.
- Fewer equipment units consume less power and steam and save energy.
- Eliminating unnecessary equipment and piping reduces the number of possible sources of contamination and other quality defects.
- Since operators have fewer equipment units to look after, operability improves and operating errors decrease.
- With fewer equipment units to maintain, maintenance costs and work-hours decrease.
- Eliminating equipment creates extra space, which yields valuable working areas and safety zones.

Process Simplification in Process Industries

Process industries keep large numbers of standby units in reserve to guard against production losses due to breakdowns. Many return lines and bypasses facilitate reprocessing, and equipment units and piping rendered unnecessary by process modifications are often simply left to deteriorate. Often equipment is used simply because it is there. Too many people, intent on maintaining the status quo, never bother to check their equipment's functions and performance thoroughly to see whether it is really needed. While boosting capacity of bottle-neck processes is a major concern in process industries, process simplification is also an important theme for focused improvement and yields excellent results.

Example of Simplification

Figure 3-12 outlines a process simplification improvement introduced at Ajinomoto's Kyūshū plant. This case study is instructive because the improvements comprehended work methods as well as equipment.

The plant used two Oliver filters in series to eliminate impurities from the monosodium glutamate solution. The improvement team wanted to eliminate one of these filters. First, they calculated the effective operating times of the two filters. These were much lower than expected; the No.1 filter operated only for 6.2 hours out of 24, while the No. 2 filter operated for 5.7 hours. Their effective operating rates were therefore 26 percent and 24 percent respectively.

The team then used a five-step know-why analysis to analyze the factors that lowered the effective operating rates. This revealed that setup and adjustment losses and failures accounted for over 40 percent of the loss, thus narrowing the improvement drive's target. Production-plan losses accounted for 30 percent of the loss in operating rates, but the improvement team felt it was not necessary to address this type of loss at that time.

The team then used know-why analysis again to analyze the origins of each type of loss and provide a starting point for improvement. Their improvement proposals included raising the capacity of the filter, reducing the slurry washing time, and taking action to prevent drive-unit failure.

These improvements produced the following loss reductions:

Elimination of filter performance losses. Remodeling the filter chamber and changing the pump pressure increased the filter capacity by 28 percent.

Elimination of setup/adjustment losses. Reducing the five-hour slurry-washing wait time decreased losses by 34 percent.

PRIOR SITUATION

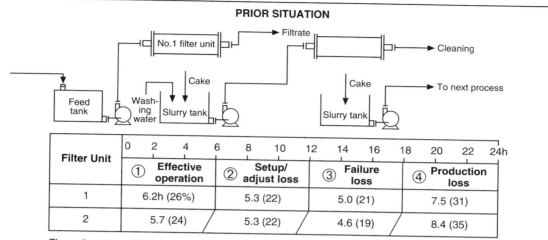

The units were originally considered to be operating to full capacity, but their operating rates were surprisingly low. Our target was to eliminate one filter unit.

IMPROVEMENT

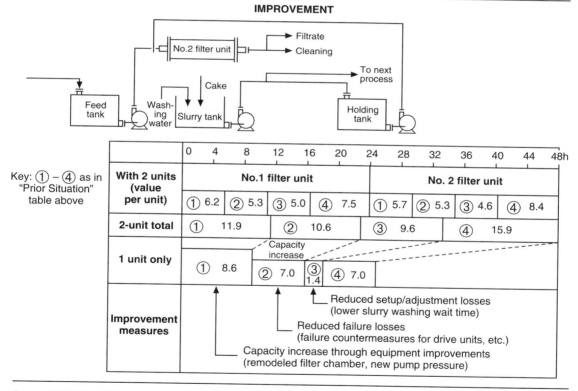

Source: 1986 National Plant Management Symposium.

Figure 3-12. Example of Process Simplification

Elimination of failure losses. Failure countermeasures targeted mainly at the drive units produced an 85 percent loss reduction.

These improvements made possible running the process with a single filter unit, thus simplifying it considerably. The effective operating time of the process with one unit, however, was 8.6 hours, still a 64 percent loss, and they had not yet achieved the zero-breakdown target. The team continued with the project with the aim of raising the level of improvement through the P-M analysis and specific engineering technology.

CONCLUSION

The key to focused improvement is to keep the approach simple. Rather than trying to apply a cocktail of complex theoretical techniques, it is far more effective to adopt the shop-floor approach: first expose and eradicate all minor flaws, restore deterioration, and painstakingly establish basic conditions. More sophisticated improvements become possible only when you solve the basic problems.

REFERENCES

Japan Institute of Plant Maintenance, ed., *National Equipment Management Symposium* (in Japanese). Tokyo: Japan Institute of Plant Maintenance, 1986.

——. *Plant Engineer*, 11 (1986) (in Japanese).

——. *TPM Development Program in Process Industries* (Seminar text in Japanese). Tokyo: Japan Institute of Plant Maintenance, 1992.

——. *TPM Development Program* (English edition). Portland, Ore.: Productivity Press, 1989.

S. Senju and Y. Futami. *Fundamentals of Engineering Economics* (in Japanese). Tokyo: Japan Management Association, n.d.

4

Autonomous Maintenance

TPM improves corporate business results and creates pleasant and productive workplaces by changing the way people think about and work with equipment throughout the company. Autonomous maintenance (maintenance performed by the production department) is one of the most important basic building blocks in any TPM program.

DEVELOPING AN AUTONOMOUS MAINTENANCE PROGRAM

Two keys to developing a successful autonomous maintenance program are *thoroughness* and *continuity*. A further decisive factor is smooth integration with two other fundamental TPM activities, *focused improvement* and *education and training*.

The Goals of Autonomous Maintenance

The production department's mission is to produce good products as cheaply and quickly as possible. One of its most important roles is detecting and dealing with equipment abnormalities promptly, which is the goal of good maintenance. Autonomous maintenance includes any activity performed by the production department that has a maintenance function and is intended to keep the plant operating efficiently and stably in order to meet production plans. The goals of an autonomous maintenance program are:

- Prevent equipment deterioration through correct operation and daily checks
- Bring equipment to its ideal state through restoration and proper management
- Establish the basic conditions needed to keep equipment well-maintained

Another important goal is to use the equipment as a means of teaching people new ways of thinking and working.

The Need for Autonomous Maintenance

In the past, plant operators in process industries were expected to keep their equipment working by checking it regularly and performing minor services. Although different companies had different practices, many expected operators to perform strip-down overhauls of equipment such as pumps. In general, plants practiced a high degree of autonomous maintenance.

During the high-growth era of the 1950s and 1960s, however, equipment became more sophisticated and complex as process plants grew larger and production technology advanced. With the introduction of preventive maintenance, equipment maintenance became increasingly specialized. At the same time, many companies were making significant technical progress in automation and centralization. Faced with two oil-price explosions in succession, Japanese companies reduced the number of plant operators in the name of reducing costs. For many years now, production departments have played an exclusively supervisory role, concentrating on production and leaving maintenance to specialists. This has bolstered the "I make — you fix" syndrome.

The future is uncertain, however, and many companies hope to survive by cutting costs to boost their competitiveness. As a result, autonomous maintenance has become an indispensable program in the drive to eliminate losses and waste from the production floor and maximize the effectiveness of existing equipment.

Advances in computer hardware and software are also intensifying the trend toward automation and unattended operation. One major obstacle, however, is the large amount of manual work required to maintain the numerous sensors that automation requires and to deal with the leaks, spills, blocks, and other problems characteristic of process industries. The best people to solve these problems are those most intimately acquainted with the workplace (the operators), so the need for autonomous maintenance is increasing.

PRODUCTION AND MAINTENANCE ARE INSEPARABLE

Today, the relationship between production and maintenance departments is often adversarial. When production stops due to equipment failures, production departments complain bitterly: "Maintenance doesn't know its job"; "It takes too long to fix the equipment"; or, "This equipment is so antiquated, no wonder it breaks down." Then they say they are too busy to do vital daily checks.

Meanwhile, the maintenance department criticizes the production department: "We prepare the standards, but they don't do the checks"; "They don't know how to operate their equipment properly"; or, "They don't lubricate their machines." The maintenance department excuses its own failings by claiming it has too many repairs and not enough people to do them. Finally, it plays its trump card: "We want to do corrective maintenance, but we don't have the money for it." With these attitudes on both sides, there is no way the goal of good maintenance — detecting and dealing with equipment abnormalities promptly — can ever be achieved.

The production department must abandon the "I make — you fix" mindset, assume ownership of its equipment, and take responsibility for preventing deterioration. Only then can the maintenance department properly carry out the specialized maintenance techniques that ensure effective maintenance. For its part, the maintenance department must discard the notion that its job is simply to make repairs. It must concentrate instead on measuring and restoring deterioration so that operators can use the equipment with confidence. Both departments must clearly define and agree to their respective roles and remove any barriers through mutual understanding and support. They must integrate their efforts until they stand like the two sides of a coin. This is the only way to create a failure-free, trouble-free workplace.

CLASSIFYING AND ALLOCATING MAINTENANCE TASKS

Activities designed to achieve optimal equipment conditions and maximize overall equipment effectiveness either *maintain* or *improve* equipment. Maintenance activities aim to keep equipment in a desired state — by preventing and correcting failures. Table 4-1 summarizes some specific maintenance techniques and activities.

Table 4-1. Maintenance Techniques and Activities

Normal Operation	Correct operation, correct adjustment, correct setting (prevention of human errors)
Preventive Maintenance	Daily maintenance (basic equipment conditions, checking, minor servicing) Periodic maintenance (periodic checking, periodic overhaul inspection, periodic servicing)
Predictive Maintenance	Condition monitoring, medium-interval and long-interval servicing
Breakdown Maintenance	Prompt abnormality detection, emergency repairs, recurrence prevention (troubleshooting)

Improvement activities, on the other hand, extend equipment life, shorten the time required to perform maintenance, and make maintenance unnecessary. Corrective maintenance, for example, focuses on reliability and maintainability improvement in existing equipment. Maintenance prevention activities promote the design of new equipment that is easier and less costly to operate and maintain as well as "vertical" startup after installation or "single-shot" startup after shutdown.

These maintenance and improvement activities are carried out simultaneously in three areas: preventing, measuring, and restoring deterioration. Zero failures cannot be achieved if any one area is neglected. Therefore, the first step in creating a maintenance system is to clarify the responsibilities of the production and maintenance departments in each of these areas and to ensure that the integrated program is free of omissions and duplications. Place particular importance on deterioration prevention (the basic maintenance activity) to build a strong foundation for planned and predictive maintenance (see Figure 4-1).

Activities of the Production Department

The production department must focus on preventing deterioration. It should build its autonomous maintenance program around the following three kinds of activities:

1. Preventing deterioration:

- Correct operation — preventing human errors
- Correct adjustment — preventing process defects (quality defects)
- Basic housekeeping (establishing basic equipment conditions) — cleaning, lubricating, and tightening
- Early prediction and prompt detection of abnormalities — forestalling failures and accidents
- Keeping maintenance records — feeding back information for recurrence prevention and maintenance-prevention design

2. Measuring deterioration:

- Daily inspection — patrol checks and five-senses checks during operation
- Periodic inspection — part of overhaul inspection during plant shutdown or shutdown maintenance

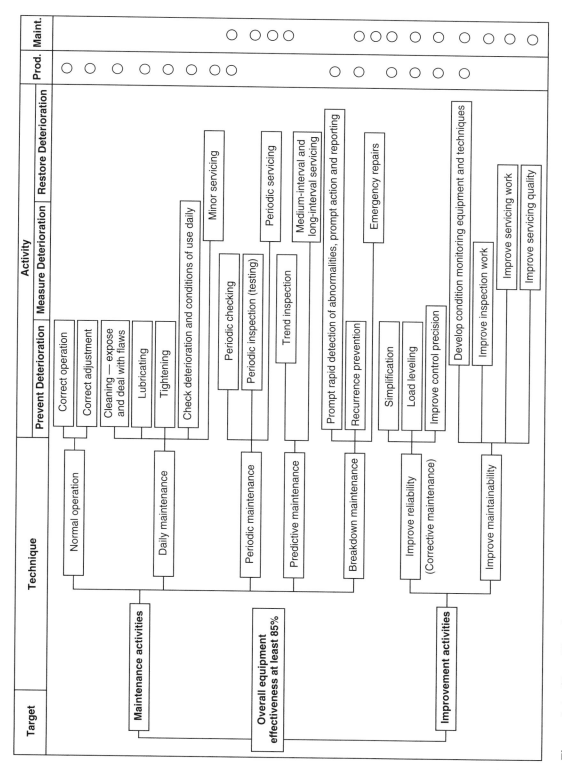

Figure 4-1. Classification and Allocation of Maintenance Tasks

3. *Predicting deterioration:*

- Minor servicing — emergency measures when abnormal conditions arise and simple parts replacement
- Prompt, accurate reporting of failures and problems
- Assistance with repairing unexpected failures

All these listed activities are important, but establishing basic equipment conditions (clean, lubricate, and tighten) is essential to prevent accelerated deterioration. Together with daily checking using the five senses, this is one of the production department's most basic responsibilities.

Maintenance-Department Activities

The maintenance department is the key player in equipment maintenance. It must put all its efforts into planned maintenance, predictive maintenance, and corrective maintenance, concentrating chiefly on measuring and restoring deterioration. It must recognize that it is not a repair shop, restoring failed equipment to its pre-breakdown condition. As an organization of specialists, its true task is to raise maintainability, operability, and safety through activities designed to identify and achieve optimal equipment conditions. This requires advanced maintenance skills and equipment technology, so maintenance departments must constantly strive to increase their technical prowess.

Support for Autonomous Maintenance

Appropriate guidance and support from the maintenance department are indispensable for establishing autonomous maintenance activities and making them an effective part of the maintenance program. The most important tasks are to:

- Provide instruction in inspection skills and help operators prepare inspection standards (checkpoints, checking intervals, and so on)
- Provide training in lubrication techniques, standardize lubricant types, and help operators to formulate lubrication standards (lubrication points, lubricant types, intervals, and so on)
- Deal quickly with deterioration, minor flaws in equipment conditions, and deficiencies in basic equipment conditions (i.e., carry out maintenance work identified by operators promptly)
- Contribute technical assistance in improvement activities such as eliminating contamination sources, making areas more accessible for cleaning, lubrication, and inspection and boosting equipment effectiveness

- Organize routine activities (morning meetings, rounds to take orders for maintenance tasks, and so on).

Above all, the maintenance department must always think, plan, and act in concert with the production department in everything that concerns equipment maintenance. Some other important activities of the maintenance department are to:

- Research and develop new maintenance technologies
- Prepare maintenance standards manuals
- Build systems for keeping maintenance records, handling maintenance data, and measuring results
- Develop and use failure-analysis techniques and implement measures to prevent the recurrence of serious failures
- Assist equipment design and development departments (participate in MP design and early equipment management activities)
- Control spares, jigs, tools, and technical data

ESTABLISHING BASIC EQUIPMENT CONDITIONS

Autonomous maintenance activities practiced by the production department focus on preventing deterioration. Establishing (and maintaining) basic equipment conditions (through cleaning, lubricating, and tightening) is an important part of this. In fact, this is the most basic maintenance activity. In TPM, basic equipment housekeeping is referred to as "establishing basic equipment conditions." This section describes what these conditions are.

Equipment Deterioration

The cause of most failures is equipment deterioration. This consists of natural deterioration, which gives equipment its inherent life, and accelerated deterioration, which occurs when equipment operates in an artificially created, harmful environment. The key to reducing failures is to prevent accelerated deterioration.

As Figure 4-2 shows, establishing basic equipment conditions means eliminating the causes of accelerated deterioration. It means *cleaning* (to remove all traces of dirt and grime and expose and eradicate hidden defects), *lubricating* (to prevent wear and burnout by keeping lubricants clean and replenished) and *tightening* (to prevent malfunctions and breakages by keeping nuts and bolts secure).

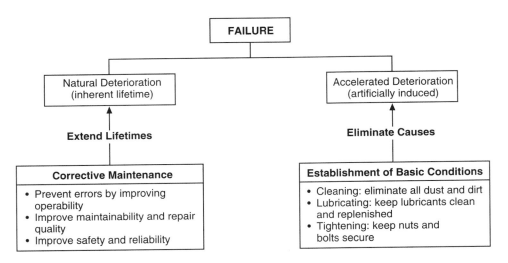

Figure 4-2. Establishing Basic Equipment Conditions Eliminates Causes of Accelerated Deterioration

What Are Optimal Conditions?

In Japanese, the word for failure or breakdown consists of two characters that mean *intentional* and *harm*. Understanding from this that machines do not break down by themselves — that people break them through their deliberate acts or omissions — our first step must be to establish the minimum conditions required to keep equipment running (basic equipment conditions). Then we strive to bring equipment to its ideal state, that is, to a level where it performs optimally. Bringing equipment to its ideal state is referred to in TPM as "establishing optimal conditions."

For example, if the bulb fails in an overhead projector, you will probably replace it right away, because the projector must have a working bulb as a condition for its operation. Suppose, however, that the bulb works, but the light it provides is weak. It functions, but only at the most basic level. You can still use an overhead projector when the light is a little dim, the focus is not very sharp, the lens is foggy, or the transparencies are dirty. In such cases, even though the projector does not fulfill all of its optimal conditions, you may accept the situation. The more you compromise, however, the farther the equipment moves from its ideal state.

Consider the optimal conditions for a quadruple V-belt:

- All four belts intact
- No cracks
- No bulging

- Clean
- Not worn
- Untwisted
- Undamaged
- Unstretched

If no one checks the equipment, these conditions will fail one by one, and the machine eventually will run on a single belt, incapable of transmitting the full driving force. All sorts of losses like this imperceptibly become chronic if you ignore optimal conditions.

The Importance of Cleaning

Cleaning consists of removing all dust, dirt, grime, oil, grease, and other contaminants that adhere to equipment and accessories — in order to expose hidden defects. It is more than a cosmetic exercise. The detrimental effects of failure to clean are innumerable. Table 4-2 lists some of the more serious ones.

Table 4-2. Harmful Effects of Inadequate Cleaning

Failure	Dirt and foreign matter penetrates rotating parts, sliding parts, pneumatic and hydraulic systems, electrical control systems, and sensors, etc., causing loss of precision, malfunction, and failure as a result of wear, blockage, frictional resistance, electrical faults, etc.
Quality Defects	Quality defects are caused either directly by contamination of the product with foreign matter or indirectly as a result of equipment malfunction.
Accelerated Deterioration	Accumulated dust and grime make it difficult to find and rectify cracks, excessive play, insufficient lubrication, and other disorders, resulting in accelerated deterioration.
Speed Losses	Dust and dirt increase wear and frictional resistance, causing speed losses such as idling and underperformance.

Key Points for Cleaning

Cleaning is a form of inspection in TPM. Its purpose is not merely to clean, but to expose hidden defects or abnormalities in equipment conditions. The key points in cleaning are:

- Clean equipment regularly as part of daily work.
- Clean deeply — remove all the layers of grime and scale built up over many years

- Open previously ignored covers, guards, and so on, to expose and re-move every speck of dirt from every corner and crevice.
- Clean attachments and accessories as well as main units, e.g., conveying equipment, control boxes, and lubricant tanks (both inside and out).
- Do not give up when a part gets dirty again soon after cleaning. Instead, carefully note how long it takes the part to become contaminated again, where the contamination is coming from, and how severe it is.

Key Points for Inspection

Practicing "cleaning as inspection" is not easy. The ability to recognize and spot deficiencies can only be developed through extensive hands-on experience. The key to detecting minor flaws in equipment conditions and other abnormalities successfully is to form a mental picture of the equipment's ideal condition and keep it in mind while cleaning. Following are some hints for finding faults:

- Search for invisible as well as visible defects, such as looseness, subtle vibrations, and slight overheating that only touch can detect.
- Search carefully for worn pulleys and belts, dirty drive chains, blocked suction filters, and other problems likely to lead to malfunctions.
- Note whether equipment is easy to clean, lubricate, inspect, operate, and adjust. Identify hindrances such as large, obstructive covers, ill-positioned lubricators, and so on.
- Ensure that all meters operate correctly and are clearly marked with the specified values.
- Investigate any leaks of product, steam, water, oil, compressed air, and so on.
- Also hunt for hidden problems such as corrosion inside insulating materials on pipes, columns, and tanks, and blockages inside chutes and ducts.

What Is Daily Checking?

The daily checks that operators perform on the production floor are more than a formality. They ensure that abnormalities are detected and dealt with as soon as possible.

Many operators in process plants perform pointless inspections based on standards others have set. The "OK" columns are often neatly ticked off a week in advance, and managers in such workplaces are deluding themselves. Ritualized checksheets are meaningless. True daily inspection means being alert enough to spot anything out of the ordinary while operating the equipment or patrolling the plant and being able to deal it with and report it correctly. It requires a high degree of skill and sensitivity. Understand that standards and checksheets are only potentially useful aids — they should not be overly relied upon as a means of preventing deterioration.

Performing meaningful daily checking, therefore, requires easily-understood standards and high operator skills. Some examples of checkpoints that are helpful for preparing standards and one-point lesson sheets are given below in Tables 4-3(1)–(7). Do not merely copy and distribute these lists, however. Use them as a guide for creating checksheets that fit your own workplace.

Table 4-3 (1). Checkpoints for Nuts and Bolts

Slight Defects	☐ Are any nuts or bolts loose? ☐ Are any nuts or bolts missing?
Bolt Lengths	☐ Do all bolts protrude from nuts by 2-3 thread lengths?
Washers	☐ Are flat washers used on long holes? ☐ Are tapered washers used on angle bars and channels? ☐ Are spring washers used where parts are subject to vibration? ☐ Are identical washers used on identical parts?
Attachment of Nuts and Bolts	☐ Are bolts inserted from below, and are nuts visible from the outside? ☐ Are devices such as limit switches secured by at least two bolts? ☐ Are wing nuts on the right way around?

Table 4-3 (2). Lubrication Checkpoints

Lubricant Storage	☐ Are lubricant stores always kept clean, tidy, and well-organized by thorough application of the 5S principles?* ☐ Are lubricant containers always capped? ☐ Are lubricant types clearly indicated and is proper stock control practiced?
Lubricant Inlets	☐ Are grease nipples, speed-reducer lubricant ports, and other lubricant inlets always kept clean? ☐ Are lubricant inlets dustproofed? ☐ Are lubricant inlets labeled with the correct type and quantity of lubricant?
Oil-level Gauges	☐ Are oil-level gauges and lubricators always kept clean, and are oil levels easy to see? ☐ Is the correct oil level clearly marked? ☐ Is equipment free of oil leaks, and are oil pipes and breathers unobstructed?
Automatic Lubricating Devices	☐ Are automatic lubricating devices operating correctly and supplying the right amount of lubricant? ☐ Are any oil or grease pipes blocked, crushed or split?
Lubrication Condition	☐ Are rotating parts, sliding parts, and transmissions (e.g. chains) always clean and well-oiled? ☐ Are the surroundings free of contamination by excess lubricant?

---

* 5S: In Japan the basic principles of industrial housekeeping and visual management are known as the 5Ss, for 5 Japanese words beginning with "S." For a list of English "S" principles and definitions, see p. 316.

Table 4-3 (3). Transmission System Checkpoints

V-belts and Pulleys	☐ Are any belts cracked, swollen, worn, or contaminated by oil or grease? ☐ Are any belts twisted or missing? ☐ Are any belts stretched or slack? ☐ Are multiple belts under uniform tension and all of the same type? ☐ Are top surfaces of belts protruding above the pulley rims? Are the bottoms of any pulley grooves shiny (indicating a worn belt or pulley)? ☐ Are pulleys correctly aligned?
Roller Chains	☐ Are any chains stretched (indicating worn pins or bushings)? ☐ Are any sprocket teeth worn, missing, or damaged? ☐ Is lubrication between pins and bushings sufficient? ☐ Are sprockets correctly aligned?
Shafts, Bearings, and Couplings	☐ Is there any overheating, vibration, or abnormal noise due to excessive play or poor lubrication? ☐ Are any keys or set bolts loose or missing? ☐ Are any couplings misaligned or wobbly? ☐ Are any coupling seals worn? Are any bolts slack?
Gears	☐ Are gears properly lubricated with the right amount of lubricant? Are the surroundings clean? ☐ Are any teeth worn, missing, damaged, or jammed? ☐ Is there any unusual noise or vibration?

Table 4-3 (4). Hydraulic Checkpoints

Hydraulic Units	☐ Is the correct quantity of fluid in hydraulic reservoirs, and is the correct level indicated? ☐ Is fluid at the correct temperature? Are the maximum and minimum permissible temperatures indicated? ☐ Is fluid cloudy (indicating air entrainment)? ☐ Are all fluid inlets and strainers clean? ☐ Are any suction filters blocked? ☐ Are any fluid reservoir breather filters blocked? ☐ Are all fluid pumps operating normally without any unusual noise or vibration? ☐ Are hydraulic pressures correct, and are operating ranges clearly displayed?
Heat Exchangers	☐ Is any fluid or water leaking from fluid coolers or pipes? ☐ Are temperature differences between fluid and water inlets and outlets correct? Are any tubes blocked?
Hydraulic Equipment	☐ Are there any fluid leaks? ☐ Are hydraulic devices properly secured without any makeshift fastenings? ☐ Are hydraulic devices operating correctly without speed losses or breathing? ☐ Are hydraulic pressures correct, and are all pressure gauges working correctly (zero points, deflection)?
Piping and Wiring	☐ Are all pipes and hoses securely attached? ☐ Are there any fluid leaks? Are any hoses cracked or damaged? ☐ Are all valves operating correctly? It is easy to see whether valves are open or shut? ☐ Are any pipes, wires, or valves unnecessary?

Table 4-3 (5). Pneumatic Checkpoints

FRLs*	☐ Are FRLs always kept clean? Is it easy to see inside them? Are they fitted the right way around? ☐ Is there sufficient oil, and are the drains clear? ☐ Is the oil drip rate correct (approximately 1 drop for every 10 strokes)? ☐ Are FRLs installed no more than 3 m from the pneumatic equipment? ☐ Are pressures adjusted to the correct value and are operating ranges clearly indicated?
Pneumatic Equipment	☐ Is any compressed air leaking from pneumatic cylinders or solenoid valves? ☐ Are all pneumatic cylinders and solenoid valves firmly attached? ☐ Are any makeshift fixings in use (wire, adhesive tape, etc.)? ☐ Are any pistons dirty, worn, or damaged? ☐ Are speed controllers installed the right way around? ☐ Is there any abnormal noise or overheating of solenoid valves, and are any lead wires chafed or trailing?
Piping and Wiring	☐ Are there any places in pneumatic pipes or hoses where fluid is liable to collect? ☐ Are all pipes and hoses clipped firmly into place? ☐ Are there any compressed-air leaks? Are any hoses cracked or damaged? ☐ Are all valves operating correctly? Is it easy to see whether valves are open or closed? ☐ Are any pipes, wires, or valves unnecessary?

Table 4-3 (6). Electrical Checkpoints

Control Panels	☐ Are the interiors of distribution boards, switchboards, and control panels kept clean, tidy, and well-organized by the application of the 5S principles? Have any extraneous objects or flammable materials been left inside? ☐ Is the wiring inside control panels in good condition? Are any wires coiled or trailing? ☐ Are all ammeters and voltmeters operating correctly and clearly marked? ☐ Are any instruments or display lamps broken? Are any bulbs faulty? ☐ Are any switches broken? Do all switches work correctly? ☐ Are control panel doors in good condition? Do they open and close easily? ☐ Are there any unused holes? Are control panels waterproof and dustproof?
Electrical Equipment	☐ Are all motors free of overheating, vibration, and unusual noise and smells? ☐ Are all motor cooling fans and fins clean? ☐ Are any attachment bolts loose? Are pedestals free of cracks and other damage?
Sensors	☐ Are all limit switches clean and free of excessive play? ☐ Are the interiors of all limit switches clean? Are any wires trailing? Are all covers in good condition? ☐ Are any limit switches incorrectly installed? ☐ Are any limit switch dogs worn, deformed, or the wrong shape? ☐ Are all photoelectric switches and proximity switches clean and free of excessive play? ☐ Are any sensors out of position? Are correct positions clearly indicated? ☐ Are all lead wires unchafed, and is insulation intact at entry points?
Switches	☐ Are all manual switches clean, undamaged, and free of excessive play? ☐ Are all switches installed in the correct position? ☐ Are emergency stop switches installed in appropriate locations, and are they working correctly?
Piping and Wiring	☐ Are any pipes, wires, or power leads loose or unsecured? ☐ Are any ground wires damaged or disconnected? ☐ Are any pipes corroded or damaged? Are there any bare wires or wires with damaged insulation? ☐ Are any wires coiled on the floor or dangling overhead?

---

* Filter-regulator-lubricator sets.

Table 4-3 (7). Checkpoints for General-Purpose Equipment

Pumps	☐ Are pumps and their stands free of unusual noise, vibration, and play?
	☐ Are pedestal bolts tight, corrosion-free, and undamaged?
	☐ Are stands and pedestals free of corrosion, cracking, and other damage?
	☐ Is any liquid leaking or spraying from gland packings?
	☐ Is any liquid leaking or spraying from pipes or valves?
	☐ Are any pipes or valves blocked?
	☐ Are all pressure gauges, vacuum gauges, flowmeters, thermometers, and other measuring instruments working properly and marked with the correct operating ranges?
	☐ Are starting current and operating current values correct? Are these clearly indicated?
	☐ Are all valves operating correctly? Is it easy to see whether whether valves are open or closed?
Fans	☐ Are fans and their stands free of unusual noise, vibration, and play?
	☐ Are all pedestal bolts tight, corrosion-free, and undamaged?
	☐ Are all stands and pedestals free of corrosion, cracking, and other damage?
	☐ Are any gland packings leaking air or gas?
	☐ Are any ducts or dampers leaking air or gas?
	☐ Are any ducts blocked or clogged?
	☐ Are all pressure gauges, vacuum gauges, flowmeters, thermometers, and other measuring instruments working properly and marked with the correct operating ranges?
	☐ Are starting current and operating current values correct? Are these clearly indicated?
	☐ Are all dampers operating correctly? Is it easy to see whether dampers are opened or closed?

IMPLEMENTING AUTONOMOUS MAINTENANCE STEP-BY-STEP

The goals of cleaning as inspection are to establish basic equipment conditions, bring equipment to its ideal state, and create workplaces that are free of equipment abnormalities, failures and stoppages, and quality defects. Accomplishing this, however, is not easy for operators entrenched in the "I make — you fix" mentality.

Adopting a step-by-step approach that everyone can easily understand permits activities to evolve slowly but thoroughly. The step-by-step approach clearly delineates each phase of the activities, allows for regular audits that secure the gains made at each step, and gives operators a sense of achievement as they proceed through the program. Spelling out the aims of each step in equipment and human terms, together with the kind of guidance managers are expected to provide, clarifies the purpose of the activities. (See Table 4-4.)

Table 4-4 outlines the autonomous maintenance steps as they have been modified for process-type production plants. It incorporates the experience of many process companies that have implemented and directed autonomous maintenance programs, including Ajinomoto Foods, Onoda Cement, Nishi Nippon Seitō, and Nissan Petrochemical.

Overview of the Seven Steps

Autonomous maintenance is implemented in seven steps, starting with initial cleaning and proceeding steadily toward full self-management. It promotes the establishment of optimal process conditions by cycling through the continuous improvement (CAPD) management cycle shown in Table 4-5.

Steps 1 through 3 place priority on abolishing environments that cause accelerated deterioration, reversing deterioration, and establishing and maintaining basic equipment conditions. The goals of these steps are to get operators interested in their equipment and help them shake off their self-image as mere switch-flickers or button-pushers. In steps 4 and 5, team leaders teach inspection procedures to their members, and general inspection expands from individual equipment units to the whole process. The goals of these steps are to reduce failures and develop operators who thoroughly understand their equipment and processes.

Steps 6 and 7 are designed to entrench and upgrade autonomous maintenance and improvement activities by standardizing systems and methods and extending the sphere of action from equipment to other areas such as stores, distribution, and so on. The ultimate goal of these steps is a robust organization and culture in which every workplace is capable of full self-management.

Adjust these steps to suit your particular industry and business conditions. Case studies are introduced later in the chapter.

Step 1: Perform Initial Cleaning

The goal of Step 1 of the autonomous maintenance program is to raise equipment reliability through three activities:

- Eliminate dirt, dust, and grime
- Expose all abnormalities
- Correct minor flaws and establish basic equipment conditions

Eliminate Dirt, Dust, and Grime

Thorough cleaning forces operators to touch every part of their equipment. This increases their interest in it and makes them resolve not to let it get dirty again. Nevertheless, initial cleaning is often slow to start because many operators do not understand why they should do it, or they believe that cleaning is

Table 4-4. The Seven Autonomous Maintenance Steps

Step	Activities	Hardware Goals (Keys for workplace audits)
1. Perform initial cleaning	• Eliminate dust and dirt from main body of equipment • Expose irregularities such as slight defects, contamination sources, inaccessible places, and sources of quality defects • Eliminate unnecessary and seldom-used items, and simplify equipment	• Prevent accelerated deterioration by eliminating the environmental stress of dust and dirt • Raise the quality of checking and repair work and reduce checking and repair times by eliminating dust and dirt • Establish basic equipment conditions • Expose and deal with hidden defects
2. Address contamination sources and inaccessible places	• Reduce housekeeping time by eliminating sources of dust and dirt, preventing scatter, and improving parts that are hard to clean, check, lubricate, tighten, or manipulate	• Increase intrinsic equipment reliability by preventing adhesion of dust and dirt and controlling them at their sources • Increase maintainability by improving cleaning, checking, and lubricating • Create equipment that does not require manual work
3. Establish cleaning and checking standards	• Formulate work standards that help maintain cleaning, lubricating, and tightening levels with minimal time and effort • Improve the efficiency of checking work introducing visual controls	• Sustain the three basic conditions for maintaining equipment and preventing deterioration (cleaning, lubricating, and tightening) • Perform accurate checking by means of visual controls such as equipment nameplates and correct operating range displays on gauges
4. Conduct general equipment inspection	• Provide inspection skills training based on inspection manuals • Get individual equipment items into peak condition by subjecting them to general inspection • Modify equipment to facilitate checking. Make extensive use of visual controls	• Improve reliability by performing general inspection and reversing deterioration for each equipment category (nuts and bolts, drive systems, etc.) • Enable anyone to inspect reliably by introducing visual controls such as equipment nameplates, V-belt specification displays, lubricant type and quantity displays, correct operating range plays on gauges, valve on-off indicators, rotation direction indicators, thermochromic tape, etc.
5. Perform general process inspection	• Provide instruction in process performance, operation, and adjustment and in methods of handling abnormalities in order to improve operational reliability by developing process-competent operators • Prevent inspection duplications and omissions by incorporating provisional cleaning and inspection standards for individual equipment items into periodic inspection and replacement standards for entire processes or areas	• Improve the overall stability and safety of processes through correct operation • Sharpen process inspection precision by extending and improving visual controls, e.g., indicators for pipe contents and flow directions • Modify equipment to make it easier to operate
6. Systematic autonomous maintenance	• Achieve quality maintenance and safety by establishing clear procedures and standards for dependable autonomous maintenance • Improve setup procedures and reduce work-in-process • Establish a system of self-management for workplace flow, spares, tools, work-in-process, final products, data, etc.	• Pinpoint relationships between equipment and quality and establish a quality maintenance system • Review and improve plant and equipment layouts • Standardize maintenance and control of transport equipment, spare parts, tools, work-in-cess, final products, data, passageways, cleaning equipment, and so on, and introduce visual controls for everything in the workplace
7. Practice full self-management	• Evolve activities and standardize improvements in line with company and plant policies and objectives, and reduce costs by eliminating workplace waste • Improve equipment further by keeping accurate maintenance records (e.g., MTBF) and analyzing the data in them	• Analyze data in various ways to improve equipment and raise process reliability, safety, maintainability, quality, and operability • Prioritize equipment improvements and extend equipment lifetimes and checking intervals by using hard data to spot weaknesses

Human Goals (Keys for SGA audits)	Roles of Managers and Staff (fostering motivation, ability, and opportunity)
• Get operators in touch with their equipment to make them more familiar with it, develop a sense of ownership and concern, and stimulate their curiosity about it • Enable group leaders to learn about leadership by implementing this step in small groups • Enable people to recognize slight defects and other irregularities	• Explain the relationship between contamination and accelerated deterioration (maintainability) — that is, explain the meaning of "optimal conditions" • Point out the most important parts to keep clean and explain the importance of basic equipment conditions (cleaning, lubricating, and tightening). Teach using nuts, bolts, and lubrication manuals • Explain the significance of "inspection through cleaning"
• Teach the philosophy and practice of equipment improvement, starting with small-scale, easily-accomplished projects • Germinate the seeds of improvement ideas through small-group activities • Let people taste the thrill and satisfaction of successful improvement	• Encourage improvement ideas and give practical hints, i.e., give technical guidance and support • Teach problem-solving techniques such as why-why analysis • Ensure that other departments respond promptly to work requests • Give guidance on the use of matchmarks and visual controls
• Ensure that operators obey standards and learn their importance (i.e., understand what workplace management is) by having them set their own • Let people learn the importance of teamwork by making them aware of their individual roles	• Give hints on writing and presenting cleaning and inspection standards • Give technical assistance in preparing lubricating standards • Describe how visual controls can simplify checking, and give practical advice
• Learn equipment structure, functions, and assessment criteria and master checking skills through hands-on checking training • Learn to deal with equipment abnormalities through on-the-spot practice • Use relay teaching to enable leaders to learn leadership and members to develop team spirit • Let people understand the usefulness of data by collecting general inspection data	• Prepare general inspection manuals and troubleshooting case studies, and train group leaders in inspection skills • Draw up inspection schedules • Give on-the-spot training in simple methods of rectifying abnormalities • Promptly perform work requested as a result of exposing abnormalities • Give guidance in improving visual controls • Give instruction in data collection and analysis • Involve group leaders in maintenance planning
• Enable operators to operate processes and deal with abnormalities correctly • Enable operators to understand the relationship between equipment and the properties of the materials being processed and master the correct adjustment and setting techniques • Make operators aware of their roles in planned maintenance and foster self-management through periodic inspection and replacement • Help operators realize the necessity for recording time-series data	• Prepare general process inspection manuals and troubleshooting manuals, and train group leaders in inspection skills • Provide on-the-job training in the correct adjustment and setting procedures • Give guidance on selecting periodic inspection and replacement items, techniques, and documentation, and give instruction on setting appropriate intervals based on hard data • Prevent planned maintenance duplications and omissions by clearly delineating the operating and maintenance departments' responsibilities
• Expand the sphere of self-management by systematizing and standardizing control items • Help people understand the relationship between equipment and quality and appreciate the importance of quality maintenance • By standardizing workplace management and collecting data, help people understand the need for improvements aimed at raising standards • Have managers and supervisors learn their true roles (improving standards and ensuring they are followed)	• Prepare system-flow diagrams for processes and give instruction in standardization • Prepare quality maintenance manuals that systematize the relationship between equipment and quality, and use these for instruction • Providing technical support for tasks such as standardizing the flow of work, and give assistance in perfecting visual controls • Give education and guidance in analysis and improvement techniques such as IE, PM, and QC
• Increase awareness of management by objectives and make everyone thoroughly cost-conscious (including maintenance costs) • Enable operators to perform simple repairs and equipment restoration by training them in repair skills • Increase operators' ability to record and analyze data, and have them master improvement techniques	• Explain the importance of management by objectives • Give hands-on repair skills training • Provide technical backup for equipment improvements, and raise operators' improvement skills by including them in improvement projects • Give guidance on standardizing improvements and participating in MP activities

Table 4-5. The Autonomous Maintenance CAPD Cycle

Step 1: Perform initial cleaning	*Check* equipment and expose irregularities	C
Step 2: Control contamination sources and improve inaccessible places	*Act* against contamination sources and inaccessible places	A
Step 3: Establish cleaning and checking standards	*Plan* and *do* checks based on standards	P, D
Step 4: Perform general equipment inspection	Repeat the C→A→P→D cycle for each category	
Step 5: General process inspection	Repeat the C→A→P→D cycle for each category	
Step 6: Systematize autonomous maintenance	C→A→P→D→C→A→P→D	
Step 7: Practice full self-management	C→A→P→D→C→A→P→D	

the job of maintenance. Even when told that initial cleaning means getting their equipment spotless, operators do not know how far to carry their cleaning activities. In the beginning, the process is one of trial and error. It is important for managers and maintenance technicians to give patient, prolonged, practical guidance and to help operators answer the following sorts of questions as they perform initial cleaning:

- What can go wrong if this part is dirty?
- What happens to this column or pipe when this part is rusty?
- How would the product be affected if this were blocked?
- This part keeps on getting dirty no matter how often I clean it. Where does the contamination come from?

Through practice, operators gradually understand how contamination causes problems. They begin to recognize the importance of cleaning, and resolve to keep their equipment spotless in the future. This, in turn, encourages them to think of ways of improving their equipment to make it easier to keep clean.

Expose All Abnormalities

An abnormality is a deficiency, disorder, slight irregularity, defect, bug, or flaw — any condition that could lead to other problems. Table 4-6 classifies abnormalities into seven types, with examples of each. Through the practical

Table 4-6. Sample Manual on Exposing Seven Types of Abnormality

Abnormality	Examples
1. Minor Flaws	
• Contamination	Dust, dirt, powder, oil, grease, rust, paint
• Damage	Cracking, crushing, deformation, chipping, bending
• Play	Shaking, falling out, tilting, eccentricity, wear, distortion, corrosion
• Slackness	Belts, chains
• Abnormal phenomena	Unusual noise, overheating, vibration, strange smells, discoloration, incorrect pressure or current
• Adhesion	Blocking, hardening, accumulation of debris, peeling, malfunction
2. Unfulfilled Basic Conditions	
• Lubrication	Insufficient, dirty, unidentified, unsuitable, or leaking lubricant
• Lubricant supply	Dirty, damaged, or deformed lubricant inlets, faulty lubricant pipes
• Oil level gauges	Dirty, damaged, leaking; no indication of correct level
• Tightening	Nuts and bolts: slackness, missing, cross-threaded, too long, crushed, corroded, washer unsuitable, wing nuts on backward
3. Inaccessible Places	
• Cleaning	Machine construction, covers, layout, footholds, space
• Checking	Covers, construction, layout, instrument position and orientation, operating-range display
• Lubricating	Position of lubricant inlet, construction, height, footholds, lubricant outlet, space
• Tightening	Covers, construction, layout, size, footholds, space
• Operation	Machine layout; position of valves, switches, and levers; footholds
• Adjustment	Position of pressure gauges, thermometers, flowmeters, moisture gauges, vacuum gauges, etc.
4. Contamination Sources	
• Product	Leaks, spills, spurts, scatter, overflow
• Raw materials	Leaks, spills, spurts, scatter, overflow
• Lubricants	Leaking, spilt, and seeping lubricating oils, hydraulic fluids, fuel oil, etc.
• Gases	Leaking compressed air, gases, steam, vapors, exhaust fumes, etc.
• Liquids	Leaking, spilt and spurting cold water, hot water, half-finished products, cooling water, waste water, etc.
• Scrap	Flashes, cuttings, packaging materials, and nonconforming product
• Other	Contaminants brought in by people, fork-lift trucks, etc. and infiltrating through cracks in buildings
5. Quality Defect Sources	
• Foreign matter	Inclusion, infiltration, and entrainment of rust, chips, wire scraps, insects, etc.
• Shock	Dropping, jolting, collision, vibration
• Moisture	Too much, too little, infiltration, defective elimination
• Grain size	Abnormalities in screens, centrifugal separators, compressed-air separators, etc.
• Concentration	Inadequate warming, heating, compounding, mixing, evaporation, stirring, etc.
• Viscosity	Inadequate warming, heating, compounding, mixing, evaporation, stirring, etc.
6. Unnecessary and Non-urgent Items	
• Machinery	Pumps, fans, compressors, columns, tanks, etc.
• Piping equipment	Pipes, hoses, ducts, valves, dampers, etc.
• Measuring instruments	Temperatures, pressure gauges, vacuum gauges, ammeters, etc.
• Electrical equipment	Wiring, piping, power leads, switches, plugs, etc.
• Jigs and tools	General tools, cutting tools, jigs, molds, dies, frames, etc.
• Spare parts	Standby equipment, spares, permanent stocks, auxiliary materials, etc.
• Makeshift repairs	Tape, string, wire, metal plates, etc.
7. Unsafe Places	
• Floors	Unevenness, ramps, projections, cracking, peeling, wear (steel deckplates)
• Steps	Too steep, irregular, peeling anti-slip covering, corrosion, missing handrails
• Lights	Dim, out of position, dirty or broken covers, not properly explosion-proofed
• Rotating machinery	Displaced, fallen off or broken covers, no safety or emergency stop devices
• Lifting gear	Wires, hooks, brakes, and other parts of cranes and hoists
• Other	Special substances, solvents, toxic gases, insulating materials, danger signs, protective clothing, etc.

action of thorough cleaning that brings hidden irregularities to light, operators learn that "cleaning is inspection." Operators, who encounter autonomous maintenance for the first time, however, cannot be expected to understand what is and is not an abnormality. They therefore need instruction on the actual equipment to enable them to answer questions like:

- What problems can occur if this nut or bolt is loose or missing?
- What problems can occur if this oil is dirty or used up?
- What problems can occur if this V-belt or chain is slack?

Provide learning aids. It is helpful to prepare learning aids for this part of Step 1. Compile a manual on the different types of abnormalities listed in Table 4-6, for example, and use it in giving hands-on guidance.

Develop one-point lessons. One-point lesson sheets are also helpful. Operators can learn to recognize abnormalities by using specially prepared sheets with simple diagrams illustrating a single point, for example, the correct and incorrect use of nuts and bolts. These are employed for "relay teaching" in autonomous maintenance teams (see Figure 4-3).

Tag abnormalities where they occur. Another technique is to tag the location of each abnormality as it is spotted, using a card that shows when it was found, who found it, and the nature of the problem. This enables everyone to see what is going on and share in the activities. Use white tags for problems that operators can handle themselves, and red tags for ones that the maintenance department will handle. Tagging takes problems out of the domain of individual autonomous maintenance circles and involves everyone, including workplace colleagues, supervisors, and maintenance department personnel (see Figure 4-4).

When the initial cleaning activities are carried out in this manner, several hundred abnormalities are usually detected in a single item of equipment. Repeated meetings and activities by autonomous maintenance circles and the guidance and action of supervisors and maintenance personnel all sharpen operators' abilities to detect bugs and rapidly increase the number they spot.

Correct Minor Flaws and Establish Basic Equipment Conditions

Correct minor flaws. It is essential to raise the reliability of equipment by establishing basic conditions. Begin by correcting minor flaws such as damage, excessive play, deformation, and wear as soon as you detect them. When serious damage is discovered — such as severely cracked or broken parts that can only be fixed by a specialist or the manufacturer — ask the maintenance department to deal with it right away.

ONE-POINT LESSON SHEET

Device name:	Bolt	**No:**	BN-51
Date prepared:	18 February 1986	**Prepared by:**	Johnson
Topic:	Types of Bolts and Screws	**Approved by:**	Section Manager

Learn the Proper Term!

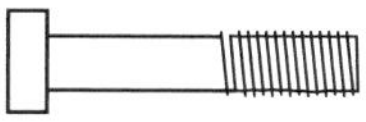

Hexagonal bolt

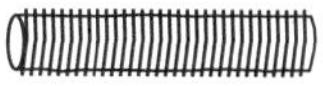

Stud bolt

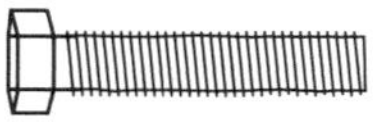

Fully-threaded hexagonal bolt

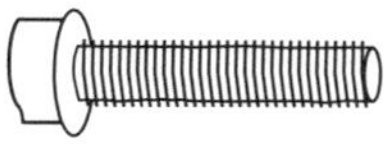

Flanged hexagonal bolt

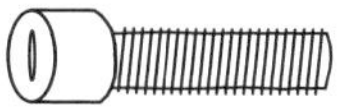

Cap screw

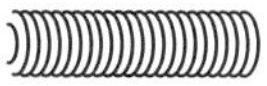

Set screw (slotted or Allen-type)

Remarks: Terminology for bolt ordering, handling and parts control to be standardized as per this sheet.

Department	CCR8	UTY2	Pckg	Cube Sugar	Prod. Cont.	Facil.	Gen. Aff.	Admin.
Date taught	/ /	/ / /	/ /	/ / /	/ /	/ / /	/ /	Passed
Name								

Figure 4-3. Sample One-Point Lesson Sheet

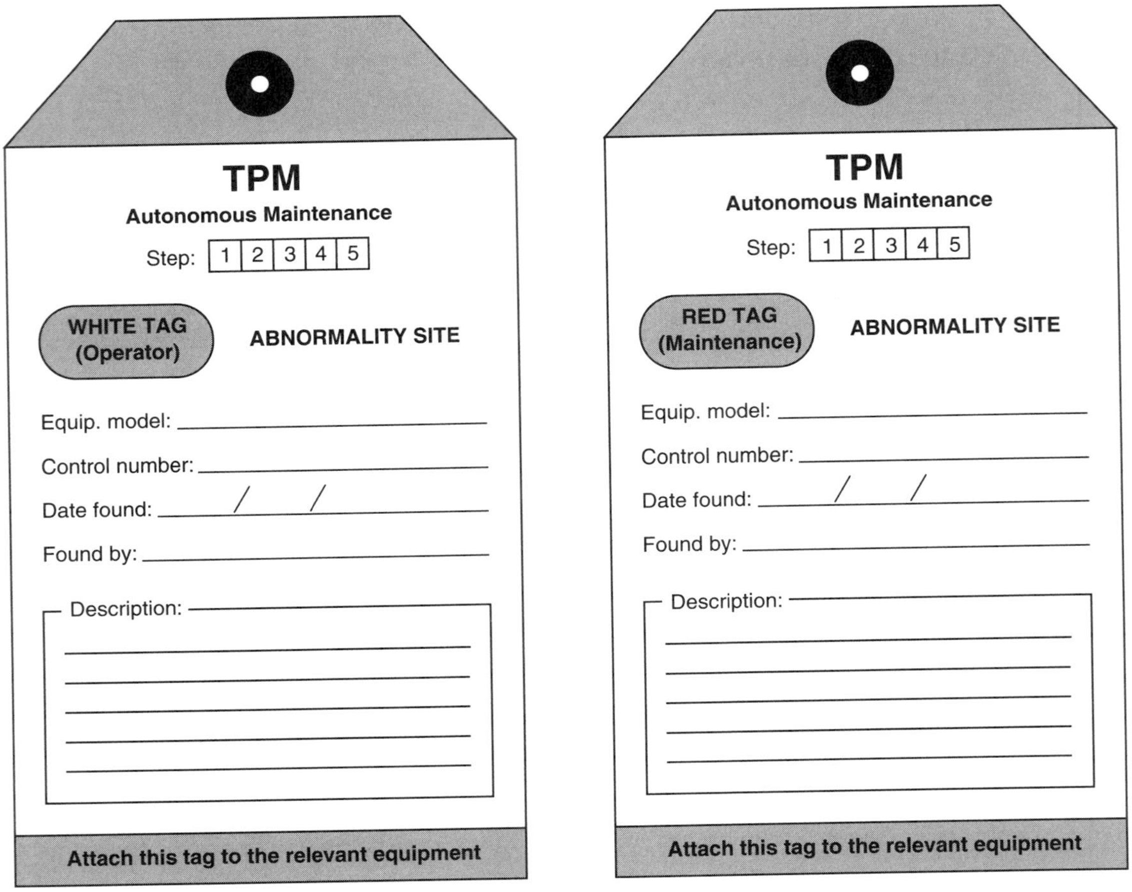

Figure 4-4. Tags for Marking Abnormalities

Lubricate. Lubrication is one of the most important basic conditions for preserving equipment reliability. It is designed to ensure efficient working by preventing wear or burnout, maintaining the operational precision of pneumatic devices, and reducing friction. Often, however, equipment is lubricated carelessly. Workplaces often operate under conditions such as the following:

- People who do not understand the necessity and importance of lubrication make statements like this: "The oil in this machine hasn't been changed for five years, but it's still going strong."
- Operators are not taught the principles of lubrication or the problems that improper lubrication can cause.
- Far too many different types of lubricant are used and too many lubrication sites are inaccessible.

- There is too much reliance on mechanical greasers and other automatic lubricating devices.
- Lubricating standards are often nonexistent or hard-to-follow.

Such conditions expose equipment to accelerated deterioration. To begin counteracting this in Step 1, perform the following activities as lubrication related abnormalities are exposed:

- Teach the importance of lubrication using one-point lesson sheets.
- Lubricate immediately whenever you find that equipment is inadequately lubricated or not lubricated at all.
- Replace all contaminated lubricants.
- Clean and repair all dirty or damaged lubricant inlets and level gauges.
- Check to see whether all automatic lubricating devices are operating correctly.
- Clean and lubricate all revolving parts, sliding parts, drive chains, and other moving parts.
- Clean and repair all manual lubricating equipment and lubricant containers.

Tighten. All machinery contains nuts, bolts, and screws as essential element of their construction. Equipment functions properly only if such fasteners are securely tightened. It only takes one loose bolt to start a chain reaction of wear and vibration. As the machine vibrates slightly, other bolts work loose, vibration feeds on vibration, the equipment starts to rattle and shake, tiny cracks widen into gaping splits, parts become damaged or snap off completely, and the result is a major breakdown.

Breakdowns and other problems are often caused by a combination of conditions acting together (see Figure 4-5). For example, a photoelectric cell probably will work satisfactorily even if it vibrates a little or its glass cover is slightly dirty. If its fixing bolts become loose, however, the vibration will increase, further loosening the bolts and magnifying the vibration. Any slight misalignment or contamination of the light receptor may then combine with this to cause a malfunction. The original looseness of the bolts, not a problem in itself, triggers the chain of events that lead to failure.

Failure analysis performed at one plant revealed that inadequate tightening contributed in one way or another, directly or indirectly, to over half of the failures. It is probably time to reevaluate the importance of tightening in many environments.

While you carry out Step 1 of the autonomous maintenance program, take the actions listed below as you search out and expose deficiencies and abnormalities that relate to nuts and bolts. They are extremely important in establishing basic equipment conditions and stamping out potential trouble sources.

- Securely tighten loose nuts or bolts.
- Replace missing nuts or bolts.
- Replace cross-threaded nuts or bolts that are too long.
- Replace damaged or severely worn nuts and bolts.
- Replace unsuitable wing nuts and washers.
- Use locking devices on important nuts that persistently work loose.

The basic housekeeping activities detailed above are pivotal. In fact, if you constantly maintain basic equipment conditions by cleaning, lubricating, and tightening as discussed here, equipment failure becomes a thing of the past.

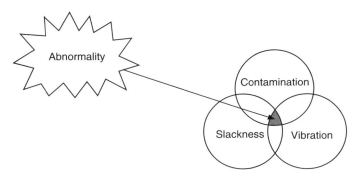

Figure 4-5. Compounding of Flaws

Expose Danger Points and Practice Accident Prevention Training

Although safety must always be paramount, injuries still occur. As indicated in Table 4-6, exposing and neutralizing all sources of danger in the equipment and the work environment prevents accidents and creates workplaces that are safe, clean, and pleasant.

The initial cleaning and improvement activities that operators perform as part of an autonomous maintenance program are not routine tasks. Operators are not accustomed to them as they are to their regular operations. Therefore, carefully consider and assure the safety of autonomous maintenance activities. Devise a program of accident prevention training using illustrations, and practice safety procedures on the actual equipment during all autonomous maintenance activities. The effectiveness of such procedures in achieving zero accidents has already been proven by many companies.

Step 2: Eliminate Sources of Contamination and Inaccessible Places

During Step 1, operators use their hands and physical senses to perform initial cleaning and detect abnormalities. During Step 2, they use their brains to devise effective improvements.

When equipment gets dirty again soon or the level of cleanliness attained through initial cleaning cannot be maintained, operators typically feel compelled to do something about it. In other words, they become improvement-conscious. They begin to think of ways of controlling leaks, spills and other contamination sources. They also try to maintain the basic equipment conditions established in Step 1, but find it takes an intolerable amount of time and effort. They become uncomfortably aware of hard-to-reach places and feel obliged to think about improving their accessibility. The goal of Step 2 is to reduce the time it takes for cleaning, checking, and lubricating by introducing these two types of improvement. (See Figure 4-6.)

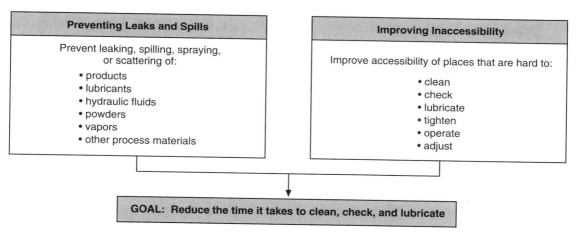

Figure 4-6. Goals for Contamination Sources and Inaccessible Places

Pinpoint and Eliminate Sources of Leaks and Spills

Production sites in process industries suffer from a wide variety of contamination sources, which often have deleterious effects on the equipment. For example:

- Powder and vapor discharges make it difficult to maintain initial cleaning levels.
- Contamination by dust and grease hampers checking bolts, nuts, oil level gauges, and so on.

- Powder contamination causes accelerated deterioration, such as excessive wear of V-belts and drive chains.
- Contamination of limit switches, photoswitches, and other sensors causes malfunction.
- Leaking liquids and vapors cause process units, stands, and other structures to corrode.
- Infiltration of control panels by powders makes control unreliable.
- General contamination impairs the working environment and lowers product quality.

Although the harmful effects of contamination are legion, very little is done about it in many workplaces for a number of reasons. For example, people rarely think about dustproofing when designing equipment such as vibrators, conveyers, and so on. Many believe it is impossible to prevent all dust and vapor from escaping, so they simply shrug their shoulders and do nothing about it. Others assume improvements cost too much money and therefore cannot be done.

From the point of view of maintaining equipment, quality, and the environment, however, not controlling leaking, spilled, and scattered powders, vapors, and corrosive liquids is inexcusable. Thoroughgoing improvement measures are needed. The following are key points for remedying contamination sources:

- Accurately ascertain the nature of the contamination and how and where it is generated.
- Gather quantitative data on the volume of leaks, spills, and other contamination (this helps operators understand the importance of measurement).
- Encourage operators to trace contamination back to its original source — blocks in dust-collecting ducts and chutes, for example.
- Localize the contamination first, then persistently reduce it through a succession of improvements. This produces the best results because one-shot improvements are impossible.
- Carry out focused improvements by project teams that include managers and technical staff. The project team approach is essential when dealing with major contamination sources that operators cannot handle through autonomous maintenance.
- Consider using novel techniques and materials for seals, joints, protective devices, and so on.

Improve Accessibility to Reduce Working Time

Even when you establish basic equipment conditions and achieve optimal conditions, you may be taking too much time and effort to maintain them, and some of the work may still be dangerous. In such cases, checking and lubricating probably will not continue for long. Optimal conditions are not truly achieved until cleaning, checking, and lubricating have become so easy that anyone can do them quickly, correctly, and safely. This involves the following improvement activities:

Reduce cleaning times. Prepare and test at-a-glance cleaning charts (draft provisional standards), reduce contamination sources, make hard-to-clean places more accessible, and devise more efficient cleaning tools.

Reduce checking times. Prepare illustrated checking charts; inspect nuts, bolts, V-belts, chains, couplings, and so on to confirm whether operators can perform checks within the allotted times; devise improved inspection tools; install quick-release covers; improve the positioning and orientation of attachments; create extra space; provide staging for operators to stand on while they check hard-to-reach places; and so on.

Identify hard-to-lubricate places. Use illustrated lubrication charts to check devices such as oil-level gauges and FRLs (filter-regulator-lubricator sets) and replenish or change lubricants.

Simplify lubrication tasks. Reposition oil-level gauges, FRLs, lubricant inlets, and so on; standardize lubricant types; improve manual lubricating devices; and take steps to prevent lubricant inlets from becoming contaminated.

Follow a similar procedure for equipment that is hard to operate or adjust. Particularly in process industries, the key to achieving remote control and unattended operation is to eliminate manual work such as unblocking chutes, clearing up spilt raw materials or products, cleaning sensors, and adjusting process conditions by manipulating controls such as valves and dampers.

Figure 4-7 is an example of a cleaning chart. Pinpointing cleaning, checking, and lubricating sites and items in the process of drawing up such charts is an important preparation for Step 3 of the autonomous maintenance program (establishing cleaning and checking standards).

Part	Job	Benchmark	Improvement 1	Improvement 2	Improvement 3	Improvement 4	Remarks
1. Upper casing	Clean	1/wk (25 min)	Improve inspection port cover (21 min)	Improve casing flange (15 min)	Seal off shaft entry point (10 min)	Improve drive chain lubrication (8 min)	
2. Lower casing	"	1/wk (30 min)	Improve inspection port cover (26 min)	Improve casing flange (20 min)	Seal off inlet port (10 min)	⟶ (10 min)	
3. Take-up section	"	1/wk (20 min)	Attach dust-proofing plate (10 min)	Improve shaft lubrication (7 min)	⟶ (7 min)	⟶ (7 min)	
4. Drive motor	"	1/wk (10 min)	Reduce lubricant leakage (5 min)	⟶ (5 min)	⟶ (5 min)	⟶ (5 min)	
Total		85 min	62 min	47 min	32 min	30 min	

Figure 4-7. Sample Cleaning Chart

Step 3: Establish Cleaning and Inspection Standards

The goal of this step is to lock into place the gains made in Steps 1 and 2, that is, to ensure maintenance of basic conditions and keep equipment in peak condition. To achieve this, operator teams must standardize cleaning and inspection procedures and take responsibility for maintaining their own equipment.

Top-Down Standards Are Never Followed

Many production workplaces have excellent inspection standards and checksheets, yet operators do not use them. Maintenance departments frequently complain that they furnish the production department with standards but the operators ignore them. Managers sigh resignedly that operators neglect to perform checks no matter how often they are reminded to do so. Some typical reasons for this from the operators' viewpoint are listed below:

- "We've been given some standards, but we don't really know why we have to do these checks."
- "We don't really understand what we have to check and how to check it."
- "If we try to perform the checks in accordance with the standards, it takes far too long and we don't make any progress."
- "The checks are hard to do because there are so many high, cramped or dark places."

Standards that are not adhered to were probably set without regard to who is to follow them or how and where the checks are to be performed. People will never follow standards properly as long as management practices a coercive "We set standards — you obey them" style of management.

Self-Set Standards Are Always Obeyed

During Step 1 of the autonomous maintenance program, operators put tremendous effort into cleaning their equipment, correcting minor flaws, and establishing and maintaining basic equipment conditions. During Step 2, they reduce the time required for these tasks by controlling sources of contamination and making cleaning, inspection, and lubrication sites more accessible. As a result, operators are well aware of the necessity and importance of keeping their equipment in its new, greatly improved state.

During Step 3, with proper guidance in preparing standards and establishing checkpoints, people will have the motivation, ability, and opportunity to formulate realistic standards for preventing deterioration during their daily checking.

Give Guidance in Preparing Standards

Provisional standards allow operators to begin performing checks easily, correctly, and without omissions. Standards, therefore, must answer the "Five Ws and One H" (Where? What? When? Why? Who? and How?) and incorporate the following points:

Inspection items. All team members should meet to decide what to clean, check, and lubricate in order to maintain the equipment's basic conditions. Supervisors should point out any omissions or duplications.

Key points. Everyone should discuss what is likely to happen if a particular part becomes contaminated, loose, or insufficiently lubricated. The purpose of this is to understand and remember the harm that can be done if the equipment's basic or optimal conditions are not satisfied. Guidance and advice from supervisors on these points are important here as well.

Method. Decide on the simplest and most appropriate method of checking. Devise clear visual controls that allow anybody to perform the checks correctly and reliably.

Tools. Decide which cleaning, lubricating, and inspecting tools to use and label them clearly.

Times. Decide how much time to allow for each housekeeping task and set achievable objectives. Shorten these times by accumulating improvements designed to simplify and minimize manual work.

Intervals. Decide on the frequency of inspections and monitor achievement of the objectives. Accumulate improvements designed to prolong the inspection intervals. Tasks such as replacing lubricants require the advice of maintenance experts.

Responsibility. Put someone in charge of each task to ensure that nothing is left out; clearly spell out people's roles to enhance their sense of ownership of the equipment.

The sample provisional standard shown in Figure 4-8 illustrates the "inspection through cleaning" philosophy in practice.

Introduce Extensive Visual Controls

The key to consistent performance of cleaning, checking, and lubricating tasks to make them easy to perform correctly by anybody. An effective way of achieving this is to use visual controls (workplace displays). Place these directly on the equipment to be controlled and clearly indicate operating conditions, rotation directions, and other information. Consider adapting the following examples for use in your own workplace:

- Mark each item of equipment with its name and number to make everyone aware of important units (Figure 4-9).
- Put matchmarks on nuts and bolts to simplify checking for slackness (Figure 4-10).
- Indicate acceptable ranges on instruments, such as pressure gauges, vacuum gauges, thermometers, and ammeters to facilitate correct operation (Figure 4-11).
- Indicate lubricant levels, types, and quantities to improve maintainability (Figure 4-12).
- Label the covers of devices such as V-belts, chains, and couplings with their rotation direction and specifications to improve maintainability and simplify checking (Figure 4-13).
- Label pipes with their flow direction and contents to improve maintainability, operability, and safety (Figure 4-14).
- Provide on/off indications on valves and switches to improve maintainability, operability, and safety (Figure 4-14).

TPM — **AUTONOMOUS MAINTENANCE STANDARD** (Cleaning, Checking, and Lubricating)

Location: CCR Equipment: Crystallizers Nos. 1-4

Group: Sprinter Leader: Hicks Tag No: MA-6810-40

Prepared: 6/25/85 Revised: 12/3/85

CHECKING THROUGH CLEANING

Part	Standard	Method	Tool	Action if abnormal	Time (min)	Dy	Wk	Mo	Yr	Resp.
1 Motor section	No dirt or oil spills	Wipe	(icon)	—	10		○			Bova
1-1 Transmission	No vibration, abnormal noise, overheating	(listen/feel)	(icon)	Inform supervisor	(1)	○				"
1-2 Oil-level gauge	Specified quantity	(look)	—	Fill to mark	(1)	○				"
1-3 Chain and sprocket	No abnormal noise, adequately lubricated	(listen/look)	—	Lubricate			○			"
2 Outboard bearing	Clean	Wipe	(icon)	—	10		○			"
2-1 Gland	No leaks	(look)	(wrench)	Tighten or replace	(1)		○			"
2-2 Bearing	No overheating or slackness	(feel/look)	—	Lubricate/observe; tighten if nec.	(1)	○				"
2-3 Cooling-water box	No leaks	(look)	(wrench)	Tighten or replace	(0.5)	○				"
3 Around inboard shaft	Clean	Wipe	(icon)	—	Wk: 12.5 Mo: 5		○			"
3-1 Gland	Not leaking	(look)	(wrench)	Tighten or replace	(1)		○		○ (Worm cover)	"
3-2 Bearing	No overheating or slackness	(feel/look)	—	Lubricate/observe; tighten if nec.	(1)	○	○			"
3-3 Gland drip pan	No accumulation	Recover	Scraper	Check gland	10		○			"
3-4 Worm bearing/worm wheel	No unusual noise, overheating, or thread deformation	(listen/look)	—	Inform supervisor	(3)		○			"

Time required (min)

LUBRICATION

Lube point	Lube type	Lube qty	Method	Tool	Time (min)	Dy	Wk	Mo	Yr	Resp.
1-1 Speed reducer	Daphne Super CS #68	12	Oil can	(icon)	10			○		Gibbs
1-3 Chain	◇	Fully oiled	By hand	◇	0.5		○			"
2-2 Outboard bearing	Grease	Turn cap 2-3 times	—	—	3			○		"
3-2 Inboard bearing	◇	◇	—	—	◇		○			"
3-5 Worm case	#220S	26	Oil can	(icon)	10				2×	"

Figure 4-8. Sample of Provisional Cleaning, Checking, and Lubricating Standard

Figure 4-9. Equipment Nameplate

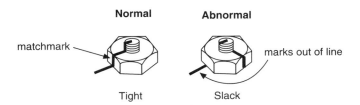

Figure 4-10. Matchmarks for Nuts and Bolts

Figure 4-11. Pressure Gauge Operating Range Indicators

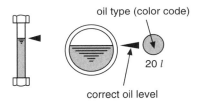

Figure 4-12. Oil Level and Type Indicators

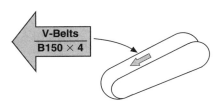

Figure 4-13. V-Belt Label and Direction Indicator

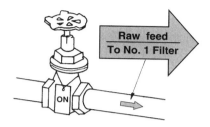

Figure 4-14. Pipes and Valves Labels and Flow Indicators

Step 4: Perform General Equipment Inspection

Operators in plants that manufacture industrial products, must be knowledgeable and confident about their equipment. It is generally believed, however, that operators need only follow instructions and run the equipment, and many companies make no effort to teach operators about their equipment. Some companies even reduce the number of operators, then tell the remaining ones that they need never lay a finger on the equipment. In such cases, operators do no more than flick switches or walk around hammering chutes and ducts to unblock them. This attitude benefits no one.

Developing Equipment-Competent Operators

On the other hand, companies where operators have become well-versed in their equipment are revolutionizing concepts of workplace management and producing outstanding results.

Equipment-competent operators should be able to do minor servicing, but their ability to detect abnormalities is even more crucial. To be truly competent, an operator should be able to spot anything out of the ordinary and immediately recognize it as abnormal.

Such abnormalities are not the effects of equipment breaking down and stopping or producing defective products. Rather, the kinds of abnormalities operators must detect are causal phenomena that presage breakdowns or signal the possibility of producing defective product at some time in the future. Operators must detect such abnormalities early enough to prevent failures and defects. An operator who is truly competent with equipment is one who can detect these causal abnormalities at an early stage and deal with them promptly and efficiently. This is the kind of operator we are trying to develop through autonomous maintenance.

Developing equipment-competent operators revolutionizes not just equipment management but every other aspect of workplace management as well.

The autonomous-maintenance training program for inspection skills described here is the first step toward developing alert, "human-sensor" operators.

Training operators is time-consuming and expensive. They must learn about all aspects of their equipment, starting with basics such as equipment functions, construction, and operating principles. They also must be trained in inspection procedures on the equipment itself. Many companies have already demonstrated that this is the only way to establish a TPM system properly and achieve excellent results. The training program described here reflects their experience.

Preparing for General Inspection Training

General inspection training must not only give each operator a firm grasp of the skills required, but also yield tangible results through general inspection of all the equipment. To accomplish both goals, the steps shown in Figure 4-15 must be implemented steadily, in the proper order, and principally through small-group activities.

Select general inspection items. Begin by determining what operators need to be taught in order to operate their equipment correctly and what they ought to inspect. To select the inspection items most appropriate to the particular workplace, consider the equipment's design specifications and the frequency of problems such as failures and defects. Always include general-purpose equipment such as valves, pumps, and fans, along with the equipment's basic functional elements (nuts, bolts, lubrication systems, drive systems, pneumatics, hydraulics, electrical systems, instrumentation, and so on).

Prepare materials for general inspection training. Detail all the items that operators ought to check through their five senses, and summarize these on a general inspection checksheet.

Next, decide what operators must learn to be able to check these items and prepare a general inspection manual for team leaders. This manual should list and describe the basic functions and structure of the equipment to be inspected, its components with their names and functions, pass-fail criteria, inspection procedures and actions to take when abnormalities are discovered.

The format of a manual is not enough to enable operators to understand this information fully. Also prepare cutaway models, easy-to-read wall charts, and actual samples of worn shafts, dirty oil, and so on. Hands-on training in matters such as the correct tightening of nuts and bolts and the proper insertion of gland-packing is also extremely effective. It is essential to prepare training workshops, jigs, tools, and instrumentation simulators to be used for this purpose.

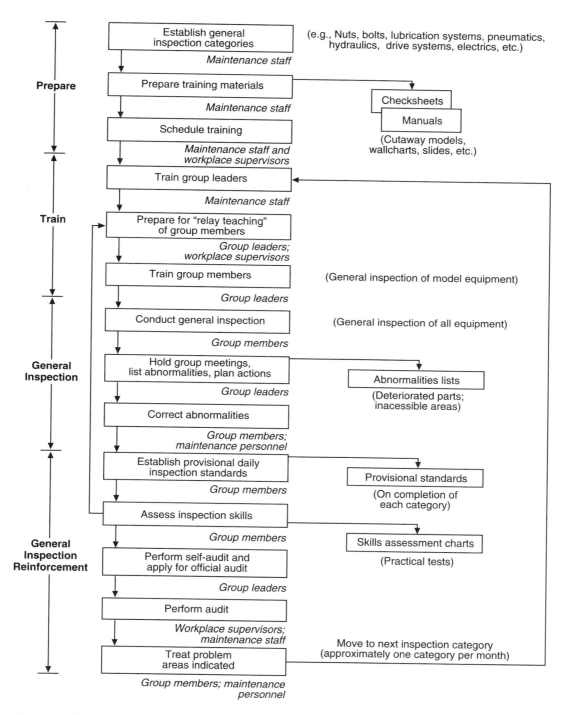

Figure 4-15. Procedure for Developing General Inspection Training Program

Draft general inspection training schedule. While compiling the curriculum and prepare teaching aids, maintenance department staff must draw up a training schedule in consultation with production managers. Allow a standard time of one month for each curriculum unit, including the general inspection performed by operators at the end of each unit. Thus, for eight curriculum units, plan the entire program to last for eight months. The procedure for each curriculum unit is:

1. Maintenance staff instruct team leaders.
2. Team leaders pass on their knowledge to team members (relay teaching).
3. Operators perform general inspection.
4. An audit is held and the team standardizes, or consolidates inspection procedures.

Figure 4-16 is an example of this procedure in action.

Category	Month 1	Month 2	Month 3	Month 4
Nuts and bolts	①②③④	① From maintenance staff to group leaders ② From group leaders to group members ③ General equipment inspection ④ Reinforcement of general inspection category		
Lubrication		①②③④		
Transmissions			①②③④	
Pneumatics				①②③④

Figure 4-16. Sample Schedule Format for General Inspection Training

Implementing General Inspection Training

The importance of "relay teaching." The "relay teaching" method is the most effective way of implementing the training program. In relay teaching maintenance staff teach team leaders, who then teach what they learned to their team members. This to allows team leaders to practice leadership and teams to develop team spirit.

Through teaching, team leaders experience the trials, tribulations, and satisfactions of leadership. Being responsible for their team's development forces them to develop their own skills in earnest. Meanwhile, team members try to support the enthusiastic efforts of their leaders and meet their expectations. This system of teaching and learning injects teams with extra energy and vitality.

Training team leaders. Maintenance staff must do more than teach team leaders the equipment knowledge that must be transferred. They should also help team leaders develop their leadership abilities and advise them on effective ways of passing on their knowledge to their members.

Preparation by team leaders. Leaders must do more than pass along the information they are given. They must prepare additional teaching materials that deal specifically with the equipment in their own workplaces and teach at a level suitable for their team members.

Relay teaching in practice. Relay teaching is a form of hands-on experience, not classroom instruction. It is on-the-job training that team leaders perform while actually carrying out general equipment inspection. Team leaders should make their teaching as effective as possible by devising ways to keep it interesting and amusing. For example, when teaching correct tightening torques for nuts and bolts, team leaders might ask their members to guess the torque required to shear off a bolt. They can also encourage greater involvement by inviting team members to prepare one-point lesson sheets.

Conducting the general equipment inspection. The goal of general inspection training is to restore deterioration and establish basic equipment conditions. This is accomplished by performing a general inspection of every item of equipment that has passed through the first three steps of the autonomous maintenance program. Repeatedly correcting abnormalities and improving hard-to-inspect and hard-to-lubricate places, improves operators' inspection skills and increases equipment reliability.

At this stage, the maintenance department will need to prepare the jigs and tools required for inspection and be prepared to respond promptly to any requests for improvement work. When teams reach the general inspection stage, morale can plummet if the necessary tools are not available or if abnormalities found through team efforts are not corrected.

Consolidation after each general inspection. On completion of each general inspection, teams must lock their gains into place and ensure that equipment remains in peak condition by reevaluating the provisional cleaning and inspection standards they prepared in Step 3 of the autonomous maintenance program. This is the first part of consolidation.

The second part of consolidation is to evaluate operators' individual skills in relation to the general inspection item just completed and to provide further instruction where needed.

The third part of consolidation is to perform an audit of the general inspection item just completed to check for improvements in equipment reliability.

Careful implementation of a training program for general equipment inspection, along with thorough maintenance and checking, eventually creates a failure-free workplace.

Step 5: Perform General Process Inspection

The goals of the first four steps of autonomous maintenance are to develop equipment-competent operators and improve equipment reliability. These accomplishments alone, however, will not ensure effective operation and control in process industries.

Developing Process-Competent Operators

In process plants, operators must operate and monitor an extremely wide range of large process units and associated equipment. The materials being handled change state frequently during the process, and properties such as concentration and purity often vary greatly as materials are subjected to extreme temperatures and pressures. A single wrong adjustment of the process or failure to rectify an abnormality properly may cause a serious accident or produce a large amount of nonconforming product.

For these reasons, operators in process industries must understand the performance and functions of their processes intimately. They should be able to perform accurate adjustments and settings based on a sound knowledge of the materials being handled; they should be capable of recognizing signs of abnormalities and taking appropriate action.

In reality, however, many operators have not be been given the opportunity by their companies to be more than switch-flickers or hammer-wielders. Knowing next to nothing about the processes or the properties of the materials being handled, they patrol the plant with no ability to recognize an abnormality when they see one. This guarantees enormous quality, reprocessing, and downgrading losses. It creates situations in which major accidents and disasters are more likely to recur. This regrettable state is often due entirely to lack of training effort on the part of the company.

The purpose of Step 5 of the autonomous maintenance program is to break out of this vicious cycle and create safe, loss-free, waste-free plants. It boosts operational reliability and equipment safety by training operators to become process-competent in operating skills and general process inspection. Table 4-7 lists the conditions that operators must satisfy to become process-competent.

Table 4-7. Necessary Accomplishments for Process-Competent Operators

Level 1
- Understands process performance and functions
- Operates process correctly

Level 2
- Understands properties of materials being handled
- Performs correct adjustment and setting

Level 3
- Detects abnormalities promptly
- Takes emergency action against abnormalities

Level 4
- Recognizes signs of abnormality
- Deals with abnormalities correctly
- Performs periodic overhaul checking and parts replacement correctly

Procedure for Developing the Process Inspection Training Program

Figure 4-17 shows three stages in developing a general process inspection training program: Step 5-1 — correct operation and manipulation, Step 5-2 — correct adjustment and setting, and Step 5-3 — correct handling of abnormalities.

Step 5-1: Correct operation and manipulation. Avoid authoritarian-style teaching that relies on existing bulky work standards. Instead, perform relay teaching using one-point lesson sheets that managers and staff carefully prepare. In teaching operators, do not focus on the performance and functions of individual equipment items — rather emphasize how processes that consist of combinations of equipment units transform materials into end products.

Avoid also the theoretical type of teaching based on classroom study. On-the-job training on the actual equipment (supported by manuals) is most effective for teaching correct operation and manipulation.

Step 5-2: Correct adjustment and setting. Use relay teaching to teach chemical engineering basics. This will help operators master correct adjustment and setting procedures based on an understanding of how the properties of the materials being processed and the changes that occur in them affect equipment and product quality.

Improve the reliability of adjustment and setting by using visual controls (indicating contents and flow directions in pipes, acceptable ranges on measuring instruments, and so on) It is important that operators know exactly why operating ranges are set as they are, how exceeding these ranges alters the properties of the materials being handled, and what effect this has on product quality and the process.

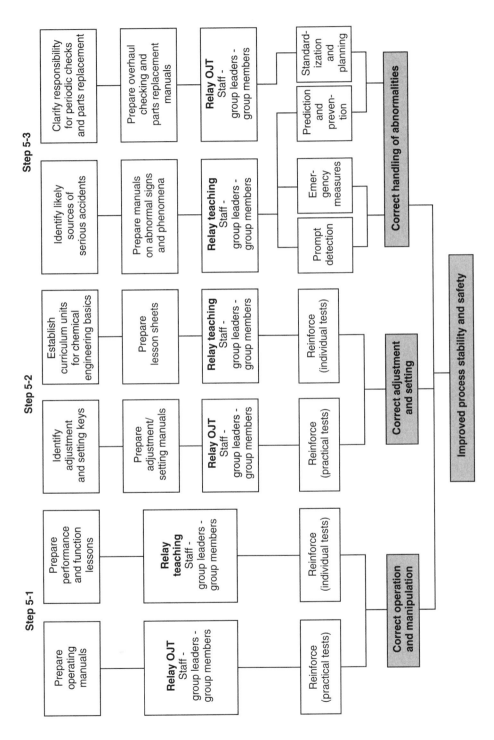

Figure 4-17. Procedure for Implementing General Process Inspection

Step 5-3: Correct handling of abnormalities. This stage consists of two separate tasks. First identify the parts of the process that can forewarn of major accidents, prepare manuals that describe the warning signs, and teach operators how to recognize and understand them so they can predict and prevent accidents.

Second, compile the provisional cleaning and checking standards developed during Steps 1–4 for individual equipment items into periodic inspection and replacement standards for whole processes or areas. This makes people aware of their roles in planned maintenance. Coordinate these standards with the maintenance department's planned maintenance program to avoid omissions and duplications. As part of this, increase the precision of process checking by teaching operators simple techniques for overhaul inspection and condition monitoring, such as monitoring the stretching of bucket elevator chains.

Preparing for General Process Inspection

Establish a curriculum unit for each equipment category. Categorize the equipment in the processes or areas operators are responsible for, and establish a curriculum unit for each category. Typical categories include rotating machinery, heat exchangers, reactor columns, screens, conveying equipment, and filter units.

When compiling the part of the program designed to teach chemical engineering basics, select topics that deepen operators' understanding of the properties of the materials being processed and how these properties change. Typical topics include properties such as viscosity, concentration, and purity, as well as their relationship with process conditions such as pH, temperature, and pressure; and the mechanisms of reaction, crystallization, separation, and dissolution.

Prepare general inspection checklists. The general process inspection performed in Steps 5-1 through 5-3 requires checklists. In preparing these, clearly distinguish between items that operators must identify and record, and items that managers and staff must record, and incorporate these into manuals. Figure 4-18 shows some examples of checklists.

Prepare teaching materials for general process inspection training. While maintenance staff help develop equipment-competent operators during Step 4, managers and staff from the production and engineering departments must cooperate to prepare teaching materials for general process inspection training and to implement the training program. Prepare the following materials:

- Process operation and manipulation manuals
- Process adjustment and setting manuals
- Material and heat balances
- Basic chemical engineering lesson sheets
- Troubleshooting sheets
- Periodic overhaul inspection manuals

Step 5-1: Performance and Functions Checklist

Item #	Process composition (equipment)	Performance Functions Role	Specs.	Relation to quality	Why necessary? Any losses?	Improvement proposals (simplification) (capacity increase)

Step 5-2: Adjustment and Setting Checklist

Item #	Adjustment/set point	Task			Change in properties	Correct range/ Reasons	Effect on quality	Action in event of abnormality
		Why?	What?	How?				

Step 5-3: Checklist Process Problems and Human Error

Item #	Past occurrences Example/location	Date/ Frequency	Problem description	Analysis (why did it happen?)	Recurrence prevention proposal

Step 5-4: Checklist for Anticipating Serious Accidents

Item #	Likely equipment/part	Anticipated accident/disaster	Warning signs/ phenomena	Projected loss/damage	Correct action

Figure 4-18. Sample General Inspection Checklist Formats

Implement general process inspection training. Using the relay teaching method, production staff can teach team leaders, who then pass on their knowledge to team members, so that people can learn from teaching others.

When training people in operation, manipulation, adjustment, setting, and accident prevention, avoid classroom study as much as possible. On-the-job training that uses the actual equipment that operators normally run is far more effective. Operators should work with maintenance personnel to learn how to perform overhaul inspection or replace parts. Maintenance personnel should also assist them in preparing standards.

Consolidate general inspection training.

- *Assess skills*: Assess operators' skill levels by administering individual tests and having them practice handling abnormalities. Include thorough follow-up training as necessary.
- *Set action criteria*: Improve maintenance quality by establishing periodic inspection and replacement criteria based on provisional cleaning and inspection standards.
- *Prepare maintenance plans*: The production department must build an effective autonomous maintenance system by preparing annual maintenance calendars and checksheets. They must cooperate closely with the maintenance department to avoid omissions and duplications.
- *Construct a recurrence-prevention system*: To prevent accidents from recurring, operators prepare abnormality report forms and action report forms and carefully gather and analyze the information.

Implementing Step 5 of the autonomous maintenance program develops process-competent operators, achieves zero-failure/zero-defect targets through correct operation and adjustment, eliminates accidents through correct handling of abnormalities, and brings entire plants closer to their ideal state.

Step 6: Systematize Autonomous Maintenance

The plant that completes the first five steps of the autonomous maintenance program, achieves optimal equipment conditions and establishes a system of standards to sustain these conditions. Equipment-competent and process-competent operators are able to detect and prevent abnormalities well in advance through proper checking and operation. Step 6 adds the finishing touches to the autonomous maintenance system.

Quality Maintenance and the Systemization of Autonomous Maintenance

One of the goals of Step 6 is to allow operators to perform sound, comprehensive autonomous maintenance of their entire process and to extend their activities into the realm of quality maintenance. Activities that promote this include standardizing various control items, preparing process flow diagrams and quality maintenance manuals, and deepening operators' understanding of the relationship between equipment and quality. Operators expose sources of quality defects by performing general quality maintenance inspection, note these on process flow diagrams and simple equipment structural diagrams, and gradually build a system that enables them to detect and promptly rectify abnormalities affecting quality.

PREPARING AN AUTONOMOUS MAINTENANCE MASTER PLAN

Production processes in process plants differ from those in fabrication/ assembly plants in a number of ways. Because TPM developed mainly in fabrication and assembly industries, some aspects of the original TPM development programs were not completely suitable for process plants. Those responsible for preparing TPM master plans in process industries were particularly challenged by the lack of concrete examples of autonomous maintenance programs and other TPM development activities that might meet the needs of their industry.

Process industries operate continuously for long periods. Accidents and breakdowns during operation can shut down entire processes, and the resulting financial losses can be devastating. Often plant conditions threaten safety and the environment. More and more companies are looking to TPM for systems that can assure safe, stable operation. The need for an autonomous maintenance development program especially designed for process industries is urgent.

The following sections propose some activity indicators based on the distinctive characteristics of process industries and outline a system for evaluating equipment and gradually bringing it under the autonomous maintenance umbrella.

Prioritize Activities by Evaluating Equipment

The principal goals and activities of autonomous maintenance are the same in any manufacturing environment: to change people's understanding and work habits using equipment as an instructional tool, and at the same time, to approach optimal equipment performance by systematically restoring and controlling deterioration and correcting abnormalities.

To maximize effectiveness and eliminate failures, an autonomous maintenance program must be both thorough and continuous. One challenge in process industries, however, is that operators handle a larger range of equipment than operators in fabrication and assembly industries. Under those circumstances, attempting to complete the autonomous maintenance program for every item of equipment within a specified period will result in incomplete improvements. If the program also omits some of the necessary audits and skills training, the program ends up as little more than a cosmetic exercise.

To ensure that the autonomous maintenance program is both thorough and sustained in plants with huge numbers of equipment units, planners must prioritize the activities based on a careful equipment evaluation. They must also come up with ways to introduce and deploy autonomous maintenance activities that will assure depth of understanding and the desired level of skill development.

Select PM Equipment through Equipment Evaluation

To select priority equipment, determine elements on which to base the evaluation, then formulate criteria for each element. Figure 4-19, for example, offers six evaluation elements: safety and pollution, quality and yield, operating status, opportunity cost, failure frequency, and maintainability. Individual companies, however, should set criteria that suit the characteristics of their plants and processes. For example, it might be necessary to add productivity or government-regulated equipment to this list. Moreover, be sure to choose criteria that can be quantified and revised upward as the activities proceed.

Evaluation element	A Rank	B Rank	C Rank
S Safety and Environmental Pollution	Failure would cause serious safety and environmental problems in surrounding area	Failure would cause some safety and environmental problems in surrounding area	Failure would cause no safety or environmental problems in surrounding area
Q Quality and Yield	Failure would cause defective product to be produced or seriously affect yield	Failure would cause quality variation or affect yield moderately	Failure would affect neither quality nor yield
W Working (operating) Status	24-hour operation	7- to 14-hour operation	intermittent operation only
D Delay Factor (opportunity cost)	Failure would shut down entire plant	Failure would shut down relevant system only	Standby unit available/more economical to wait for failure and then repair
P Period (failure interval)	Frequent stops (every six months or more)	Occasional stops (approximately once a year)	Hardly any stops (less than once a year)
M Maintainability	Repair time: 4 hr or more Repair cost: over $1,600	Repair time: 1-4 hr Repair cost: $400 - $1,600	Repair time: less than 1 hr Repair cost: less than $400

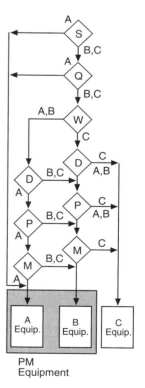

Figure 4-19. Equipment Evaluation Criteria

After establishing criteria, evaluate all the equipment. In Figure 4-19, equipment is classified in three ranks (A, B, and C) in accordance with the flowchart. Items ranked A or B are designated as PM equipment. In this example, equipment ranked A in terms of safety and pollution and quality and yield is automatically ranked A overall, so the remaining elements need not be evaluated. In practice, modify the procedure shown in the flow diagram to suit your particular industry and business conditions.*

Table 4-8 and Figure 4-20 show how a certain process plant selected PM equipment. Only 44.3 percent of all units have PM equipment status, but the average number designated for autonomous maintenance is still fairly high at 9.6 units per operator.

Table 4-8. Sample PM Equipment Chart

Machine/Device	All Equipment		Units	
	% of total	PM Equipment	Units	PM rate (%)
1. Columns and tanks	375	31.0	38	10.1
2. Rotating machinery	299	25.0	194	64.9
3. Transport equipment	280	23.0	121	43.2
4. Centrifugal separators	17	2.0	17	100.0
5. Filters and sieves	40	3.0	29	72.5
6. Crystallizers and kilns	11	1.0	11	100.0
7. Heaters and coolers	59	5.0	23	39.0
8. Weighers and metal detectors	44	4.0	39	88.6
9. Packagers and sewing machines	40	3.0	35	87.5
10. Boilers	3	0.3	3	100.0
11. Other	42	3.4	26	61.9
Total	**1,210**		**536**	**44.3**

---

* This type of evaluation can also be used in designing a planned maintenance system or in selecting and prioritizing equipment for vibration monitoring and other forms of predictive maintenance.

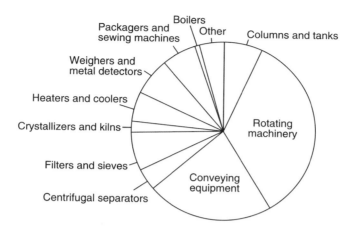

Figure 4-20. PM Equipment

Measure the Autonomous Maintenance Load

When introducing autonomous maintenance for the first time, select a particular item of equipment to use as a model (referred to in TPM as "model equipment"). Then, tackle the first three autonomous maintenance steps listed in Table 4-5. To determine the best way to proceed after the model or pilot stage, calculate the potential "autonomous maintenance load" — the average number of items of equipment designated for autonomous maintenance per operator. Calculate this average for each of the small teams that will actually perform the autonomous maintenance — not for large organizational units such as an entire plant, department, or section. Display the results on a chart such as that shown in Table 4-9. This sort of chart is useful for working out how to deploy the autonomous maintenance program and also for plotting progress. Each item of equipment can be struck off as its autonomous maintenance program is completed.

Clarification of Maintenance Responsibilities

Responsibility for periodic maintenance. As autonomous maintenance activities progress, the range of equipment that operators maintain gradually increases. Take care not to overload operators with equipment units or tasks as they proceed through the autonomous maintenance steps. In particular, clearly distinguish between the responsibilities of the production and maintenance departments for periodic maintenance activities other than inspection (see Table 4-10).

Table 4-9. Autonomous Maintenance Load Table

Group	Members	Total	Equipment Load (PM equipment)		Total/ Load
			A Rank	B Rank	
Challenger	O'Toole Chan Gast * Arvin (leader)	4	1. Feed conveyor 1 2. Feed conveyor 2 3. Feed elevator 3 4. Feed belt scale 5. Feed centrifugal separator ↓ 20. Instrumentation compressor	1. Feedstock heating-water pump 2. Feedstock pump 1 3. Filter washer pump 4. Filter compressor 5. Feedstock stirring tank ↓ 18. Carbon stirrer	38/95
Target	Danko Figis Marks * Meany (leader)	4	1. Activated charcoal recycling kiln 2. Activated charcoal adsorption column 3. Screw dewaterer 4. Nash pump 5. Lift pump 2 ↓ 23. Recycling kiln exhaust fan	1. Rotary product drier 2. Vibrating product conveyor 3. Dust-collector suction fan 4. Product screen 5. Steel-belt recovery conveyor ↓ 19. Product bottle chiller unit	42/10.5
⋮	⋮	⋮	⋮	⋮	
Total for subsection		20	115 units	108 units	223/11.1

Table 4-10. Sample Allocation of Responsibility for Periodic Maintenance

Task	Autonomous Maintenance	Specialized Maintenance
Replace pump shaft packing	Gland packing	Mechanical seals
Replace V-belts and chains	Models B and below, JIS 100 and below	Models C and above, JIS 120 and above
Replace lubricant	15 kW and below	18.5 kW and above
Overhaul pump	PM equipment, 3.7 kW and below	PM equipment, 5.5 kW and above

Equipment maintenance system and policy. As operators proceed through the autonomous maintenance steps, cleaning up their equipment and eliminating accelerated deterioration, production managers must envision the type of maintenance system that will be needed when the production floor has reached its ideal state. The purpose of autonomous maintenance is not merely to eliminate dust, dirt, and accelerated deterioration. Over time, it contributes significantly to maximizing overall plant effectiveness and reducing costs, as spelled out in Table 4-7. So what roles will production and maintenance workers play in maintaining these higher levels of performance? Bear in mind that as companies minimize operator numbers and move increasingly toward unattended operation, the amount of periodic maintenance and repair work that operators can do by themselves will be limited.

The master plan formulated when TPM is introduced, of course, includes the creation of an overall equipment maintenance system. Therefore, it is essential to incorporate personnel plans based on the company's mid- and long-range business plans. Figure 4-21 is a proposal for a maintenance system drafted with an eye to the company's mid- and long-range investment and staffing plans. This plan envisions the autonomous maintenance activities performed after completion of the seven development steps as consisting mainly of inspection.

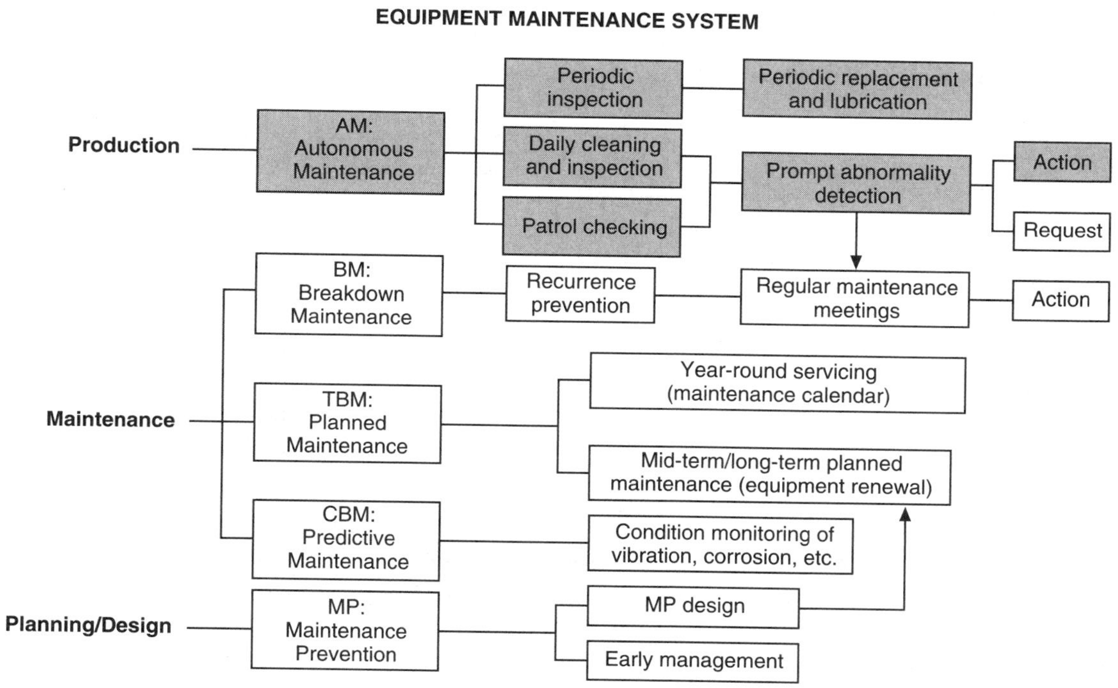

EQUIPMENT MAINTENANCE SYSTEM

Figure 4-21. Sample Maintenance System

Adapting the Autonomous Maintenance Development Steps

In process industries, the high ratio of equipment to operators is a large obstacle to developing an autonomous maintenance program. Prioritizing equipment and working out autonomous maintenance loads are two ways to overcome this difficulty and find the best way of deploying the full seven-step autonomous maintenance program. This section offers practical examples of how the development steps can be effectively adapted.

The Basic Seven-Step Development Pattern

When the autonomous maintenance load is three units per person or less, the basic autonomous maintenance development pattern consisting of the seven steps shown in Table 4-4 is satisfactory. A master plan like that shown in Figure 4-22 is then usually adopted.

Model deployment consists of selecting a single item of equipment with a high failure rate or a large number of contamination sources as a model on which to practice. The goal is to teach autonomous maintenance through painstaking repetition of activities and audits. Operators then take the techniques they master during the model deployment phase and apply them to the rest of their equipment. This second phase is known in TPM as *lateral deployment*.

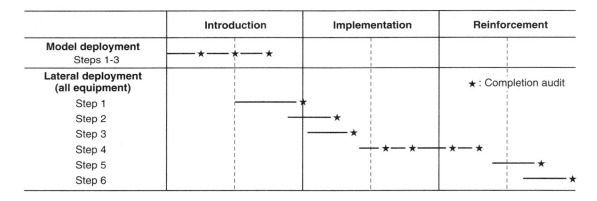

Figure 4-22. Sample Autonomous Maintenance Master Plan

Difficulties Arising from High Autonomous Maintenance Loads

What sorts of difficulties and problems can arise when a company develops a typical autonomous maintenance program in an environment where the load will be five units or more per operator. Imagine a six-member team, responsible for thirty pieces of equipment, attempting to follow the basic pattern. In theory, they select one item of equipment for model deployment, then apply the techniques they learned to the remaining 29 units in the lateral deployment phase.

Figure 4-23 shows what happens. They selected Unit A as the model, then the team members proceed through Step 1 (initial cleaning), Step 2 (addressing contamination sources and inaccessible places), and Step 3 (establishing cleaning and checking standards), with an audit on completion of each step. As they do so, they remove all dirt and grime, establish basic equipment conditions, restore deterioration, eliminate contamination sources and inaccessible places, and perform checks based on provisional standards. Then the team members reach a point where they are able to maintain their model equipment near its optimal state.

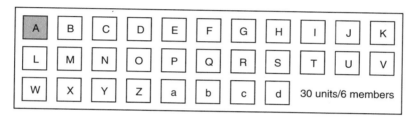

Figure 4-23. Equipment Load per Group

Now the activities enter the lateral deployment phase, where team members must apply the techniques learned to the other equipment in their area. The members start by performing initial cleaning on unit B. Once they remove all dirt and grime on Unit B, they clean units C, D, E, and F in sequence. Unfortunately, however, no one has eliminated contamination sources and inaccessible places yet, so the team finds it difficult to maintain the level of cleanliness they attained in Step 1. By the time they start on unit G, unit B is dirty again and they must go back and repeat the process from the beginning. In this way, the team never gets beyond the initial cleaning stage.

This predicament is more prevalent in process industries, with their many high-volume contamination sources. When activities fail to proceed vigorously, however, operators lose their motivation and the autonomous maintenance program may collapse.

Block Deployment and Area Deployment

Extending autonomous maintenance from model equipment to the remaining equipment requires considerable ingenuity to keep completed units up to scratch while dealing with the ones that remain. Figure 4-24 illustrates how one process plant accomplished this. After model deployment, the team extended activities to blocks of similar equipment. Although they implemented the first three autonomous maintenance steps in sequence during the model deployment phase, they performed the steps *simultaneously* in the "block deployment" phase. They then extended the activities to equipment areas and simultaneously implemented Steps 1 to 4 there. This last phase is known as "area deployment."

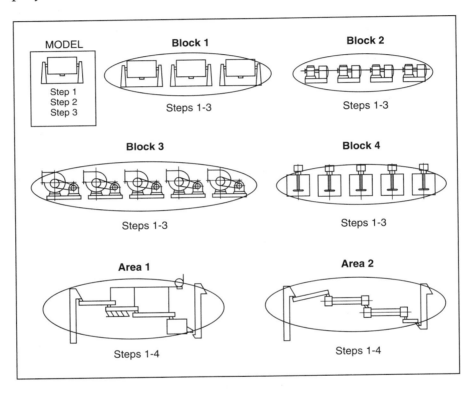

Figure 4-24. Model — Block — Area Deployment

"Point" activities (model deployment). As Figure 4-24 shows, model deployment in this example consisted of selecting a single item of equipment as a model and performing the first three autonomous maintenance steps on it in sequence. Step 1 consisted of thorough initial cleaning, including strip-down overhaul, followed by an audit. Once the participants successfully completed this audit, they started Step 2. In this step, they eliminated or controlled contamination sources, improved inaccessible places, and restored the equipment to better than mint condition. They then implemented Step 3 (preparation of provisional inspection standards), keeping the equipment in its pristine state by periodically cleaning, checking, and lubricating it. As Figure 4-25 shows, the model deployment process took nine months. During that time 19 teams worked on 27 items of equipment.

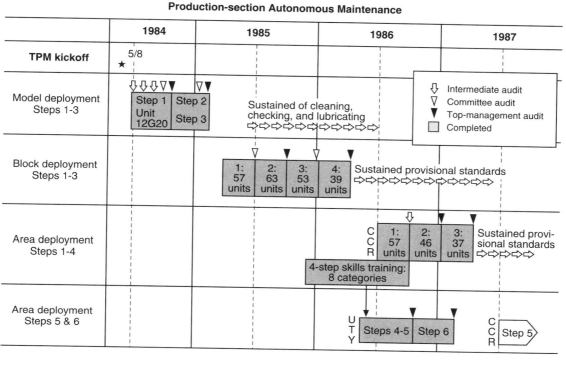

Figure 4-25. Sample Results Achieved through Autonomous Maintenance

"Surface" activities (block deployment). To deploy laterally the improvement techniques they mastered during the model deployment phase, the teams selected blocks of similar equipment for the block deployment phase.

They performed Steps 1 to 3 simultaneously on an initial block of three units, bringing all three to the same maintainable level as the model. They then implemented the same activities on a second block of four units. In all, they implemented four blocks in this way, until they improved all the units in all the blocks to a consistently maintainable level.

The level of improvement of contamination sources and inaccessible areas rose steadily as they completed each block thereby eliminating wasteful repeat cleaning. An audit covering all three steps was performed on completion of each block.

As Figure 4-25 shows, it took thirteen months to complete blocks 1 to 4. Forty-two people in ten teams dealt with 212 separate items of equipment during this time. The approach adopted enabled them to extend and accelerate the autonomous maintenance program. During the block deployment phase, the autonomous maintenance load was 5.05 items per person.

"Volume" activities (area deployment). In the final phase, area deployment, the team split the production process into separate areas, with one team in charge of each area. Their aim was to look three-dimensionally at the equipment problems, quality irregularities, and other disorders within the areas and lay the foundations for an autonomous maintenance program specially tailored to the needs of a process industry.

The area deployment in this example had several distinctive features. To prevent activities from becoming ritualized and to develop their knowledge of their equipment, operators learned maintenance skills that covered eight topics (nuts and bolts, transmissions, bearings, and so on). They added Step 4 of the autonomous maintenance program (general equipment inspection) to the first three steps, and implemented Steps 1 to 4 simultaneously. Area 1 consisted of seven equipment units. After bringing this area to its optimal state by implementing Steps 1 through 4, they similarly extended activities to Area 2, as shown in Figure 4-24. As Figure 4-25 shows, the company took 12 months to complete Areas 1 to 3, with 35 people in 5 small teams dealing with 140 equipment items. The autonomous maintenance load during the area deployment phase was 4 items per person. Steps 1 to 4 were audited together as each area was completed, and operators were tested on each skills training topic to evaluate their grasp of the training.

Figure 4-26 outlines the aims of developing the activities from "point" to "surface" to "volume" in this way. In this workplace, teams raised the plant to its optimal condition by completing Steps 1 to 4 for all 379 PM equipment items, and achieved excellent results in terms of minimizing failures and manual work. The autonomous maintenance load increased to 9.59 items per operator during this time.

Reviewing Standards in Step 5

Teams prepared a provisional standard for cleaning, inspection, and lubricating for each of the 379 equipment items involved in the program described above. The total number of standards came to 1,137. After consolidating individual cleaning, inspection, and lubricating standards and eliminating duplicate standards for identical units, the number of standards was reduced to 300.

Although the operators tried to formulate standards that they themselves would use, there were simply too many to follow in a workplace where staffing levels had already been reduced. In Step 5 of the autonomous maintenance program (general process inspection), the teams further streamlined and standardized the system. Realistic standards were established that could actually be adhered to. (See Figure 4-27.)

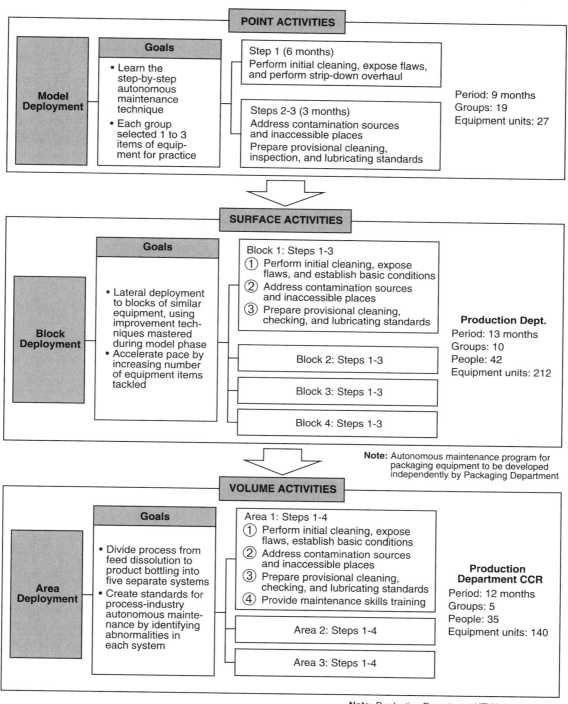

Figure 4-26. From "Point" to "Surface" to "Volume"

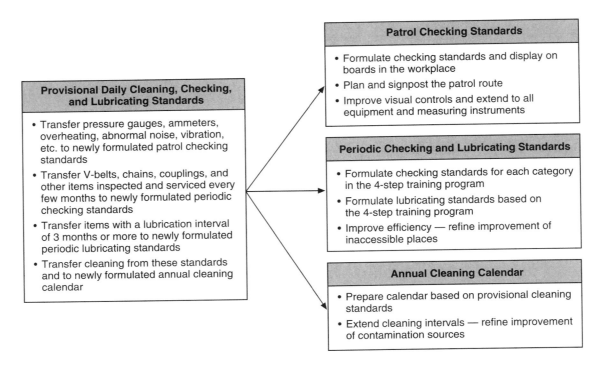

Figure 4-27. Streamlining Autonomous Maintenance Standards

AUTONOMOUS MAINTENANCE AUDITS

Developing an autonomous maintenance program in steps, as described above, has two advantages that make the program especially effective:

- Activities produce concrete results as they proceed
- Results are confirmed as part of the program

The single most important factor in the success of an autonomous maintenance program is conducting a careful audit on completion of each step to confirm the results achieved and point the direction for further work. The audit provides guidance where needed and gives people a sense of achievement. While the step-by-step approach makes the program easier for teams to understand as they progress through it, the audits serve as milestones on the journey and help to consolidate the gains made at each step.

Autonomous maintenance audits provide more than opportunities for assessing progress and giving guidance. They also act as signposts that indicate how far to carry each phase of the activities. They include presentations in which all team members participate, so they also help develop disciplined people who can speak their minds. These are important features not seen in other types of small-group activities. Audits are in fact the most effective management tool for ensuring that an autonomous maintenance program proceeds with vigor.

Audits may be self-audits, section-level audits, or top-management audits. Self-assessment audits promote effective monitoring and evaluation of progress; section-level audits keep activities bubbling by providing guidance and assistance; top management audits foster motivation through recognition. Figure 4-28 shows a flow diagram for an auditing system.

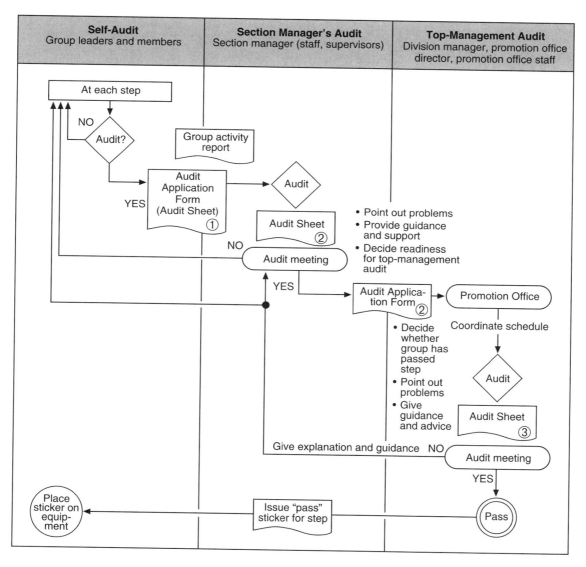

Figure 4-28. Autonomous Maintenance Audit Diagram

5
Planned Maintenance

Planned maintenance should establish and maintain optimal equipment and process conditions; it should also be efficient and cost-effective. In a TPM development program, planned maintenance is the deliberate, methodical activity of building and continuously improving such a maintenance system.

EQUIPMENT MANAGEMENT IN PROCESS INDUSTRIES

Equipment management in a process industry is profoundly influenced by its unique types of equipment, the nature of its process and equipment failures, and the skill levels and roles of its maintenance personnel.

Equipment Characteristics

Production plants in process industries consist of static equipment, such as columns, tanks, and heat exchangers, all connected by pipes to rotating equipment such as pumps and compressors. Measuring instruments and control devices that keep conditions constant or vary them according to a preset program continuously or intermittently control and monitor processes. Individual equipment units that are systematically combined and integrated subject raw materials to various chemical, physical, and biological changes as they undergo the process that transforms them into final product. Ancillary equipment, installed at each end of the production process, receives and stores the raw materials, and packages, warehouses, and ships the final product. Using the production system fully requires careful control of all this equipment.

Some equipment in process industries is very large, and the stored energy of its contents can be enormous. As rotating equipment become bigger and

145

faster, plants often operate them under conditions that push their structural materials to the limits of their performance. Maintaining the intrinsic and operational reliability of such equipment at high levels is therefore essential.

Most of the equipment in process industries is designed and fabricated separately and installed on site. Consequently, it has not usually benefited from a lengthy program of refinement and improvement. Uncorrected design and installation weaknesses often handicap its operation. Additionally, many plants were fitted with distributed digital control systems in recent years, and software bugs or spurious control signals sometimes cause process problems. Maintaining control devices and software, therefore, is also important.

Table 5-1 indicates some of the special features of process-industry equipment. Shutdown losses due to equipment failures are generally very high, so equipment weaknesses should be corrected systematically to ensure effective operation and prevent accidents, failures, and quality defects.

Table 5-1. Characteristics of Process-Industry Equipment

Equipment	Characteristic	Weakness
Static equipment	• Increasing size • Use of novel materials	• Different design and operating conditions (due to diversification of raw materials, etc.) • Problems often invisible until they break out
Rotating machinery	• Bigger and faster • No standby equipment	• High early failure rate • Long MTTR
Measuring and control equipment	• Increasingly digitalized	• More and more "black boxes"

Equipment Failure and Process Problems

In addition to equipment problems, process industries are plagued by process problems such as blocks, leaks, contamination, and powder spills. Preventing sudden plant shutdown due to such problems is crucial.

Process problems are often chronic, resulting from a complex combination of causes. For example, the external shape or internal construction of a piece of equipment may create local nonuniformities in fluidity, dispersion, temperature, composition, or other properties of the substances being processed, and this in turn may produce unwanted physical or chemical changes.

Equipment failures and process problems (losses) in process industries can be classified into five broad categories:

- Equipment failures or process problems that cause shutdown
- Quality abnormalities

- Unit-consumption abnormalities
- Capacity reductions
- Safety and environmental problems

Most of these problems result from equipment disorders or abnormalities. A plant can prevent them by bringing equipment and processes into their ideal state. Figure 5-1 shows these main problems together with the equipment disorders and hidden defects that cause them.

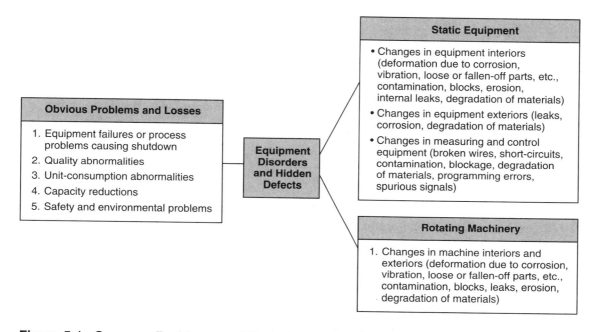

Figure 5-1. Common Problems and Their Causes

Maintenance Personnel in Process Industries

The ratio of maintenance professionals to equipment is generally small in process industries, and the maintenance department's principal task is planning and organizing. Its role is mainly administrative, with subcontractors performing most of the actual repair and maintenance work. Company maintenance personnel often receive insufficient training to improve their skills.

PLANNED MAINTENANCE FOR PROCESS INDUSTRIES

In TPM, planned maintenance is based on the twin foundations of autonomous maintenance by the production department and specialized maintenance by the maintenance department. Within a planned maintenance system, maintenance personnel conduct two types of activities:

- Activities that improve equipment
- Activities that improve maintenance technology and skill

These activities should evolve systematically and organically. Figure 5-2 illustrates the relationship between the two. A step-by-step procedure for evolving the activities appears later in this chapter.

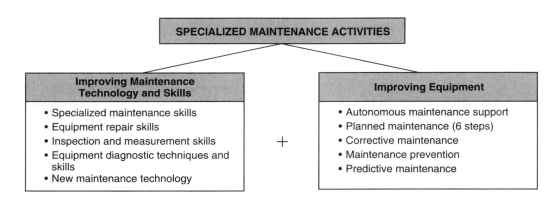

Figure 5-2. The Twin Activities of Specialized Maintenance

Maintenance Regimes

Figure 5-3 shows the different maintenance regimes used today. An efficient planned maintenance program combines time-based maintenance (TBM), condition-based maintenance (CBM), and breakdown maintenance (BM) as rationally as possible.

Time-based maintenance (TBM). Time-based maintenance consists of periodically inspecting, servicing, and cleaning equipment and replacing parts to prevent sudden failures and process problems. It should be part of both autonomous maintenance and specialized maintenance activities.

Condition-based maintenance (CBM). Condition-based maintenance uses equipment diagnostics to monitor and diagnose moving machinery conditions continuously or intermittently during operation and on-stream inspection (OSI — checking the condition of static equipment and monitoring signs of change by nondestructive inspection techniques.) As its name implies, condition-based maintenance is triggered by actual equipment conditions rather than the elapsing of a predetermined interval of time.

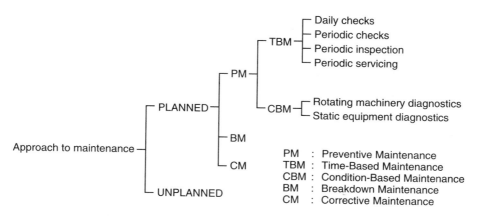

Figure 5-3. Types of Maintenance

Breakdown maintenance (BM). Unlike the preceding two systems, breakdown maintenance means waiting until equipment fails to repair it. Breakdown maintenance is used when failure does not significantly affect operation or production or generate any financial losses other than repair costs.

Preventive maintenance (PM). Preventive maintenance combines time-based and condition-based methods to keep equipment functioning by controlling equipment components, assemblies, subassemblies, accessories, attachments, and so on. It also maintains the performance of structural materials and prevents corrosion, fatigue, and other forms of deterioration from weakening them.

Corrective maintenance (CM). Corrective maintenance improves equipment and its components so that preventive maintenance can be carried out reliably. Equipment with design weaknesses must be redesigned.

Role of Planned Maintenance in Equipment Management

Equipment management ensures that equipment functions and performs as expected throughout its life, from planning through fabrication, installation, and operation until final scrapping. Figure 5-4 shows the position of planned maintenance within the life cycle of an item of equipment.

The useful life of most ordinary equipment is not clearly specified at the design stage. Consequently, it is more often determined not by the equipment's physical life span but by the decrease in economic performance of the process to which the equipment contributes. The useful lives of measuring equipment and control devices may also be determined by how long parts are still available after the devices themselves are no longer manufactured.

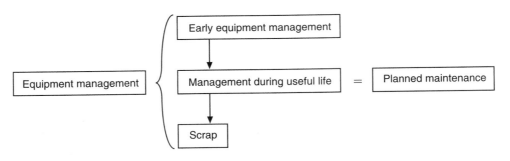

Figure 5-4. Planned Maintenance as Part of a Machine's Life Cycle

Planned maintenance is extremely important for equipment life. It can even determine the success or failure of a line of business over the long term. Like those of other industries, products in process industries are changing with the times, and process plants must continuously revamp so they can produce products that meet contemporary needs. Changes in raw materials or process conditions create unexpected equipment and process problems that can lead to reduced production, lower yields, or even serious accidents. Therefore, planned maintenance tailored to the characteristics of particular equipment and processes is essential.

In this regard, a particularly important aspect of planned maintenance is ensuring that improvements achieved through corrective maintenance are incorporated in subsequent designs. To achieve this, collate information on maintainability and design weakness improvements and store it for use as MP data.

Planned Maintenance — Who Is Responsible?

Figure 5-5 shows how the different maintenance regimes mentioned earlier fit into a planned maintenance system. It indicates the responsibilities of each department and outlines the maintenance technology, control technology, and control systems the company needs to support the planned maintenance system.

Time-based Maintenance in Planned Maintenance

The goals of planned maintenance are to eliminate equipment failures and process problems and minimize losses. The first step toward achieving those goals, is time-based maintenance, that is, performing maintenance tasks such as those shown in Figure 5-6 according to a fixed schedule. Deciding what maintenance to perform on which equipment will depend on a company's policies,

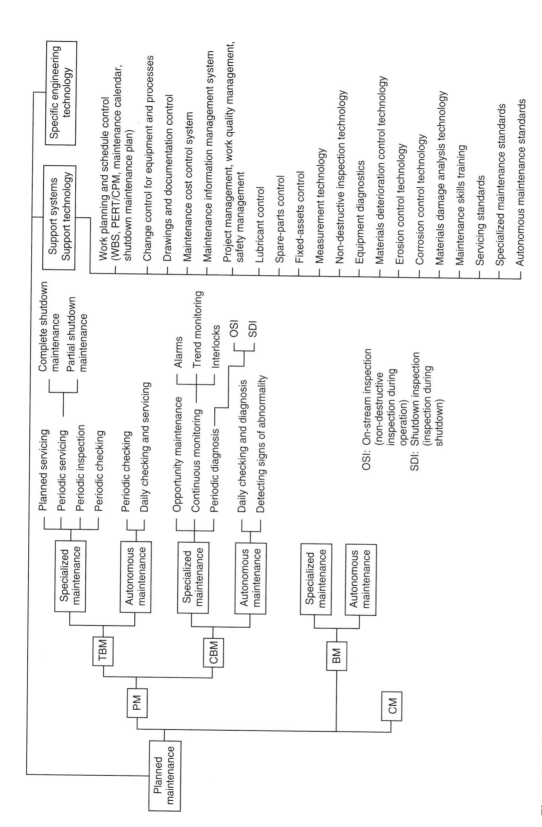

Figure 5-5. Planned Maintenance System Showing Allocation of Responsibility

long- and mid-range plans, annual plans, and so on. To maintain equipment and processes in their ideal state, however, it is vital to use all available maintenance data and technology. Close cooperation between the maintenance department and other departments is, therefore, essential.

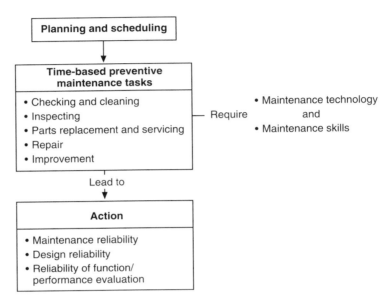

Figure 5-6. Preventive Maintenance Tasks in TBM

Condition-based Maintenance in Planned Maintenance

The second principal activity of planned maintenance, condition-based maintenance, has two main thrusts:

- Condition monitoring: This must occur while equipment is running to gauge its functions and performance accurately.
- On-stream inspection (OSI): This helps increase the precision of shutdown maintenance planning. In process plants, many maintenance tasks are performed during annual shutdown maintenance. If inspections during shutdown maintenance reveal defects that must be corrected, maintenance personnel must modify the shutdown maintenance plan. This can cause a delay in restarting the plant among other problems.

Time-based and condition-based maintenance control the condition of the assemblies, subassemblies, and components that comprise a piece of equipment. It is critical to accurately identify and control all those components whose failure might lead to equipment breakdown or lost performance, cause quality defects, compromise safety, or harm the environment.

Breakdown Maintenance in Planned Maintenance

The third main activity of planned maintenance, breakdown maintenance, consists of replacing parts or performing other repair work after equipment breaks down. To facilitate prompt repairs and prevention, make it easy for operators to detect abnormalities when they perform their daily checks or routinely monitor the equipment.

THE PLANNED MAINTENANCE SYSTEM

Close cooperation between production and maintenance departments is the single most important factor for ensuring that planned maintenance is carried out effectively. Effective maintenance also requires, at different times, the active support of other departments, such as production management, production engineering, safety and environment, administration, personnel, finance, development, and marketing. These departments must also cooperate and coordinate closely with maintenance.

Companies organize their specialized maintenance functions differently, depending on their size, type of business, staffing arrangements, past history, and so on. Table 5-2 shows some characteristics of maintenance systems used in different industries at present. Consider what features will best suit the needs of your particular plant.

Table 5-2. Present Use of Maintenance Systems

	Mechanical	Electrical	Instrumentation	Equipment diagnostics	Construction
Centralized	◯	◎	◎	◎	◎
Decentralized	◯	△	△	—	—
Mixed	◯	△	△	—	—

◎ Commonly used   ◯ Sometimes used   △ Rarely used

In a *centralized* maintenance system, maintenance technicians are assigned permanently to a maintenance center managed by the maintenance department. The technicians go out to the shopfloor or production site as required. This system is common in medium-sized plants with few maintenance personnel.

In a *decentralized* system, maintenance technicians are assigned permanently to different workplaces. This system is common in large plants. Even in large plants, however, only mechanics are usually decentralized; electrical and instrumentation maintenance personnel typically remain centralized.

In a *mixed* system, some maintenance personnel are assigned permanently to different workplaces, while the rest are based in a maintenance center. Again, plants usually adopt the mixed system for mechanical maintenance and the centralized system for electrical and instrumentation maintenance.

Each of the three systems has advantages and disadvantages, as Table 5-3 shows. In a "line maintenance system" (decentralized, with maintenance personnel reporting to production), for example, problems of skill and motivation can arise, reducing maintenance quality. Select a system only after assessing the whole situation, including the need for job rotation.

Table 5-3. Advantages and Disadvantages of Different Maintenance Systems

	Advantages	Disadvantages
Centralized	• Skills and technology easily disseminated • Problems easily investigated	• Collaboration with operating department difficult • Incomplete collection of operating data
Decentralized	• Good communication with operating department • Speedy maintenance response	• Difficult to share technology and skills • Requires more people • Job rotation difficult
Mixed	• Good communication with operating department • Skills/technology dissemination and problem investigation possible	• Management somewhat difficult • Job rotation requires ingenuity

IMPROVING MAINTENANCE EFFECTIVENESS

To improve maintenance effectiveness, start by reducing equipment failures, process problems, and losses such as quality defects, high unit consumption, underproduction, and safety and environmental problems.

The basic indicator for effectiveness is output divided by input. First measure existing effectiveness using the following improvement indicator:

$$\frac{\text{Results (cumulative annual cost savings)}}{\text{Maintenance costs} + \text{annual depreciation of improvement investment}}$$

Where maintenance costs = costs of TBM, CBM, BM, and unexpected failure repair

Next, strive for a breakthrough in effectiveness by reducing the cost of the inputs (the denominator of the preceding improvement indicator) by optimizing the overall TBM/CBM/BM system. You might need to explore new approaches to maintenance to assist with this, such as reliability-centered maintenance (RCM).*

How is maintenance effectiveness being measured by most companies? A 1989 JIPM survey reveals the measures commonly used in Japanese companies. (See Figure 5-7.)

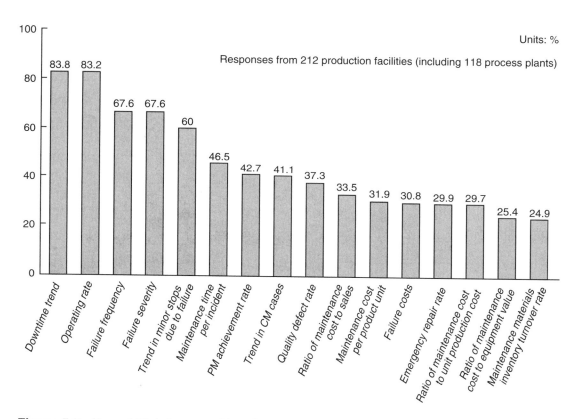

Figure 5-7. Use of Maintenance Results Indicators

---

* Reliability-centered maintenance is "a process used to determine what must be done to ensure that any physical asset continues to fulfill its intended functions in its present operating context." John Moubray, *Reliability-centered Maintenance* (New York: Industrial Press, 1992), p.7. It is a highly structure framework, initially developed in the civil aviation industry, that enables users to determine the most appropriate maintenance strategy for different assets.

BUILDING A PLANNED MAINTENANCE SYSTEM

The goal of TPM is to strengthen a company's basic constitution by achieving zero defects, zero failures, and zero accidents, and eliminating every kind of loss. The most important of these is zero failures.

Achieving Zero Breakdowns

Most serious accidents in production plants occur in the course of responding to problems such as equipment failures. Very few occur when processes operate normally and operators merely monitor or check their equipment.

Likewise, most process defects and product defects occur when plants shut down because they fail, are under repair, or are restarting. Defect rates are naturally very low in plants that continue to operate normally for long periods. In other words, achieving zero breakdowns is the quickest way to eliminate accidents and defects.

To prevent accidents and defects, prevent the possibility of serious failures that shut down major systems or complete processes. The key is to construct a planned maintenance system that combines various specialized maintenance activities.

The Six Zero-Breakdown Measures

As discussed in Chapter 3 in connection with loss reduction, many plants neglect basic equipment conditions (cleaning, lubricating, and tightening bolts) and do not comply with conditions of use. Equipment in such plants is subject to accelerated deterioration. Idling, minor stops, and minor failures are rife, and failure intervals vary widely. It is pointless to attempt to carry out periodic or predictive maintenance in such a situation.

The maintenance department cannot achieve zero breakdowns through planned maintenance alone. Nor can the production department achieve it solely through autonomous maintenance. Both can achieve significant results, however, by combining planned and autonomous maintenance and painstakingly implementing the six zero-breakdown measures detailed earlier on pp. 64–66.

The Four Phases to Zero Breakdown

The six zero-breakdown measures introduced earlier involve tremendous work. Implementing all at the same time is well-nigh impossible. Even if you could put all six into effect at once, you would still waste time trying to carry out periodic maintenance on dirty, unlubricated equipment exposed to accelerated deterioration. Equipment that breaks down before its next service is due forces you to set ridiculously short service intervals. In either case, periodic maintenance fails. Predictive maintenance is subject to the same limits. No matter how good your diagnostic techniques, optimal service intervals cannot be predicted in an environment where failures persist as a result of loose nuts and bolts, operator errors, and so on.

Many production plants have found that the most effective way of successfully implementing the six zero-breakdown measures is to distribute them among four phases and proceed through those four phases systematically. (For a detailed discussion, see Chapter 3, pp. 66–75.)

Four Phases to Zero Breakdowns for Static Equipment

Common in process industries are the many pieces of static equipment to be controlled such as columns, tanks, pipes, heat exchangers, and furnaces. Another feature is the static nature of common failure modes such as corrosion, leaks, and blocks. Zero-breakdown activities in process industries must consider these characteristics. Table 5-4 shows an example of the four phases applied to achieve zero failures in static equipment. Use it as a guide in developing the most suitable program for your own particular industry or process.

Implementing Maintenance Activities Step-by-Step

An important issue for the maintenance department is how to plan and systematically implement the various planned maintenance activities over time. The generic activities and step-by-step approach offered below distill the practical experience of many successful TPM companies by companies.

The goal of the maintenance department in carrying out planned maintenance is, of course, to eliminate failures. The six zero-breakdown measures and the four phases to zero failures described in Chapter 3 form an excellent basis

Table 5-4. Four Phases to Zero Breakdowns for Static Equipment

Columns, tanks, piping, heat exchangers, furnaces, valves, measuring instruments, etc.

Phase 1:
 	
Establish
Basic
Conditions
	A. Exteriors (parts in contact with the outside environment)
	  1. Remove corrosion products and keep surfaces dry
	  2. Replace damaged, discolored thermal insulation; investigate reasons for deterioration
	  3. Check for corrosion inside insulation; dry affected parts
	  4. Investigate/repair leaks and seepage
	  5. Check for damaged piping supports
	  6. Investigate causes of vibration and shock (water hammer, etc.)
	  7. Remove corrosion products from beams, supports, and other structures, repair where necessary
	B. Interiors (parts in contact with process fluids, steam, water, etc.)
	  1. Investigate/repair internal corrosion, deformation, slackness, fallen-off parts
	  2. Investigate/repair corrosion and cracking of main units
	  3. Investigate/remove contamination, scaling, blocks, etc.
	  4. Investigate variations in operating conditions and equipment conditions

Phase 2:
 	
Correct
Weaknesses
	A. Exteriors (parts in contact with the outside environment)
	  1. Repair and prevent local corrosion
	  2. Repair and prevent rainwater ingress
	  3. Repair and prevent leaks and seepage
	  4. Alleviate or prevent vibration and shock
	  5. Improve beams, supports, and other structures
	B. Interiors (parts in contact with fluids, steam, water, etc.)
	  1. Relieve stress concentrations (static loads, dynamic loads, thermal stress)
	  2. Relieve and improve thermal fatigue
	  3. Correct and prevent local corrosion
	  4. Correct and prevent leaks and seepage
	  5. Introduce improvements to prevent contamination and scaling
	  6. Introduce improvements to prevent blocks
	  7. Introduce improved methods of adding process-problem prevention agents
	    (such as polymerization inhibitors)
	C. Common Items
	  1. Investigate and adopt novel anticorrosion and antierosion coatings
	  2. Investigate and adopt novel corrosion-resistant materials
	  3. Improve gasket coatings
	  4. Introduce improved repair techniques such as thermal spraying

Phase 3:
 	
Restore
Deterioration
	A. Exteriors (parts in contact with outside environment)
	  1. Check exteriors regularly
	  2. Rustproof and paint exteriors periodically
	  3. Periodically renew insulation and supports
	B. Interiors (parts in contact with process fluids, water, steam, etc.)
	  1. Perform periodic overhaul inspection
	  2. Periodically replace internal parts
	  3. Periodically repair and renew deteriorated parts
	  4. Descale periodically
	  5. Plan and implement medium-term and long-term renovation plans for piping, tanks, heat exchangers, etc.
	  6. Identify relationships between rate of equipment deterioration and process conditions such as raw material properties and operating conditions

Phase 4:
 	
Predict and
Extend
Equipment
Lifetimes
	A. Predict materials deterioration and extend lifetimes
	  1. Perform non-destructive material tests
	  2. Perform destructive tests and microstructure tests on samples
	  3. Investigate and analyze deterioration mechanisms by destructive and non-destructive testing
	  4. Develop and introduce internal corrosion monitoring devices and technology for equipment such as piping
	  5. Develop novel materials and technology to extend equipment life
	  6. Investigate repair and fabrication techniques such as welding and thermal spraying
	  7. Review and improve operating conditions
	B. Predict process failures and lengthen descaling intervals
	  1. Lengthen descaling intervals by monitoring contamination and adhesion and employing initial in-line cleaning
	  2. Extend continuous operation by analyzing changes in raw materials, operating conditions and equipment conditions, and relating these to the occurrence of contamination and adhesion

for any step-by-step program. Table 5-5 shows how a six-step program for developing maintenance department activities coordinates with the overall four-phase approach to zero breakdowns and the autonomous maintenance program described in Chapter 4. The goal of this program is to build a solid and effective planned maintenance system.

The advantages of the step-by-step approach are that concrete results accumulate as the activities unfold and they are checked and reinforced as an integral part of the program. To utilize these advantages fully, the planning team must spell out clearly what is to be done at each step. Table 5-6 lists typical activities performed at each step, and Table 5-7 shows a master plan for these activities.

Table 5-5. The Six Steps for Building a Planned Maintenance System

Phase	① Stabilize failure intervals	② Lengthen equipment life	③ Periodically restore deterioration	④ Predict equipment life	
Autonomous Maintenance	Step 1: Perform initial cleaning Step 2: Improve contamination sources and inaccessible places Step 3: Establish cleaning and checking standards	Step 4: Perform general equipment inspection	Step 5: Perform general process inspection	Step 6: Systematize autonomous maintenance Step 7: Practice full self-management	
Specialized Maintenance	**Step 1: Evaluate equipment and understand situation** **Step 2: Restore deterioration and correct weaknesses** (support autonomous maintenance and prevent recurrences)	**Step 3: Build an information management system**	Establish as corrective maintenance Establish as periodic maintenance **Step 4: Build a periodic maintenance system**	**Step 5: Build a predictive maintenance system**	**Step 6: Evaluate the planned maintenance system**

Table 5-6. Step-by-Step Development Process

Step	Activities
Step 1: Evaluate equipment and understand situation	1. Prepare or update equipment logs 2. Evaluate equipment: establish evaluation criteria, prioritize equipment, and select PM equipment and components 3. Define failure ranks 4. Understand situation: measure number, frequency, and severity of failures and minor stops; MTBFs; maintenance costs; breakdown maintenance rates; etc. 5. Set maintenance goals (indicators, methods of measuring results)
Step 2: Reverse deterioration and correct weaknesses	1. Establish basic conditions, reverse deterioration, and abolish environments causing accelerated deterioration (support autonomous maintenance) 2. Conduct focused improvement activities to correct weaknesses and extend lifetimes 3. Take measures to prevent identical or similar major failures from occurring 4. Introduce improvements to reduce process failures
Step 3: Build an information management system	1. Build a failure data management system 2. Build an equipment maintenance management system (machine-history control, maintenance planning, inspection planning, etc.) 3. Build an equipment budget management system 4. Build systems for controlling spare parts, drawings, technical data, etc.
Step 4: Build a periodic maintenance system	1. Prepare for periodic maintenance (control standby units, spare parts, measuring instruments, lubricants, drawings, technical data, etc.) 2. Prepare periodic maintenance system flow diagram 3. Select equipment and components to be maintained, and formulate a maintenance plan 4. Prepare or update standards (materials standards, work standards, inspection standards, acceptance standards, etc.) 5. Improve shutdown maintenance efficiency and strengthen control of subcontracted work
Step 5: Build a predictive maintenance system	1. Introduce equipment diagnostics (train diagnosticians, purchase diagnostic equipment, etc.) 2. Prepare predictive maintenance system flow diagram 3. Select equipment and components for predictive maintenance, and extend gradually 4. Develop diagnostic equipment and technology
Step 6: Evaluate the planned maintenance system	1. Evaluate the planned maintenance system 2. Evaluate reliability improvement: number of failures and minor stops, MTBF, failure frequency, etc. 3. Evaluate maintainability improvement: periodic maintenance rate, predictive maintenance rate, MTTR, etc. 4. Evaluate cost savings: decrease in maintenance expenditures, improvement in distribution of maintenance funds

The activities selected will depend on the level of equipment maintenance in the particular plant. Plants with a weak maintenance system and frequent failures must implement every step. Plants that already have a fairly strong system should focus on the steps designed to reduce failures and upgrade performance by eliminating weaknesses.

Audits

The key to the success of a step-by-step approach is to lock in improvements by auditing results on completion of each step When preparing audit checksheets, clarify what must be done and what results must be achieved at each step. Table 5-8 provides a sample audit checksheet for Step 1. It is important to proceed through the program in a controlled way, decisively marking the end of each step and the beginning of the next.

Specialized maintenance audits require expert knowledge and are, therefore, more difficult than autonomous maintenance audits. They are useful learning opportunities, however, so senior managers at the department level and above should attend them.

STEP-BY-STEP IMPLEMENTATION OF PLANNED MAINTENANCE

Setting up a planned maintenance system requires careful preparation and hard work. Trying to do everything at once is ineffective. Develop the activities in the following sequence, with all relevant departments cooperating at each step:

Step 1: Evaluate equipment and understand current conditions.

Step 2: Restore deterioration and correct weaknesses.

Step 3: Build an information management system.

Step 4: Build a periodic maintenance system.

Step 5: Build a predictive maintenance system.

Step 6: Evaluate the planned maintenance system.

Table 5-7. Sample Planned Maintenance Master Plan

Step	Activity	Preparation (3, 6, 9)	Introduction (12, 3, 6, 9)	Implementation (12, 3, 6, 9)	Consolidation (12, 3, 6)
Step 1: Evaluate equipment and understand current conditions	Prepare or update equipment logs	⊢⊣			
	Formulate and implement equipment evaluation standards	⊢ PM equipment ⊣			
	Define failure ranks	⊢⊣			
	Understand situation (number of failures, etc.)	⊢⊣			
	Set maintenance goals	⊢⊣			
Step 2: Restore deterioration and correct weaknesses	Establish basic conditions and reverse deterioration		⊢ Support autonomous maintenance		
	Abolish environments causing accelerated deterioration		⊢ Deal with major contamination sources		
	Take measures to prevent identical or similar major failures		⊢ Build systems ── Evolve activities		
	Lengthen equipment lifetimes by correcting weaknesses		⊢────	Corrective maintenance work	
	Reduce process failures and improve manual work		⊢────		
Step 3: Build an information management system	Build failure data management system		Construct CMMS	System startup	
	Build equipment maintenance management system		Construct CMMS	System startup	
	Build equipment budget management system			Construct CMMS	
	Build systems for controlling standby units and spares			Construct CMMS	

Consolidation: Special guidance for PM Prize; PM Prize on-site audit

Prepare for periodic maintenance

Prepare periodic maintenance worksheets

Select equipment and components for periodic maintenance

Prepare periodic maintenance calendar

Reinforce work management (prepare standards)

Improve shutdown maintenance efficiency

Strengthen control of subcontracted work

Step 4: Build a periodic maintenance system

Introduce equipment diagnostics

Prepare predictive maintenance worksheets

Select equipment, components for predictive maintenance; extend gradually

Step 5: Build a predictive maintenance system

Evaluate planned maintenance system

Evaluate reliability and maintainability

Evaluate overall cost reduction

Step 6: Evaluate the planned maintenance system

Chart labels: Lubricants, spare parts, drawings, etc. — Design work flow — Set maintenance intervals — Perform periodic maintenance — Train diagnosticians — Introduce equipment — Design work flow — Select equipment — Perform predictive maintenance — Evaluate recurrence prevention — Evaluate periodic maintenance — Perform comprehensive evaluation

Note: CMMS = computerized maintenance management system

Table 5-8. Sample Audit Sheet for Planned Maintenance Step 1

PLANNED MAINTENANCE AUDIT
Step 1: Evaluate Equipment and Understand Conditions

Location: _____   Self-Audit (90+): _____

Date: _____   Section Mgr. Audit (85+): _____

Auditor: _____   Sr. Mgt. Audit (80+): _____

Activity	Key Audit Points	Max. Pts.	100%	80%	60%	Remarks
1. Prepare equipment logs	• Logs prepared for every item of equipment?	10				
	• Logs include failure histories?	5				
	• Logs include repair histories?	5				
2. Evaluate equipment and select PM equipment	• Are equipment evaluation attributes and criteria formulated? Are they appropriate?	5				
	• Has all equipment been evaluated?	5				
	• Is selection of PM equipment and components appropriate?	5				
	• Is PM equipment clearly marked as such?	5				
3. Perform failure ranking	• Are equipment failures appropriately defined?	5				
	• Are idling and minor stops appropriately defined?	5				
	• Are process failures appropriately defined?	5				
4. Understand conditions and level of maintenance	• Are failures and minor stops tallied and graphed?	10				
	• Are failure frequencies and severities known?					
	• Are MTBFs known?					
	• Are major and intermediate failures recorded on charts?	5				
	• Are maintenance costs known? Are their application categories clear?	5				
5. Benchmark and set goals	• Are benchmarks and reduction goals for failures, idling, and minor stops set appropriately?	5				
	• Are MTBF benchmarks and goals set appropriately?	5				
	• Are benchmarks and goals for breakdown maintenance rates and periodic maintenance rates set appropriately?	5				
6. Prepare action plan	• Is there an action plan for step-by-step development?	5				
	• Have preparations been made to proceed to Step 2 and are responsibilities clearly allocated?	5				

Step 1: Evaluate Equipment and Understand Current Conditions

Process plants use many different types of equipment. Even equipment units of the same type can differ in importance depending on their functions in the process. To decide which equipment receives planned maintenance, prepare equipment logs and prioritize the equipment in accordance with pre-estabished criteria.

Equipment Logs Should Provide Data for Equipment Evaluation

Equipment logs are raw data for evaluating equipment. They must give design data and show the equipment's operating and maintenance history. The sample log in Table 5-9 suggests items to include.

Table 5-9. Equipment Log Format

1. Asset # : _____

2. Equipment name:_____ Model # :_____ Drawing # :_____ Spec. # :_____

3. Location:_____ Factory:_____ Plant:_____ Process:_____ Record of movements:_____

4. Manufacturer:_____ Mftr. date:_____ Installation date:_____ Test operation date:_____ Startup date:_____

5. Record of specification changes

Date	Equipment Specification	Operating Condition

6. Maintenance record

Date	Periodic Service	Corrective Maintenance	Major Failures

7. Specifications of main ancillary equipment

Evaluate and Prioritize the Equipment

Evaluate each piece of equipment in terms of its effect on safety, quality, operability, maintainability, and so on. Rank equipment (as A, B, or C, for example) and perform planned maintenance on all units ranked A or B, as well as those for which zero failure is a legal requirement. Ranking criteria will vary depending on the process, so the maintenance, production, production engineering, and safety departments must cooperate in scoring each attribute.

Figure 5-8 shows a sample flow-sheet for selecting equipment for planned maintenance. Table 5-10 offers sample criteria for assessing equipment characteristics.

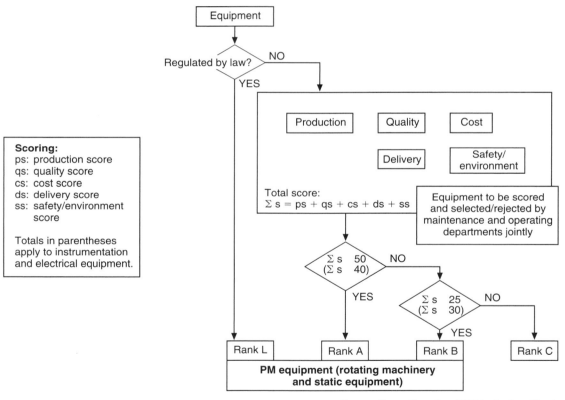

Source: Nippon Zeon Co., *PM Prize Lecture Digest.*

Figure 5-8. Flow Diagram for Selecting PM Equipment

Table 5-10. Criteria for Evaluating Equipment Characteristics

Attribute	Evaluation Criterion	Rank
Safety: Effect of failure on people and environment	Equipment failure poses explosion risk or other hazards; equipment failure causes serious pollution	A
	Equipment failure might adversely affect the environment	B
	Other equipment	C
Quality: Effect of failure on product quality	Equipment failure has a major effect on quality (could lead to product contamination or abnormal reactions and produce out-of-spec product)	A
	Equipment failure produces quality variations that can be put right by the operator comparatively quickly	B
	Other equipment	C
Operation: Effect of failure on production	Equipment with major effect on production, without standby provision, whose failure causes previous and subsequent processes to shut down completely	A
	Equipment failure causes only partial shutdown	B
	Equipment failure has little or no effect on production	C
Maintenance: Time and cost of repair	Equipment takes 4+ hours or costs $2,400+ to repair, or fails three or more times per month	A
	Equipment can be repaired in under 4 hours at a cost of between $240 and $2,400 or fails less than three times per month	B
	Equipment costs less than $240 to repair or can be left unrepaired until a convenient opportunity arises	C

Source: Nippon Zeon Co., *PM Prize Lecture Digest.*

Rank Failures

Rank failures as major, intermediate, or minor depending on their effect on equipment. For major and intermediate failures, implement measures to prevent their recurrence and, also, to prevent similar failures from occurring in other equipment.

Understand the Failure Situation and Set Maintenance Goals

To grasp the current situation, obtain data on failure numbers, frequencies, and severities, and on MTBFs (mean times between failures), MTTRs (mean times to repair), maintenance costs, and so on. Then set goals for reducing these through planned maintenance. Table 5-11 suggests some planned maintenance goals.

Table 5-11. Examples of Planned Maintenance Goals

Indicator	Improvement Goal
Failures by equipment ranking	• A equipment ➝ 0 • B equipment ➝ 1/10 of baseline 1/10 • C equipment ➝ 1/2 of baseline 1/2
Failures by failure ranking	• Major failures ➝ 0 • Intermediate failures ➝ 1/10 of baseline 1/10 • Minor failures ➝ 1/2 of baseline 1/2
Process failures	• Leaks, contamination, and blocks ➝ 0 • Abnormal pressures, temperatures, and flow rates due to complex causes ➝ 1/2 of baseline
Equipment failure severity	$\dfrac{\text{Failure downtime}}{\text{operating time}} \times 100$ ➝ (A equipment: 0.15 or less)
Equipment failure frequency	$\dfrac{\text{Failure stops}}{\text{operating time}} \times 100$ ➝ (A equipment: 0.1 or less)
PM achievement rate	$\dfrac{\text{PM jobs completed}}{\substack{\text{total planned maintenance} \\ \text{jobs scheduled}}} \times 100$ ➝ (90% or more)

Step 2: Restore Deterioration and Correct Weaknesses

Until a plant establishes autonomous maintenance, equipment exposed to accelerated deterioration for many years can fail unexpectedly at irregular intervals. Maintenance departments often have no time to perform planned maintenance because they are too busy dealing with such failures. It is impossible to force through a program of planned maintenance in such a situation. The first step in the planned maintenance program is therefore to support operators' autonomous maintenance activities by restoring accelerated deterioration, correcting design weaknesses, and restoring equipment to its optimal condition.

To support Steps 1 through 3 of the autonomous maintenance program, help operators restore deterioration. At the same time, correct weaknesses and lengthen equipment life, prevent failure recurrence, and reduce process failures. Each of these activities is described in more detail below.

Help Operators Restore Deterioration

Help operators understand and overcome the effects of deterioration in their equipment in the following ways:

• Deal promptly with any deterioration or irregularities that operators discover but cannot deal with themselves.

- Prepare one-point lesson sheets and teach operators about the structure and functions of their equipment.
- Give hands-on guidance to operators on inspection, restoring equipment, and making small improvements.

To abolish environments that promote accelerated deterioration:

- Advise operators on how to address contamination sources and hard-to-lubricate places.
- Eliminate major contamination sources.

To establish basic equipment conditions:

- Prepare visual control standards and help operators implement them.
- Assist operators in preparing provisional daily checking standards.
- Teach operators about lubrication and standardize lubricant types.

Correct Weaknesses and Lengthen Equipment Life

In addition to accelerated deterioration, equipment may also suffer from inherent weaknesses generated during design, fabrication, and installation. Weaknesses may also become apparent when equipment is operated outside its design conditions. Teams should use techniques such as FMEA (failure mode and effects analysis) and P-M analysis to analyze failures due to such weaknesses and then correct them. Otherwise, unexpected failures will undermine any benefits planned maintenance might be expected to have.

Prevent Recurrence of Failure

Use failure analysis to deal with the type of major and intermediate failures that halt production lines. Also investigate the possibility of similar failures that occur in other equipment and take steps to prevent them. The flow-sheet in Figure 5-9 outlines a procedure for preventing the recurrence of unexpected major and intermediate failures. Table 5-12 offers a format for reporting failure analyses and preventive measures taken.

Reduce Process Failures

Process failures are usually caused by combinations of equipment and process factors such as:

- Corrosion, cracking, blocks, leaks, and accumulation of foreign matter in static equipment; vibration and blocking of pipes; perforation of heat-exchanger tubes; and so on
- Changing properties of raw materials and subsidiary materials, disrupted services, misoperation, catalyst deterioration, and other process disorders

Table 5-12. Unexpected Failure Recurrence-Prevention and Action Report Form

<table>
<tr><td colspan="8" align="center">UNEXPECTED FAILURE
REPORT NO. _____</td></tr>
<tr><td colspan="4">Division Manager ☐
Supervisor   ☐
Team Leader   ☐</td><td colspan="4">Equipment Section Manager ☐
Supervisor   ☐
Team Leader   ☐</td></tr>
<tr><td colspan="5">Failed equipment: ____Heating oil pump____
Occurred on: ___/___/___ Time: _____ (min.)
Repaired on: ___/___/___ Time: _____ (min.)</td><td colspan="3">Model No: ____P-XXX____   Total
                                                     time ☐
                                                     (Min.)</td></tr>
</table>

Description:

The pump was stopped to replace the mechanical seal. When the pump was restarted, the coupling ruptured, so the pump stopped again.

Pump P-XXX pumps heating oil at a normal temperature of 200 - 250 °C. Since the mechanical seal was leaking, the pump was stopped to replace the seal after first switching over to standby pump P-XXX. The coupling ruptured when the pump was restarted after the seal had been replaced.

Failure Analysis: (Direct causes • Indirect causes • True causes)

1. The coupling had cooled down while the mechanical seal was being replaced. The pump was restarted after connecting the coupling to the pump shaft, which was still hot.

2. The state of attachment of the coupling was not checked.

Action and Countermeasures:

1. Preheat a spare coupling and attach it when the temperature difference between it and the pump shaft is within the specified range.

2. Specify a method for checking the state of attachment of the coupling after installation, and write this into the work standards.

Action to Prevent Similar Failures:

Location	Equipment	Action plan'd	Action compl.	Location	Equipment	Action plan'd	Action compl.
	Heating-oil pump P-X	/	/			/	/
	High-temperature pump P-X	/	/			/	/
	High-temperature rotating machines	/	/			/	/
		/	/			/	/
		/	/			/	/

(Nishi Nippon Seitō)

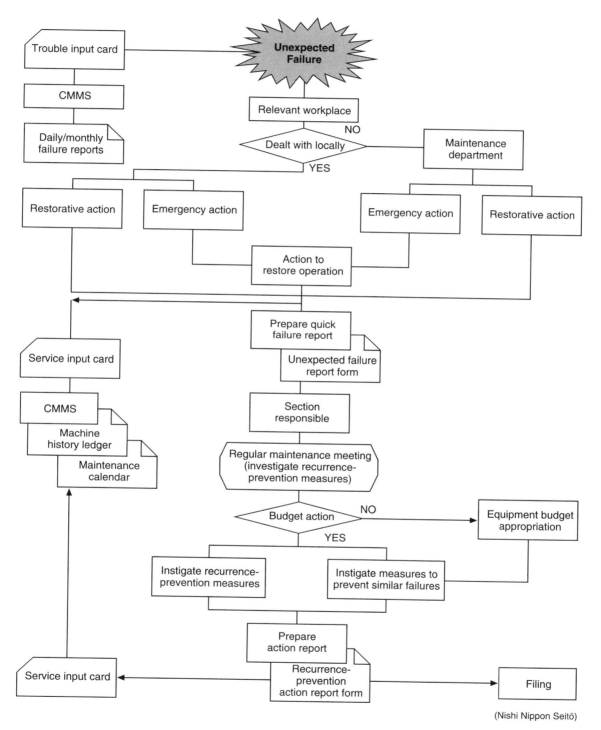

Figure 5-9. Flow Diagram for Preventing Recurrence of Unexpected Failures

(Nishi Nippon Seitō)

Since causes of process failures are combinations of factors, it is often difficult to pinpoint where and when they start. The causes of a failure may disappear by the time someone notices the failure. Then only the obvious phenomena can be analyzed, and measures to prevent recurrence are hard to implement.

To minimize process failure losses, restore process conditions to normal as soon as possible after spotting signs of impending failure. To facilitate process failure prediction:

- Make sure the people involved accurately understand the process status. Calibrate measuring instruments carefully and check them regularly to maintain their accuracy.
- Overhaul control systems and constantly confirm that they are functioning correctly.
- Study past failures. Use the results to train operators to restore disrupted processes to normal as quickly as possible.
- For every process failure that occurs, prepare a detailed report that describes warning signs, the nature of the failure, and the action taken.
- Analyze each failure using FMEA, P-M analysis, or other techniques, and recast the failure report form in the light of the results.

A basic approach to reducing process failures is to select the most suitable system of maintenance for each functionally important component or equipment item. Use the reliability-centered maintenance (RCM) approach to determine this, based on failure records and physical principles.

Step 3: Build an Information Management System

In process industries, an enormous variety of equipment needs maintenance, and different processes require different maintenance regimes. Managing this colossal amount of information manually is impossible. The company must set up a computerized data-processing system. Consider the following key points about computerization:

- Before committing to a system, evaluate and improve the existing maintenance system and decide which data are necessary.
- Determine the degree of computerization required.
- Devise simple data-entry methods for those responsible for maintenance.
- Start with personal computers. As the level of data management required rises, consider designing a comprehensive data management system to be run on a mainframe computer.

- A computerized maintenance management system (CMMS) cannot function effectively if major and intermediate failures persist. Construct a failure data management system, first. Build the equipment maintenance management system only when major and intermediate failures no longer recur.

Building a Failure Data Management System

A failure data management system should include certain information, which shift operators must enter in the database. Such information includes date and time; failure rank (major, intermediate, minor); equipment model; failed component (shaft, coupling, bearing, etc.); nature of failure (vibration, abnormal noise, overheating, corrosion, wear, etc.); cause; action taken; effect on production; and time and number of personnel required for repair.

The system should be able to generate reports with this information each morning for discussion at morning meetings. The team can analyze minor failures at these meetings. At weekly maintenance meetings they should reanalyze major and intermediate failures that were fixed temporarily and consider measures to prevent their recurrence.

This data should be analyzed and made available at regular intervals in the form of periodic failure summaries and equipment failure lists. These help teams determine failure frequency, downtime, and so on for individual processes or types of equipment. The information also helps prioritize improvements and prevent recurrence. Equipment failure lists also facilitate more penetrating analyses of the causes of mechanical and process failure for different ranks of equipment and failure.

Figure 5-10 shows an example of a periodic failure summary; Figure 5-11 shows an example of an equipment failure list.

Case 5-1: A Small Computerized Maintenance Management System

When management at a certain company installed a mainframe computer, they decided to use the opportunity to develop a maintenance management system to increase the effectiveness of autonomous and specialized maintenance. They built the system from three subsystems: failure management, equipment management, and budget management. The system was designed to allow operators on the production floor to enter data using personal computers.

The primary goals of the system were:

- To accelerate analysis of major and intermediate failures in order to prevent their recurrence
- To strengthen the maintenance system by enabling everyone to share the maintenance data
- To reduce the number of personnel required to collect and analyze maintenance data
- To improve maintenance work and budget management

PERIODIC FAILURE SUMMARY

Monthly total: 8/1/89 - 8/10/89   Department Manager _____
Cumulative total: 5/13/89 - 8/10/89   Section Manager _____

Mechanical Failures	PM Equipment				All Equipment					
Equipment	Monthly total	Monthly %	Cum. total	Cum. %	Monthly total	Monthly %	Cum. total	Cum. %	Down-time	Repair hours
Mixers and minglers	0	0.0	2	1.5	0	0.0	2	1.3	.00	.00
Separators	3	23.1	49	36.6	3	23.1	49	31.0	.00	.17
Filters	2	15.4	3	2.2	2	15.4	4	2.5	.00	18.00
Pumps	1	7.7	14	10.4	1	7.7	17	10.8	.00	.00
Fans	1	7.7	8	1.5	1	7.7	3	1.9	.00	.33
Tanks	0	0.0	2	1.5	0	0.0	15	9.5	.00	.00
Crystallizers	2	15.4	6	4.5	2	15.4	6	3.8	.00	2.00
Screens	0	0.0	2	1.5	0	0.0	2	1.3	.00	.00
Elevators	0	0.0	9	6.7	0	0.0	9	5.7	.00	.00
Vibrating conveyors	0	0.0	4	3.0	0	0.0	4	2.5	.00	.00
Screw conveyors	0	0.0	8	6.0	0	0.0	9	5.7	.00	.00

Figure 5-10. Periodic Failure Summary

EQUIPMENT FAILURE LIST

Printout date: 8/31/89
Period: 4/1/89 - 8/15/89

Prod. #	Equipment	Fail date	Rank	Component	Description	Failure	Remarks
C F-7302	No. 2 separator	4/4/89	C	Unloader	Stopped		Unloader limit-switch abnormality
C F-7302	No. 2 separator	4/5/89	C	Unloader	Stopped	Failed to unload	
C F-7302	No. 2 separator	4/11/89	C	Unloader	Cycle time exceeded	Failed to unload	Occurred twice, poss. cause friction around upper end
C F-7302	No. 2 separator	4/14/89	C	Unloader	Stopped	Other	Failed to return to horizontal at unloader upper limit
C F-7302	No. 2 separator	4/20/89	C	Unloader	Stopped	Jammed	

Figure 5-11. Equipment Failure List

Figure 5-12 shows the structure of the computerized maintenance management system.

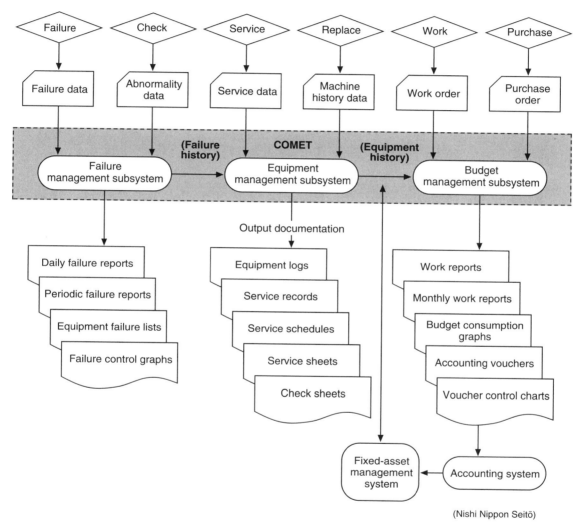

Figure 5-12. A Computerized Maintenance Management System (CMMS)

Case 5-2: A Large Computerized Maintenance Management System

After a company computerizes production management, cost control, fixed-asset management, and personnel management systems, it must clarify the relationships between these and the maintenance information management system. Figure 5-13 shows an example.

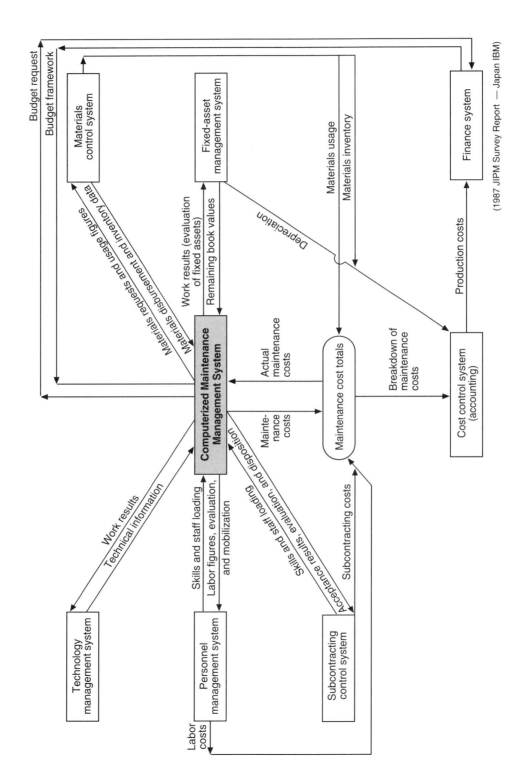

Figure 5-13. Information Flows Between CMMS and Other Systems

(1987 JIPM Survey Report — Japan IBM)

Human judgment plays a larger part in computerized maintenance management systems than in other systems, and things do not always go according to plan. A company cannot expect the benefits of systematization to show themselves immediately. To make the transition smoother, keep the following in mind:

- Ensure that data leads to action and use the outcomes of any action to revise standards.
- Start with a system that matches the existing level of control and upgrade it in stages.
- Make the system as effective as possible for front-line maintenance personnel.

Figure 5-14 illustrates the functional organization of a computerized maintenance management system.

Computerizing Maintenance Budget Management

A computerized management system for the maintenance budget compiles, apportions, and totals maintenance budgets. It must generate the following kinds of information:

- Budget summaries for different types of maintenance work that compare budgeted and actual expenditure over the same period in different years for different types of maintenance work or budgeting systems.
- Work and materials usage schedules that provide information on work plans, costs, projected materials usage, and materials inventories. You can also use this information for forecasting when maintenance funds need to be disbursed.
- Job priority lists that include information on maintenance work priorities, projected downtimes, costs, and so on.
- Equipment life forecasts that help ensure that maintenance is performed appropriately. The system should generate past MTBF data along with details about equipment that is due to reach the end of its useful life.
- Charts that compare predicted downtime losses with maintenance costs and help measure maintenance effectiveness. The system should generate data that compares the cost of maintaining equipment with the predicted losses that arise from its failure.

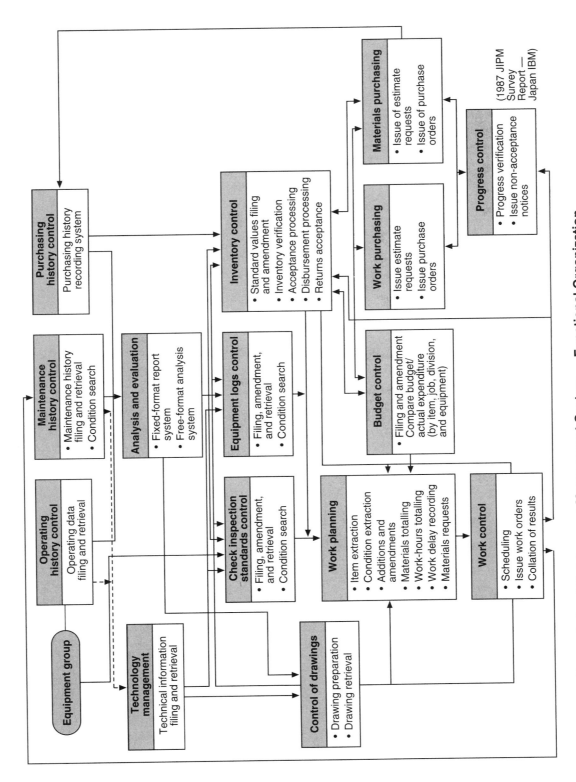

Figure 5-14. Computerized Maintenance Management System — Functional Organization

Building a System for Controlling Spare Parts and Materials

To analyze reasons for holding long-term stocks and to cut down on the labor required for calculating total usage and keeping track of issues and receipts, the following information is necessary:

- Lists of long-term stocks that include equipment and component models, specifications, order numbers, order months, expected month of use, stock months, months elapsed, quantities, and reasons for stocking
- Materials usage tables for calculating totals for different procurement systems, different equipment models, and so on
- Receipts/issues comparison tables that show the status of spare parts and materials receipts and issues

Building a System for Controlling Technical Information and Drawings

A technology management system should control all information that relates to maintenance, including design standards, technical reports, important literature, checking standards, mechanical design calculation programs, equipment diagnosis criteria, and structural analysis data.

Design the drawing control system to file and retrieve maintenance drawings, equipment drawings, equipment logs, detailed drawings of parts to inspect, piping layouts, flow diagrams, wiring diagrams, drawing lists, catalogs, and so on.

Step 4: Build a Periodic Maintenance System

In periodic (or time-based) maintenance, standby units, spare parts, inspection equipment, lubricants, and technical information such as drawings may be required to carry out the scheduled work. Maintenance work proceeds smoothly only if these resources are properly prepared in advance.

Periodic Maintenance Procedure

As the flow-sheet of Figure 5-15 shows, equipment can be overmaintained if work is scheduled unthinkingly at rigidly set intervals. Whenever you perform a maintenance job, consider whether the interval and the type of work scheduled are appropriate. When equipment fails before the set maintenance interval elapses, analyze the reasons and use the results to revise the maintenance interval and tasks before the next service.

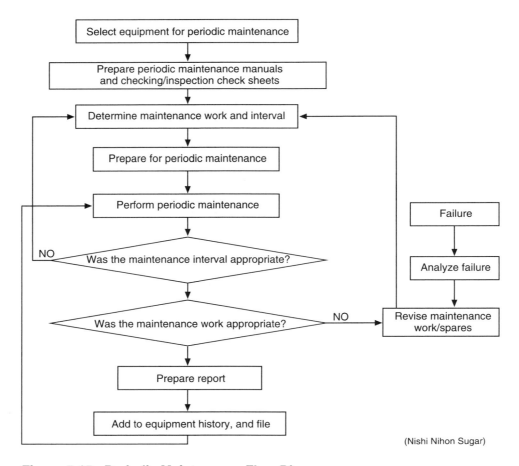

Figure 5-15. Periodic Maintenance Flow Diagram

Selecting Equipment and Components for Periodic Maintenance

Assess the equipment designated for planned maintenance and select equipment from the following categories for periodic maintenance:

- Equipment that, by law, requires periodic inspection
- Equipment with maintenance intervals determined by experience
- Equipment that requires regular checking because of its importance to the process
- Equipment with an established replacement interval based on the serviceable life of its components
- Equipment, such as heat exchangers, whose performance begins to deteriorate after a known period as a result of scale buildup and so on
- Important equipment for which it is difficult or impossible to detect or correct abnormalities during operation

Preparing Maintenance Plans

Base maintenance plans on mid-range (approximately five-year) production plans. Detail the shutdown maintenance for the entire plant or section along with the periodic maintenance required for individual equipment items. Include shutdown maintenance plans; annual, monthly, weekly, and daily plans; individual plans; and plans for "opportunity maintenance" (maintenance performed on machines whenever they are shut down for other reasons).

When drawing up periodic maintenance plans, try to incorporate the following:

- Set up and fabricate in advance to reduce the time the actual maintenance work takes.
- Minimize personnel movement during maintenance work by multi-skilling maintenance technicians and outside workers.
- Prepare everything in advance (scaffolding, lighting, materials, electrical power, compressed air, water supplies, purging and opening-up of equipment, etc.).
- The severity of equipment deterioration depends on the operating conditions since the equipment's last service. Before drawing up the maintenance plan, examine information such as daily checking records and note any changes in operating conditions.

Formulating Periodic Maintenance Standards

To ensure that people perform periodic maintenance accurately and efficiently and to build up a solid base of maintenance technology within the company, formulate the following kinds of standards and update them as necessary:

Materials selection standards. Even though the best materials may have been selected when equipment was originally designed, subsequent process changes or changes in the properties of raw materials and auxiliary materials can alter the situation. In such cases, revise the original standards.

Work estimating standards. Assume the use of the latest maintenance techniques, equipment, and materials to establish standard work-hours and materials and equipment costs for standard maintenance tasks such as:

- *Rotating machinery*: assembly and disassembly, parts replacement, centering and adjustment, lubricant replacement, etc.
- *Columns and tanks*: removing and replacing covers, internal cleaning, internal parts removal and replacement, etc.

- *Heat exchangers*: assembly and disassembly, internal cleaning, checking for tube-bundle leaks, etc.
- *Furnaces*: removal and replacement of burners, cleaning and replacement of heating tubes, repairing furnace walls, etc.
- *Piping*: attachment and removal of flanges and valves; repair, replacement, and internal cleaning of pipes; etc.
- *Electrical equipment and instrumentation*: testing, servicing, replacement, etc.

Spare-parts control standards. Spare parts are essential for assuring equipment reliability, extending equipment life, and reducing equipment downtime. On the other hand, unnecessary stocks tie up capital and increase warehousing costs, so it is vital to establish effective control standards.

Classify and control spare parts in accordance with a scheme such as the following:

- *Standby units — pumps, motors, and other standby equipment.* The maintenance department should control and keep constantly ready for use.
- *Priority components — rotating parts of important machinery, etc.* The maintenance department should control and check regularly.
- *General parts — regularly-issued items such as bearings, nuts, and bolts.* The stores department should control, using a fixed-number system to issue items such as bearings, and the package/batch system to issue items such as nuts, bolts, and so on.
- *Tools and testing equipment.* The maintenance department should control tools and issue them on loan. Testing equipment should be controlled by the department that uses it.

Lubricant control standards. Compared with other petrochemical products, there are many more brands of lubricants available than discrete product specifications Most companies simply buy the brand specified by the machine manufacturer. This may be necessary at first so as not to invalidate the machine's performance warranty. It gradually increases the number of different types of lubricant in use, however, which makes it difficult to keep track of them all. Equipment users must learn to assess the suitability of different types of oil for different conditions of use so that they can prepare lubricant-type control standards and reduce the number of different brands they use. Some companies have succeeded in reducing the number of different brands from fifty to ten, which greatly facilitates lubricant control.

Lubricant-supply control standards. People often use lubricants, particularly grease to excess. This contaminates equipment and encourages the adhesion of dust and dirt. Rubbing surfaces actually consume very little lubricant:

In one instance, carefully observing a 60-mm diameter rolling bearing over one year revealed that it operated trouble-free even when the operator applied only 0.2 cc of lubricant three times per month.

Safety standards. Draw up safety standards for maintenance work. Review and partially revise these annually, and revise them completely at least once every five years. Include the following items:

- Duties of workers and supervisors
- Action before starting work
- Action in the event of an accident
- Safety procedures during work
- Standards for *seiri* (sort out the unnecessary) and *seiton* (set in order — arrange efficiently)
- Handling radioactive substances
- Electrical safety precautions

Table 5-13 is an example of a safety standard to be applied before commencing maintenance work.

The most important preparations for ensuring the safety of maintenance workers are:

- Draw up standards that cover specific problems in the area where they are to work
- Allow workers to inspect the worksite in advance
- Make the worksite safe for the use of naked flames

Table 5-14 is an example of a maintenance work commencement authorization and completion report.

Improving the Efficiency of Shutdown Maintenance

It is standard practice in the chemical industry to perform shutdown maintenance at least once a year, and this helps to improve operational safety. Some other process industries also improved their efficiency when they introduced planned shutdown maintenance in place of maintenance after working hours or on holidays.

Shutdown maintenance can consume up to half of a company's annual maintenance budget. This is because it includes equipment modification, the cost of stopping and restarting the plant, as well as the cost of maintaining equipment (such as columns, tanks, heat exchangers, and piping) that cannot be opened up during normal operation. Companies also carry out capital investment projects during the shutdown maintenance period, therefore improving the efficiency of shutdown maintenance is important.

Table 5-13. Sample Safety Procedures Completed before Starting Maintenance Work

I. Duties of Work and Inspection Supervisors

Para. 110: Work and inspection supervisors ("supervisors") shall endeavor to prevent danger and injury by:

- observing all legal requirements and plant regulations
- taking all safety precautions directed by the safety manager or the relevant equipment manager
- and ensuring that those performing the work do likewise

II. Procedure to be Followed Before Commencing Work

Para. 111: Supervisors will not order work or inspection to begin unless the following actions have been taken and confirmed with the safety manager, the manager of the section in which the relevant equipment is located, and those carrying out the work.

1. When working in dangerous areas in the presence of petrochemical products or reagents and gases used in refining processes or performing special tasks such as moving heavy loads:
   — The work plan is only drawn up *after* the area has been checked and all questions of safety have been settled in respect of schedule, techniques, setup procedures, and supervision and direction of the work;
   — A specific person has been placed in charge of the work;
   — Workers have been fully informed of the contents of the work plan and given any necessary safety training.

2. In accordance with "Work Commencement Authorization Regulations", authorization tags permitting work to begin or equipment to be opened up have been attached to the relevant equipment.

3. Safety devices and protective clothing required for the work have been overhauled and placed ready.

4. When pumps or compressors are to be repaired, the relevant drive motors have been switched off at both the worksite and the substation. Furthermore, a notice is displayed in the substation stating that work is being carried out.

5. When air-fin coolers and tank mixers are to be repaired, the relevant drive motor is switched off at the workplace. Furthermore, the workplace switch is chained to prevent it being operated, and a notice is displayed stating that work is being carried out.

6. The equipment about to be worked on is verified as the right equipment.

7. Pressure has been released and volatile materials have been purged from any equipment that must be dismantled or opened up; moreover, valves and stopcocks on chemical equipment have been tightly closed or blanking plates installed, in order to prevent dangerous substances or high temperature steam from being discharged into the work area; these valves, stopcocks, or blanking plates have also been chained, and either they carry notices stating that they must not be opened, or a person has been appointed to stand guard over them.

8. In addition, the procedures and conditions specified in "Procedures for Performing On-Site Work" have been complied with.

9. When commencing work, adequate precautions, particularly the connection of equipment to ground, have been taken to prevent discharges of static electricity when performing steam cleaning, kerosene washing, painting, or other spraying work.

Table 5-14. Work Commencement Authorization and Completion Report

Date:_____ Work #:_____ Auth. tag #:_____

		Use of naked flame?
JOB	Facility:_____ New ☐ Continued ☐ Work description:_____ Instructions:_____ Attendance required? ☐ ☐ Yes No	☐ ☐ Yes No Auth. tag #_____

Subcontractor:_____ Work superintendent:_____ | Scheduled start time
Work director:_____ # of workers:_____ |
Work site:_____ Equip. name:_____ | Scheduled finish time

PRE-COMMENCEMENT CHECKPOINTS	Prod. Dept.			Works Dept.		
	Yes	No	Signed	Yes	No	Signed
1. Has person in charge checked details of the work?						
2. Is equipment properly purged; is internal pressure equal to atmospheric?						
3. Is equipment properly tagged?						
4. Are procedures for detecting flammable, toxic, and asphyxiatory gases completed?						
Flammable gases ___ %						
Toxic gases ___ ppm						
Asphyxiatory gases ___ O_2%						
5. Are blanking plates correctly attached to valves and other equipment?						
6. Is equipment switched off?						
Are switched-off signs attached? (on substation switch and workplace switch)						
7. Are drains properly sealed?						
8. Have flammable materials been removed or placed under guard?						
9. Are signs stating that naked flames are temporarily in use displayed in the workplace?						
10. Has permission been received for vehicles to be driven into danger zones?						
11. Are fire extinguishers installed?						
12. Are workers legally qualified?						
13. Is scaffolding correctly installed or scheduled to be installed?						
14. Are all relevant workplaces informed?						
15. Have steps been taken to assure safety even if measuring instrument circuits are interrupted?						
16. Is protective clothing provided?						
(artificial resuscitation equipment, gloves, safety belts, safety goggles, face masks,						
rubber boots, gas masks, respirator masks, and hose masks)						
17. Are work commencement authorization tags attached?						

Safety Confirmation | I have checked the condition of the equipment, materials, and surroundings, and I confirm that it is safe to carry out the work.

Prod. Foreman/Team Leader:_____ Prod. Supervisor:_____
Works Supervisor:_____

Large Vessels | When large vessels are to be opened, entered, or sealed, obtain authorization in accordance with Work Commencemen Authorization Regulations

Inspection Manager:_____ Prod. Sect. Manager:_____
Works Sect. Manager:_____ Safety/Security Manager:_____

Completion Checkpoints	Works Dept./Subcontractor			
	Sect.	Comp.	Signed	Remarks
1. Have all flames been extinguished after use?				
2. Are all gas hoses and cables neatly and unobstructively arranged?				
3. Are switches on distribution boards and elsewhere turned off?				
4. Are temporary installations, e.g., scaffolding, fireproof walls, protective sheets, etc.				
satisfactorily secured against wind?				
5. Are equipment, materials, spares, etc. clean, tidy, and neatly arranged?				
6. Have you informed the Production Department that the day's work has been completed?				

Confirmation | I confirm that I have completed the above checks.

Works supervisor/subcontractor work director:_____

I confirm the results of the above checks
Production Department — Confirmed by:_____ Time:_____

Copies to: Prod. Sect. Manager, Works Sect. Manager, Safety/Security Sect. Manager, Subcontractor

(Kyokutō Petroleum)

Work Breakdown Structure for Shutdown Maintenance

Shutdown maintenance is the most extensive maintenance activity for any process plant. It involves much work, starting with shutting down production, purging the system, checking safety, performing and accepting the maintenance and construction work, preparing for startup, and finally, restarting production. It involves almost every department within the company, including safety, purchasing, and accounting, as well as production, maintenance, inspection, and engineering. Omission-free, error-free shutdown maintenance is impossible unless the entire process is carefully planned. List every single maintenance task, regardless of size, and relate each to the each others by means of a work breakdown structure (WBS) diagram. Figure 5-16 shows a WBS diagram. For additional information about this activity, see *New Directions for TPM*, published by Productivity Press.

The WBS method includes the following activities:

Prepare an on-site work operation sheet in network form. On-site work during shutdown maintenance is usually delayed by a multitude of unanticipated events such as the discovery of unexpected deterioration, late arrival of materials, and adverse weather conditions. The bar-type of operation sheet is less useful in such cases because it conceals the relationships among different tasks and the effect of delays on the overall project.

To avoid this, prepare a network diagram that clearly shows the relationships among different tasks. Keep a constant check on the critical path (the bottleneck for the overall process). This is the key to expediting the process effectively.

Prepare a network diagram. Use a network scheduling method such as PERT (program evaluation and review technique) or CPM (critical path method) to prepare an on-site work operation sheet showing the tasks detailed in the WBS diagram. Highlight the bottleneck processes.

Shorten the process. Shorten the bottleneck process by giving it first claim on personnel and materials, reducing delivery times of purchased materials, and devising external setup techniques, that is, gathering and setting up tools, materials, parts, and equipment needed for the work as much as possible before actual shutdown. Use the network diagram to assess the effect of these efforts and identify the next bottleneck process. To shorten the overall schedule, keep repeating this procedure.

Reduce shutdown maintenance costs. Eliminate unnecessary expenditures for personnel, materials, electrical power, equipment hire, and so on, for each

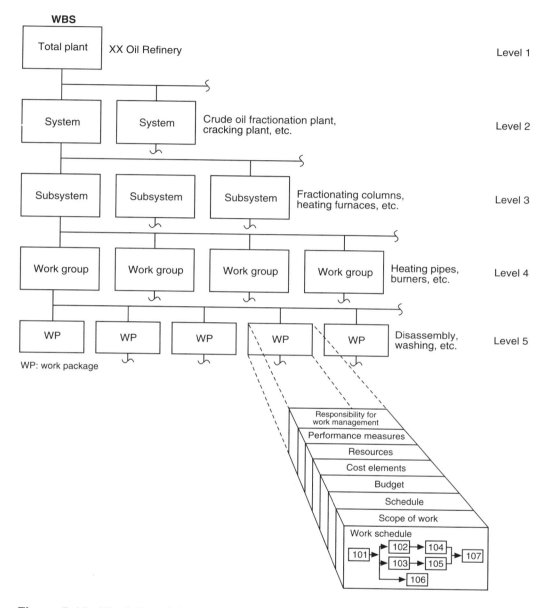

Figure 5-16. Work Breakdown Structure (WBS)

task. In particular, watch out for waste in personnel costs and equipment hire costs resulting from schedule changes. Below are some ideas for improving work efficiency:

- Juggle the schedule to level the numbers of outside workers on the site each day.

- Make effective use of float times and spare labor capacity.
- Reduce the amount of overtime and holiday work by setting aside specific rest days during the shutdown maintenance period.
- Make effective use of subcontract workers normally employed on daily maintenance.
- Rationalize the use of heavy equipment such as cranes.
- Order out-sourced items far in advance.
- Select subcontractors by competitive tendering based on shutdown maintenance work standards.

Progress Control

Advance preparation. Advance preparations for shutdown maintenance include:

- Making early arrangements for materials and equipment
- Reviewing the schedule
- Providing scaffolding, lighting, and power; positioning materials and equipment where they are needed
- Installing temporary piping for internal purging

The production department must plan purging operations carefully and ensure their safety. Successful purging ensures that maintenance personnel can open up the equipment at the right time and also keeps internal cleaning costs down. It also greatly affects the safety and efficiency of the maintenance work and the time taken for its completion.

Safety management. After starting work, the most important thing is safety management. Over 50 percent of serious accidents in process plants occur during shutdown maintenance. With the support of other departments, the maintenance department must control safety, the environment, the quality of the work, and the schedule. In managing subcontract work, give priority to the following:

- Exercise strict control during shutdown maintenance to ensure safety.
- Because the nature of the work and site conditions change daily, all managers must meet each day to discuss and agree on the next day's tasks.
- Employees and subcontractors must carry out safety patrols and daily accident prevention activities together.
- Inspect the safety of all machinery that subcontractors bring on site. Do not allow equipment in that fails inspection.

- Make every effort to level the number of people who enter the site during shutdown maintenance each day. Set an upper permissible limit.
- Before starting shutdown maintenance, give safety training and issue attendance certificates to everyone who will be entering the site.
- In addition, take the safety measures described earlier on pp. 183–85.

Concluding Shutdown Maintenance

At the conclusion of shutdown maintenance, prepare a report that details the work accomplished, the progress made, the organization used, the budget, and so on. Be careful to report all problems that concern safety, progress, and budget, and use this information in planning the next shutdown maintenance project.

The length of this report varies with the size of the shutdown maintenance project, and in some cases may run into dozens of pages. Table 5-15 lists the general information the report should generally include, and Table 5-16 shows an example of the type of weekly progress report that the shutdown maintenance project manager should submit to the plant superintendent.

Case 5-3: Shutdown Maintenance Management

Figure 5-17 shows how Daicel Chemical Industries' Aboshi Plant improved the quality of its shutdown maintenance management. The company not only reduced the time and cost of shutdown maintenance; it also achieved excellent results in increasing the number of focused improvement projects accomplished and reducing failures and defects. This success was probably due to the careful practice of collecting data needed for planning shutdown maintenance and incorporating it into the plans.

For example, as part of their autonomous maintenance program, operators at the Aboshi plant hold daily "ZT Meetings" ("zero-trouble" meetings) at which they discuss "trouble cards" (cards with brief descriptions of problems found). Any problems the operators have not addressed by the time shutdown maintenance is due are incorporated into the shutdown maintenance plans.

Sometimes shutdown maintenance rivals the scale of a small construction project, but it remains, nevertheless a maintenance task. No matter how skillfully personnel carry out the work, the result cannot be fully effective from the maintenance viewpoint, unless information gathered during operation and relevant to the work is taken into consideration in the plans. The maintenance department at this plant has established a reliable system for incorporating into shutdown maintenance plans critical information from focused improvement activities and from planned periodic checks and inspections.

Table 5-15. Items Recorded on Shutdown Maintenance Report

1. Shutdown maintenance schedule	• Planned (network diagram) — indicate critical path • Actual (network diagram) — indicate actual critical path, with reasons • Planned (calendar) — daily worker numbers, cranes, heavy machinery, government inspections • Actual (calendar) — actual daily worker numbers, cranes, heavy machinery, government inspections, weather
2. Shutdown and startup schedule	• stop operation • commence work • planned and actual • problems **Work completion:** • normal operation • scheduled and actual • problems
3. Organization for shutdown maintenance	• actual organization employed • points to incorporate in next shutdown maintenance plan
4. Description of principal work performed 5. Safety and environmental problems 6. Work problems, improvement measures adopted	
7. Budgeted and actual expenditure	• materials costs • subcontracting costs
8. Subcontracted work	• work undertaken by each subcontractor • planned and actual numbers of workers entering site
9. Government inspections	
10. Shutdown maintenance inspection	• problems (attach separate inspection report)
11. Shutdown maintenance debriefing (SDM)	• schedule for next SDM
In principle: **SDM debriefing** **Scheduling meeting for next SDM** **Planning meeting for next SDM** **Work meeting for next SDM**	• within two months after completion • three months before date • within four months after completion • two months before date
12. Other items to note in planning and implementing next SDM	

Table 5-16. Sample Weekly Shutdown Maintenance Report

GENERAL
- No injuries to company or subcontractors' employees
- Progress of shutdown maintenance work: 97-98%

SHUTDOWN MAINTENANCE

Plant C: A tube leak test revealed leaks in the ends of three reactor discharge oil/feed heat exchangers. One was due to a leak in the sealing weld of a tube plug. The other two were due to cracked tube ends. All have been repaired. Reactor catalyst charging has been completed.

Plant B: Based on the results of γ-radiation inspection of the heating furnace tubes after decoking, the decoking operation was repeated.

Plant A: Tray leak test satisfactory; inspection cover replacement commenced. None of the above problems has affected overall progress.

NEW WORK

Plant B: Testing revealed that several of the 32 tray-washing spray nozzles were blocked. A 10-mesh strainer will be attached to the pump outlet, and the line scoured by air jet. The work is on schedule.

GOVERNMENT INSPECTIONS

Plant C: 8/22 fire safety

Plants D and E: 8/25 fire safety, high-pressure gas

Plant B: 8/26 fire safety

Plant A: 8/29 fire safety

SPECIAL ITEMS
None

Step 5: Build a Predictive Maintenance System

While unexpected failures decrease once periodic maintenance is established, they still occur, and maintenance costs may increase. This is because periodic maintenance is time-based and assumes a hypothetical rate of equipment deterioration. Optimal service intervals cannot be set without measuring the extent of actual deterioration in individual items of equipment. This requires a condition-based approach, in which the timing and nature of the maintenance required is based on the extent of actual deterioration as confirmed through equipment diagnostics. To conduct condition-based or predictive maintenance, it must be possible to measure characteristics that indicate deterioration reliably (known as "substitute characteristics"). Such characteristics might include vibration, temperature, pressure, flow rate, lubricant contamination, wall thickness decrement, metallurgical defect growth, corrosion rate, and electrical resistance.

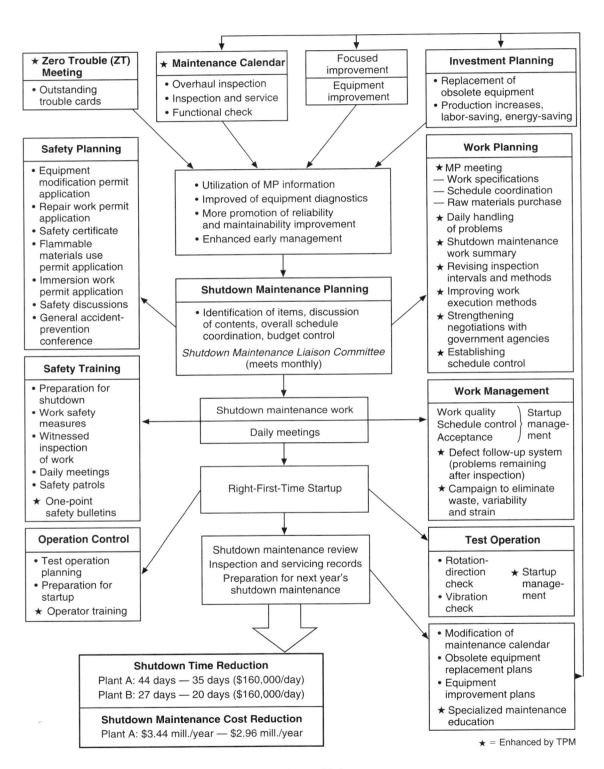

Figure 5-17. Enhanced Planning of Shutdown Maintenance

Introducing Equipment Diagnostics

Predictive maintenance involves the use of equipment diagnostics. It is best to start with vibration diagnostics, which is a technique developed in the steel and chemical industries. First establish the following system of diagnostics for rotating machinery, then use the same method to introduce diagnostics for static equipment.

Introducing Vibration Diagnostics for Rotating Machinery

Step 1: Establish a core team by training people likely to make good vibration diagnosticians.

Step 2: Designate certain items of equipment as models for practicing vibration diagnostics. Core team members practice their skills on this equipment and then pass on their knowledge to others.

Step 3: Designate certain items of equipment within each workplace as models for implementing vibration diagnostics. In process industries, feed pumps or gas compressors are probably the most suitable types of equipment for this, as their operating conditions and the properties of the materials they handle are fairly stable.

Step 4: Set provisional periods and criteria for measuring the vibration of the model equipment. To begin with, set periods of approximately one month, two months, or three months.

Step 5: Monitor the model equipment intensively for the set period. When a large degree of dispersion occurs in the measurements, check the state of the measuring surface to find out whether the measuring point moved or the attachment pressure of the measuring instrument changed. Also check whether the machine's load has changed, the machine's rotation rate has varied, or the machine is resonating. Then repeat the measurements.

Step 6: Have the core team meet to discuss the diagnostic techniques and results. Prepare case-study materials and use these for training.

After training a number of diagnosticians in this way, establish a comprehensive diagnostic system, perform diagnostic measurements, analyze and collate the results, and disseminate the technique throughout the organization.

Introducing Diagnostics for Static Equipment

Static equipment in process industries ranges in size from small stirrers and separators to huge columns and tanks. If overlooked, small materials defects or weld defects in such equipment may grow into large ones that can halt production and even cause major disasters. It is therefore vital to use equipment diagnostics to discover, diagnose, and predict deterioration. Table 5-17 shows some examples of diagnostic techniques for columns/tanks and piping/heat exchangers, while Table 5-18 shows an example of the diagnostic techniques used during normal operation and shutdown maintenance at a particular chemical plant.

Table 5-17. Diagnostic Techniques for Static Equipment

Abnormality	Cause	Diagnostic technique	Equipment
COLUMNS/TANKS **Leaks**	Corrosion, cracking, leaky packing	Visual inspection, soapy-water test, gas detection, wall-thickness measurement	Color-forming or foaming liquids, magnetic-powder flaw detectors, ultrasonic thickness gauges, gas detectors
Vibration	Transmission from outside	Vibration measurement	Vibration meter
	Abnormal gas/liquid flow	Analysis of operating conditions	Frequency analyzer, operating records
Internal contamination	Corrosion, abnormal internal fluids	Check operating conditions, analyze discharge	Radioscope, operating records
Internal damage	Loosening due to abnormal flow	Vibration, sound	Vibration meter, stethoscope, radioscope
PIPING **Leaks**	Corrosion, erosion, perforation	Visual inspection, gas detection, foaming liquid test	Gas detector, magnetic-powder flaw detector, ultrasonic thickness gauge
	Leaky packing and gaskets	Thickness measurement	
Blocks	Stuck valves, foreign matter, accumulated sludge	Pressure-drop measurement, radioscopy	Pressure gauge, radioscope
Vibration	Resonance with rotating machinery vibration	Vibration measurement	Vibration meter
	Abnormal fluids flow	Investigate operating conditions	Operating records
	Abnormal supports	Visual inspection, vibration measurement	Vibration meter
Deformation, bending	Abnormal hangers and supports	Displacement measurement	Scale, level gauge, transit theodolite
	Abnormal external force, thermal stress	Check external forces and temperatures	Operating records

JIPM Seminar: "Assessing Equipment Health"

Table 5-18. Equipment Diagnosis During Plant Operation and Shutdown

Diagnosis during Operation	Diagnosis during Shutdown
Principally rotating machinery and static equipment abnormalities diagnosed from process abnormalities. Usually done by operators monitoring the process or performing roving checks. Factors analyzed include: • Equipment abnormality (from instrument panel readings) • Vibration in rotating machinery and other equipment • Leaks • Abnormal sound • Abnormal temperature • Lubricant • Odor • Blocks	Principally of static equipment. Includes long-term diagnosis of materials deterioration (hydrogen attack, creep, carburization, stress corrosion cracking, fatigue). Types of inspection include: • Overhaul of static equipment • Overhaul of large rotating machines not provided with backup • Materials degradation in static equipment (hydrogen attack, creep, carburization, stress corrosion cracking, fatigue, etc.) • Welds • Wall thickness in high-temperature piping

Work Flow for Predictive Maintenance

Once you introduce equipment diagnostics and select equipment for predictive maintenance as described, prepare a predictive maintenance flow diagram. Figure 5-18 is an example. When applying this to static equipment, treat "simple diagnosis" as discovering abnormalities and "precision diagnosis" as diagnosing them.

Step 6: Evaluate the Planned Maintenance System

The goal of planned maintenance in process industries is not merely to plan the timing and techniques of maintenance, but also to plan methods for effectively maintaining equipment's expected functionality and reliability. Basically, planned maintenance systematizes the most effective maintenance techniques for eliminating failures that lead to degradation or total loss of the equipment's production functions.

As Figure 5-19 shows, the crux of maintenance system evaluation is assessing how well the maintenance and production departments work together. It should be a two-pronged system: The maintenance department is responsible for periodic maintenance in accordance with the maintenance calendar and predictive maintenance using equipment diagnostics and condition monitoring; The production department is responsible for keeping the equipment in peak condition through regular daily checks.

To assess the efficiency, timeliness, and economic feasibility of maintenance, look at what actually happens to the equipment in the workplace. To gauge whether the planned maintenance system is permanently in place, check whether the various supporting subsystems — control standards, technical standards, and so on — are properly established.

Chapter 12 contains a detailed discussion on evaluating maintenance results (see also the basic maintenance improvement indicators described on pp. 154–55, 168 of this chapter).

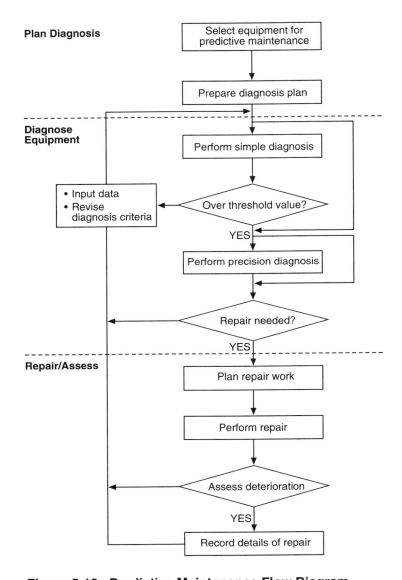

Figure 5-18. Predictive Maintenance Flow Diagram

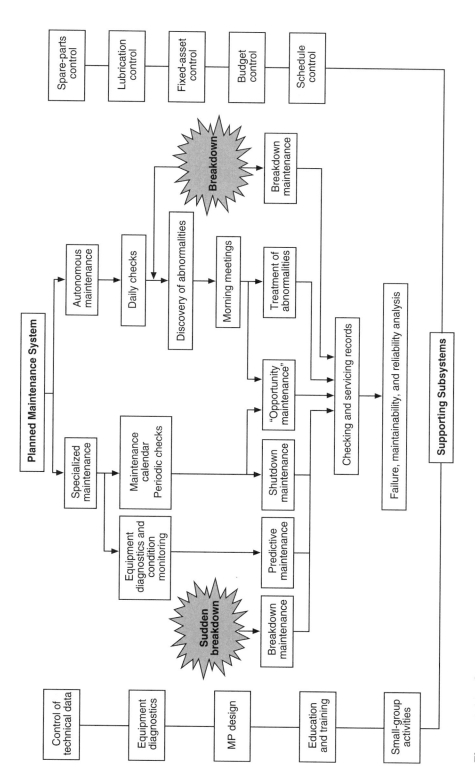

Figure 5-19. Outline of Planned Maintenance System

REFERENCES

E. Oshima, ed. *A Practical Dictionary of Equipment Diagnostics and Predictive Mainte-nance.* (in Japanese).: NTS Fuji Technosystems, n.d.

Y. Sakaguchi. *Plant Engineer,* Vol. 3: 8 (1990).

T. Suzuki. *New Directions for TPM.* Portland, Ore.: Productivity Press, 1992.

6
Early Management

As products diversify and their life cycles become shorter, finding ways to make new-product development and equipment investment more efficient grows in importance. The goal in TPM is to reduce dramatically the time from initial development to full-scale production and to achieve *vertical startup* (a startup that is fast, free of bugs, and right the first time).

THE NEED FOR EARLY MANAGEMENT

It is vital to develop products of readily assured quality that anticipate users' needs, products that are competitive, easy to sell, and easy to produce — and to do this efficiently. At the same time, however, the transition from development to full-scale production must be rapid and problem-free. To accomplish this, you must identify the production inputs (equipment, materials, people, and methods) required to bring the products to the market, eliminate the losses associated with equipment that produces them, and maximize return on investment. In other words, you must ensure that production equipment is easy to use, easy to maintain, highly reliable, and well-engineered. With such equipment, assuring product quality is simple.

Particularly in process industries, major equipment items are often customized to individual specifications; they are often designed, fabricated, and installed in a rush. Without strict early management, such equipment enters the test operation phase with many hidden defects. The truth of this is borne out by the frequency with which maintenance and production personnel discover defects generated in design, fabrication, and installation during shutdown maintenance and startup.

Early management is particularly important in process plants because large amounts of money are invested in their linked processing units and management expects the plant to operate for a considerable number of years. Also, after each period of shutdown maintenance, the restart operation must be managed by the same procedure followed when the plant was first commissioned. To accomplish this, all departments must cooperate closely — not only R & D, design, engineering, production, and maintenance, but also planning, marketing, finance, and quality assurance.

TPM gives equal importance to early product management, early equipment management, and the other TPM activities. The basis of early management is of course economic performance evaluation (optimizing life-cycle costs) and maintenance-prevention (MP) design.

LIFE-CYCLE COSTING

Consider first the basic philosophy of life-cycle costing (LCC) as it is understood and propounded by the LCC Committee of the Japan Institute of Plant Maintenance.

Life-Cycle Cost Defined

The *life-cycle cost* of a product, equipment item, or system is its total cost over the whole of its life. The U.S. Office of Management and the Budget defines it as: "The sum of the direct, indirect, recurring, non-recurring, and other related costs of a large-scale system during its period of effectiveness. It is the total of all costs generated or forecast to be generated during the design, development, production, operation, maintenance, and support processes."*

What Is Life-Cycle Costing?

JIPM's LCC Committee defines life-cycle costing as: "A systematic decision-making technique that incorporates life-cycle cost as a parameter at the design stage, performing all possible trade-offs to ensure an economic life-cycle cost for the user's system or design."

---

* *Major System Acquisitions.* U.S. Office of Management and Budget. Circular #A-109. Washington, D.C., 1976.

A general procedure for life-cycle costing a given system consists of the following steps:

Step 1: Clarify the system's mission.

Step 2: Formulate several alternative proposals capable of fulfilling the mission.

Step 3: Identify criteria for evaluating the system and techniques for quantifying these.

Step 4: Evaluate the proposals.

Step 5: Document the analytical results and processes.

MP DESIGN

MP design activity minimizes future maintenance costs and deterioration losses of new equipment by taking into account (during planning and construction) maintenance data on current equipment and new technology and by designing for high reliability, maintainability, economy, operability, and safety.

Ideally, MP-designed equipment must not break down or produce nonconforming products. It should be easy and safe to operate and maintain. The MP design process improves equipment reliability by investigating weaknesses in existing equipment and feeding the information back to the designers.

The Importance of MP Design

Even when the design, fabrication, and installation of new plant and equipment appear to have gone smoothly, problems often emerge at the test operation and commissioning phases. Production and maintenance engineers struggle to get the plant working properly, and they achieve normal operation only after repeated modifications.

After the plant has begun operating normally, checking, lubricating, and cleaning to prevent deterioration and failure may be awkward and difficult to carry out, as may be setup, adjustment, and repair. When equipment is not designed for ease of operation and maintenance, operators and maintenance personnel tend to neglect routine housekeeping, setup and adjustment take far too long, and even the simplest repairs necessitate shutting equipment down for unconscionably long periods.

When designing process plants, the block plan (plant layout) and plot plan (ancillary equipment and piping layout) are very important. Neglecting MP design considerations at these stages inflates operating costs and impairs operability and maintainability during test operation and shutdown maintenance.

Some people claim that numerous problems at the initial operation stage are inevitable in view of the rapid advance of technology and the increased size, speed, and automation of equipment. Never try to justify the problem like this. Equipment engineers must incorporate new processing and operating conditions into the equipment's design conditions. To ensure that equipment is highly reliable, maintainable, operable, and safe, avoid relying on outside purchasing. Make full use of the in-house technology that your own production, design, and maintenance engineers have accumulated from problems they overcame in the past. The thoroughness of the investigations performed at the design stage largely determines the amount of maintenance a plant requires after installation.

The Practice of MP Design

Equipment management consists broadly of project engineering and maintenance engineering. MP design is a significant aspect of project engineering that serves as the interface between project and maintenance engineering.

Consider this in more detail, referring to the equipment technology system outline shown in Figure 6-1. This example systematizes equipment technology using four main subdivisions:

- Equipment investment planning (techniques for evaluating the economics of equipment investment)
- Early equipment management (MP design technology)
- Operation and maintenance (technology for maintaining and improving existing equipment)
- Rationalization measures (technology for developing and modifying) equipment

Under this system, MP design activities are integral to early equipment management (from design to commissioning). As the diagram shows, teams conduct MP design activities during the following stages and engage in debugging (discovering and correcting errors and abnormalities) at each stage:

- Design
- Fabrication
- Installation and test operation
- Commissioning (establishing normal operation while producing actual product)

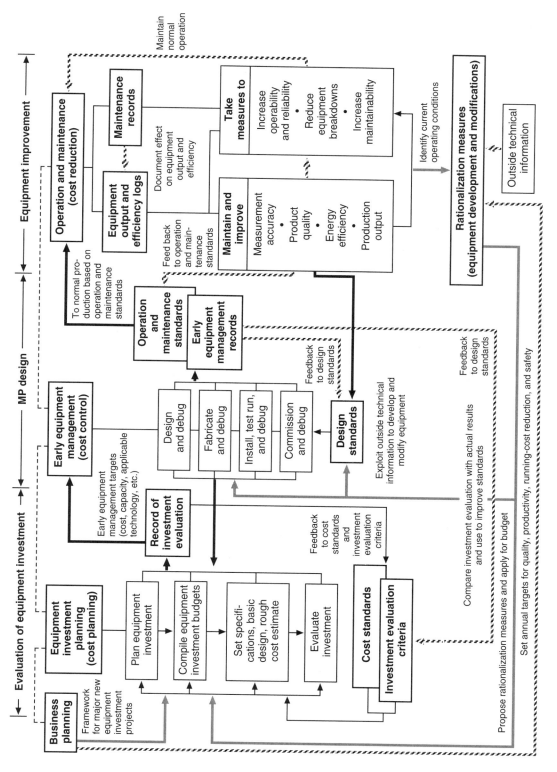

Figure 6-1. Equipment Technology System Outline

MP design activities are subject to the following constraints established at the equipment investment planning stage:

- Technology (production technology and equipment technology)
- Quantitative and qualitative equipment capacity
- Basic equipment specifications
- Capital budget
- Running costs (operator labor, raw materials yields, maintenance costs, energy costs, etc.)

Their objective is to achieve the following goals within the above restrictions:

- Reduce the time taken from design to stable operation
- Accomplish the transition efficiently with minimum labor and a balanced workload
- Ensure that equipment is designed to be highly reliable, maintainable, economical, operable, and safe

To achieve these goals, engineers from the production technology and equipment design departments responsible for equipment development must be highly skilled and sensitive. They should make full use of all available technical data, combining its application with technology derived from in-house research and development, and incorporating the results into new equipment designs.

THE EARLY MANAGEMENT SYSTEM

The following procedure ensures that early management of products and equipment evolves comprehensively and effectively.

Step 1: Investigate and Analyze the Existing Situation

To pinpoint problems, investigate and analyze the approach to early management in use for the past one to two years:

1. Plot the current early management work flow.
2. Identify problems in the flow.
3. Clarify the mechanisms employed to prevent predicted problems at each commissioning stage.

4. Establish what problems occurred during pilot production, test operation, and full-scale startup and what corrective actions were taken.
5. Identify any delays that occurred during pilot production, test operation, and full-scale startup.
6. Find out what information is being collected for the purpose of designing products and equipment with high levels of usability, manufacturability, ease of quality assurance, maintainability, reliability, safety, and competitive effectiveness.

Step 2: Establish an Early Management System

Use the information obtained in Step 1 to build a new, improved early management system that is closer to the ideal. Do this in the following steps:

1. Investigate and outline the basic structure of the early management system required and define its scope of application.
2. Investigate and establish a system for accumulating and using the information required for early management.
3. Design or revise the standards and forms needed for operating the systems in 1 and 2.

Step 3: Debug the New System and Provide Training

Initiate model projects to enhance the system and improve everyone's performance. Select enough topics for all designers to experience the new system, and ensure that the topics are within the designers' capabilities.

1. Evolve the activities step-by-step for each early management phase and each topic.
2. At the same time, train people in the standard techniques required to implement the new system.
3. At each step, evaluate the new system in terms of how well people understand it, how skillfully they use the techniques, how well the feedback works, and so on.
4. Use the results of this evaluation to augment or modify the system and the various standards and documents.
5. Document the benefits gained by using the system.

Step 4: Apply the New System Comprehensively

1. Apply the new system across the board (expand its scope of application to all areas).
2. Optimize life-cycle costing and enhance the use of information in MP design.
3. Identify problems that occur at each early management stage and each topic to which the new system is applied. Tally the number of feedback items incorporated in new designs, the number of commissioning problems that occur, the number of months that new plants falls behind schedule, and so on. Total these annually or semi-annually to provide an overview of the benefits of the new system. Analyze any problems that occur after the plant has been commissioned. Investigate and standardize methods of plugging the gaps during the early stages and try to achieve on-schedule vertical startup.

Early Product Management

As user needs diversify and competition on quality, price, and delivery intensifies, it is essential to efficiently plan, schedule, develop, design, and create prototype products that satisfy customer quality requirements and that the plant can make quickly and cheaply. One company found that 80 percent of its product costs were determined at the design stage, and that over 80 percent of losses from manufacturing problems could be traced back to poor design as well. Poor design is a major cause of reduced profitability, impaired production efficiency, and low overall equipment effectiveness.

In process industries, particularly the chemical industry, early product management is closely concerned with the properties of the product. Make every effort to manage the initial production of new products skillfully by studying the equipment failures and quality defects that occurred when similar products were manufactured. The life-cycle cost of a product can be greatly influenced by the early application of production technology, particularly in the mechanical processing, packaging, and distribution stages. This makes it essential to speed up pilot production and achieve right-first-time startup during commissioning by building quality, manufacturability, ease of quality assurance, and usability into the product at the preceding conceptual and detailed design stages. Of course, it is still necessary to perform market surveys and investigate in-house technical capabilities at the planning and scheduling stages in order to develop competitive, salable new products.

Designing Easy-to-Make Products at the Development Design Stage

Problems arise with the manufacture and use of a new product if a company does not pay careful attention to its manufacturability at the development design stage. This section briefly discusses design for manufacturability, one of TPM's main activities in the product development and design fields.

What Is an Easy-to-Make Product?

An easy-to-make product is one for which the means of production are easily secured and cheap. A company can produce it under safe conditions using simple operations and equipment. For example, products or components manufactured mainly by machining must satisfy the conditions listed below to achieve a high level of manufacturability. Molded and packaged process-industry products also must satisfy these conditions, with additional attention paid to materials flow.

- Easily established reference planes
- Easy to clamp
- Easy to position in fixtures
- Tends to stay centered
- Resists damage
- Rarely forms burrs
- Easy to machine
- Easy to measure
- Easy to distinguish from other products or components
- No ingress of chips
- Easy to dechip
- Easy to assemble
- Easy to automate

Five Strategies for Achieving Manufacturability

Use the following five strategies to design and develop easily manufactured products:

- Before starting to design the product, collect and utilize information on the manufacturability of existing products.
- Analyze the processes by which existing products are made to identify and plan for manufacturability requirements.

- Perform process analysis for the new product at the conceptual and detailed design stages to identify and plan for manufacturability requirements.
- During new product design reviews, analyze potential quality defects in order to identify and plan for robustness (low defect) requirements.
- Research and predict production problems at the pilot production and test stages in order to identify and plan for manufacturability requirements.

Carrying out these five strategies requires:

- Applying volume-production conditions
- Developing new evaluation methods to expose hidden problems
- Performing product reviews using standardized checklists and other tools
- Systematically employing and developing highly-skilled, competent personnel

Early Product Management Systems

Development, design, pilot production, and volume production of new products can cover a wide range of product types and forms. Moreover, development may vary from completely new products to partially new products, as when a new or improved function or performance is added to an existing product. Product development teams need a flexible process that can be fine-tuned to meet diverse needs. Figure 6-2 shows an example of an early product management system.

Most companies have an established quality management system, but such systems frequently are not thoroughly applied during the initial early management stages. Investigation and analysis are inadequate, and technology is not properly accumulated and applied. This prolongs the development stage and leads to frequent problems when full-scale production starts. Each company must develop an early product management system appropriate to its particular needs. The system must enable a company to incorporate information about potential problems and requirements early in the development process, so that right-first-time startup and problem-free volume production can be achieved.

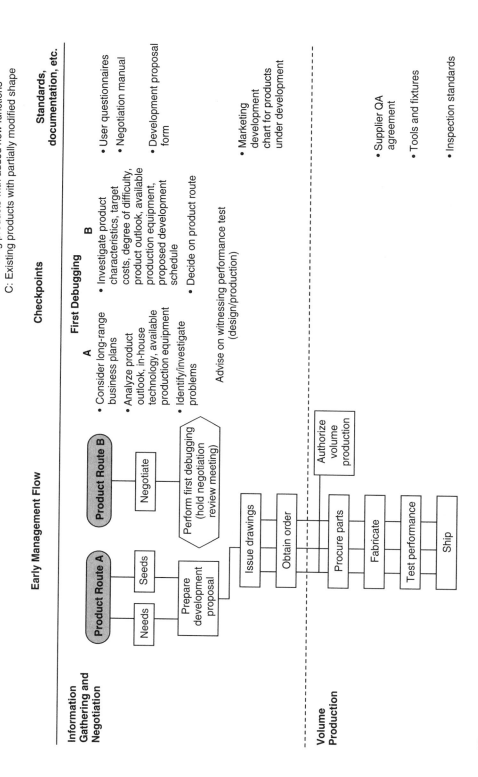

Figure 6-2. Example of Early Product Management System

Selecting and Evaluating Product Development Projects

Developing competitive, salable products is the key to corporate success. When deciding whether to develop a particular product, carefully investigate and evaluate the company's technical capability and capacity. Evaluate factors such as the product (price competitiveness, market size, novelty, life cycle, profitability, etc.), the company's development capability (development technology, processing and assembly technology, raw-materials handling technology, etc.), the development schedule in relation to available labor, conformance to company policy, and the possibility of product evolution. Establish a set of basic development policy specifications for evaluating these factors. Break down what must be developed into separate elements and identify any obstacles that must be overcome to complete the project successfully.

Table 6-1 is an example of a checksheet used for selecting development projects. The people responsible for the project score each item. Then they investigate the items with the lowest scores to identify problems and direct the subsequent design and pilot production.

In fulfilling a new product's basic specifications (functions) and rapidly designing, test-producing, and bringing to market new, easily quality-assured products, it is important that no defects or claims arise after test production. To avoid this, fabricate prototypes at the conceptual (assembly) design and production (component) design stages and build in manufacturability at these stages.

Normally, when a development project is initiated, the design team receives a list of requirements and begins to design the product with reference to design standards and information on competing products or other products with similar functions. Input from departments such as engineering, equipment design, and production is very important at this stage. When a product proves difficult to make during pilot production, or when many defects appear after volume production begins, the cost of rectifying the situation in terms of time, labor, and equipment effectiveness can be enormous. Using analytical techniques such as FMEA (failure mode and effects analysis) at this stage can highlight potential problems and generate ideas for that will prevent unnecessary losses later. This is a very effective way of improving reliability. Figures 6-3 and 6-4 show examples of FMEA checksheet formats.

Using the outline drawings, working drawings, and FMEA results, designers, production engineers, quality assurance engineers, and others follow debugging routines to detect and eliminate anything in the design that may hamper the product's performance or make it difficult to manufacture. Doing this builds manufacturability and quality assurance into the product design from the start.

Table 6-1. Checksheet for Selecting Development Projects

ASSESSMENT CRITERIA

Marketability: 40 points						
	1	2	3	4	5	Total
1. Price				✳△○□		4
2. Competitiveness			○	✳△ □		3.75
3. Market size				✳△○□		4
4. Novelty/originality			△○□	✳		3.25
5. Future prospects				○	✳△ □	4.75
6. Life cycle				△○□	✳	4.25
7. Profitability				○□	✳△	4.5
8. Patentability				○□	✳△	4.5
Remarks						33/82.5%

Development Capacity: 30 points						
	1	2	3	4	5	Total
1. Technical capability required	New technology	Current technology	New proprietary technology ✳△○□	Outgrowth of current proprietary technology	Proprietary technology	3
2. Personnel required			Collaboration among engineers from different fields	Existing project team ✳△○□	Within existing departments	4
3. Processing technology			□	△○□		3.75
4. Assembly technology			✳△○□			3
5. Materials technology				✳△○□		4
6. Materials/components supply capacity				✳△○□		4
Remarks						21.75/72.5%

Development Schedule: 15 points						
	1	2	3	4	5	Total
1. Schedule	1.5 years+	1 year	10 months	6 months ✳△○□	3 months	4
2. Labor		2 full-timers	1.5 full-timers	1 full-timer ✳ ○□	In tandem with other projects △	4.25
3. Priority				✳△	○□	4.5
Remarks						12.75/85%

Other: 15 points						
	1	2	3	4	5	Total
1. Conforms to company policy and plans	Under 60%	60%	75%	90%	100% ✳△○□	5
2. Ability to evolve into further products		△○□	✳			2.25
3. Improvement of corporate image			○	△○□		3.75
Remarks						11/73.3%

Total: 78.50

OVERALL ASSESSMENT

This product has a high projected marketability of 82.5%. Its development schedule rating is also high, and it conforms 100% to company policy. Based on this evaluation, it has been decided to proceed with the development at high priority.

✳,△,○,□: evaluators

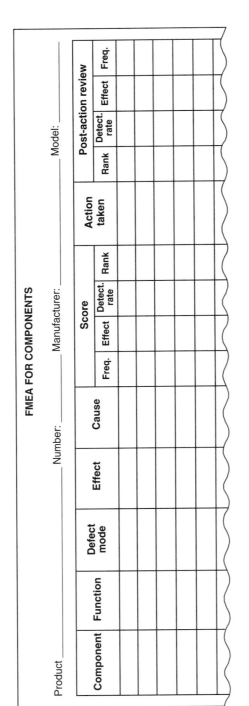

Figure 6-3. FMEA for Components

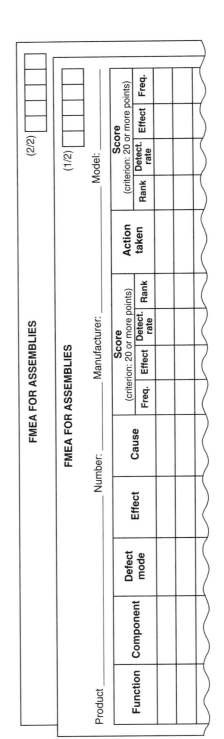

Figure 6-4. FMEA for Assemblies

Building in Quality by Early Management

During test production or at the start of full-scale production, the production department must control stringently the first products of each production run (first-of-run control) to ensure that no nonconforming products are made or shipped. Figure 6-5 outlines a first-of-run control process. Under this system, the quality assurance department examines the production drawings and decides whether first-of-run control is required. If it is, the production department performs FMEA and other checks, then submits the first production batch to the quality assurance department together with FMEA sheets, measurement data, and other information. The quality assurance department verifies whether the product conforms to the drawings. It also determines whether the production process is properly standardized and under control. If all the requirements are met, QA removes the product from the first-of-run control list. This system prevents shipping any product if any of the first-of-run control requirements are not satisfied. Apply this system both to new products and to the first products a plant produces when it is restarts after shutdown maintenance or other repairs.

Using Defect Information Generated During the Early Product Management Phase

Even when a company makes strenuous efforts to build in quality and manufacturability at the design stage, internal and external problems can still causes losses during equipment fabrication, assembly, and installation, pilot production, and initial full-scale production. To prevent such problems from recurring in the future, obtain accurate information on them, investigate their causes, feed the results back to the previous stage, and take appropriate preventive action. Figure 6-6 shows a *problem control* (PC) system for using this kind of information, and Figure 6-7 shows an example of a PC sheet. Develop a comparable system to suit your own company.

THE PRACTICE OF EARLY EQUIPMENT MANAGEMENT

When equipment is remodeled or newly installed, problems arising at the commissioning stage often delay completion and lower overall effectiveness. This occurs when project teams fail to build in reliability, maintainability, operability, economy, safety, and ease of quality assurance during the early

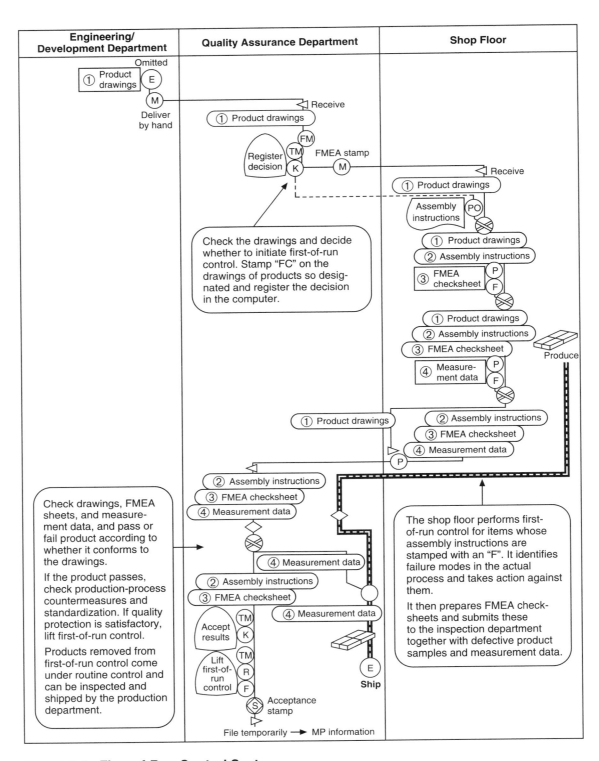

Figure 6-5. First-of-Run Control System

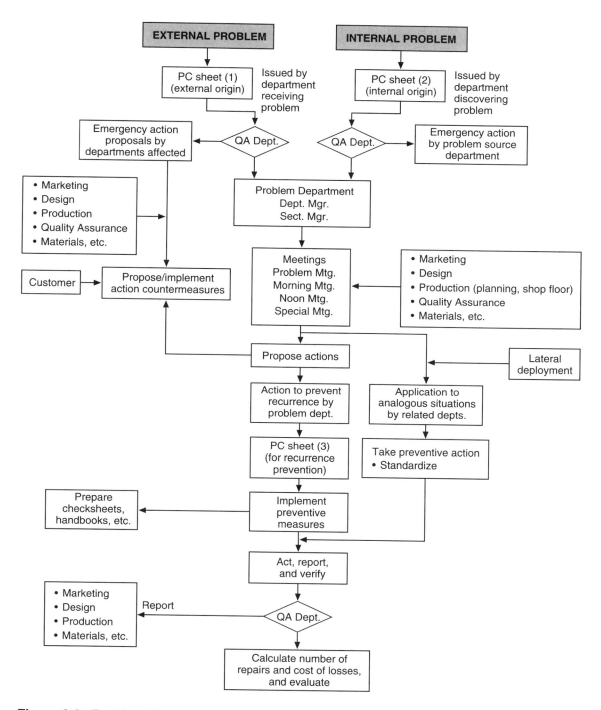

Figure 6-6. Problem Control (PC) System

PC SHEET (3)
Recurrence Prevention

To: _____   File # : _____
                                        Date: _____
QA → Problem Dept. → QA → Related Depts.   Section: _____

Problem: _____   Problem Department: _____
_____   Section Manager: _____
Item: _____   Inspector: _____
_____   Person responsible: _____

Discussion date: _____ Time: _____
Participants: _____
Discussion Leader: _____
Discussion/training (if applicable): (list documents) _____
_____

Cause	Countermeasure

Problem department — costs incurred:

Indirect cost:	Direct cost:	Loss code

Action (Who?)	When?	By when?	Why?	What?	Sect. Mgr.	QA Dept.
					☐ confirm	☐ confirm

Lateral deployment to:
☐ General Affairs   ☐ Marketing

Figure 6-7. Problem Control (PC) Sheet

management phase. To shorten test operation and commissioning and achieve immediate, problem-free startup, use all available technical capabilities to weed out potential problems at the planning and design stages.

Basic Equipment Requirements

The goal of MP design is to break free of the equipment-centered design mentality. It adopts a "human-machine" system-approach to design problem-free, safe equipment that makes quality assurance easy. When conducting MP design, address the basic attributes that equipment must possess: reliability, general maintainability, operator maintainability, operability, resource economy, safety, and so on. Be sure to define these characteristics clearly; otherwise everyone will interpret them differently. Table 6-2 gives some sample definitions.

Table 6-2. Basic Equipment Attributes and their Definitions

Attribute	Definition	Details	
Reliability	Is immune to function-deterioration and function-loss failure	• Low failure rate • Low idling and minor stops • Low quality defect rate • Corrosion-proof • Highly-reliable control system	• Needs little adjustment • Stable machine cycle time • Static and dynamic precision easily-measured • High weld quality
General Maintainability	Deterioration is easily measured and corrected	• Failures easily detected and located • Parts easily replaced; functions easily restored • Easy to inspect • Readily accessible for maintenance	• Deteriorated parts easy to detect • Lubricants easily replenished and replaced • Easily overhauled
Operator Maintainability	Operators can rapidly and easily perform maintenance tasks such as cleaning, lubricating, and checking.	• Easy to clean, lubricate, and check • Chips easy to collect • Sources of contamination and scattering easy to contain • Easy to inspect and patrol	• Lubrication checks easy to perform • Simple quality maintenance (precision, etc. easily measured)
Operability	Can be set up and operated rapidly and reliably	• Easy to set up and adjust • Tools and grinding wheels easy to replace; accompanying adjustments easy to execute • Easy process control	• Easy push-button operation (height, position, number, shape, color, etc.) • Easy transportation and installation
Resource Economy	Efficient use of operating resources such as energy, tools, grinding wheels, lubricants, etc.	• Low unit consumption of energy and other resources	• High level of resource recycling
Safety	Does not directly or indirectly endanger life or limb	• Little non-standard work in dealing with failures, idling, minor stops, and quality defects • Moving parts securely guarded	• Few projections, sharp corners, etc. • Easy escape routes • Process or equipment abnormalities easy to detect

An Early Equipment Management System

Figure 6-8 outlines the flow of an early equipment management system. Teams detect potential problems at each step from planning to commissioning and take action to prevent them. The aim in doing this is to create nearly perfect equipment that is capable of "one-shot startup" and therefore requires only a short commissioning period. Debugging activities carried out during the first three steps (initial planning, action planning, and design) are particularly important in reducing startup time.

At these three stages, make full use of equipment technology capabilities and analytical techniques to build quality, reliability, and other desirable characteristics into the equipment. Assemble qualified people to hold debugging reviews at each step. Doing this reduces the number of defects produced during test operation and later stages and shortens the commissioning period (Figure 6-9).

The time required to commission an item of equipment from installation to stable operation affects its life-cycle cost. Today, with technical innovation proceeding at a bewildering pace, failure to keep production on schedule is a serious management problem. This is why equipment effectiveness losses during startup and the startup period itself are treated as MP design items.

The goal of debugging is to identify problems that slipped through the MP design net and eliminate them before the equipment comes on stream. It is one more activity designed to achieve vertical startup. Debugging is most important at the design stage and becomes relatively less important through fabrication, test operation, and installation. Thus, the key to success is thorough debugging at the design stage.

The next section explains how to proceed with two particularly important stages: action planning and design.

Action Planning

After careful commercial investigation, set the equipment design and fabrication specifications. Then use debugging to increase planning precision and ensure that no items have been omitted (Figure 6-10).

Analytical tools that support this activity include:

Production process chart. This shows the order in which processes take place and the boundaries between different processes. (It divides the overall process up into separate subprocesses.)

Process QA matrix. This shows the relationship between product quality and individual subprocesses. Figure 6-11 provides a sample format.

Production-input (4-M) analysis. For each process the QA process matrix identifies as being closely associated with defect production, clarify the relationships with the production inputs (equipment, materials, people, and methods), and identify the equipment conditions that will not produce defects (Figure 6-12).

Process FMEA. For problematical processes identified in the production-input analysis, use process FMEA to assess the risk. This provides useful information for evaluating equipment concept designs and for planning countermeasures to deal with any items that fail the evaluation criteria (Figure 6-13).

Reflect Results in Equipment Specification Concepts

Countermeasures against problems identified through the preceding analyses must be incorporated into the equipment specification concepts. Use a table format such as that shown in Figure 6-14 for recording the information fed back and the action taken.

Preliminary Evaluation Through Feedback to Equipment Specification Concepts

When evaluating equipment specification concepts, record predictions relative to the goals set at the initial planning stage. If these do not match, rethink the equipment specification concepts. Figure 6-15 offers a format for an equipment specification table.

Cooperating departments use the preceding analyses and tables to expose and solve early on potential problems involving production capacity, reliability, flexibility, and so on. The next section describes how the information developed during this stage is incorporated in equipment designs.

An Example of the Design Stage

Engineering teams design equipment based on equipment design and fabrication specifications, concept drawings prepared at the action planning stage, and common equipment specifications. Then they subject this design to an equipment FMEA review to find out how failure of any of the equipment's subassemblies or components might affect product quality, system operation, and safety.

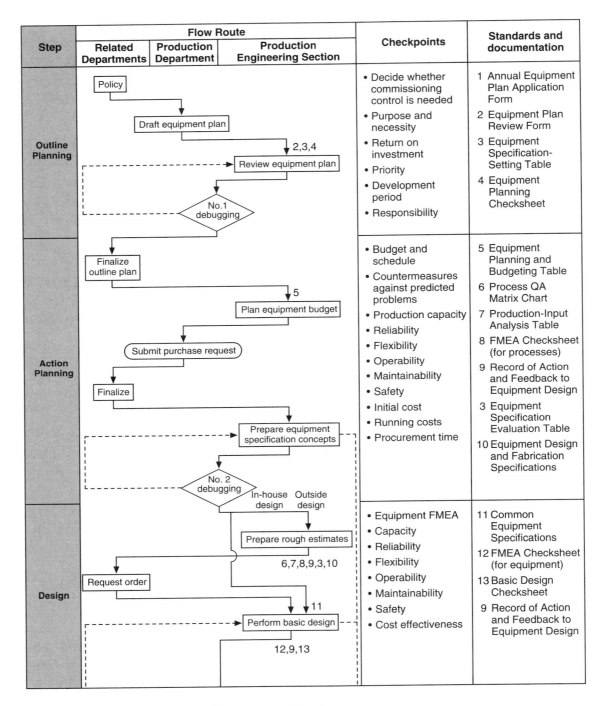

Step	Flow Route			Checkpoints	Standards and documentation
	Related Departments	Production Department	Production Engineering Section		
Outline Planning		Policy → Draft equipment plan → Review equipment plan (2,3,4) → No.1 debugging		• Decide whether commissioning control is needed • Purpose and necessity • Return on investment • Priority • Development period • Responsibility	1 Annual Equipment Plan Application Form 2 Equipment Plan Review Form 3 Equipment Specification-Setting Table 4 Equipment Planning Checksheet
Action Planning		Finalize outline plan → Plan equipment budget (5) → Submit purchase request → Finalize → Prepare equipment specification concepts → No. 2 debugging	In-house design / Outside design	• Budget and schedule • Countermeasures against predicted problems • Production capacity • Reliability • Flexibility • Operability • Maintainability • Safety • Initial cost • Running costs • Procurement time	5 Equipment Planning and Budgeting Table 6 Process QA Matrix Chart 7 Production-Input Analysis Table 8 FMEA Checksheet (for processes) 9 Record of Action and Feedback to Equipment Design 3 Equipment Specification Evaluation Table 10 Equipment Design and Fabrication Specifications
Design		Request order	Prepare rough estimates (6,7,8,9,3,10) → (11) Perform basic design (12,9,13)	• Equipment FMEA • Capacity • Reliability • Flexibility • Operability • Maintainability • Safety • Cost effectiveness	11 Common Equipment Specifications 12 FMEA Checksheet (for equipment) 13 Basic Design Checksheet 9 Record of Action and Feedback to Equipment Design

Figure 6-8. Early Equipment Management System

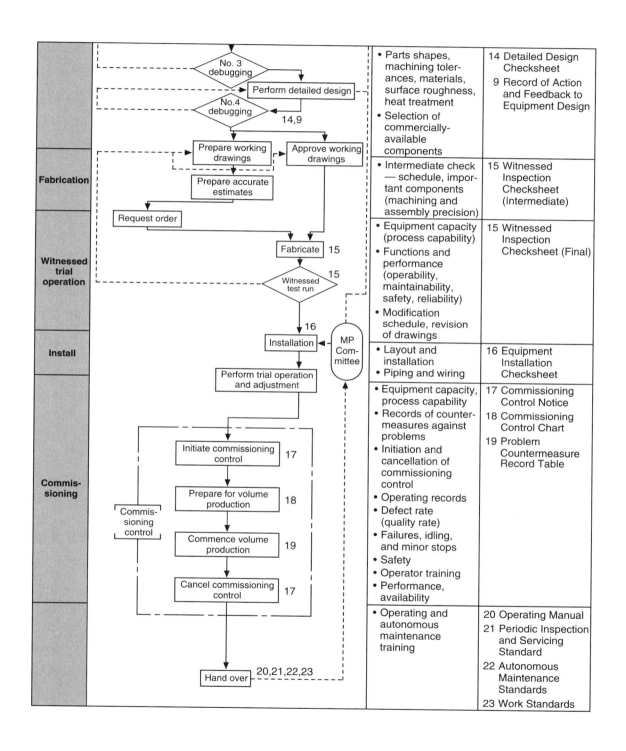

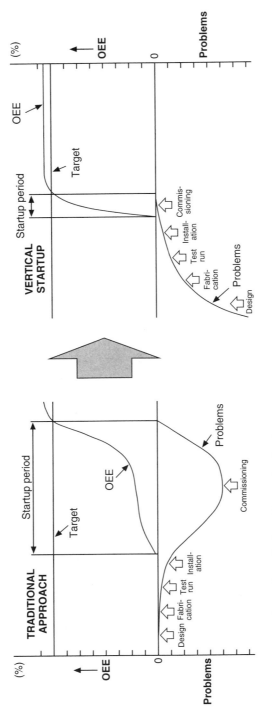

Figure 6-9. Debugging during Commissioning

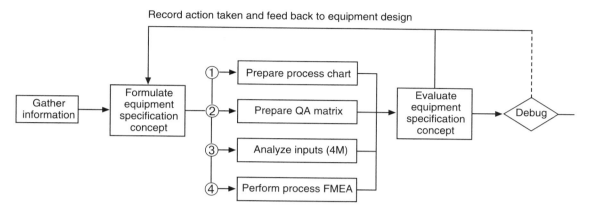

Figure 6-10. Detailed Flow Diagram for Action Planning

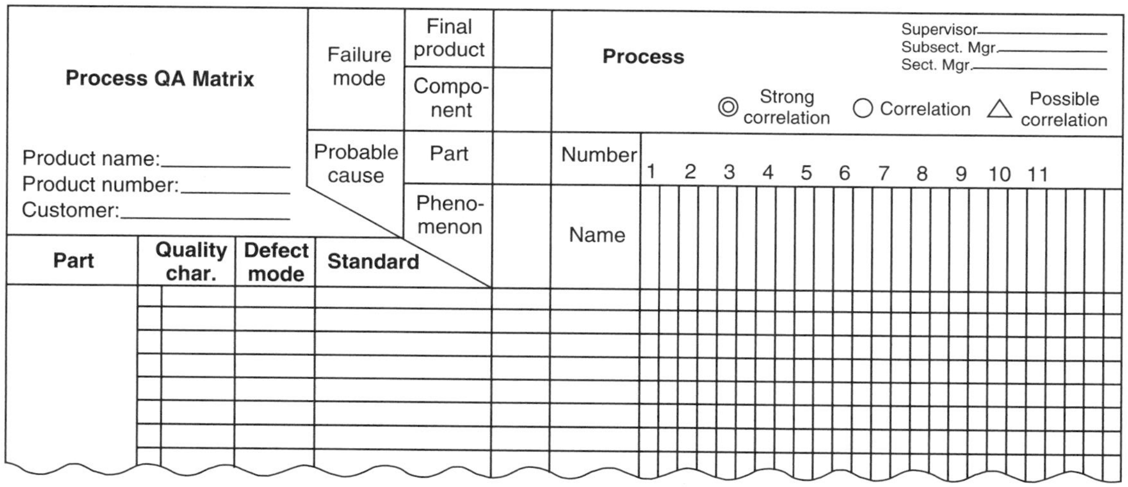

Process QA Matrix				Failure mode	Final product		Process										Supervisor_____ Subsect. Mgr._____ Sect. Mgr._____		
					Compo-nent		⊚ Strong correlation ◯ Correlation △ Possible correlation												
Product name:_____ Product number:_____ Customer:_____				Probable cause	Part		Number	1	2	3	4	5	6	7	8	9	10	11	
Part	Quality char.	Defect mode	Standard		Pheno-menon		Name												

Figure 6-11. Process QA Matrix

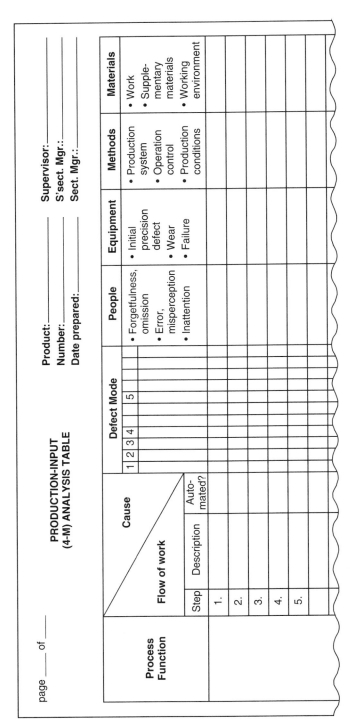

Figure 6-12. Production-Input Analysis (4-M)

FMEA FOR PROCESSES

Purpose: _____

Prepared by: _____
Date: _____

Equipment: _____
Important product: _____ Work name and number: _____
Important process: _____ General product: _____
Supervisor: _____ General process: _____

	5	4	3	2	1
A. Frequency	Chronic (every lot)	Sporadic (1/mo)	Occasion (1/3 mos)	Possible, but rare	Could not possibly occur
B. Importance	Critical fault (end strength actuation, water penetration, durability)	Major fault (strength, dimensions, or durability outside safety range)	Cannot be installed in final product (wrong part, incorrect assembly, defect)	Surface blemish (scratch, misplaced color protector, etc.)	Unimportant
C. Detection Difficulty	Impossible to observe externally	Only by human senses	By instrument	Only during assembly	Before assembly

Process	Function	Failure mode	Failure effect	Failure cause	25+ points: action req'd.			Action taken	Schedule	Dept. Resp.	Checked by (sign)
					A × B × C = risk						
					Bef Aft	Bef Aft	Bef Aft				

Figure 6-13. Process FMEA

ACTION/FEEDBACK TO EQUIPMENT DESIGN

Equipment: _____
Destination Section: _____
Accepting department: _____
Subsection manager: _____

Production Engineering Section: _____
Supervisor: _____
Subsection Manager: _____
Section Manager: _____

Prepared by: _____
Date: _____

At time of:
☐ Specification Concept
☐ Basic Design
☐ Detailed Design
Issued on: _____

No.	Date	Source (A)	Priority (B)	Problem/ request	Action	Date	Action (C)	Cause (D)	Result	Feed to (E)	Details (F)	Person resp.	Remarks
1													
2													
3													
4													
5							1	1	OK				
6							1	4	OK				
7							1	1	OK				
8							1	1	OK				
9							1	1	OK				
10							1	1	OK				
11							1	1	OK				
12							1	1	OK				
13							—	1	OK				
14							—	1	OK				

Key

A. Information Source	B. Priority	C. Action	D. Cause	E. Feedback destination	F. Feedback details
1 Fabrication dept. (in-house) 2 Fabrication dept. (external) 3 Design dept. (in-house) 4 Design dept. (external) 5 User dept.	1 Incorporation mandatory 2 Incorporate as far as possible 3 Reference requested	1 Modify structure/ mechanism 2 Modify action/function 3 Modify control circuitry 4 Modify surface/ heat treat 5 Modify material/shape	1 Planning error 2 Design error 3 Fabrication error 4 Specification change	1 This machine only 2 This machine/ subsequent models 3 This machine/ subsequent and similar models	1 Increase process capability 2 Increase capacity 3 Improve reliability 4 Improve maintainability (durability) 5 Improve cost-effectiveness 6 Improve safety 7 Improve operability

Figure 6-14. Record of Action and Feedback to Equipment Design

EQUIPMENT SPECIFICATION TABLE
TARGET SETTING/CONCEPT EVALUATION

Equipment:_____

Accepting dept:_____

Date prepared:
At outline planning _____ / _____ / _____
At detailed planning _____ / _____ / _____

	Outline Planning	Detail Planning
Prod. Eng'ring Sect.		
Supervisor	☐	☐
S'sect. Mgr.	☐	☐
Sect. Mgr.	☐	☐
Accepting Dept.		
Supervisor	☐	☐
Manager	☐	☐

Item	Contents	At outline planning	At action planning	
		Target	Planning forecast	Evaluation
Production capacity	Cycle time, production volume			
	Usage rate (%)	(%)	(%)	
Reliability	Quality (quality rate) (%)	(%)	(%)	
	Durability	(Yrs)	(Yrs)	
Overall Evaluation				
	_____			
	_____			
	_____			
	Key: A: Target exceeded B: On target C: Below target	When overall evaluation is C, rethink proposal		

Figure 6-15. Equipment Specification Concept Evaluation Table

The team then modifies the design to forestall potential problems identified by FMEA. This is accomplished by gathering all the relevant departments together for a debugging review. The review team examines the design drawings and FMEA data to see whether the design incorporates all feedback, eliminates potential failures and latent defects identified through analysis, and conforms to standards.

COMMISSIONING CONTROL

During commissioning control (also known as initial flow control), teams deal with problems and strive to achieve rapid stable operation. The commissioning control period begins with the start of actual production after equipment installation and test operation. (Sometimes commissioning also includes installation and test operation.) It also applies when introducing new products into existing equipment.

Repeated debugging reviews during the previous stages help build quality, reliability, and other desirable characteristics into the equipment and ensure that no problems pass on to the commissioning stage. Commissioning is the final opportunity to detect and prevent problems unforeseen at previous stages. The occurrence of many failures and defects indicates that technical capabilities were not fully exercised at the previous stages.

Debugging during commissioning should focus on process capability, quality problems, and materials flow problems. Another important activity is preparing to hand over the equipment to the operation and maintenance departments. This involves formulating standards for operation, setup, and maintenance (e.g., lubricating, checking, periodic servicing, and so on), and training operators and maintenance technicians.

Sample Commissioning Control System

Figure 6-16 is an example of a flow diagram for a commissioning control system. This system clearly defines the roles of the production, maintenance, and planning (design) departments and the activities they carry out cooperatively. Commissioning acts as the interface between design, operation, and maintenance. It is easy to imagine how badly things can go without a system like this.

This system also clearly defines commissioning control initiation and cancellation procedures. Cancellation criteria such as production performance, stoppage frequency and severity, quality rate, and so on are specified when commissioning control is initiated.

COLLECTING AND USING PRODUCT DESIGN TECHNOLOGY AND MP DESIGN DATA

Figures 6-17 and 6-18 are examples of flow diagrams for systems that collect and use product design technology data and MP design data. These systems are designed to standardize and feed back to previous stages in-house and outside information on factors such as quality requirements, production technology, maintenance, and safety. Such systems ensure that all relevant information is incorporated into checksheets, design standards, and other documentation at every step.

Design Standardization

The main reason information on reliability, operability, and maintainability does not find its way into the design and improvement of products and equipment is that companies fail to compile and communicate this information.

Compiling and Communicating Information

Compiling technological information involves more than simply squirreling away raw, untreated technical data. In such a form it is little more than organized scrap paper. The most highly-experienced, highly-qualified designers cannot help raise the technical abilities of their experienced colleagues if their knowledge exists only in their heads. The technology derived from this information and experience must be standardized and used to improve designers' development capabilities. It should be compiled in handbook format to prevent design errors.

Parts Proliferation

One of the most troublesome design problems is parts proliferation. It impairs maintenance efficiency and complicates component fabrication and assembly. The number of parts with exactly the same function multiplies over time as a result of varying customer requirements or manufacturers' styles. This increases unit fabrication costs and inventories. It also leads to long stoppages due to parts stockouts and increases the likelihood of assembly and repair errors.

Standardizing designs and using common components wherever possible controls parts proliferation. Since parts proliferation is partly the result of designers' zeal, it is not altogether bad, but designers should take care not to become "catalog fiends" or pursue novelty for its own sake.

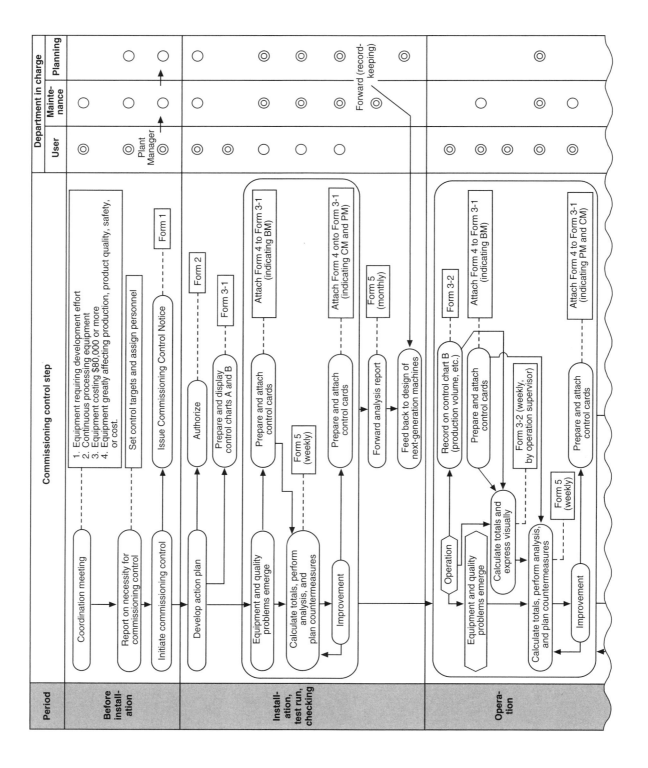

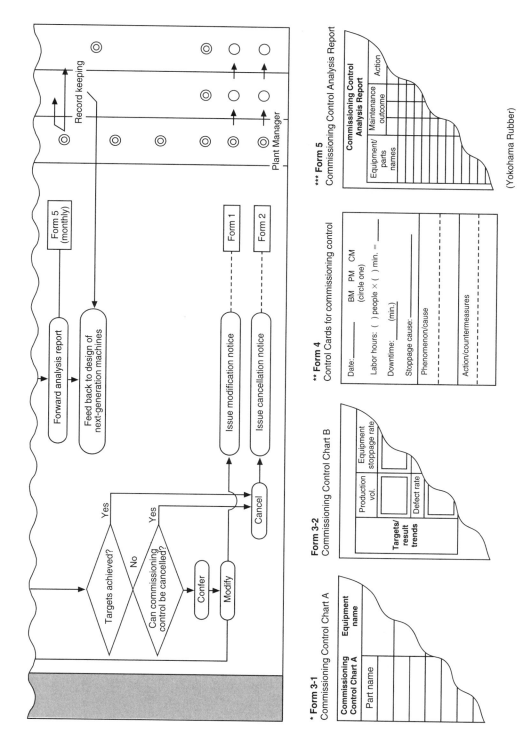

Figure 6-16. Commissioning Control Flow Diagram

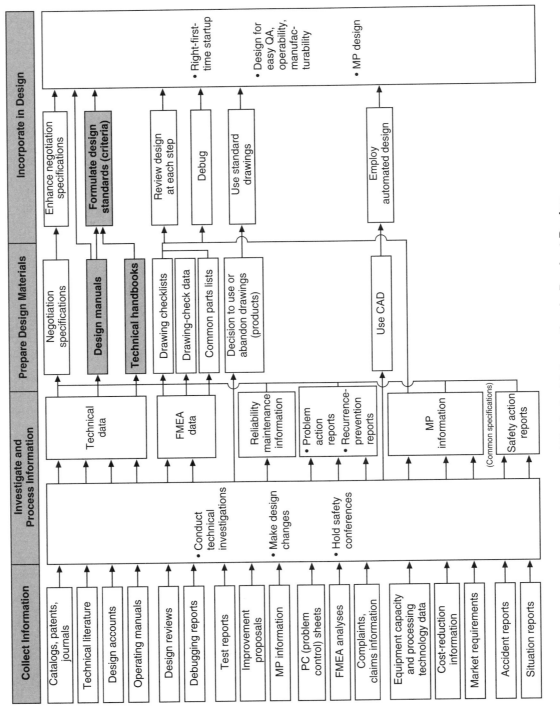

Figure 6-17. Collection and Utilization of Technical Information in Product Design

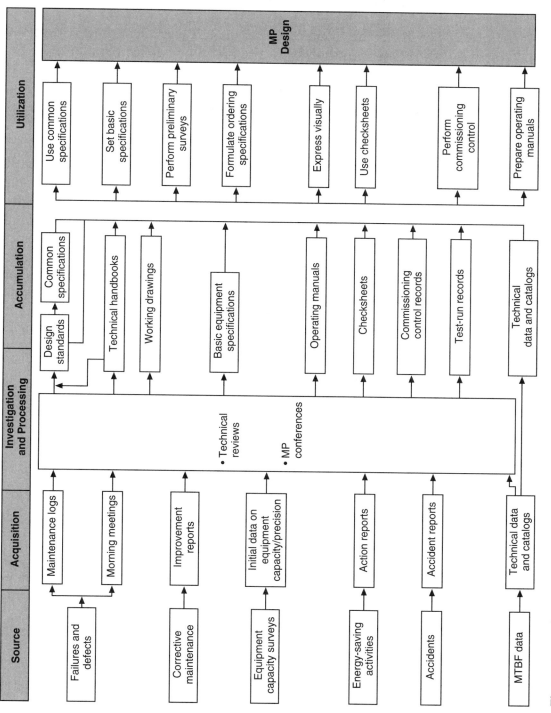

Figure 6-18. Collection and Utilization of MP Information

Compile Information in the Most Useful Forms

It is pointless to go to the trouble of preparing design standards and then neglect to use them. Design standards are often not fully used, however, because they are too bulky, hard to use, or out of date. Preparing a set of design standards is only the start of the job. Compile their contents into study texts, revise them on the basis of new information, and improve them constantly while using them in actual design work.

Designers' checklists reflecting design standards at each stage (planning, design, fabrication, installation, test run, and commissioning) combined with debugging by everyone involved helps ensure that design standards are used effectively and nips potential problems in the bud. Debugging is incomplete, however, if designers use standardized checklists that do not include items unique to particular machines. It is essential to study the details of the checks and the actions taken at each stage, predict potential problems, and identify priority items for checking at the next stage. Standardize items common to all equipment in the form of common specifications and develop complete individual standards for designing and purchasing particular types of equipment.

7
Quality Maintenance

As equipment takes over the work of production, quality depends increasingly on the condition of the equipment. Quality maintenance evolved as a major TPM activity in certain fabrication and assembly industries that are becoming increasingly automated. In environments where human intervention is decreasing, the goal of quality maintenance is to maintain and constantly improve quality through effective equipment maintenance.

In process industries, quality has always been built into the product through the process. The pace of new product development, however, is accelerating, and the greater diversity of raw materials and products currently necessitates ever more frequent changeovers. To cope with this, production departments must review their quality assurance systems with the aim of tackling quality through equipment management.

QUALITY MAINTENANCE IN PROCESS INDUSTRIES

In process industries, the process comes first. Quality is built into the product through processes that provide the conditions needed for transformations such as reaction, separation, and purification of materials as they become product. Equipment complexes known as process plants implement such processes.

To produce perfect products, it is necessary to set appropriate process conditions (temperature, pressure, flow rate, catalyst quantity, and so on) for the particular properties, compositions, and volumes of the raw materials, reagents, and other substances being handled. To achieve this, the equipment units that make up the plant and their component modules and parts must be installed and maintained so they function optimally and create no quality defects.

235

Process industries always aim for this, but the results often leave much to be desired. Quality defect losses and reprocessing losses (two of the eight major plant losses) still occur and substandard product often has to be recycled, salvaged by mixing it with good product, or downgraded. Customer complaints and dissatisfaction are a perennial problem.

Meanwhile, in plants where chemical reactions take place, poor control of conditions not only affects quality but is also dangerous. To create safe plants that produce only flawless products, a company must analyze processes and equipment rigorously to identify and maintain conditions that do not lead to defects ("defect-free conditions"). This is the role of quality maintenance.

A *quality defect* is a property that falls outside the specified range. Table 7-1 lists some of the ways in which quality defects appear in process industries.

QUALITY MAINTENANCE IN TPM

Quality maintenance consists of activities that establish equipment conditions that do not produce quality defects, with a goal of maintaining equipment in perfect condition to producing perfect products. Quality defects are prevented by checking and measuring equipment conditions periodically and verifying that the measured values lie within the specified range. Potential quality defects are predicted by examining trends in the measured values, and prevented by taking measures in advance.

Rather than controlling results by inspecting product and acting against defects that have already occurred, quality maintenance in TPM aims to prevent quality defects from occurring altogether. This is accomplished by

Table 7-1. Quality Defect Modes

Quality Defect Mode	Description (Example)
1. Deviation from specified composition, physical properties, etc.	Chemical composition, properties such as thermal stability, impurities
2. Contamination	Rust, dust, splinters, hair, bacteria, broken machine parts, tools, wrong pallets
3. Nonuniformity and dispersion	Color variation, irregular grain size, uneven thickness, unequal plate flatness
4. Visual defects	Discoloration, cloudiness, precipitation, coagulation, crystal clumping, other visible deformities
5. Packaging defects	Underweight, improperly sealed, burst sack, wet, decomposed, mislabeled, etc.

identifying checkpoints for process and equipment conditions that affect quality, measuring these periodically, and taking appropriate action (Figure 7-1).

The approach illustrated in Figure 7-1 focuses on the four production inputs (equipment, materials, people, and methods) as sources of quality defects. "Establishing conditions" means setting the range of material, equipment, method, or operating conditions that must be maintained to produce flawless product. Once set, these conditions are maintained and controlled by "competent operators," extensively trained in production technology as part of autonomous maintenance activities (see right side of the figure). Setting and controlling conditions in this way eliminates process defects.

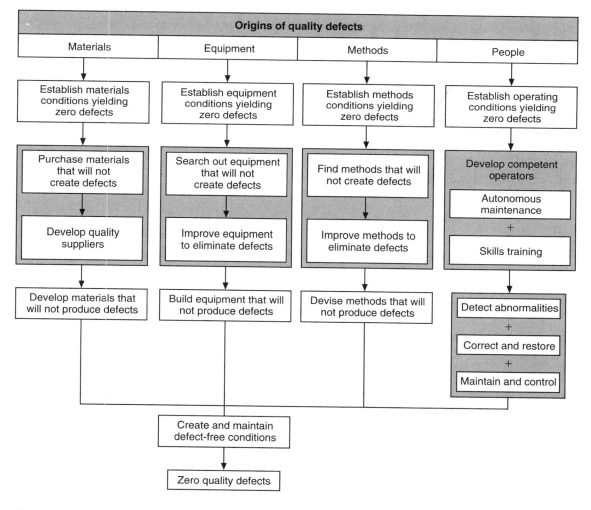

Figure 7-1. Basic Philosophy of Zero Defects

PRECONDITIONS FOR SUCCESSFUL QUALITY MAINTENANCE

A quality maintenance program builds upon gains achieved through fundamental TPM activities such as autonomous maintenance, focused improvement, planned maintenance, and operation and maintenance skill training. There are several preconditions for a successful quality maintenance program, however: abolish accelerated deterioration, eliminate process problems, and develop competent operators.

Abolish Accelerated Deterioration

When equipment is subject to accelerated deterioration, its modules and components have a short life span. The equipment is unstable and fails unexpectedly. Progress toward zero quality defects is painfully slow when equipment is continually breaking down. Before quality maintenance can work, accelerated deterioration must be abolished and unexpected failures minimized through the activities in TPM implementation Step 7 — focused improvement, autonomous maintenance, planned maintenance, and operation and maintenance skills training. (See Chapters 3, 4, and 5.)

Eliminate Process Problems

Process industries are plagued by process failures such as blocks, leaks, spills, composition changes, and other enemies of stable operation. Blocks, leaks, and stoppages are the bane of any process plant. If any of these occur frequently, eliminate them through focused improvements or operator-initiated autonomous maintenance improvements. Only then can quality maintenance be effective.

Develop Competent Operators

Developing process-competent and equipment-competent operators has already been discussed at length in Chapter 4, and Chapter 8 gives further details. Operators must be trained to promptly spot and correct any defect-presaging abnormalities in the causal system.

In TPM activities, great importance is attached to the "three actualities" — actual location, actual object, and actual phenomenon. This is because quality defects arise at specific locations where the process is taking place, and the actual objects (defective product or parts of equipment) and phenomena — details of how the problem manifested — provide the best clues for locating their sources.

As we saw in Chapter 6, the ideal system creates defect-free plants at the product and equipment design stages. Before tackling quality maintenance, clarify its relationship with the seven other main TPM activities, including the early management of new products and equipment (see Figure 7-2).

BASIC ELEMENTS OF A QUALITY MAINTENANCE PROGRAM

Causes of Quality Defects

The first step in practicing quality maintenance is to clarify relationships between the product's quality characteristics and the four production inputs shown in Figure 7-1. Quality defects emanate from at least four sources:

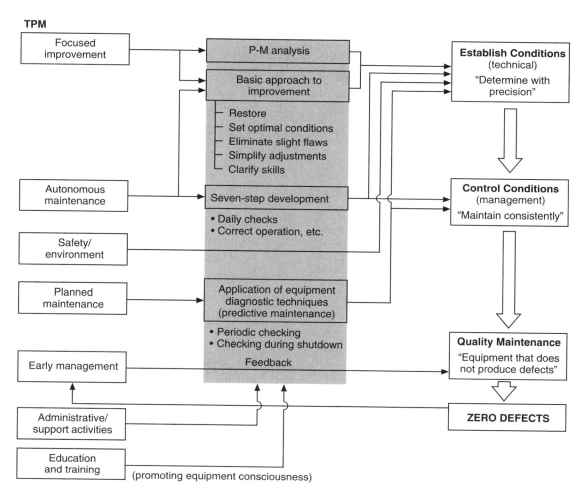

Figure 7-2. The Relation between Quality Maintenance and the Other TPM Mainstays

equipment, materials, people, and methods. Some companies add a fifth input — measurement of quality characteristics. (See Table 7-2.)

Relationship between Equipment and Quality

In process industries, product is produced by a combination of equipment units. Each unit consists of modules, which in turn are made up of components. Units, modules, and components govern different types of quality. It is essential to clarify the relationships among them (Table 7-3).

Equipment Control Conditions

The next step in maintaining quality is to establish the equipment's control conditions. To achieve this, analyze the causes of past quality problems using why-why analysis and P-M analysis. Equipment components that affect a product's quality characteristics are called "quality components." Prevent defects

Table 7-2. Production Inputs and Quality Characteristics

Production Inputs / Quality	Quality Characteristics				
	1···	2···	3···	4···	5···
People	◯		◯		◯
Equipment		◯		◯	◯
Materials	◯		◯		◯
Methods	◯	◯		◯	◯

Table 7-3. Relationship between Plant and Quality Characteristics

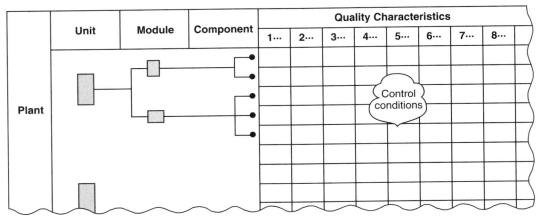

from occurring by maintaining such components in their specified condition. This is the basis of quality maintenance. Table 7-4 shows the format of a quality maintenance checksheet.

What Are Quality Components and Conditions?

Figure 7-3 illustrates the construction of the seal section of an oil-sealed process-gas compressor. This compressor was causing a quality defect: process gas contaminated by sealant oil. A block in the pipe leading to the sealant-oil trap prevented the sealant oil from draining completely, so it infiltrated the impeller side of the seal and contaminated the process gas. In this case, the *quality component* is the trap system. The *condition* (that does not cause a quality defect) is that it must discharge a specific quantity of spent oil. This can be checked by measuring the amount of spent oil.

Table 7-4. Quality Maintenance Checksheet

Quality Maintenance Checksheet			
Quality Component	Control Conditions		
	Condition	Checking method	Checking standard
①			
②			
③			
④			

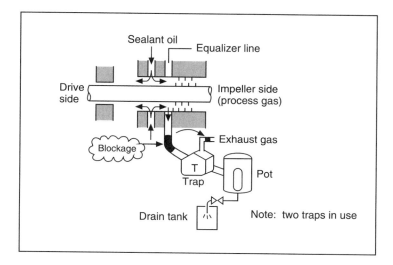

Figure 7-3. Schematic Diagram of Gas-Compressor Seal

Table 7-5 shows a control table for this quality component. The basic aim is to investigate the causes of the problem and through improvements enable the component to operate normally for long periods. (In this case, the pipe was blocked by products of a reaction occurring between the process gas and additives in the oil.)

Process Condition Control

In process industries, quality is governed by process conditions as well as quality components. Daicel Chemical Industries (Otake Plant) uses an "MPQ Matrix" to control process conditions (see Table 7-6). "Q" is the quality check item, such as a sensory check for defect modes such as abnormal odors caused by overheating. "M" is the machine or equipment where the defect mode appears. "P" is the control "point," such as temperature range, through which the quality condition (a specific setting) can be achieved.

Table 7-5. Quality Component Control Table (Example)

Quality Component / Quality Characteristic			Oil contamination						Production Dept.				Maintenance Dept.				Remarks
									Check				Check		Repair		
Unit	Compo-nent	Phenom-enon							Interval	Approach	Method	Replace or repair	Interval	Approach	Spares	Method	
C104	Oil trap	Blockage	◎						1x/wk	Measure quantity discharged		Switch	1x/mo		Stand-by unit	Switch	Fail if XX ppm or above

Table 7-6. MPQ Matrix (Control Table)

Quality Item	Defect Mode	Defect Mechanism	Equipment (M)	Control Point (P)	Control Condition
Sensory Test	Odor	Impurities generated by overheating	Separator (1)	Temperature	< 100°C
	Odor	Impurities formed because of poor reaction startup	Reactor (2)	Temperature distribution	Peak ① ~ ②
	Odor	Unreacted materials remain because of incomplete reaction	As above	Temperature distribution	Temperature difference within 20°C

Quality Maintenance Step-by-Step Implementation

Figure 7-4 is a flow diagram that illustrates the steps in implementing a quality maintenance program. Table 7-7 describes each step in detail.

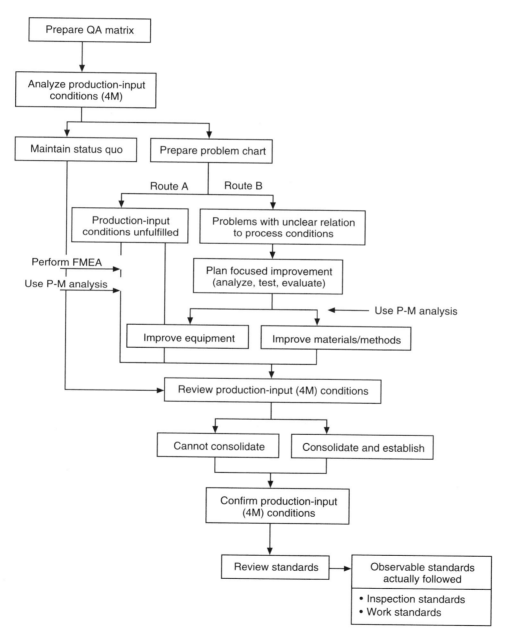

Figure 7-4. Flow Diagram for Implementing Quality Maintenance

Table 7-7. Procedure for Implementing Quality Maintenance

Step	Details
1. Prepare QA matrix	Analyze relations between quality and processes/equipment: • Check quality characteristics • Investigate defect mode and subprocess where defect occurs • Assess seriousness of defect mode
2. Prepare production-input condition analysis table	• Check deficiencies in production-input conditions for each defect mode in each subprocess • Check whether standards exist and are being followed
3. Prepare problem chart	• Clarify production-input conditions for problems in each subprocess • Act promptly against problems that can be tackled on the spot. Carefully work out countermeasures for problems that cannot be dealt with immediately • Stratify defect modes, devise investigation techniques, and plan countermeasures
4. Evaluate seriousness of problems (FMEA 1)	This step directs the equipment improvement effort: • Prioritize problems by assessing their impact on the quality defect mode • Decide on the assessment scale in advance
5. Use P-M analysis to track down causes of problems	• For the most serious problems in the preceding step, clarify the actual phenomena • Investigate using techniques such as P-M analysis and propose countermeasures
6. Assess impact of proposed countermeasures (FMEA 2)	• Perform a preliminary evaluation of the post-improvement situation using FMEA
7. Implement improvements	
8. Review production-input conditions	• Review the production-input conditions identified in Step 2 • Check whether the production-input conditions are appropriate and correct
9. Consolidate and confirm check points	• Use the results of Step 8 to summarize the inspection items • Prepare a quality check matrix
10. Prepare a quality component control table and assure quality through strict condition control	• Standards must be numerical and observable

QUALITY MAINTENANCE IMPLEMENTATION: CASE STUDY

This section outlines the steps taken in a quality maintenance program implemented for the production of a certain product at Tokuyama Sekisui Industries' Nanyō Plant.*

---

* A full description of this implementation appears in Japanese in the proceedings of the *1989 National Equipment Management Symposium*, edited by the Japan Institute of Plant Maintenance.

Figure 7-5 shows the relevant part of the production process. PVC slurry made by polymerizing vinyl chloride monomer in the previous process enters the slurry tank shown on the left side of the diagram. The slurry is dried to form the product, which is then used as a raw material for plastic moldings.

Step 1: Prepare a QA (Quality Assurance) Matrix (Table 7-8)

Preparing a QA (quality assurance) matrix involved the following four substeps:

1. Investigate the types of defects occurring in each process.
2. Classify the product's quality characteristics precisely and identify the all defect modes related to each characteristic.
3. Rank the defect modes according to their seriousness and indicate which ones have caused problems in the past as frequent or occasional. When assessing the seriousness of defect modes, be sure to include a member of the quality assurance department in the discussion.

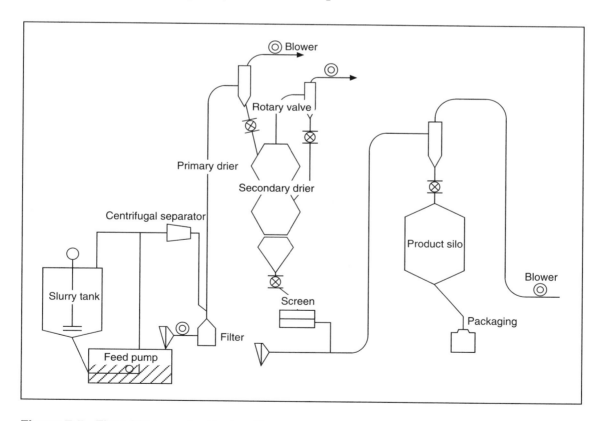

Figure 7-5. Flow Diagram for Drying Process

4. Divide the process into the smallest possible units (subprocesses) and indicate the relationships between these and the defect modes. (See Table 7-8.)

Step 2: Analyze Production-Input Conditions (Table 7-9)

After preparing the QA matrix, analyze the production-input (4M) conditions and organize the data in a table format. (See Table 7-9.)

For each defect mode in each subprocess, identify all the conditions for equipment, materials, people, and methods which when established do not give rise to defects. Be sure to check conditions on the spot, not from behind a desk. Next, determine whether standards for these quality conditions exist and whether people follow them. Again, be sure to investigate the level of standardization and adherence through on-the-spot observation.

Table 7-8. QA Matrix for Drying Process

Main interm. processes	Sub-process	Quality Characteristic — Defect mode Seriousness / Past occurrences / Product inspect. / Process inspect. / Supp. process		Contamination						Polymerization		Moisture content	
				Inorg. matter	Wood splinters	Scale	Burnt deposits	Iron/ stain. steel	Large foreign objects	High	Low	High	Low
				▲	▲	▲	▲	▲	▲	●	●	●	▲
					☆	☆	★	☆		☆	☆	★	★
Drying/ Feed	Recirc.	Recirc. pump		◎			×	×					
		Gland		◎			×	×					
	Transfer	Transfer pump		◎			×	×					
		Gland		◎			×	×					
	Feed	Feed selector		◎									
		Feed pump		◎			×	×					
		Gland		◎			×	×					
Drying/ dewater		Centrifugal separator		◎		×	×	×					
		Feed DCV						◎					
		Feed adjust. meter											
		Vibrat'g conveyor											
		Pulverizer					×	◎					
		PVC pocket					×	◎					

Findings. In this case, investigation revealed that standards were unclear, and that each operator ran the process differently. Only 45 percent of the subprocesses in the drying process were performed in accordance with standards. The standards were impossible to follow in 27 percent of cases and not strictly adhered to in 4 percent. In the remaining 24 percent, standards were needed but had not been set.

Step 3: Prepare a Problem Chart (Table 7-10)

Prepare a problem chart by listing any irregularity uncovered in the process by problem type. Note how it is investigated and the results and use this information as a basis for proposing countermeasures. (See Table 7-10.) Also consider any subprocesses which the production-input conditions analysis revealed were not properly standardized (marked with an Δ, ×, or ⊗ on Table 7-9).

Table 7-8. (continued)

Bulk density		Granularity					Glass parts.		C-test		Initial thermal stab.	Residual VCM*	Appear-ance White powder		Gelation		
		Distribution			Large parts.												
					PVC	Other											
High mois-ture	Static elect.	Coarse parts.	Fine parts.	Broad	Coarse parts./ flakes	Large parts.	Glass parts.	Scale parts.	Low	High	Dis-colored	High	Dis-col-ored	For-eign mat-ter	Fast gela-tion	Slow gela-tion	Diff. torque
●	●	▲	▲	▲	▲	▲	▲	▲	▲	▲	▲	▲	▲	▲	●	●	●
★	★	★	★	☆			☆	☆	☆	☆		☆	☆	☆			

Correlation Analysis

○ Process where the problem occurred (where it was actually discovered)

× Process directly related to the problem (when something goes wrong, the problem always occurs in the next process)

◎ Process where the problem is predicted to occur

◇ Process where process inspection is performed

◆ Process where product inspection is performed

Seriousness

● Develops into major defect

▲ Managable through countermeasures

Past Occurrence

★ Frequent

☆ Occasional

* vinyl chloride monomer

Table 7-9. Production-Input Conditions Analysis Table for Drying Process

PRODUCTION-INPUT CONDITIONS ANALYSIS: DRYING PROCESS

○ : According to standard △ : Standards not properly followed × : Standards impossible to follow ⊗ : Standards needed

Main Process	Sub-process	Defect Mode	Raw Material		Equipment		Method (people)	
Drying/ Storage	Storage	Foreign matter	Concentration: 30% Temperature: 70° C or less	○ ○	V11-2-D rubber lining: no rust V11-3-D stainless steel: no rust V11-4-D PVC lining: no rust V11-5-D stainless steel: no rust	○ ○ ○ ○	Check for internal corrosion Storage temperature: 70° C or less Use: V11-4-D for product R V11-1, 2, 3, 5-D for other products	⊗ ○ △
Drying/ Feed	Recirc. • Transfer • Feed	Foreign matter	PVC slurry: Concentration: 30% Temperature: 70° C or less FW turbidity standard	○ ○ ○	P11-1, 2, 3, 4-D: no gland leaks P11-1, 2, 3, 4-D: no gland heating P11-1, 2, 3, 4-D: gland water supply quantity P11-1, 2, 3, 4-D: gland water supply pressure Output pressure of gland water supply pump: 5 kg/cm² or above	× △ ⊗ △ △	Gland leak rate standards Gland heating check: once per shift Gland water supply rate check Gland checking standard Gland water supply pressure check Gland water supply pump output pressure check: once per shift	⊗ △ ⊗ ⊗ △ ○

Investigate the problems noted and propose countermeasures. As far as possible, express the results quantitatively.

For simple problems, decide what action to take, assign responsibility, and act immediately. For more difficult problems, clearly record the investigation methods and results, but don't jump to hasty conclusions about solutions. For these problems, use FMEA analysis to rank defect modes in terms of the seriousness of their effects and prioritize the problems for action. Then take time to develop appropriate countermeasures through P-M analysis.

Findings. Through this process, teams pinpointed problems in each subprocess and identified the unfulfilled production-input conditions for each defect mode. Quantifying the problem investigation results made it possible to decide whether each problem could be immediately tackled or not and helped focus the improvement countermeasures.

Table 7-10. Problem Chart for Drying Process

Process	Production Inputs (3M)	Problem	Defect Mode	Investigation Technique	Investigation Result	Suggested Action	Person Resp.
Recirc. • Transfer • Feed	Equipment	P11-D: leaky gland P11-D: overheated gland P11-D: gland water supply rate unknown P11-D: gland water supply pressure varies P14-D: gland water supply pump output pressure varies, reducing to under 5 kg/cm²	Foreign matter	Gland leak rate Gland replacement frequency Gland water supply rate → P-M analysis of causes of variation in water supply pressure	P-M analysis results: Pressure drops when water is used by other processes: • Product changeover in compounding and drying processes • Opening, polymerization and drying processes	• Isolate from changeover washing water supply, and ensure sufficient washing water is stored Improvement to be investigated and implemented by FW production group.	Kramer Bills Kramer
	People • Methods	• No gland leak rate tolerance standard • Procedure for checking gland heating unclear • No gland replacement standard • No water supply rate standard	Foreign matter	• Check gland leak rate standards and inspection procedures • Investigate reasons for overheating • Investigate gland replacement frequency • Investigate pressure variation	• Rate of 50 cc/mo. would be acceptable, but gland is currently leaking at 2 l/mo because of overheating in the past. The gland is also replaced often because of problems • The cause of the pressure variation is as noted	• Replace gland periodically or according to leak rate • Mark face of pressure gauge with appropriate values	Lu Marks
Centrifugal separator	Equipment	• PVC adhering to the decanter cover, leaking out and forming congealed lumps • Interior of bearing is being contaminated by liquid PVC PVC adhesion	Foreign matter	Investigate causes of PVC adhesion Check which products form lumps → P-M analysis of causes of foreign matter Check foreign matter generation frequency	P-M analysis results: Comes in contact with carbon inside the bearing, forming discolored contaminant	• Prevent PVC from entering bearing	Davies

Step 4: Evaluate Seriousness — Perform FMEA (1) (Table 7-11)

Examine the problems on the problem chart and rank them in terms of their effects on the defect modes. Then, prioritize the problems by scoring their frequency of occurrence, effect, and difficulty of detection. Determine the assessment criteria in advance. Multiply the scores for each problem together and use the results to prioritize the improvement effort. (See Table 7-11.)

Step 5: Use P-M Analysis to Devise Improvement Measures

For more challenging problems, use P-M analysis to clarify the observed phenomena and develop improvement proposals. In applying P-M analysis, carefully analyze and understand the phenomena in terms of physical principles and steer the improvement plan in the right direction by checking, analyzing, and measuring.

- Begin by stratifying phenomena in terms of their type and mode of occurrence. Analyze them physically, and identify the conditions that produce them.
- Be sure to uncover and consider all the necessary conditions in producing a given problem. If improvement teams overlook vital conditions at this step, they may fail to eliminate defects, even after confirming and eliminating numerous causes.
- List all the conditions that tend to produce the phenomenon, regardless of their magnitude.

In this case, P-M analysis helped the team to formulate an improvement plan for preventing the generation of foreign matter by the feed pump gland (Table 7-12). Tables 7-12 and 7-13 show the results of the P-M analysis in this case.

Findings. Analysis of the causes of the problem for all the production-input conditions revealed that the condition of the filtered water (FW) supplied to the feed pump gland was very important. Supplying the filtered water to other processes and equipment by the same pump, however, caused its pressure to vary greatly, which resulted in insufficient cooling and the risk of back flow. This suggested the need for a feed pump that was not affected by fluctuations in water pressure (Figure 7-6).

Table 7-11. FMEA (1) for Drying Process

FMEA FOR PROBLEMS IN DRYING PROCESS

Problem	Defect mode	Fre-quency	Effect	Detect-ability	Serious-ness	Process where defect is detected	Detection method
19. Generation of foreign matter by feed pump gland	Foreign matter	3	4	3	36	Process inspection	Contamination measurement
20. Lumps formed during dewatering process	Black contamination Discolored contamination Scale Fish eyes	2	4	3	24	Process inspection	Contamination measurement
21. Feed control unstable	Moisture content Bulk density (BD)	4	3	2	24	Process inspection	Moisture content measurement BD measurement
22. PVC pocket, foreign matter in primary entrainment pipe	Burnt deposits	4	2	3	24	Process inspection	Contamination measurement

Frequency

1	2	3	4
Occurred in past	Occurs 1x/year	Occurs 1x/6 mos.	Occurs 1x/mo.

Effect

1	2	3	4
Does not cause defects	May cause defects	Indirect cause	Defect cause

Detectability

1	2	3	4
By control room or during routine operation	By operation control	By process control	By product inspection

Table 7-12. P-M Analysis for Drying Process

P-M ANALYSIS FOR DRYING PROCESS	Generation of Foreign Matter by Slurry Feed Pump

Phenomenon	Physical Principles	Conditions Producing Problem	Relation to Equipment, People, Materials, and Methods	Optimal Conditions
Gland heating	1. Friction between pump shaft and gland produces heat	1-1 Insufficient cooling water 1-2 Lack of clearance between gland and shaft	• Cooling-water line blocked • Excessive gland leakage • Water-seal ring displaced • Water-seal ring blocked • Shaft damaged • Gland overtightened • Drop in cooling-water pump capacity	Revise drying operation work standard Gland retainer · Gland packing · Water-sealing ring · Water inlet
Burnt PVC appears between shaft and gland	2. Friction heating carbonizes PVC	2-1 Increased gland leakage, reducing amount of water on casing side 2-2 Drop in cooling-water supply pressure, causing backflow of slurry	• Gland wear • Small number of gland insertions • Water supply valve not fully opened • Drop in water supply pressure due to use by other equipment • Pump started incorrectly	Investigate gland construction, locate precise point where foreign matter is generated, and remodel gland so it no longer generates foreign matter

Table 7-13. Results of P-M Analysis of Drying Process

P-M ANALYSIS RESULTS FOR DRYING PROCESS

○ : no abnormality
△ : review
✕ : implement countermeasure

Investigation	Assess Investigation Results		Propose and Implement Improvements
Investigate causes of insufficient cooling:			
1. Blockage in cooling-water line	No blockages exist, but there is a danger of backflow due to decreased water supply pressure	○	**Countermeasures against gland problems:** • Insufficient cooling arises from variations in the water supply pressure and flow rate due to sharing of the FW (filtered water) by other processes. • Change to a self-flushing-type mechanical seal unaffected by water-pressure fluctuations.
2. Increased gland leak rate	• Gland leakage increased as a result of gland packing wear	✕	
	• Burnt PVC was found in the gland packing section	✕	
	• Leak rate: 2.0 l/m		
3. Displaced water-sealing ring	No displacement	○	
4. Blocked water-sealing ring	PVC adheres to water-sealing ring, causing PVC backflow	✕	**Countermeasure against pressure variation in FW supply:**
5. Damaged shaft	No damage to shaft	○	• Take as much as possible of the washing water for other equipment and processes out of the shared line, and install dedicated pumps for product changeover. • Remodel FW production plant to increase supply.
6. Reduced capacity of water supply pump	Water supply pump capacity normal (6 kg/cm^2 during normal operation)	○	
Investigate pressure drop occurring when water is used by other processes:			**Self-flushing Mechanical Seal**
1. Changeover in compounding process	6kg/cm^2 → 5kg/cm^2 2x/mo.	△	
2. Washing at beginning and end of opening process	6kg/cm^2 → 4kg/cm^2 15x/mo.	△	
3. Supply of water to V15-K	6kg/cm^2 → 5kg/cm^2 15x/mo.	△	
4. Changeover in drying process	6kg/cm^2 → 4kg/cm^2 4x/mo.	△	
5. VCM removal	6kg/cm^2 → 5kg/cm^2 80x/mo.	△	
6. Changeover from FW to PW	6kg/cm^2 → 2.5kg/cm^2 3x/mo.	✕	

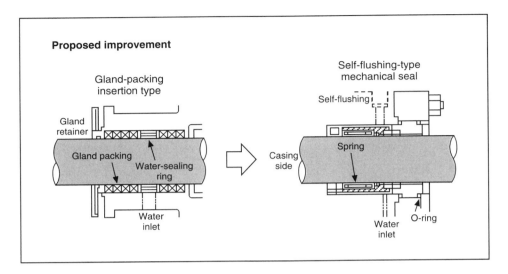

Figure 7-6. Pump Construction Before and After Improvement

Step 6: Assess Impact of Proposed Countermeasures — FMEA (2) (Table 7-14)

Use FMEA again to assess the effects of implementing the improvement proposals based on P-M analysis and the other investigation results. (See Table 7-14.)

Step 7: Implement Improvements

In this case, a second FMEA on the improvement proposals based on the P-M analysis and investigation results showed that the best plan was to replace the feed-pump gland with a self-flushing mechanical seal. (See Figure 7-6.) Benefits of the new seal included:

- The new seal is self-flushing, so there is no need to supply water during the operation.
- The seal is not affected by water use in other processes.
- Operators need to check water pressure only at startup and shutdown.
- No foreign matter is produced.
- The seal does not leak, so the surroundings stay clean.

The team improved the equipment as described above. (See Figure 7-6.) They followed the same procedure for irregularities they could not definitely

Table 7-14. FMEA (2) Evaluation of Improvement Proposals

FMEA FOR PROBLEMS IN DRYING PROCESS

Problem	Failure Mode	Fre-quency	Effect	Detect-ability	Serious-ness	Process Where Detected	Detection Method	Proposed Countermeasure	Serious-ness	Fre-quency	Effect	Detect-ability
19. Generation of foreign matter by feed-pump gland	Foreign matter	3	4	3	36	Process inspection	Contamination measurement	Change to mechanical seal, less liable to leak or generate contamination	4	1	2	2

link to production-input conditions, and classified improvements as either equipment improvements or materials and methods improvements.

Step 8: Review Production-Input Conditions (Table 7-15)

Review and update the Production-Input Conditions Analysis Table (Table 7-9) to determine whether the production-input conditions are appropriate and correct, whether any deficiencies remain in the standards, and whether conditions are being satisfied. In this case, solving the easy problems identified on the Problem Chart (Table 7-10) and implementing the equipment improvements indicated, satisfied all the production-input conditions. (See Table 7-15.)

Step 9: Consolidate and Confirm Checkpoints

Use the results of Step 8 to consolidate and establish checkpoints for production-input conditions. Draw up a quality check matrix, standardize quality,

Table 7-15. Production-Input Conditions Review Table for Drying Process

| PRODUCTION-INPUT REVIEW FOR DRYING PROCESS | | | ○ : According to standard △ : Standards not properly followed | | X : Standards impossible to follow ⊗ : Standards needed | |

Main processes	Sub-process	Defect mode	Raw material		Equipment		Method (people)	
Drying/ Storage			Temperature: 70° C or less	○	V11-3-D stainless steel: no rust	○	Storage temperature: 70° C or less	○
					V11-4-D PVC lining: no rust	○	Method of use: V11-4-D dedicated to product R.	○
					V11-5-D stainless steel: no rust	○	V11-1, 2, 3, 5-D for other products	○
Drying/ Feed	Recirc. • Transfer • Feed	Foreign matter	PVC slurry: Concentration: 30%	○	P11-1, 2, 3, 4-D: no gland heating	○	Gland heating check: 1x/shift	○
			Temperature: 70° C or less	○	P11-1, 2, 3, 4-D: gland water supply rate: 2 l/m	○	Gland water supply rate check: 1x/shift	○
			FW turbidity standard	○	Output pressure of gland water supply pump: 5 kg/cm² or above	○	Gland water supply pump output pressure check: 1x/shift	○
	Centri- fugal sepa- rator	Foreign matter	PVC slurry		PVC scraper cycle: once every 4 sec.	○	Check scraper operation	

people, and checking procedures, and ensure that standards can be followed without difficulty. (See Table 7-16.)

Step 10: Prepare a Quality Component Table (Table 7-17)

To establish visual control and ensure that checks are carried out, quantify substitute characteristics using the quality check matrix, developed in Step 9 and prepare a quality component table to set practical standards (Table 7-17).

Quality components. Determine which components affect quality and mark them down for special treatment as *quality components.*

Quality component table. To ensure that quality components receive priority for maintenance, prepare a quality component table and develop practical standards.

Table 7-16. Quality Check Matrix

Equipment Part	No. 1 Feed Pump				
Check Item	Gland temperature	Gland water supply pressure	Gland water supply rate	Pump current	Output pressure
Standard	30° C or less	5 kg/cm^2 or more	2 l/m or more	10.5 ± 0.5 A	2 kg/cm^2 or more
Checking Interval	1x/shift	At startup and shutdown	At startup and shutdown	1x/shift	At startup
Foreign Matter	○	○	○		

Table 7-17. Quality Component Table

Quality component: water supply rate
Checking interval: At startup and shutdown
Checking standard: 2 l/m or more
Checking method: Visual check of flowmeter
Result: Record flowmeter reading on daily operating log for No.1 drying unit

Case Study Results

The action that eliminates quality defects originating in the drying-process feed pump has been described. Teams used a similar procedure to develop countermeasures against contamination from other sources in this process. Figure 7-7 shows the resulting defect rate decrease. In this instance, defect losses and inspection hours dropped to 1/10 and 1/5 of their original values.

WHO IS RESPONSIBLE FOR QUALITY MAINTENANCE?

The quality control department must be responsible for promoting quality maintenance throughout your company or plant. Quality maintenance projects vary considerably in difficulty, however. Projects spanning a wide range of processes or requiring advanced technology should be tackled by project teams headed by section managers. Easier projects can be addressed by small groups in the workplace. After teams establish the conditions for zero defects, operators should maintain and control most of these conditions as part of autonomous

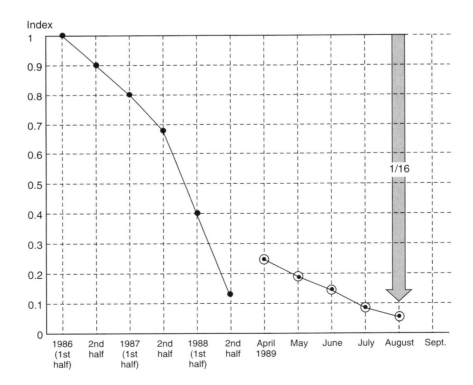

Figure 7-7. Defect Trend in Drying Process

maintenance. More difficult problems should be attacked by project teams from the production department with participation from departments such as product design, production engineering, equipment engineering, maintenance, and quality assurance.

BUILDING IN QUALITY THROUGH EARLY MANAGEMENT

When building a production plant, initial planning to set fundamental design conditions precedes basic equipment design. When reviewing the initial plans, first evaluate the process to highlight anything that is unclear, undecided, or causing concern. To build quality in through the process and the equipment, review quality at the same time. The different groups responsible for production, maintenance, and design must conduct a thorough preliminary investigation and agree clearly on what is required. Figure 7-8 is an example of a flow diagram for conducting a preliminary assessment at the basic equipment design stage in manufacturing a certain product.

Preliminary Investigation Items

- Clarify the targets that the equipment must achieve.
- Clarify the process sequence and interfaces between processes.
- Clarify the relationship between each process and product quality.
- Detect all possible causes of defects in each process.

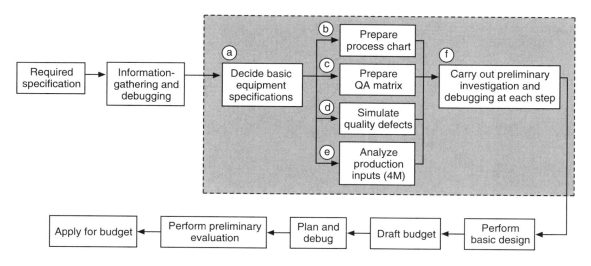

Figure 7-8. Preliminary Investigation Flow Diagram

- For defect causes that quality simulation detects, clarify the equipment conditions in each process that will not cause defects.
- List all points still unclear after production-input analysis, and all other points that require checking. Decide who will be responsible for solving these problems, when they must solve them, and how they should solve them.

REFERENCES

T. Suzuki. *New Directions for TPM*. Portland, Ore.: Productivity Press, 1992.

Japan Institute of Plant Maintenance (ed.), Proceedings. *1989 National Equipment Management Symposium* (in Japanese). Tokyo: Japan Institute of Plant Maintenance, 1989.

Nachi-Fujikoshi Corp. (ed.). *Training for TPM*. Portland, Ore.: Productivity Press, 1990.

8
Operating and Maintenance Skills Training

Companies flourish by ceaselessly developing their human resources and ensuring that all employees exercise their full potential. TPM aims to create corporate environments able to respond positively to the changing business climate, technological advances, equipment sophistication, and management innovation.

Essential in this environment are competent people who understand their equipment intimately. Front-line operators closest to the equipment must be willing and able to look after it themselves. Meanwhile, maintenance personnel must acquire the requisite technology and skills to act as its professional custodians. Similarly, equipment designers and production engineers must master engineering technology, management techniques, and managerial abilities to fulfill their required functions. Without this, the benefits of a full-scale TPM effort remain a pipe dream.

In practice, production departments tend to focus exclusively on production in its narrowest sense, while maintenance departments drown in a sea of breakdowns. Companies that neglect maintenance technology and skills training invite equipment failures, idling, minor stops, and equipment-originated quality defects. Reduced operating rates, poor productivity, and unsafe conditions are not far behind. Meanwhile, the equipment design and production engineering departments struggle desperately to commission equipment that is ill-suited to workplace conditions, difficult to use, awkward to maintain, and regularly breaks down or spews out defectives. All this demonstrates a low level of technology, skill, and managerial ability in every department.

EDUCATION AND TRAINING IN TPM

TPM frees companies from this vicious cycle. It only pays off, however, when the approach to implementation or promotion raises the managerial, technical, and practical skills of each individual involved. In fact, all PM-prize-winning companies have responded to the accelerating growth of technology and skill requirements by establishing education and training systems designed to maximize the potential of every employee. Such companies devote enormous effort to operating and maintenance skills training. Such training must begin from day one of any company's TPM program and take into account the company environment and the needs, aptitudes, character, and special skills of individual trainees.

The Basic Philosophy of Education and Training

In TPM, the two basic approaches to training are on-the-job training (OJT) and self-development. Fundamentally, improving the abilities of individuals not only helps the company's bottom line, but also increases people's zest for life and pride in their work. Off-the-job training and support activities, of course, are also important in ensuring training efficiency.

To achieve this, all line managers and supervisors must be dedicated to educating the people in their care. They must devote a considerable portion of their energy to developing equipment-competent personnel through TPM.

What Is Skill?

Skill is the ability to do one's job, to apply knowledge and experience correctly and reflexively in all kinds of events over an extended period (Figure 8-1). Systematically accumulating training, experience, and information enables a person to exercise good judgment and act appropriately. The more swiftly a person can deal with an abnormality, the higher the skill level.

Skill is the product of personal motivation and thorough training. The end result is mastery. To enable people to achieve mastery, companies must develop the most effective training methods.

The Four Skill Levels

The first step in any training program is to identify the level of knowledge, technology, skill, and competence people need to fulfill and progress in each

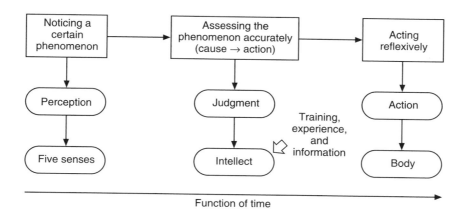

Figure 8-1. What Are Skills?

type of task, specialization, or position. Existing skill levels should also be assessed. Table 8-1 identifies four skill levels:

Level 1: Lacks both theoretical knowledge and practical ability (needs to be taught)
Level 2: Knows in theory but not in practice (needs practical training)
Level 3: Has mastered practice but not theory (cannot teach to others)
Level 4: Has mastered both theory and practice (can teach to others)

Training should be designed to meet all of these needs. Much training is ineffective, either because the content or timing is inappropriate. Often, opportunities for supervised application and achieving mastery through teaching others are simply not available. Training should be thorough and practical, and it should address clearly understood needs one step at a time.

Equipment-Competent Operators

What abilities can we expect from equipment-competent people, that is, from operators coping with automation, electronic control, and other advanced technologies?

Operators' work is in transition, from hands-on operation toward more monitoring and supervision. Operators must acquire the four abilities listed on p. 266; they should be so familiar with their equipment that it becomes an extension of their own brains and bodies. These abilities are acquired through on-the-job training, autonomous maintenance, and focused improvement activities.

Table 8-1. Example of Skills Evaluation

Work Classification	Knowledge/Skill Item	Briggs	Meyer	Baker	Orloff	Jenkins	Jain	Saito	Gruber	Moss
Basics	1 Use/knowledge of tools	○	○	△	○	○	○	○	○	○
	2 Use/knowledge of nuts and bolts	○	○	△	○	○	○	○	○	○
	3 Use/knowledge of keys	○	□	△	□	□	△	□	□	□
	4 Knowledge of bosses and shafts and their fixing methods	△	□	●	△	△	□	△	△	□
Workshop Skills	5 Theory/practice of scribing	○	○	△	○	○	○	○	○	○
	6 Theory/practice of filing	○	●	●	●	□	□	△	○	□
	7 Theory/practice of grinding	○	●	●	●	□	□	△	□	□
	8 Theory/practice of welding	△	○	△	○	□	□	△	□	□
Assembly	9 Use/knowledge of cams, ratchets, and Geneva drives	□	△	●	□	○	○	○	○	○
	10 Use/knowledge of racks, pinions, and gears	□	□	△	□	○	○	△	△	○
	11 Use/knowledge of clutches and brakes	○	△	△	○	□	△	△	△	△
	12 Installation, adjustment, and knowledge of equipment for special-purpose machines	△	●	●	△	△	△	△	△	□
	13 Ability to assess and act against unexpected failures	△	△	△	△	△	○	△	△	○
Pneumatics/ hydraulics	14 Use and knowledge of speed controllers, flow controllers, and check valves	△	△	●	△	○	○	△	○	○
	15 Use/knowledge of FRLs	△	△	●	○	○	○	△	○	○
	16 Use/knowledge of solenoid valves	△	△	●	○	○	○	△	○	○
	17 Use/knowledge of cylinders	△	△	●	○	○	○	△	○	○
	18 Use/knowledge of hydraulic and pneumatic piping and connectors	△	●	●	△	○	○	△	○	○
	19 Knowledge of pneumatic piping layouts	△	●	●	△	○	○	△	○	○
Drawings	20 Knowledge of drawings	○	○	□	○	○	○	○	○	○
Lubrication	21 Knowledge of lubrication	△	△	●	△	□	△	△	△	△
Background knowledge	22 Knowledge of materials and their applications	○	●	●	●	●	●	●	○	●
	23 Use/knowledge of measuring instruments	○	△	●	△	△	○	○	△	○
Other	24 Use/knowledge of motors and transmissions	△	●	●	△	△	□	△	△	△
	25 Use/knowledge of drive pumps and hydraulic pumps	△	●	●	●	●	□	●	△	□
	26 Use/knowledge of parts feeders and feed tables	●	●	●	●	□	□	●	□	□
Consumable Parts	27 Use/knowledge of bearings	○	●	●	●	□	□	□	□	□
	28 Use/knowledge of O-rings and packings	△	△	●	●	△	△	△	△	△
Safety	29 Knowledge of and attention to safety	○	○	○	○	○	○	○	○	○
	Score (max. 29) Knowledge	24	19	24	19	20	19	9	16	26
	Score (max. 29) Skill	19	25	24	19	20	19	9	16	26

● Knowledge and skill both unsatisfactory
△ Knowledge satisfactory
□ Skill satisfactory
○ Knowledge and skill both satisfactory

Item Symbol	2. Use/Knowledge of Nuts and Bolts
Knowledge/ System	1 Knows difference between ISO and JIS standards
	2 Knows nut and bolt types
	3 Knows differences in materials used in different types of nuts and bolts
	4 Knows pitches and leads for different nut and bolt sizes
	5 Knows standards and applications for fine screws
	6 Knows types and applications of pipe threads, trapezoidal threads, and square threads
Skill (Application)	19 Can tighten bolts of different types and sizes correctly
	20 Can fabricate and use slotted nuts as locking devices
	21 Can lock nuts correctly using wire stoppers
	22 Can prevent nuts and bolts from seizing

Item Symbol	16. Use/Knowledge of Solenoid Valves
Knowledge/ System	1 Knows symbol for solenoid valves on pneumatic circuit diagrams
	2 Knows functions and types of solenoid valves
	3 Knows structure and characteristics of spool-type solenoid valves
	4 Knows structure and characteristics of poppet-type solenoid valves
	5 Knows where single solenoid valves are used
	6 Knows where double solenoid valves are used
Skills (Application)	21 Can repair displaced spools or damaged O-rings in spool-type solenoid valves
	22 Can remove dust and dirt from solenoid valves without contaminating solenoid
	23 Can remove oil from solenoid valve exhaust outlets
	24 Knows how to reduce solenoid valve exhaust noise

1. Equipment-competent operators can detect equipment abnormalities and effect improvements. They must be able to:

- Detect equipment irregularities
- Understand the importance of lubrication and can lubricate correctly, and check the results
- Understand the importance of cleaning as inspection and can do it correctly
- Understand the importance of minimizing the scattering of product, raw materials, and other contaminants and can develop improvements to address them
- Correct or improve irregularities they detect

2. Equipment-competent operators understand equipment structure and functions and are able to discover the causes of abnormalities. They must be able to:

- Understand key points of equipment construction
- Maintain equipment performance by inspecting through cleaning
- Know the criteria for recognizing abnormalities
- Understand the causes of abnormalities
- Judge correctly when to shut down equipment
- Diagnose failures to a certain extent

3. Equipment-competent operators understand the relationship between equipment and quality and can predict quality abnormalities and discover their causes. They must be able to:

- Analyze phenomena from physical principles
- Understand the relationship between equipment and product quality characteristics
- Understand and check properly static and dynamic equipment precision tolerances
- Understand the causes of defects

4. Equipment-competent operators can understand and repair equipment. They must be able to:

- Replace components
- Know component lifetimes
- Postulate failure causes
- Take emergency action
- Assist in equipment overhauls

Equipment-Competent Maintenance Personnel

In many industries, equipment quality significantly affects productivity, product quality, safety, and so on. This is why excellent maintenance skills are so badly needed. To meet this demand, maintenance technicians must acquire a wider range of abilities.

Maintenance professionals must be able to:

- Instruct operators in correct handling, operating, and daily maintenance
- Correctly assess whether equipment is operating normally or not
- Trace the causes of abnormalities and restore normal operation correctly
- Improve equipment and component reliability, lengthen equipment lifetimes, and curb abnormalities and failures
- Understand equipment diagnostics and use and standardize them
- Optimize the preceding activities and make them as cost-effective as possible

As equipment becomes more sophisticated and automated, the need for safe and environmentally friendly operation, low energy consumption, and completely assured quality increases. It is, therefore, essential to establish and maintain equipment conditions that build quality into the product. Clarify the technology and skills your company requires to achieve these goals, then tailor a well-organized, effective training system that combines both in-house and outside training to help meet them.

Importance of Self-Development

To ensure that people develop the skills to cope with sophisticated equipment, create an environment that encourages them to learn for themselves rather than to passively receive teaching. Much classroom training is ineffective because it is a one-way process. Trainers deliver information with little regard for the trainees' usual working environment. By contrast, step-by-step autonomous maintenance development and focused improvement activities provide far more effective training because most learning takes place directly in the workplace.

In classroom training, it is important to use the self-development approach illustrated in Figure 8-2 to ensure that each person masters the required skills. Frequent opportunities for group discussion and practical application and reflection are important keys. And, of course, the trainer must continually assess how well each trainee is acquiring the skills and give individual coaching as needed.

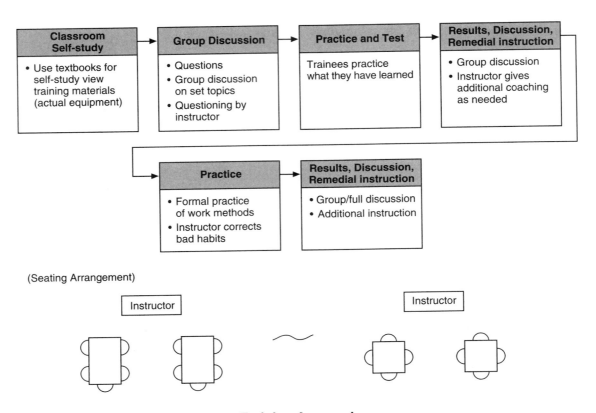

Figure 8-2. The Self-Development Training Approach

Meanwhile, for on-the-job training, managers and supervisors must realize the importance of their role in increasing skill levels. They must create an environment that supports development through work and avoid exerting undue pressure for results. They must know the skills of each of their subordinates and understand classroom objectives so they can assign work of appropriate difficulty to support that learning.

SIX STEPS TO BOOST OPERATING AND MAINTENANCE SKILLS

To ensure that training for operating and maintenance skills is effective, develop it systematically in the following six steps, which are discussed in detail below:

1. Evaluate the current training program and set policy and priority strategies.
2. Design a program for improving operating and maintenance skills.

3. Implement operating and maintenance skills training.
4. Design and develop a skill-development system.
5. Foster an environment that encourages self-development.
6. Evaluate the activities and plan for the future.

Step 1: Analyze the Current Program and Set Policy and Priority Strategies

Most companies give their employees some form of training. Very few companies, however, possess cadres of truly equipment-competent individuals, who are professionals in their chosen fields and rival their competitors. In most firms, training is secondary to the pressure of daily work; when training occurs, it is ritualized and piecemeal. Take a hard look at your company's training program and its effect on raising skills among individuals and specializations. Go back to the basics, review the situation, and identify the persistent problems. Then work out clear policies, goals, and priorities for a training program that solves these problems and suits the particular circumstances of your company. Use these policies, goals, and priorities to guide you through the remaining steps. Table 8-2 is an example of one company's policies, goals, and priorities for training.

Table 8-2. Sample of Training Policies, Goals, and Priorities

> **BASIC POLICY**
>
> This plant's training policy is to develop specialist skills through an active program of on-the-job training and self-development, supported by off-the-job training. Our basic belief is that raising individual skills not only helps improve our company's business results but also increases our zest for life and pride in our work.
>
> **GOALS**
> - To foster equipment-competent and administration-competent people through TPM
> - To nurture human resources that will meet workplace needs over the long term
>
> **PRIORITIES**
> To accomplish these goals, we have reviewed the training system. Priority is now placed on:
> 1. Developing equipment-competent people
>   - Develop maintenance personnel with more advanced skills and analytical abilities.
>   - Establish a maintenance-skills training center and develop equipment-competent operators.
>   - Foster specialist abilities by sending people to outside training courses.
> 2. Developing administration-competent people
>   - Develop administration-competent people through step-by-step autonomous maintenance development and training in office automation.
> 3. Establishing an ability-development program
>   - Evolve an ability-development system that focuses on essential skills to develop, systematically, truly equipment-competent and administration-competent people.

Step 2: Design a Training Program for Improving Operating and Maintenance Skills

Production technology and skills are advancing at a bewildering pace and rapidly becoming obsolete. The introduction of industrial robots, numerical control, and flexible manufacturing systems is quickly eliminating the need for human operation, and the production department's role is shifting more toward supervision and maintenance.

Meanwhile, maintaining this sophisticated, electronically controlled equipment has become a major headache. In response, companies are acquiring or training more engineers and technicians well-versed in equipment and mechatronics technology. People on the front line need to grow from single-skilled technicians into multi-skilled masters of theory and practice. This cannot happen overnight, however. To develop equipment-competency at every level, the company must construct a program of training that progresses in steps from elementary through basic, intermediate, and advanced skills, and so on. Table 8-3 is an example of one company's overall training curriculum, while Figure 8-3 is an example of a maintenance training program.

Each company should devise its own particular system to suit its own equipment. If your company has neglected equipment maintenance training in the past, it must consider how to improve maintenance skills from the most basic level and up.

Step 3: Implement Operating and Maintenance Skills Training

This section describes how to improve operating and maintenance skills to the level required for effective TPM promotion.

Training Curriculum

Start by developing a curriculum. Consider the equipment your company owns, clarify the skill levels required, then decide what specific items to teach and how long to spend on them. Table 8-4 is an example of a maintenance skills training curriculum. The company that developed it achieved good results by covering two units in one week, followed by two weeks' practical application in the trainees' own workplaces. It is no good trying to rush through the program with a couple of hours for each unit — proper understanding takes time.

Table 8-3. Overall Training System

Training Milestone		Introduction (New Entrants)	Basic Skills (Grades 1-2)	Specialized Skills (Grade 3)	Management Skills (Grades 4-5)	Advanced Management Skills (Grade 6)	Basic Business Management Skills (Grades 7-8)
OJT		Departmental training	Departmental training	Departmental training	Departmental training	Departmental training	Departmental training
Self Development		← • Video training courses • Training video rental system			• Introduction of training texts • Correspondence-course system →		
Off-JT:	Maintenance	• Introduction to equipment maintenance (1)	• Introduction to equipment maintenance (2)	• Maintenance classroom (elementary)	• Maintenance classroom (intermediate)	• Maintenance classroom (intermediate)	
	Technology and Skills	• Practical workplace training • Interpreting drawings (1)	• Interpreting drawings (2)	• Industrial engineering course (1) • Numerical control course • Mold and die design course • Plastic molding course • Cable characteristics course (1)	• Industrial engineering course (2) • Plastic molding course • Cable characteristics course (2) • Financial statements course (1)	• Financial statements course (2)	
	Management	• Accident prevention training (1) • Office automation course (A) • QC course (introductory)	• Accident prevention training (2) • Office automation course (B) • QC course (elementary)	• Cost control course (1) • Management-by-objectives training (1) • Office automation classroom (elementary) • QC circle leaders' course (elementary) • QC course (intermediate)	• Cost control course (2) • Management-by-objectives training (2) • Office automation classroom (intermediate) • QC circle leaders' course (intermediate) • QC course (advanced)	• Office automation classroom (advanced) • QC circle leaders' course (advanced)	• Office automation classroom (advanced)
	Grade-Specific Training	• President's training (1) • Follow-up training • Customer-contact course (1) • Group training for new entrants • Pre-entry training	• President's training (2) • Graduates' residential training • Customer-contact course (1)	• President's training (3) • Group leaders' course (introductory) • Management training program (introductory) • Customer-contact course (2)	• President's training (4) • Group leaders' course (advanced) • Management training program (introductory) • Technical Research Institute training • Top-management lecture	• Director's seminar • Management training program (intermediate)	• Senior management training • Managers' seminar • Management training program (advanced) • Management seminar • Departmental seminar

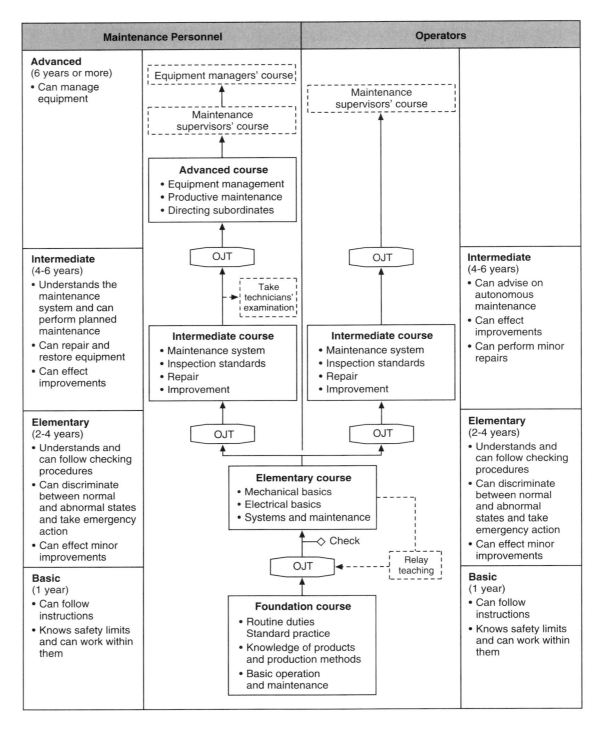

Figure 8-3. Maintenance Training System

Lesson Plans and Materials

An effective training program requires a good learning model. The self-development approach is best, because it emphasizes learning through practice. A good rule of thumb is 70 percent practice and 30 percent lectures and discussions. For each topic, draw up a lesson plan specific to your particular company, compile in-house self-study texts, and prepare the training aids and materials trainees will need for practical training (e.g., cutaway models, diagnostic equipment, practice machines and tools). (See Table 8-5.)

Provide enough training aids and practice equipment to enable every trainee to perform practical training. Two or three trainees can share expensive items at one time (transmissions, electronic hydraulic control systems, etc.).*

Classrooms

While practical instruction should be given one-on-one, 6 to 10 trainees to each trainer is a good ratio for classroom instruction. Classroom environments must be conducive to learning and equipped with practical training aids.

Training

Train personnel in accordance with the lesson plans. Focus on practice rather than theory and use the self-development approach described earlier. Link the training as much as possible to actual activities of the workplace to help trainees acquire skills more effectively. Figure 8-4 is an example of a training flow plan that requires trainees to apply what they have learned in the workplace and to document and report on their experiences.

To deepen understanding and promote rapid mastery, have trainees use what they have learned in the training to prepare one-point lesson sheets for each curriculum unit, tailored to their various workplaces. Trainees should then use these materials to teach their colleagues what they have learned. The lessons should communicate points of basic knowledge, tips for preventing problems, and keys to effective improvement activity related to the topic. (See Figures 8-5 and 8-6.) Lessons describing solutions to actual problems and improvements are particularly effective.

---

* In Japan, TPM companies send potential instructors to outside courses on maintenance skills offered by the Japan Institute of Plant Maintenance and other organizations. With this foundation in the basic content and methods, they can then develop programs, texts, and teaching aids suited to their own companies.

Table 8-4. Maintenance Skills Training Curriculum

ADVANCED CURRICULUM (16 units)

① **Company and Organization**	② **Duties of Front-line Supervisors**	③ **Equipment Management**	④ **Maintenance Management**
• Company and objectives • Company and organization • Organization and management	• Line and staff • Self-assessment	• Importance of equipment to company • Equipment management and its function	• Relation between maintenance management and production • Functions of maintenance management (technical and financial)
⑤ **Equipment Life and Processing Costs**	⑥ **Production Budget and Its Function**	⑦ **AM Practice I:**	⑧ **AM Practice II:**
• Life-cycle cost • Processing-cost reduction topics	• Systems and functions • The role of line and staff	Measuring and analyzing the status quo	Measuring and analyzing the status quo • Analyzing problems • Proposing and implementing countermeasures
⑨ **PM Practice I:**	⑩ **PM Practice II:**	⑪ **PM Practice III:**	⑫ **PM Practice IV:**
Measuring and analyzing the status quo • Technical activities • Economic activities	Measuring and analyzing the status quo • Analyzing problems • Proposing and implementing countermeasures	Measuring and analyzing the status quo • Designing and applying maintenance standards • Evaluating status and effectiveness	Measuring and analyzing the status quo • Drafting and implementing maintenance work plans • Evaluating status and effectiveness
⑬ **PM Practice V:**	⑭ **Maintenance Budget Control**	⑮ **Manager Skills I**	⑯ **Manager Skills II**
Measuring and analyzing the status quo • Assessing maintenance records and reports and using them for failure control and improvement	• System and use • Reducing maintenance costs • Measuring and evaluating results	• In-house training • Ability development	• Using training plans • Progress control (skill inventory) • Skill assessment techniques

INTERMEDIATE CURRICULUM (20 units)

① **Equipment Mainte-nance Approaches**	② **Understanding Maintenance Systems**	③ **Applied Statistics**	④ **Maintenance Planning**
• Preventive maintenance • Corrective maintenance • Maintenance prevention • Breakdown maintenance	• Daily maintenance • Checking standards • Periodic inspection • Repair standards	• Abnormality and failure records and their application (implementation and control)	• Use of maintenance calendars
⑤ **Maintenance Skills Practice**	⑥ **Developing and Applying Checking and Inspection Standards**	⑦ **Piping Fabrication and Installation**	⑧ **Mechatronics Overview**
• Revision and augmentation of key maintenance skills		• Formulating piping fabrication and installation work standards	• Data flow • Machine construction and actions
⑨ **Failure Detection Techniques**	⑩ **Condition-Monitoring and MTBF**	⑪ **Detecting Abnor-malities and Failures**	⑫ **"Worst" Case Analysis**
• The relation between deterioration and abnormality/failure; countermeasures • Statistics and their use in failure reduction	PdM practice • Noise • Vibration • Temperature • Insulation resistance	• Case studies	• Presentation of "worst five" examples in trainees' own workplaces • Investigation of countermeasures

AM = autonomous maintenance
PM = planned maintenance

(13) **Equipment Checking and Maintenance**	(14) **Equipment Inspection**	(15) **Equipment Repair Practice**	(16) **Injection Molders**
• Checking and maintaining components • Periodic checking and maintenance	• Preparing process tables • Preparing inspection checksheets • Dynamic and static inspection • Disassembly and cleaning	• Understanding equipment construction and functions; practice in performing and recording repairs in accordance with block diagrams	• Clamps • Injectors • Controllers
(17) **Hydraulic Equipment and Circuits**	(18) **Hydraulic Equipment Maintenance**	(19) **Mechanical Adjustment Skills**	(20) **Electrical Circuits**
• Hydraulic systems (injection molders and presses) • Structure and operation of hydraulic equipment • Hydraulic device actuation and circuits	• Daily and periodic checks • Maintenance • Troubleshooting	• Checking and trial operation • Adjustment and setting of parts • Control devices	• Interpreting elementary wiring diagrams • Sequencers • Troubleshooting

ELEMENTARY CURRICULUM (16 units)

(1) **Basic Nuts and Bolts**	(2) **Applying Correct Tightening Torques**	(3) **Lubrication Basics**	(4) **Basic Seals**
• Use and maintenance of nuts and bolts	• Practice in performing workplace checks	• Use and maintenance of lubricant oils and greases • Practice in assessing lubricant deterioration	• Use and maintenance of packings and gaskets • Practice in performing workplace checks
(5) **Interpreting Mechanical Drawings**	(6) **Basic Keys and Couplings**	(7) **Basic Gears**	(8) **Review Practice**
• Basic fitting • Materials symbols	• Basic knowledge, use, and maintenance of bearings	• Use and maintenance of belts and chains	• Disassembly, assembly, and test operation of practice equipment
(9) **Basic Electricity**	(10) **Basic Sequencing**	(11) **Limit Switch Circuits**	(12) **Basic Electrical Maintenance**
• Electrical devices and symbols • Interpreting sequence diagrams • Use of electrical testing devices	• Practice in circuit wiring • Holding circuits • Motor start-stop circuits • Thermal relay circuits	• Timer circuits • Interlock circuits • Motor forward-reverse circuits • Circuit fault detection	• Safety • Practice in performing workplace checks
(13) **Basic Hydraulics and Pneumatics**	(14) **Hydraulics Structure and Functions**	(15) **Hydraulics and Electrical Systems**	(16) **Fault Detection**
• Basic hydraulic and pneumatic circuits • Disassembly of practice hydraulic systems	• Assembly and test operation of practice equipment • Preparation of hydraulic cycle line diagrams	• Hydraulic circuits and electrical circuits • Preparation of timing charts	• Fault detection using practice hydraulic systems • Practice in performing workplace checks • Summary

BASIC CURRICULUM (3 units)

(1) **Principal Equipment Units**	(2) **Ancillary Equipment**	(3) **Dies**	
• Types and names of injection molders • Guided tour of production equipment • Equipment safety	• Types and names of ancillary equipment • Guided tour of ancillary equipment	• Types and names of injection molding dies • Types and names of metal press dies	

Table 8-5. Example of Lesson Plan

INTRODUCTORY MAINTENANCE COURSE		Date:_____ Preparer:_____
Maintenance of Drive Devices: **(4-2) Basic Bearings** (4 hrs)		

Goals:
- Understand the function of bearings
- Install and remove bearings correctly
- Check bearings and detect abnormalities
- Use puller blocks and lubricants; use listening rods and thermochromic labels

Materials:
1) Texts
2) Bearings of various types
3) Model systems

Topics	Materials	Time	Format
• Types and function of bearings	Text 2-3	30	D
• Rolling bearings	Bearings of various types		
• Structure, classification, and labeling	Text 2-3	30	L
• Key points in handling (precautions, installation, removal, fitting)	Model system, puller blocks	90	P
• Lubricant types and amounts; lubricating methods	Lubricants	20	L
• Key maintenance points (noise, vibration, temperature)	Listening rods and thermochromic labels	30	P/D
• Sliding bearings			
• Characteristics; comparison with rolling bearings	Bearings	30	P/D
• Key handling points; lubrication			
• Key maintenance points			
• Bearing checks; explanation of one-point lesson sheet topics		10	L

L: lecture
D: self-study and discussion
P: practice

Step 4: Design and Develop a Skill-Development Program

Basic training for production and maintenance personnel should emphasize on-the-job training and self-development in the workplace. At the same time, a sustained, long-term skill-development program tailored to the needs of individuals and individual workplaces is essential to enable people to cope with today's rapid technical progress and advancing automation.

In the long run, the best way for a company's various departments to achieve their objectives is to develop people with excellent skills and abilities, tap into their unlimited potential, and encourage them to take on higher and

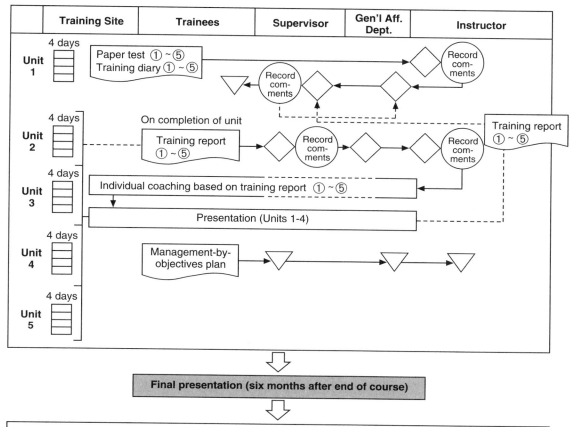

Final presentation (six months after end of course)

Notes to Instructors:

- Ask students to record in their training diaries details of knowledge and skills acquired together with impressions and self-reflections.
- Test each key point in writing.
- The three-week interlude between course units is for workplace practice and relay teaching. Have students submit a report on this.
- Based on these reports, interview trainees individually and give appropriate advice and guidance.
- Evaluate and score trainees on their mastery of the training and on their reports. Summarize your findings on a training report, and submit this to the trainees' supervisor.
- Issue a management-by-objectives training plan (period: 6 months) to trainees on the final day of the course.
- After six months, hold a presentation meeting for trainees to report on the implementation of their training and the results achieved.

Figure 8-4. Training Flowsheet

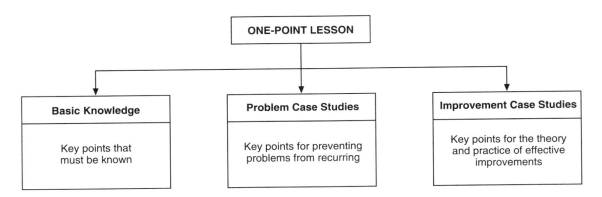

Figure 8-5. Types of One-point Lesson

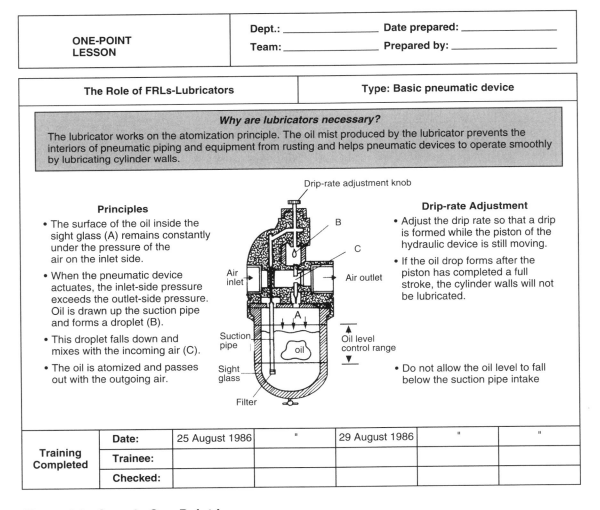

Figure 8-6. Sample One-Point Lesson

higher challenges. Off-the-job training in maintenance skills will be useless, however, if it fails to support the individual's self-development goals. Therefore, evaluating subordinates' skills and helping plan individual training programs are two important tasks for line managers and supervisors. Figure 8-7 outlines a system for administering an individual skill development program.

In this example, the first step is to draw up a long-term (three-year) plan to develop skills. Employees perform self-evaluations and discuss their desired career paths and skill development routes with their supervisors, who then work out long-term training policies based on each employee's present abilities, aptitudes, characteristics, and future prospects.

Annual skill development programs are also planned and implemented. Each employee reports on his or her progress, weaknesses, and aptitudes, and discusses these with the supervisor. To determine appropriate training, the

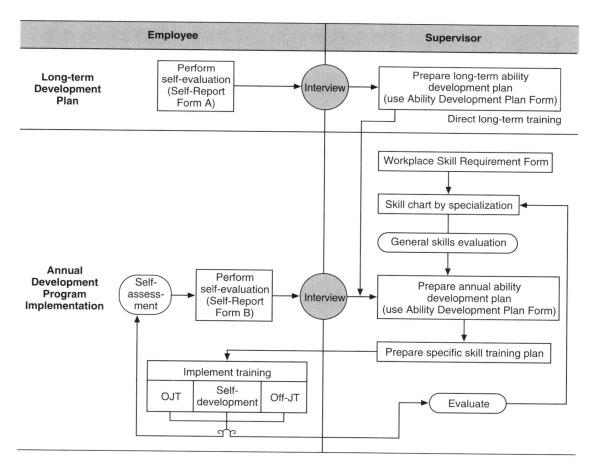

Figure 8-7. Ability Development System

supervisor conducts a general skills evaluation using a skill chart based on skill requirements reported from each work area. During this evaluation the supervisor gives due weight to the employee's long-term skill-development plan and the results of the interview. The supervisor then designs a specific skill-training plan for the employee for the year that appropriately balances on-the-job training, self-development, and off-the-job training.

At the end of each financial year, this individual training program is evaluated and the results are used to draft the next year's training plan. Supervisors also use these evaluations to help determine promotions or salary increases.

Referring to this example, devise a system that suits the characteristics of your own company and systematically nurtures the skills that each specialization and job grade requires over the long term. This will enable you to develop a robust maintenance system that can respond appropriately to any situation it faces.

Although this discussion focuses on the operating and maintenance departments, training is important in every department, including marketing, research and development, production engineering, and administration. The strategies suggested here for ensuring effective training are appropriate for every discipline.

Step 5: Foster an Environment that Encourages Self-Development

It is important for employees to strengthen their weaknesses and develop their skills on their own through their daily work. This is the principle behind on-the-job training. When people are too busy with routine tasks, however, self-development takes a back seat. In addition to offering self-development planning and appropriate training, companies must create an environment where employees feel they can pursue their individual goals freely. Some companies foster an environment conducive to self-development by introducing correspondence courses, making video programs and books available, or offering financial assistance with training, as shown in Table 8-6. Others use a management-by-objectives approach, which assigns each employee to a self-development project every six months.

Step 6: Evaluate the Activities and Plan for the Future

Assess training activities periodically and see what progress individuals are making toward skill development goals for their specializations and grades. Employees must be able to keep up with and even anticipate the rapid advances

Table 8-6. Schemes for Encouraging Self-Development

Training Item	Cost to Employee	Course Unit	Eligibility
Correspondence Course	Half of course fee	• Set by correspondence course institution • Recommended by employee's supervisor	All employees (courses start in January and July)
Video Training (rental system)	Free	Over 250 training videos available	All small groups and individuals from home company and suppliers
Designated Video Training Courses	Free	Monthly	Anyone (monthly topic chosen by company and announced at beginning of month). Each video lasts 40 minutes and is screened after working hours

in technology, equipment, and management. Periodically review the skills, training systems, training processes, and curricula your company requires, and strive for a program that will develop people who know their jobs and their equipment inside out. This is the way to achieve lasting corporate growth.

9

TPM in Administrative and Support Departments

Thanks to advanced computers and communications technology, massive amounts of real-time data now wash constantly around the globe. The growing availability of information encourages market fragmentation and accelerates changes in consumer lifestyles. This results in greater product diversification and individualization accompanied by ever-shrinking product life cycles, making business management increasingly complex. Many companies desperately need to restructure and reform to survive the merciless competition and thrive amid today's chaotic business environment.

THE NEED FOR TPM IN ADMINISTRATIVE AND SUPPORT DEPARTMENTS

Companies must map out a clear strategy to respond to this maelstrom of change and dramatically shorten their product time-to-market. At the same time, they must distinguish themselves from their competitors in both quality and cost. These are the most important challenges facing managers today.

Eighty percent of a product's quality and cost is already determined at the development, design, and production stages. Development, design, and all other staff departments must cooperate unstintingly to ensure that the production department does not produce useless or wasteful products. Meanwhile, companies must set up manufacturing plants in a way that enables the production department to fill orders on time, at the quality and cost that the development and engineering departments prescribe. This is not the responsibility of the production department alone—it requires a TPM program that embraces the entire company, including the administrative and support departments.

TPM activities in administrative and support departments do not involve production equipment. Rather, these departments increase their productivity by documenting administrative systems and reducing waste and loss. They can help raise production-system effectiveness by improving every type of organized activity that supports production. Their contributions to the smooth running of the business should be measurable.

The Role of Administrative and Support Departments

Unlike production departments, departments such as planning, development, engineering, and administration do not add value directly. As experts in their particular area, their primary responsibility is to process information, advise on and assist with the activities of the production department and other departments, and help reduce costs.

Their second task is to enable the company to respond rapidly to changes taking place in the social and business environment and to outperform the competition. This means improving their own productivity, cutting costs, and helping the company accomplish the strategic developments that senior management envision.

Their third task, based on the preceding, is to win customer confidence and create an outstanding corporate image.

To pursue these goals through TPM, administrative and support departments must define their mission by answering the following questions:

- How do we support the TPM activities of the production department and other departments?
- What issues must we address to maximize our own efficiency?

Improving the Organization and Management of Administrative and Support Departments

The function of administrative and support departments can be improved in two ways:

- Improving efficiency so each department can perform its particular function satisfactorily.
- Developing people able to sustain and continuously improve the new, more efficient system.

Figure 9-1 shows the relation between these two approaches.

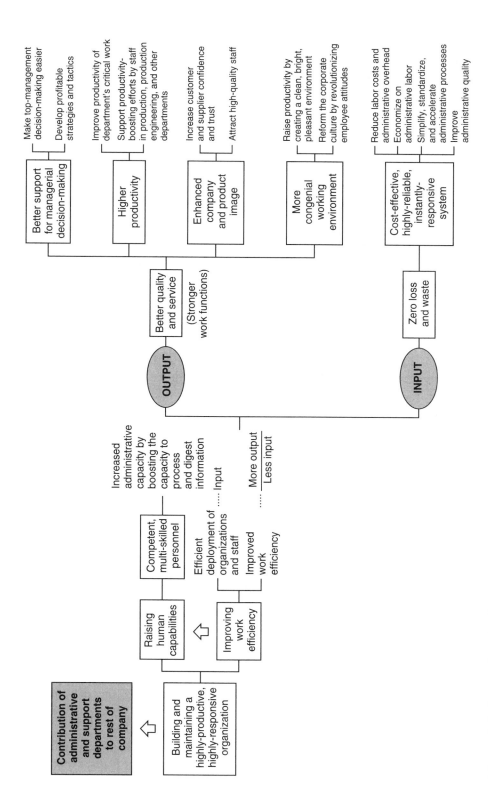

Figure 9-1. Improving the Organization and Management of Administrative and Support Departments

Improving efficiency means boosting output while reducing input. Boosting output means eliminating anything that reduces production-system efficiency to enhance work functions and raise their effectiveness. Reducing input means eliminating administrative losses associated with the work and creating a cost-effective administrative system able to provide high-quality, timely, and reliable information.

These are the ostensible goals of improving the organization and management of administrative and support departments. An even more fundamental goal is to use the activities to develop administrators who are extremely effective at processing information.

Each company must tackle this challenge differently, however. A firm's present and future problems and needs depend on its type, scale, management history, present circumstances, and business environment. Each company must work out the best approach for its own situation.

Figure 9-2 outlines the various losses that impair administrative efficiency. In this figure, a *work function* is a particular task. For example, two work functions of shipping are checking and allocating stock. *Administrative functions* are tasks required to ensure the work is processed accurately. In shipping, this might include checking stock ledgers and making entries. In general, administrative functions have three aspects: decision-making, communication, and data processing.

IMPLEMENTING TPM IN ADMINISTRATIVE AND SUPPORT DEPARTMENTS

Information from departments such as engineering and administration triggers action in the production department. The quality, accuracy, and timing of this information, therefore, profoundly affect what the production department does.

How this information is handled is the main concern of TPM in administrative and support departments. In TPM the work in such departments is treated as analogous to a production process, (i.e., as the manufacture of information), with administrative procedures viewed as counterparts of production equipment.

The approach described below systematizes the experiences of many companies that have implemented TPM in their administrative and support departments. The main elements, elaborated later, are:

- Begin with the concept of creating "information factories."
- Apply the equipment approach to administrative and support work.
- Create a vision of what each department should be like (i.e., its optimal conditions) and strive to realize this ideal.

- Implement TPM through the five core activities.
- Strive to achieve measurable results.

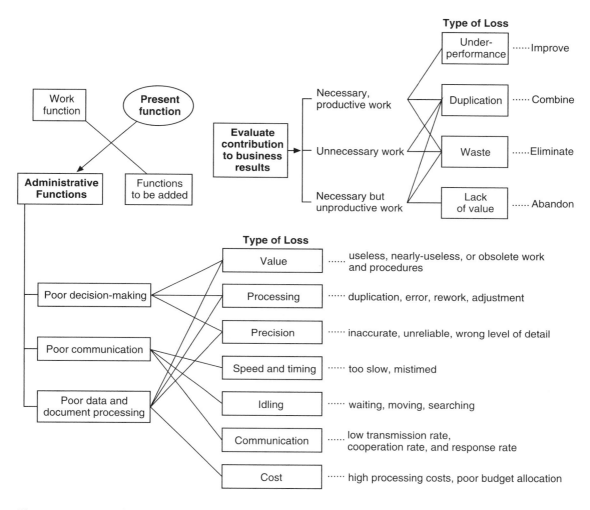

Figure 9-2. The Concept of Efficiency Losses

Create Information Factories

An administrative department manufactures information. Ideally, it takes in raw data and adds value to it by processing and compiling it. The information it provides must be high-quality, accurate, low in cost, and supplied in a form that is useful to those who need it. Good timing is equally important. To achieve this, the processes that produce the information, like production processes, must be easy to see and monitor, i.e., visible and easy to control.

Apply an Equipment Approach to Administrative Procedures

To make administrative work visible and controllable, think of administrative procedures as production equipment. When engineers study a complex machine's functional reliability, they section it into appropriately sized, functionally connected modules. In the same way, the improvement team can analyze administrative procedures functionally. Figure 9-3 summarizes the application of this approach to administrative functions.

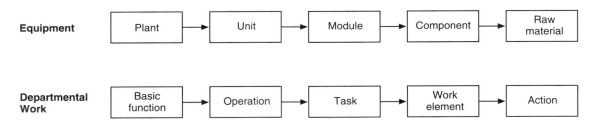

Figure 9-3. Comparison between Administrative Work and Equipment

A department's work can be divided and subdivided down to the level of discrete actions. The subdivisions at each stage are called *work units* (WU). Improvement teams can identify and investigate functions, characteristics, and workloads in terms of these work units. Figure 9-4 shows an example.

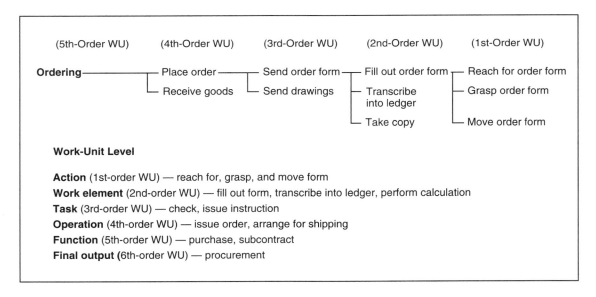

Figure 9-4. The Work Unit (WU) Concept

When defining work units, remember the following:

- Make each unit independent to avoid duplicating work measurements.
- Make units easy to understand by supervisors who must measure, plan, allocate, and organize the work.
- Make it easy to estimate the work count (the workload generated for each unit).
- Given sufficient time, ensure satisfactory reproducibility.
- Ensure that workloads can be set economically.

Envision Optimal Conditions for the Department (Vision and Mission)

The first step in breaking down a department's work into work units is clarifying the basic function of the department and its members within the overall organization. Each department has an essential function to fulfill and a specific level to attain within the total system. Applying an equipment approach means establishing optimal conditions for the administrative functions of the department that will clarify what improvement is needed and how to achieve it. A department's vision and mission must articulate these conditions.

A department's *vision* is an ideal image of its required functions, based on the nature of the company's business. Establishing a clear vision is the duty of the department's senior managers. Its *mission* is the work that it must perform in order to realize its vision. The mission establishes how the department ought to perform in order to fulfill its essential functions. A department's statement of its vision and mission, therefore, maps out the department's optimal condition or ideal state.

To formulate a department's vision and mission, investigate its basic functions in terms of the following:

- The ideal state required at present (to reliably maintain present functions)
- The ideal state required to meet future changes (as new functions evolve through innovation)

Establishing Departmental Visions and Missions

The goal of any department's TPM campaign is to bring its vision and mission into reality, and this ultimate purpose must guide all its activities. If, however, the functions of different departments do not mesh smoothly without gaps or discontinuities, various losses can arise during the production system's life cycle. These losses hamper efforts to improve the system's overall effectiveness. When promoting TPM in an administrative and support department, it is important to establish a vision and mission compatible with those of other departments.

Every department functions in concert with others. Thus, no one department can establish its vision and mission in isolation from the rest. Establish departmental visions and missions using the following procedure:

1. Invite each department to submit vision and mission proposals.
2. Integrate the proposals of all the departments and build an overall consensus.
3. Obtain the approval of top management.

In the first step, senior managers of each department must hammer out their department's vision and mission. This is done by identifying the department's essential functions (primary and secondary) and working out its current and future roles based on these. Table 9-1 illustrates the relationship between the functions and ideal state (vision and mission) of an engineering subcontracting department. The department's basic function is to eliminate impediments to the firm's production by rendering technical assistance to subcontractors.

Implementing the Five Core Activities

Develop TPM in administrative and support departments through the following five activities: focused improvement, autonomous maintenance, education and training, flexible staffing, and performance measurement. Table 9-2 provides goals and descriptions for each of the five core activities.

Focused Improvement

After establishing a vision and mission for the department, eliminate chronic losses and painstakingly pursue efficiency in all aspects of the department's existing work. Departmental work rarely takes place in a vacuum; it usually closely involves other departments as well. Start by selecting a task that affects other departments and appears likely to yield significant improvement results. Set up a team that includes managers and staff from those other departments, and initiate a focused improvement project aimed at eliminating losses.

Table 9-1. Relation Between Functions and Ideal State (Vision and Mission) in Engineering Subcontracting

VISION

- Eliminate production holdups by preventing supplier quality and delivery problems.
- Solve supplier problems at source. Help suppliers become independent by showing them how to solve quality problems by themselves.
- Gradually reduce the cost of supplier guidance as suppliers become more self-reliant. Disband the supplier support section as soon as possible.

MISSION

- Drastically reduce quality and delivery problems.
- Achieve trouble-free, rapid startup.
- Never allow a problem to recur for the same reason.
- Bolster suppliers' independence and make them self-managing.
- Transfer the section's engineers to other duties as soon as possible consistent with achieving the preceding objectives.

Primary	FUNCTIONS Secondary
Assist in solving quality problems	• Troubleshooting and follow-up • Quality checking systems • Quality systems • Inspection systems
Advise on design changes	• Construction methods • Layouts • Work methods • Inspection procedures
Expedite production	• Workload • Labor • Transport
Advise on processing technology	• Mold and jig design • Working conditions • Working methods • Process quality points
Support early management	• Startup plans • Mold and jig fabrication • Preparatory activities • First-of-run control • Troubleshooting

Table 9-2. The Five Core Activities for Administrative TPM

Mission

Improve the organization and management of administrative and support departments, strengthen their basic capabilities, and create a system able to respond to change while adhering to fundamental standards

Core Activity	Goal	Description
Increase work efficiency through focused improvement • Enhance and improve functions • Rationalize and automate administrative procedures	• Probe the work's functional value in light of departmental vision and mission statements, and create a lean administrative system by eliminating losses	Evolve in five stages based on departmental vision and mission 1. Clarify subject 2. Identify relationships and isolate problems 3. Identify and prioritize improvement topics 4. Formulate basic improvement concept 5. Implement improvement
Build a system of administrative autonomous maintenance • Administrative functions (the "soft" aspect) • Administrative environments (the "hard" aspect)	• Develop competent administrators • Create highly-efficient office environments • Develop the ability to maintain and improve functions	Implement the seven basic steps 1. Do initial cleaning and stocktaking 2. Identify and address problems 3. Tackle contamination sources 4. Prepare standards and manuals 5. Educate and train 6. Perform general inspection 7. Establish full self-management
Improve administrative capacity through education and training	• Upgrade people's grasp of the knowledge and skills they require for their work • Promote multiskilling	• Identify the knowledge and skills required to perform the department's work • Establish evaluation categories and achievement criteria • Prepare teaching materials and manuals, and train instructors • Compile training curricula • Establish training methods • Train • Evaluate achievement
Create an efficient staffing system	• Allocate staff flexibly to suit fluctuating workloads	• Divide widely fluctuating work into constant and variable elements • Estimate the load and unit processing time for the constant element, and use this to create a flexible staff allocation system
Develop a work evaluation system	• Set targets based on the department's vision and mission • Measure achievements and assess the rate of attainment of targets	• Identify performance categories for each function based on the department's vision and mission • Establish evaluation points and performance indicators for each function • Establish measurement and evaluation techniques for each function • Measure performance • Evaluate and follow up target achievement rates

Autonomous Maintenance

Autonomous maintenance, one of TPM's hallmarks, is another key to successful TPM in administrative departments. Developing a program of administrative autonomous maintenance is essential for efficient, trouble-free work execution.

Approach the design of this program from two angles: administrative function and administrative environment. The goal of the first is to reduce costs and boost work effectiveness by improving the quality of the administrative system. The aim of the second is to raise administrative efficiency by eliminating psychological and physical stress and alleviating strains on office equipment and environments. Its ultimate goal is to create environments in which people can maintain these higher efficiency levels.

Education and Training

The information revolution is changing the world at blinding speed. Developing people with superior information-processing capabilities is a vital issue for businesses. Companies that train their employees unsystematically, by having them watch others or learning by trial and error, for example, are unlikely to grow or even survive. Establish a detailed training program that covers all specializations and grades, set standards for acquiring the necessary knowledge and skills, and devise effective training curricula. Ensure that your training program adds real value to your company's human assets.

Flexible Staffing

The most effective way of raising the efficiency of administrative and support work is to be aware constantly of the relationship between work and cost. Labor costs account for the lion's share of administrative and support expenses, so effective use of human resources is a top priority. Administrative and support workloads vary over time in response to changing conditions. It is wasteful to keep an office continuously staffed with enough people to handle the peaks in work volume. Rather, adopt a system of flexible staffing, and match personnel to workloads by multiskilling and leveling fluctuations in the workload.

Performance Measurement

As part of its mission, each department must achieve certain results, some quantified, some qualitative. It must attain tangible, measurable results in the areas of cost effectiveness, functional effectiveness, and increased productivity and creativity. Adopt and track performance indicators such as problem reduction rate, cost reduction rate, lead-time reduction rate, and inventory reduction rate.

Each department must also clearly identify the relationship between overall performance and the functions and tasks expected of its various sections and subsections, and constantly measure and evaluate results. Assess a department's overall performance by the extent to which it achieves its mission within a certain time frame. Measuring the results achieved and the degree of attainment of targets linked to indicators such as those listed above reveals the direction for future activities and management priorities. Table 9-3 shows an example of performance measurement indicators for improvement in cost-effectiveness, functional efficiency, and creativity.

PROMOTING TPM IN ADMINISTRATIVE AND SUPPORT DEPARTMENTS

Figure 9-5 shows the overall structure of a system that promotes TPM in administrative and support departments.

IMPROVING FUNCTIONAL WORK

Improving a department's effectiveness requires the department to ensure that all work contributes to achieving of its mission. The approach to this goal is both quantitative and qualitative.

The quantitative approach involves decreasing the amount of nonproductive work, raising the operating rate, and increasing the amount of productive work completed per unit time. The qualitative approach involves reducing functional disharmony and increasing precision and effectiveness.

Improving Work Efficiency in Three Phases

Work efficiency is improved in three phases with administrative autonomous maintenance. (See Figure 9-6.)

Table 9-3. Measuring TPM Results

Improvement	Indicator	Examples	Measures
Cost Effectiveness	Cost reduction	Cost of consumables, inventory, communication, transport, subcontracting, etc.	Cost saving, percentage cost reduction
	Labor-cost reduction	Headcount reduction	Headcount reduction × unit labor charge (cumulation of labor-hours saved)
	Reduction of processing time and lead time	Processing time, recovery time	Time saved × unit time charge, percentage
Functional Efficiency	Improved fitness for purpose	Contribution target, e.g. trouble elimination, availability, smooth operation	Number, utility rate, achievement rate, questionnaire evaluation
	Quality improvement	Errors, rework, duplication, tightness of control, number of adjustments/changes	Number, precision, probability
	Effective human resource utilization	Number of transfers, workload increase, upgrading of knowledge and skills	Number, work processed per unit time, target achievement rate, qualifications acquired
Creativity	Environmental improvement	5S for movable equipment, fixtures/fittings, utilities	MTBF, diagnosis, maintenance implementation rate
	Workplace vitality	Number of suggestions, number and nature of circle activities	Number, frequency, and adoption rate of suggestions
	Higher morale	Attitude, speech, behavior, personal appearance, discipline	Audits, questionnaires

Phase 1: Improve System

Phase 1 is implemented in conjunction with autonomous maintenance over a period of one to two years to lay the groundwork. During this phase, focus on identifying the roles and objectives that must be met through the departments current work and on raising quality and achievement rates to acceptable levels. Goals for Phase 1 include:

- Make work more productive by investigating its functional value and eliminating losses.
- Eliminate disorder and waste from administrative functions and the administrative environment.
- Promote standardization and prepare written guidelines and specifications to create a firm foundation for office task automation.

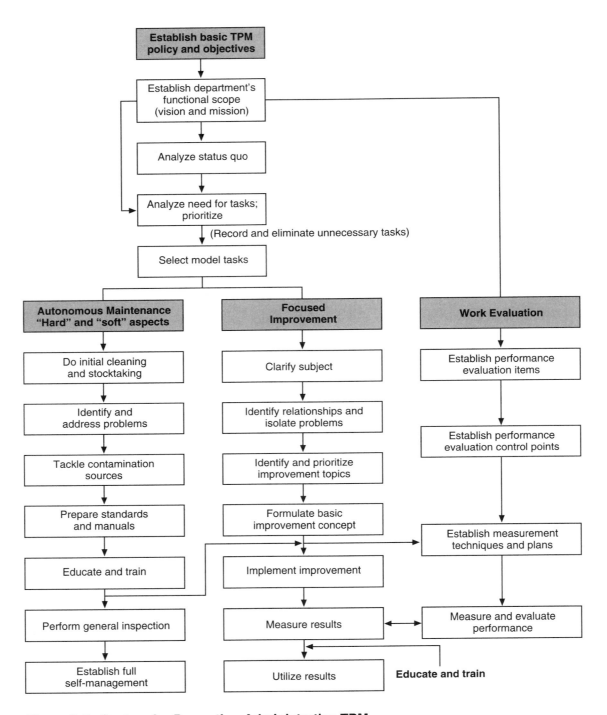

Figure 9-5. System for Promoting Administrative TPM

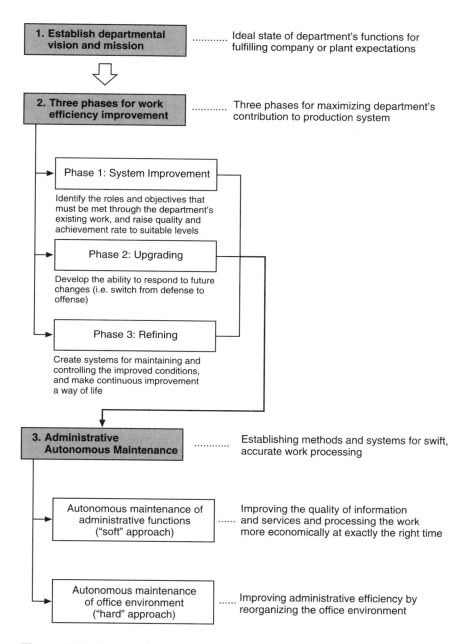

Figure 9-6. Developing the Work Function Approach

Phase 2: Upgrade System

In Phase 2, focus on developing the ability to respond to future changes. Goals for Phase 2 include:

- Review and reinforce the activities of Phase 1.
- Systematize new functions and tasks and integrate with current tasks that need overhauling.
- Review and revise systems for standardization and automation.
- Review and revise systems for performance measurement and evaluation.

Phase 3: Refine System

Design systems to maintain improved conditions at new high levels and to make continuous improvement a part of daily work. Goals for Phase 3 include:

- Review the organization and its functions.
- Establish and maintain more appropriate staffing levels.
- Establish a management-by-objectives system.
- Institutionalize performance measurement and evaluation systems.

ADMINISTRATIVE FOCUSED IMPROVEMENT

Focused improvement activity is a cross-functional project team activity designed to focus attention and expertise on critical problems for thorough as well as expedited solutions. (See Chapter 3 for a detailed discussion of this activity in the context of process and equipment problems.) Implement focused improvements in administrative and support departments in the five stages shown in Table 9-4. This section describes the key points of each stage.

Stage 1: Clarify the Subject

Study the work procedure in question in terms of its expected contribution to business results and performance. This requires a thorough understanding of how work is performed at present. Analyze the current system and determine what work is unnecessary and what work must be improved.

Table 9-4. Administrative Focused Improvement

Stage	Description	Keys
1. Clarify subject	Evaluate the work from the standpoint of its expected contribution to business results and performance	1-1 Analyze status quo • Comprehensively review the work system and workloads • Analyze workloads to understand the nature of the work 1-2 Investigate necessity of work • Assess the work's functional value • Perform a trade-off to decide which tasks are needed and which not 1-3 Assess the work • Record unnecessary tasks to provide information for improvement • Prioritize necessary tasks for improvement
2. Identify relationships and isolate problems	Clarify functional relationships between tasks, treating gaps between existing and ideal work states as a problem	2-1 Isolate problems through function deployment 2-2 Structure problems by From-To analysis
3. Identify and prioritize improvement topics	Classify topics to decide order of priority	3-1 To prioritize, examine individual topics and decide whether they are likely to yield results quickly or slowly and whether they constitute a system improvement or upgrade
4. Formulate basic improvement concept	Focus the improvement by identifying requirements, constraints, and relationships	4-1 Structure relationships between topics 4-2 Design procedure for implementing improvement 4-3 Identify requirements and constraints
5. Implement improvement	Control progress based on the implementation procedure designed in the previous step, and measure and standardize the results	5-1 Control progress of improvement 5-2 Measure and utilize results 5-3 Standardize and follow up

1. Analyze the Current System

Thoroughly review the work system and workloads. To obtain an overview, analyze the work and workloads within your department's functional domain. Use this overview as a reference point for subsequent activities. Start by investigating how work is distributed among the members of the organization. Table 9-5 is an example of a work allocation table.

Table 9-5. Work Allocation Table

Function (5th-order WU)	Section Manager	Subsection Manager	Labor Affairs Adviser	Labor Affairs Clerk
Labor Relations	Directing strategy and negotiating with labor union	Proposing strategy and negotiating with labor union	Gathering information, publishing monthly labor affairs bulletin, preparing conference materials, taking minutes	Compiling reference materials, preparing articles for labor affairs bulletin, assisting conference preparation, etc.
Government Relations	Directing and supervising negotiations with government agencies	Preparing materials for submission to government agencies, advising on negotiations with government agencies	Advising on interpretation and application of official regulations, interpretation and application of labor law, and execution of official procedures	Surveying employment conditions, applying employment and public service regulations, investigating accidents
Salaries and Budgets	Approving and managing the budget	Preparing budget proposals and operating the budget		
Salary Payment	Directing and supervising	Advising and monitoring		
Other	Directing and supervising	Advising and monitoring	Preparing daily labor reports and researching labor law	Administering safety training, organizing files, and preparing daily work reports

Based on this overview, each member of the organization uses work-unit analysis to clarify his or her current duties and workloads (the time needed to perform each task). A survey form such as that shown in Table 9-6 may be used.

Identify work characteristics at the section and subsection levels. Collate the findings from the previous survey and calculate the monthly workloads (Figure 9-7) and peaks (Figure 9-8) for each section and subsection. Together, these two diagrams show the degree of variation in monthly workloads and indicate underloaded or overloaded individuals. The point of this exercise is to identify the scope for smoothing out workload variations and distributing the work more equitably.

Measure departmental running costs. Identify the number of people in the department together with its labor costs, cost of consumables, and nonlabor administrative costs such as communication costs. Then calculate indicators such as cost per person, cost per time, or holiday-work/overtime rate, as a basis for cost-reduction activities. Table 9-7 is an example of a departmental cost analysis table.

Table 9-6. Work Survey Form

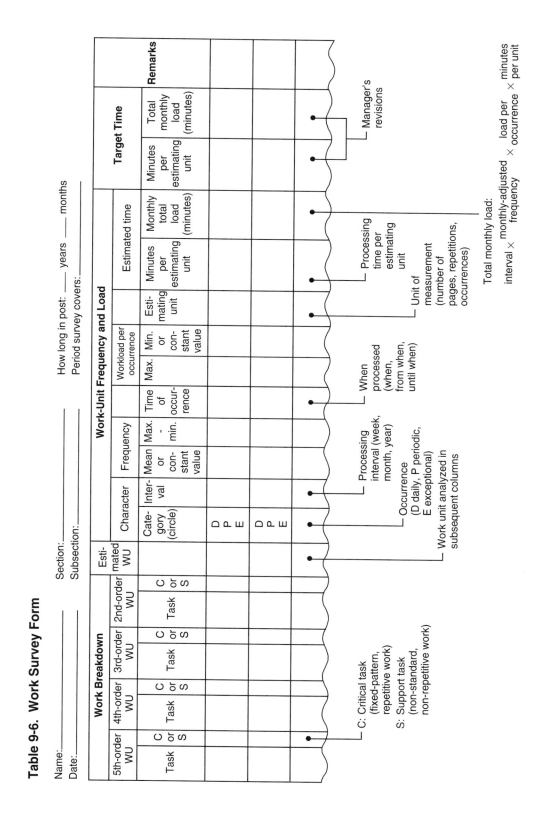

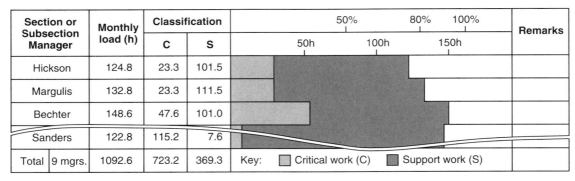

Section or Subsection Manager	Monthly load (h)	Classification		50% 80% 100%	Remarks
		C	S	50h 100h 150h	
Hickson	124.8	23.3	101.5		
Margulis	132.8	23.3	111.5		
Bechter	148.6	47.6	101.0		
Sanders	122.8	115.2	7.6		
Total 9 mgrs.	1092.6	723.2	369.3	Key: ☐ Critical work (C) ☐ Support work (S)	

Monthly availability per person = average days per month × operating hours per day
= 22 days/month × 7.5 h/day
= 165 h/person/month

$$\text{Section (subsection) operating rate} = \frac{\text{Total average monthly load per section}}{\text{Monthly availability per person}} \times \text{\# of people in section or subsection} \times 100\ (\%)$$

$$= \frac{1092.6}{1485} \times 100 = 73.6\%$$

Figure 9-7. Monthly Workload Total Chart

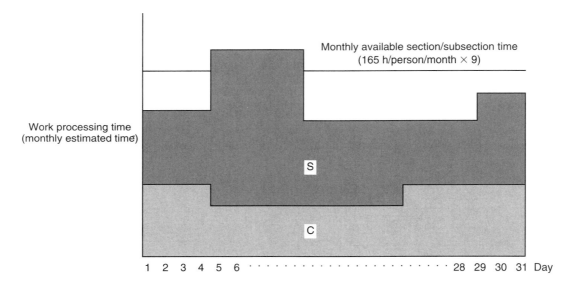

Figure 9-8. Monthly Workload Variation Chart

Table 9-7. Departmental Cost Analysis Table

Item / Date	Reference date	Actual date	+/−	Actual date	+/−	

1. Staffing
   Managers
   Workers
						(Rest omitted)

2. Labor costs
   Standard
   Non-standard
   Out-of-hours						

3. Non-labor costs
   • Maintenance costs
   • Office consumables						

4. Per-person running costs (2 + 3)						
5. Labor-cost rate $\left(\dfrac{2}{2+3}\right)$						
6. Holiday work and overtime (h)						
7. Holiday work and overtime rate						

2. Investigate the Necessity of the Work

Assess the functional value of the work. The aims of administrative work are to ensure a smooth business flow and improve the firm's operating results. In other words, work is behavior directed at accomplishing these aims. The more effective this behavior, the greater its value. Table 9-8 summarizes this thinking. Adopt this viewpoint to evaluate your department's current work, and use the results to discriminate between necessary and unnecessary tasks.

Perform work trade-off. As Figure 9-9 shows, the improvement team must subject the work to two screening stages or evaluations: first, by the department that provides the work, then by the department that receives the work. After evaluating the work, the departments must negotiate whether it is really necessary. A cooperative approach is important here, because work assessment can put people on the defensive. They may try to protect work that is not useful, that is produced to an unnecessarily high standard, or that pleases supervisors but does not fulfill the department's essential functions. Consultation between the work supplier and its customer helps to avoid such distortions and eliminates inconsistencies between the two parties' requirements.

Table 9-8. Assessing the Functional Value of Work

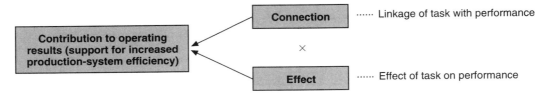

Assessing functional value: Effective work has a significant impact on the production system.
Assess this in terms of what would happen if the work were stopped.

Relation to Performance	Rank	Item evaluated
Criteria	1	• Essential to corporate competitiveness and position in society • Inevitably accompanies business activities • Should be stopped, but impossible to do so at present
	2	• Probably necessary • Might cause problems if stopped • Would cause inconvenience if stopped
	3	• Could be stopped without any problem • Irrelevant • Could be stopped on orders from above
Effect	a	• Immediate effect • Gradual effect
	b	• Probable effect • Long-term effect
	c	• Irrelevant • Done for convenience; has no direct effect on performance

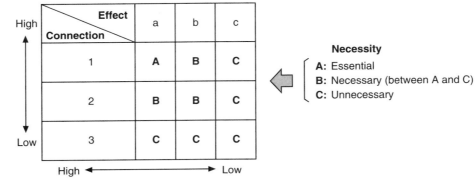

Functional Value Assessment Matrix

Effect / Connection	a	b	c
1	A	B	C
2	B	B	C
3	C	C	C

High ↕ Low (Connection)
High ← → Low (Effect)

Necessity
A: Essential
B: Necessary (between A and C)
C: Unnecessary

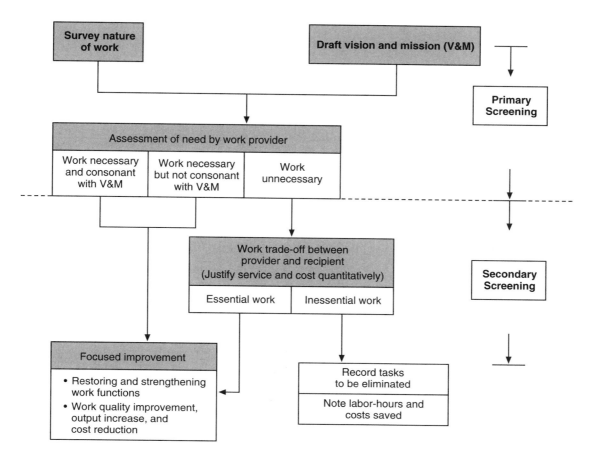

Figure 9-9. The Work Trade-Off Approach

The purpose of this trade-off is to assess the functional value (both quantitative and qualitative) of the department's present work and reach the best compromise between the value of providing each service to a realistic standard and its cost.

Following the procedure illustrated in Figure 9-9, assess your department's work and trade-off with the department that receives the work. Table 9-9 lists the necessary tasks that remained after such a trade-off.

Table 9-9. Table of Necessary Tasks

Section: Purchasing   Subsection: Volume-Production

(5th-order WU) Function	Vision	Mission	4th-order WU	Rank	3rd-order WU	Rank	Key Control Point	Time required per month Now Max.	Time required per month Now Min.	After improvement	Remarks
Cost control (of purchased items)	I Purchase by competitive tender from at least three companies (where possible, avoid purchasing from nominated suppliers)	1. Gather market information on functions, products, prices, suppliers, characteristics, etc., and organize it more effectively									
		2. Prepare and apply clear supplier selection criteria to expedite prototype fabrication and development									
		3. Make purchasing more effective by establishing basic standards for evaluating competitive tenders	1. Prepare a purchasing plan	A	1-1 Investigate costs	A	Calculate appropriate cost	1,550	570		
					1-2 Investigate capacity	A	Assess supplier capacity	1,350	490		
					1-3 Investigate quality	A	Obtain quality information	850	290		
		4. Promote cost control by monitoring the cost history of designated articles	2. Control purchasing records	A	2-1 Prepare a table of outstanding credit purchases	A	Assess purchasing performance	120	120		
					2-2 Prepare a distribution table	A	Assess distribution performance	5	5		
					2-3 Check details of miscalculations	A	Discover causes of miscalculation	60	40		
					2-4 Check purchase orders	A	Check parts number	3,000	2,500		
	II Create a global purchasing system that includes overseas sourcing	1. Set clear standards for purchased items	3. Prepare a unit-price schedule	A	3-1 Check schedule	A	Check details of errors	2,500	5		
					3-2 Check revisions to schedule	A	Identify components, distribution, and unit prices	400	40		

3. Assess the Work

Record and use the details of unnecessary tasks. When you eliminate the unnecessary tasks that the trade-off procedure identifies, be sure to record the cost reductions and labor hours saved. Note them down immediately and use this information for reducing holiday and overtime work and smoothing out workload variations. Table 9-10 is an example of a record sheet used for this purpose.

Prioritize the necessary tasks that need improvement. Once you eliminate the unnecessary tasks, only the necessary ones remain. Attempting to improve them all at once, however, invites failure. Prioritize these improvements by taking into account the effect each task has on other departments. Give the highest priority to those that appear likely to yield the best results in the shortest time. In Stage 2 these prioritized tasks are actually improved.

Stage 2: Identify Relationships and Isolate Problems

Begin this stage by clarifying the functional relationships between each task under consideration and its related tasks. For example, Table 9-11 shows the visions and missions of various departments in relation to the task of cost control.

Isolate Problems through Function Deployment

To understand how to improve the efficiency of a particular type of work, study the work's mission and consider how to fulfill it. Specifically, quantify the gap between the work's current level and its ideal state, then treat this gap as the problem to solve. Use a function deployment analysis table such as Table 9-12.

Perform From-To analysis. A department by itself, cannot solve all the problems the previous step identifies. The solutions lie in connections with other work functions. For example, the sales department cannot speed up its estimating work without the cooperation of departments such as engineering and production management. Use From-To analysis to analyze problems that occur at the interfaces between your own department and other departments. *From* represents a connection with a previous process and *To* a connection with a next process, or customer. Table 9-13 is an example of a From-To analysis table.

Table 9-10. Record of Results

Control #	Operation (4th-order WU)	Task (3rd-order WU)	Final Trade-off (Details)	Type of trade-off result (circle)							Total Monthly Savings		Date Recorded and Measured
				Meeting	Distri-bution	Report	Advice	Document Data	Nego-tiation	Decision	Labor-hours	Cost	

(Identify results by department and task)

Office-Cost Record Table

Function: _____ Department: _____

Current Task				Monthly labor-hours reduction	Monthly Cost Saving					Improvement Focus							
										Improve task mechanism, method, or means							
Mem-bers	WU	Task	Load (processing labor-hours)		Labor costs	Com-muni-cation	Travel and trans-port	Printing	Abolish task	Sim-plify	Save labor	Improve timing	Stan-dardize	Accel-erate	Amal-gamate	Correct	Dele-gate

Table 9-11. Cost Control Visions and Missions

Department	Vision	Mission
Planning	Build a system for supplying the right information at the right time to managers and other departments. Prepare for the future.	• Compare final selling prices with estimates. Analyze and evaluate overall profit for each series of models. • Analyze differences between selling prices and unit purchasing costs. Set target costs and inform relevant departments.
Sales	Accelerate and improve the efficiency of estimating work by rationalizing the estimation tasks arising at each product development stage.	• Standardize calculations by setting the specification level (depth, detail) and method of calculation for each product development stage and factor estimated. • Establish internal regulations for cost calculation criteria and methods. Build a system for evaluating conformity.
Purchasing	Construct a system for enabling cost calculations to be performed more quickly, easily, and accurately.	
Production Control		
Engineering		**Creating the "ideal situation"** Build a system that permits the timely supply of needed cost data to relevant departments. To do this, improve the reliability and productivity of the entire estimating task by clarifying, simplifying, and standardizing the criteria for calculating estimated costs.

Table 9-12. Function Deployment Analysis Table

1st-order Function (5-4th-order WU)		2nd-order Function (4-3rd-order WU)	Ideal State (mission)	Current Existing Work Level	Need	Problems and Losses	Relation among Problem Causes					
							Organization	People	Systems	Methods	Means	Locations

Table 9-13. Speeding Up Estimating by From-To Analysis

From To	Sales	Production Control	Engineering
Sales	(Aim to rationalize estimation at each product development stage) • Preparing estimates take too long and often inconveniences customers	• Processes and process sequences change frequently between the development and trial production stages • Obsolete cost tables • Inaccurate cost tables	• Product and parts drawings submitted late
Production Control	• Competitors' cost data not sought	• Finalizing processes and process sequences takes too long (due to lack of staff)	• Drawings finalized too late • Too many drawing changes
Engineering	• Customers' opinions and wishes communicated late and inaccurately • Final negotiations with customers too imprecise		

Stage 3: Identify and Prioritize Improvement Topics

As mentioned, departmental improvement topics are always related to other tasks and departmental functions. Therefore you should not approach improvements unilaterally nor regard them simply as optimal solutions for a particular department. Try to achieve the best result for the overall system. Table 9-14 is a table of prioritized improvement topics showing their relationships with other departments.

Each improvement project has its own particular character. Some can yield quick results, while others take longer. Some address current difficulties, while others are future-oriented. Good progress is far more likely if improvement topics are classified and prioritized by a scheme such as that illustrated in Table 9-15.

Table 9-14. Improvement Topic Relationship Table

Function	Vision	Mission (or 4th-order WU)	Present Problems	Improvement Topics	Rank	Type of Improvement
Purchasing/ subcontracting	• Energetic cost reduction	1. Review annual plans and identify cost-reduction priorities (topics, targets, etc.) 2. Create a system for planning cost reductions and evaluating results • Make cost calculation work faster, easier, and more accurate • Rationalize price-setting by identifying suppliers' cost margins 3. Review VA and VE proposal systems and make quantitative use of them (make consideration of VA and VE proposals mandatory when determining purchase prices)	★ Cost reduction is difficult because of insufficient grounds for requesting discounts during negotiations with suppliers ★ The evaluation system has been reviewed, but there is considerable variation in VA and VE proposals received from suppliers	☆ Clarify and enforce cost targets ☆ Repromote evaluation system	4 4	Production engineering and production control (in-house and outside) In-house and outside
	• Build a system for faster, easier, and more accurate cost calculation	1. Prepare cost tables • Make pricing decisions efficiently 2. Establish a system for updating cost tables 3. Standardize the establishment of cost calculation criteria and techniques	★ Cost calculation criteria are unclear, making independent pricing impossible	☆ Prepare item-ized cost tables (obtain unit consumption figures) and use them routinely	9	Production control Production engineering Planning Sales Development
Order/Delivery Control (subcontractors)	• Eliminate problems before they reach the production line by establishing a control system able to cope with startup, sharp production increases, and other delivery variations	1. Establish a system able to accurately gauge suppliers' capacities (production capacity, control capability, and processing characteristics)	★ Trouble occurs during production because suppliers' long-term capabilities have not been clearly identified	☆ Establish unified capacity appraisal criteria	1	Manufacturers Development Production engineering Sales Computing Production control
Purchasing/ Subcontracting		1. Review and improve ordering system	★ Because the number of rolls required is not known	☆ Establish a system for identifying the number of rolls required	2	Manufacturers Computing

Table 9-15. Prioritizing Improvement Topics

Nature of Topic

Type \ Appearance of effects	a Immediate	b Delayed
A System-improvement	A • a	A • b
B Upgrading	B • a	B • b

Topic Priority

1. A • a
2. B • a
3. A • b
4. B • b

Stage 4: Formulate a Basic Improvement Concept

Focus the improvement by identifying requirements, constraints, and relationships among the elements of the improvement.

Plot the relationships among the elements of the improvement topic. Table 9-16 shows an example of a chart that depicts the relationships among the various elements of an improvement topic.

Devise a procedure for implementing improvement. To implement an improvement, establish the main approach routes and map out the required tasks sequentially. Use a chart like that shown in Figure 9-10 to control the progress of the improvement. Such charts are indispensable tools for expediting and controlling improvement projects. In this example, the two main approaches to improving estimating precision are: "Investigate Estimating Methods" and "Systematize Estimating Data."

Identify requirements and constraints. Identify conditions and requirements for carrying out the improvement project as follows:

- External constraints
- Internal constraints
- Topic requirements
- Required system characteristics
- Control points to incorporate
- Intended effects and tolerances
- Connection with other topics (caveats)

Figure 9-11 shows an example of an improvement procedure based on these considerations.

Table 9-16. Improvement Topic Structure Chart

	Resp. Section	①② 3 4 5 6 7 ⑧⑨ 10 11 12 13 14 ⑮⑯ 17
• Improve sewing/cutting labor-hours tables	Production Control	Process analysis
• Establish standard labor charges	Planning	Collect garment-industry data

• Improve sewing method chart • Improve assembly process • Improve manufacturers' estimating forms		1 2 3 4 5 ⑥⑦ 8 9 10 11 12 ⑬⑭ 15 16 17 18 19 ⑳㉑ 22
• Improve standard estimation	Analysis	Compare with present labor-hours table
• Improve material width tables	Collate data	Collate results
		Prepare table of standard charges
• Lamination	Prepare and use lamination tables	Improve assembly process charts
		Improve manufacturers' estimating forms
• Pattern estimating		○○ Improve cutting-out estimating forms
• Auxiliary materials	Investigate materials use	Prepare and implement standard tables
• Layout		Prepare standard tables
• Improve patterns		
• Improve exploded diagrams		
• Improve and computerize materials layout diagrams		
• Improve samples	Development	

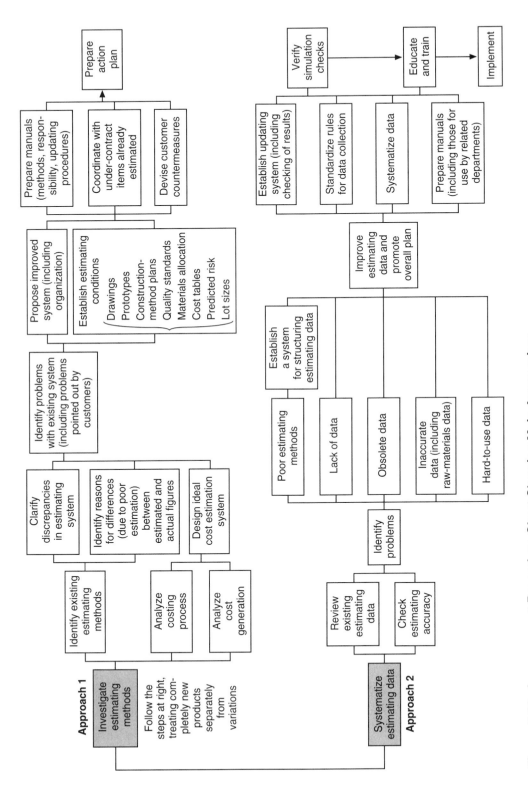

Figure 9-10. Improvement Procedure Chart Showing Main Approaches

Document/drawing: Layout diagram

Purpose: For calculating material costs, pattern costs, and cutting-out costs.

Contents: Decide optimal layout based on pattern. Calculate length of material required and length of perimeter of each part per unit.

Preparation:

1. Receive pattern and exploded diagram from prototype group.
2. Input into CAD system based on pattern, exploded diagram, and material width table, and prepare layout diagram.
3. Return pattern to prototype group, and file material width table with production engineering group.
4. Make two copies each of layout diagram and exploded diagram.
5. File original exploded diagram and layout diagram with production engineering group.
6. Send layout diagram and exploded diagram copies to sales and purchasing (1 set each).

FLOW CHART

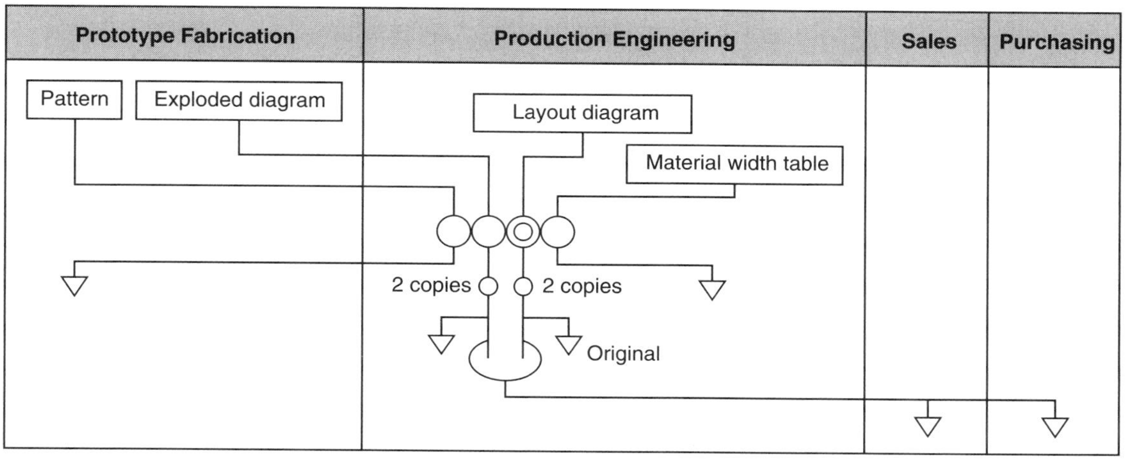

Schedule	Month	7	8	9
Introduce CAD		→7/9		
Train		→7/20		
Formulate improvement proposals		→8/11		
Explain			8/14	
Finalize and implement			8/17→	

BENEFITS

1. Document movements are simpler
2. Less sales-section labor is required
3. CAD makes information transmission more accurate
4. Preparing estimating data takes less work
5. Preparation time has dropped from 31 to 17 hours (a reduction of 14 hours, or 45%)

Figure 9-11. Setting Improvement Topic Conditions and Requirements

Stage 5: Implement Improvement

As the preceding discussion implies, improving work efficiency means solving problems by making full use of the best available techniques, such as work analysis, administrative flow-chart analysis, work-function analysis, value engineering (VE), and industrial engineering (IE), as well as one's own original techniques. Figure 9-12 illustrates how using these tools resulted in an improved estimating procedure.

ADMINISTRATIVE AUTONOMOUS MAINTENANCE

Administrative autonomous maintenance addresses both administrative functions and administrative environments with the following goals:

- Eliminating all losses and problems from administrative procedures
- Creating a working environment that permits efficient administration
- Building a system for maintaining improved efficiency levels and raising them even higher

The administrative-function ("soft") approach focuses on improving work allocation, administrative procedures, and tasks such as visitor reception. Many of the methods and procedures detailed earlier for administrative focused improvement activity are appropriate here. The administrative-environment ("hard") approach, on the other hand, improves office layouts and equipment (computers, copiers, desks, lockers, etc.) so people can work at peak psychological and physical efficiency. From this perspective, the autonomous maintenance steps and 5S principles implemented on the plant floor are easily translated to the office environment

The 5S's are the foundation of workplace management. Administrative autonomous maintenance integrates each of these principles in step-by-step improvement activities:

- Sort — eliminate the unnecessary
- Stabilize — establish permanent locations for the essential
- Shine — find ways to keep things clean and inspect through cleaning
- Standardize — make adherence easy
- Sustain — self-discipline

Table 9-17 details the steps to follow to establish an administrative autonomous maintenance program for both administrative functions and environment. It is important to proceed step by step to ensure that program goals do not degenerate into mere window dressing. Take one step at a time, master

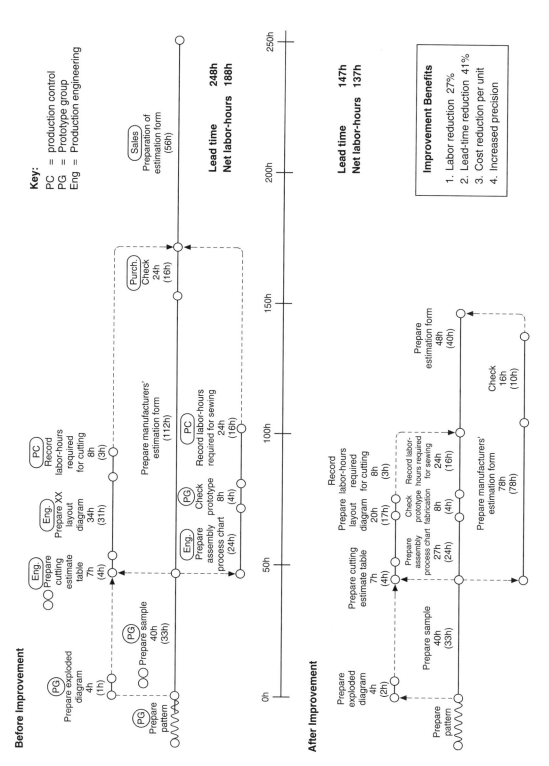

Figure 9-12. Estimation Work Before and After Improvement

it completely, and pass the official audit before proceeding to the next step. It is also far more effective to engage the creativity and involvement of everyone working in the area, rather than leaving improvements up to a small group of staff with specialize skills.

Table 9-17. Seven Steps for Developing Administrative Autonomous Maintenance

Step	Improving Administrative Environment	Improving Administrative Functions
1. Do initial cleaning and stocktaking	Eliminate unneeded items from offices and communal facilities, and eliminate all dust and dirt • Environment: Check temperature, humidity, ventilation, natural and artificial lighting, soundproofing, etc. • Location/object/layout: Clean, check, and rearrange desks, tables, office machines, filing cabinets, toilets, etc.	Use the work function approach to identify administrative scope, function, purpose, and effect. Review means and methods. • Review work flow, allocation of responsibility, processes, labor-hours, and costs, and analyze administrative flow charts and filing systems • Analyze forms, documents, and reference materials. Review filing and storage
2. Identify and address problems	Identify and correct hidden defects, deficiencies, and losses (Look for hidden, overlooked, and unnoticed faults, and defects disguised by dirt and trash) Examples: • Local "cold spots," noisy air conditioners • Poorly positioned office equipment, wrong-height chairs, poor operation, breakdowns • Poor illumination and ventilation, unsuitable color schemes • Mismatched furniture and equipment, poor passage layouts • Damaged and stained floors and walls	Thoroughly investigate losses. Identify and rectify problems associated with administrative functions and tasks. — Conformance to objectives — Work organization and allocation — Assignment of labor-hours and costs — Setup and other procedures — Documents, forms, and other means of communication — Information accuracy, preparation time, and timing
3. Tackle contamination sources	Eliminate sources of trash, dirt, and losses. Make hard-to-inspect places more accessible. Reduce the number of places that must be cleaned and checked, and shorten the time required. Eliminate losses at source.	Remove obstacles to improvement by examining relationships among mechanisms, methods, allocation of responsibility, and timing. Maintain system quality and reliability. Prevent backsliding.
4. Prepare standards and manuals	Formulate action standards that allow reliable cleaning, checking, and loss prevention.	Standardize administrative procedures and rules, and prepare office manuals.
5. Educate and train	• Compile training curricula by reviewing and systematizing the necessary knowledge and skills. Implement and follow up the training program, and constantly upgrade it by researching better training methods.	
6. Perform general inspection	• Use checking manuals to give training in checking skills. Identify and eliminate causes of deficiencies through general inspection. • Enhance visual control • Review and enhance systems, and prepare final standards and manuals. Promote office technology.	
7. Establish full self-management	• Increase administrative performance and efficiency through improvements tackled on employees' own initiative. • Maintain and improve visual control.	

Table 9-18 shows an example of the application of this process to filing. Table 9-19 illustrates the procedure for auditing and evaluating each step. This example details the points to check when you audit the first step (initial cleaning) of an autonomous maintenance program for improving the work environment.

Table 9-18. Autonomous Maintenance of Filing System

Step	Activity	Key Point

1. Do initial cleaning and stocktaking	• Remove dirt and dust from around tables, lockers, and cabinets. Abolish unnecessary items and personal articles
	• Eliminate unnecessary forms, documents, etc., and measure quantities abolished
	• Record details of remaining documents on a filing survey table
	• Sort forms and documents by fiscal year and reference materials and drawings by type. Decide on storage locations, and store temporarily
		Survey status quo (establish benchmarks)
		(1) Note types and quantities of furniture (desks, tables, general-purpose cabinets, filing cabinets, bookshelves, drawing cabinets, etc.)
		(2) Note types and quantities of files (binders, envelopes, folders, letters, bound volumes, etc.)
		(3) Record quantities of documents and reference materials scrapped
		(4) Take dated photographs
		(5) Sort files and store temporarily:
		  • Current financial year — desk drawer or filing cabinet
		  • Previous financial year — filing cabinet or cupboard
		  • Earlier years — records room or storage center

2. Identify and address problems	• Pinpoint and tackle problems with organizing, retrieving, and using filed data	• Pinpoint and tackle problems with file formats, storage locations, control methods, storage periods, allocation of responsibility, etc.
3. Tackle contamination sources	• Investigate effectiveness and usefulness of documents and data, and take necessary action	• Investigate and address why files are created, how long they are kept, what would happen if they were abolished, what problems occur with their use, and whether they need to be made communal. Do this for your own and other departments (i.e. your customers).
4. Prepare temporary standards and manuals	• Perform filing • Prepare provisional filing standards, specifications, and usage manuals	• Devise effective file indexes, organization/storage formats, and information retrieval guides • Establish a filing-clerk system
5. Perform general inspection	• Identify and address problems and causes of lost files, based on provisional filing standards, specifications, and usage manuals • Promote communal use and centralized control	• Perform checks using checksheets • Enhance visual control • Automate information retrieval • Review provisional filing manuals and establish final standards
6. Establish full self-management	• Maintain and control • Standardize and institutionalize improvements	• Maintain and constantly improve an uncluttered, easily-understood filing and storage environment • Maintain easily-retrieved and returned files • Identify and address problems on own initiative

Table 9-19. Initial Cleaning Audit Procedure

Audit Item	Key Points	Assessment Procedure
1. Individual lockers and desks (inside and out)	• Free of trash, dust, dirt, and graffiti • Free of slack, play, and dents	Are top surfaces clear? • (Check for dust by stroking surfaces with a bare hand.) • Any dirt or cleaning residue on the floor? • Are lockers labeled? • Do keys work? • Any graffiti? • Are lockers and desks steady?
	• Free of unnecessary objects • Free of spare office supplies • Tidy and well-organized	• Has the group decided what items are not needed? • Has the group decided which office supplies will be individual or and which communal? Is this documented? • Are individual desk drawers tidy and well-organized? • Are business-card holders indexed? • Are files and other documents clearly labeled?
2. Filing cabinets, forms, and documents	• Free of trash, dust, dirt, and graffiti • Free of slack, play, and dents	• Are any cleaning residues around the base? • Is a list of contents displayed clearly inside or outside? • Are cabinets steady?
	• Have all unnecessary objects been removed? • Are documents filed correctly? • Are files tidy and well-organized? • Do any forms or documents remain unused for long periods?	• Has the group agreed on unnecessary items? • Has the group decided on correct filing methods? • Are files and other documents clearly labeled? • Has the storage procedure for each type of file been decided, and is it being followed?
3. Equipment, fixtures, and fittings (including computers, telephones, etc.)	• Free of trash, dust, and dirt?	See Item 1
	• Has permanent positions been decided? • Are items where they belong? Are they accurately positioned and aligned?	• Has placement of communal equipment items been decided, and are they clearly labeled? • When they are borrowed for long periods, is the name of the borrower displayed?

Note:

☆ When auditing tidiness and organization, open everything including individual desk drawers.

☆ Listen to group members as well as the group leader.

☆ When the group is discussing initial cleaning, note whether they remember where they are heading with the subsequent steps of the autonomous maintenance program.

4. Surroundings	• Are floors, walls, panels, and skirting boards free of trash, dust, and dirt? • Are storage-areas clear and uncluttered? • Are concealed areas also clean (above, below, behind, back surface)?	• Are corners of the room clean? • Are areas around copiers and other office equipment clean? • Are kitchens and other communal areas clean? • Are window frames, sashes, and window panes clean (interior only)?
	• Are emergency exits clear? • Are regularly-used passageways clear? • Are fire extinguishers in their designated places?	• Are passageways at least 800 mm wide and 2 m high? • Are passageways free of piping and wiring? • If any pipes or wires do cross passageways, are they properly bridged? • Are fire-extinguisher notices clearly visible from inside the room?
5. Inaccessible areas and contamination sources	• Is there a plan for dealing with hard-to-clean places? • Is there a plan for dealing with hard-to-eliminate unnecessary items?	• Has the group discussed and planned countermeasures? • Has the group discussed and decided on the disposal of unnecessary items?
	• Has a system for maintaining tidiness and good order been established? • Have countermeasures been devised to prevent backsliding?	• Is this a temporary show of cleanliness put on specially for the audit? • Has the group thoroughly discussed and agreed on measures to prevent backsliding?

Evaluation Level	2 Points	4 Points	6 Points	8 Points	10 Points
Things	Hardly done at all	Done in visible places only	Also done in some concealed places	Done in visible and concealed places	Thorough cleaning and checking; some improvements commenced
People	Everyone apathetic	Done by group leader only	Group members active in some simple areas	Almost all group members active	Duties clearly allocated and carried out

Note:

While the evaluation considers both things and people, full participation is the key, so give more weight to the people aspect when scoring. For example:

(1) things: 10 points
     people: $\underline{4 \text{ points}}$
     score: $\overline{(10 + 4)}/2 = 7 \rightarrow 6$ points

(2) things: 4 points
     people: $\underline{10 \text{ points}}$
     score: $\overline{(4 + 10)}/2 = 7 \rightarrow 8$ points

REFERENCES

T. Suzuki. *New Directions for TPM.* Portland, Ore.: Productivity Press, 1992.

S. Murakami. *Deciding Factors for Organizational Reform* (in Japanese). Tokyo: Japan Management Association, n.d.

H. Oda. *Performance Measurement and Evaluation in Administrative and Support Departments* (in Japanese). Tokyo: Japan Management Association, n.d.

S. Takahara. *Office Management* (in Japanese). Tokyo: Hitotsubashi Shuppan, n.d.

Japan Institute of Plant Maintenance. *Administrative Efficiency* (seminar text in Japanese). Tokyo: Japan Institute of Plant Maintenance, n.d.

1989 Digest of PM Prizewinners. Acceptance Reports (proceedings in Japanese). Tokyo: Japan Institute of Plant Maintenance, 1989.

Japan Management Association, ed., *Office Improvement* (course text in Japanese). Tokyo: Japan Management Association, n.d.

10
Building a Safe,
Environmentally Friendly System

Eliminating accidents and pollution is a mandatory requirement for winning the PM prize in Japan. The safety records of prize-winning operations are, in fact, significantly better than before they introduced TPM. Review your own safety and environmental management system at the end of the TPM implementation phase, and establish an environment that permanently maintains the improved safety record. Your goal must be zero accidents and pollution.

TPM AND SAFETY AND ENVIRONMENT MANAGEMENT

Ensuring equipment reliability, preventing human error, and eliminating accidents and pollution are basic tenets of TPM. This is why safety and environmental management is a key activity in any TPM development program. Fully implementing TPM improves safety in many ways, for example:

- Faulty equipment is a common danger source, so zero-failure, zero-defect campaigns also improve safety.
- Thorough application of 5S principles (as part of autonomous maintenance) eliminates leaks and spills and makes workplaces clean, tidy, and well-organized.
- Autonomous maintenance and focused improvements eliminate unsafe areas.
- TPM-trained operators look after their own equipment and are better able to detect abnormalities early and deal with them promptly.
- Operation of equipment and processes by unqualified people ceases.

323

    • Operators take responsibility for their own health and safety.
    • Standards and regulations developed in a TPM program are adhered to more thoroughly.

Practicing TPM builds safety into the work. It also contributes greatly to a healthy, hospitable working environment. Figure 10-1 shows how one company (Japan Cable Systems) worked to improve both productivity and safety simply by practicing five of the eight TPM core activities.

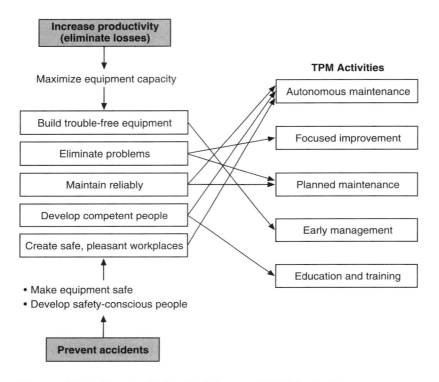

Figure 10-1. Productivity, Safety, and TPM Activities

ZERO ACCIDENTS AND ZERO POLLUTION

Perfect safety and environmental cleanliness are basic manufacturing requirements. In practice, however, there is always a possibility of plant or equipment causing accidents and pollution. The potential for disaster is always present, even in a plant with a perfect safety record.

Causes of Accidents and Pollution in Plants

Plants that handle large quantities of flammable, explosive, or toxic materials, use high pressure gases, consume large amounts of energy, or operate under other extreme conditions are particularly at risk. The danger of fire and explosion is ever-present, and accidents may affect the surroundings as well as the plant itself. Pollution due to in-plant accidents or process problems is also highly undesirable, since it can harm local environments and communities. Eliminate these risks by taking the same approach that you take to improve safety.

Since major accidents and disasters are so rare, zero-accident momentum is easily dissipated. Stay alert for blind spots, and remember the following two points:

- A tiny defect or problem can develop into a serious accident or pollution incident, so focus daily zero-failure activities toward zero accidents and zero pollution as well.
- A company may neglect safety and environmental considerations to increase competitiveness, particularly by reducing costs. Over-enthusiastic cost-cutting can lead directly to accidents and forcibly remind us to put safety first. No company wants that kind of reminder.

Attack and Defense

To minimize the possibility of accidents and pollution, develop people who know their equipment intimately and are consistently safety-conscious. Begin by ensuring that everyone understands the importance of establishing, implementing, and constantly improving the safety and environmental management system. Adopt a two-pronged strategy: Actively attack — by taking steps to minimize the possibility of accidents and pollution. At the same time, defend — by creating a reliable damage-limitation procedure for accidents or pollution incidents that do occur.

KEY STRATEGIES FOR ELIMINATING ACCIDENTS AND POLLUTION

A production plant is a vast human-machine complex. To eliminate accidents and pollution, take specific steps to strengthen the organization and management of both people and equipment. Build a companywide management system that can support, promote, and direct the creation of safe, pollution-free, hospitable workplaces.

Two factors help people acquire a zero-accident, zero-pollution mindset — daily practice as part of workplace and materials management on the plant floor and strong, visible companywide support. There are limits to what can be accomplished if plant personnel are always entirely responsible for preventing accidents and pollution. Plant personnel and staff must understand each other and work together effectively. Figure 10-2 illustrates a system designed to eliminate accidents and pollution.

STEP-BY-STEP PROCEDURE FOR ELIMINATING ACCIDENTS AND POLLUTION

The specific strategies listed in Figure 10-2 will be discussed later. Most are based on common sense, and every workplace probably implements them to some degree. In practice, however, strategies often fall short of desired results. Accidents and pollution still dog many workplaces, and safety activities are often meaningless rituals. This happens when activities are unsystematic, sporadic, and not properly institutionalized.

Figure 10-3 is a model of a three-year plan for reviewing safety as an integral part of a TPM development program. This company implemented safety activities as part of their autonomous maintenance and planned maintenance programs. Because accidents and pollution originate in the workplace, the program designers determined that an effective safety and environmental management program should start with a step-by-step development plan based on the workplace and the actual objects and materials in it. All employees participate in the activities, which are promoted and enhanced through self-audits and senior-management audits.

Although safety and environment management are comprehensively reviewed in Step 11 of the new TPM development program (after full implementation), safety awareness needs time to sink in. It is important to begin addressing it from the preparation phase. (See Figure 10-3.)

Promoting Safety Awareness in Conjunction with Autonomous Maintenance

In the first autonomous maintenance step, operators clean working equipment and stationary equipment. Because they probably have not done this before, it entails considerable risk of injury. These risks can be lessened if the following steps are taken at the outset:

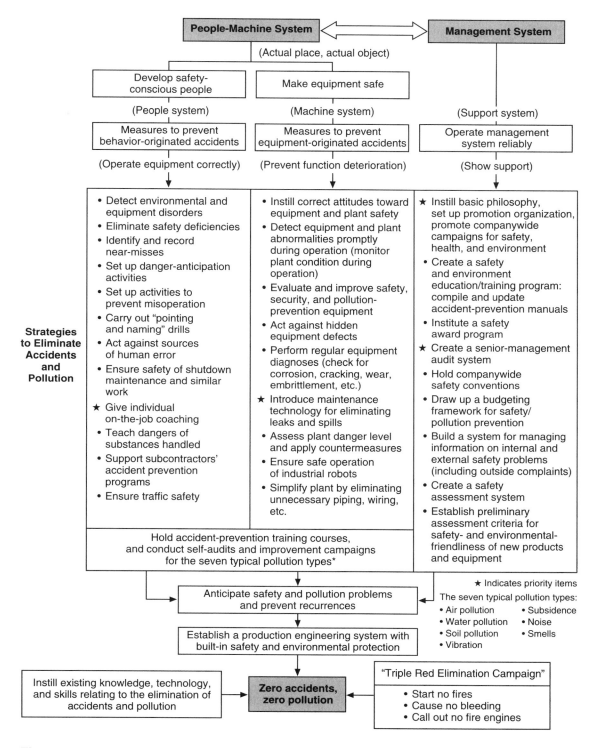

Figure 10-2. System of Activities for Eliminating Accidents and Pollution

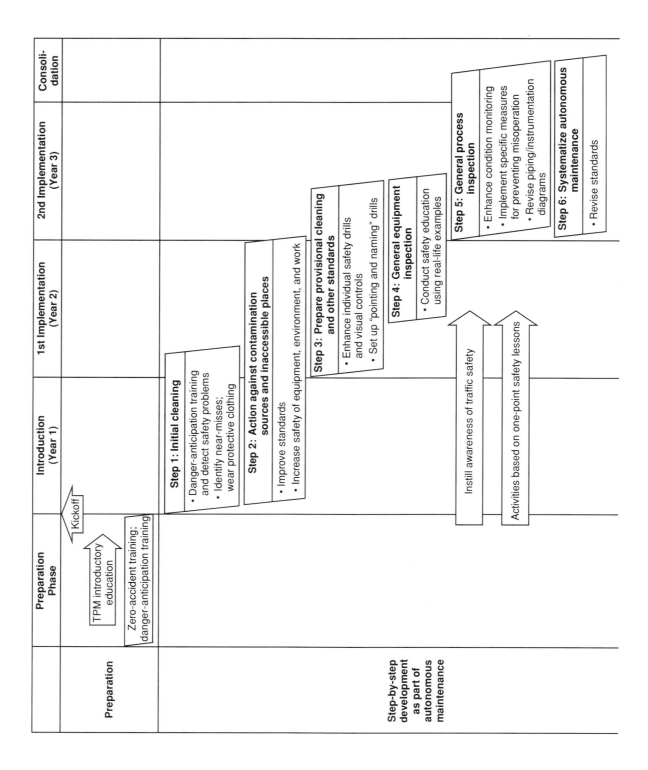

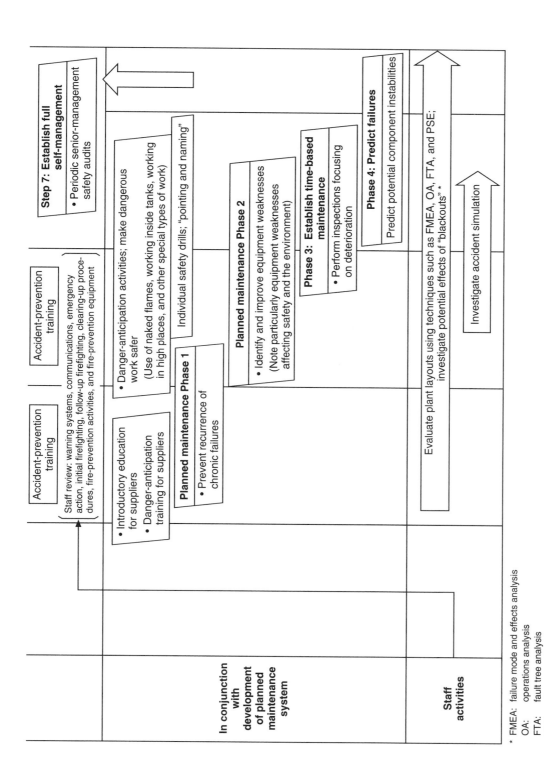

Figure 10-3. Step-by-Step Safety Development Program

* FMEA: failure mode and effects analysis
OA: operations analysis
FTA: fault tree analysis
PSE: plant security evaluation

- Start by teaching the zero-accident philosophy. Make people understand the overriding importance of safety.
- Train operators to anticipate danger.
- Avoid having operators clean rotating parts or high (2.5 m or more) places.

Steps 1–3: Establish Basic Safety Requirements

Incorporate safety and pollution awareness into the first three steps of autonomous maintenance in the following ways:

Step 1: As part of initial cleaning, detect and correct any problems that might affect safety or the environment.

Step 2: Improvement activity to facilitate cleaning and inspection also improves safety and the environment by eliminating sources of leaks, spills, and dust. Deal with major contamination sources through focused improvement. Many companies have reformed their plant environments and created clean, tidy workplaces through focused crusades such as a "Zero-Leak Campaign."

Step 3: Include key safety procedures in provisional cleaning and checking standards. Since one-person operation is so common today, also establish individual safety routines.

Pursue the five fundamental activities for a safe workplace. The include 5S improvements, safety checks, visual controls, danger limitation, and traffic safety.

1. 5S. Use the first three S's: *Sort*, (eliminating the unnecessary), *Stabilize* (establishing a permanent place for everything essential), and *Shine* (find ways to keep things clean) — to eliminate leaks and spills and keep everything in its proper place.

2. Perform safety checks. Safety checks should be included in daily cleaning and inspection activities. The time required for these decreases with practice.

3. Visual control. Visual systems such as color-coding make abnormalities more apparent and improve workplace safety.

4. Damage limitation. Implement damage-limitation systems. Check safety equipment regularly, and conduct periodic safety drills.

"Traffic" safety. Conduct zero "traffic-accident" campaigns (treat "traffic safety" as the basis of workplace safety). While it is important to follow the

rules, to achieve safety in a rapidly changing environment, actively eliminate all sources of danger. This helps to sharpen people's sense of safety.

Steps 4–5: Develop Equipment and Process-Competent People

The more people know about their equipment and processes, the more safely they can work. Link safety education and training to skills training through the use of accident case studies. The number of accidents rises in proportion to the number of minor stops, so attack accidents and problems by enhancing condition monitoring of equipment and plant.

Steps 6–7: Consolidation

Take each step in turn, without rushing or omitting anything, until everyone becomes confident and knowledgeable about safety.

One-point Safety Lessons

Starting at Step 1, collect examples of near misses and compile them into one-point lesson sheets. Use these to improve safety knowledge and consciousness. Do the same for traffic safety.

Phase-by-Phase Development and Planned Maintenance

Today, companies contract out more and more major maintenance work. When introducing TPM, companies should also give refresher training in accident prevention to subcontractors. Focus on preferred subcontractors first.

Planned maintenance aims to eliminate unexpected failures, and operating levels gradually improve as the four implementation phases are completed. It entails much dangerous activity, however, such as introducing new equipment, large-scale rebuilding, shutdown maintenance, and nonroutine work. Design a safety program for such tasks, and implement it in conjunction with subcontractors. Make preliminary discussions particularly thorough, and identify the more dangerous types of work (both joint and individual).

Most serious accidents and pollution incidents are equipment-related. Rank failures and problems in terms of their danger and environmental impact, and institute a systematic safety program for priority equipment that decreases failure frequencies and deterioration rates. Figure 10-3 shows how to develop a safety program in conjunction with a planned maintenance program.

Staff Activities

Process plants can be particularly dangerous. When confronted with complex engineering problems concerning process or equipment safety, draw on the specialized knowledge of your company's engineering department or equipment manufacturers. The bigger the plant, the more important it is to avert mishaps.

Safety engineers have established systems for dealing with safety and environmental problems. Staff departments must prepare comprehensive safety checklists and ensure that no potential problems have been overlooked. This is a vital part of risk management. For example, the blackout simulation noted in Figure 10-3 means investigating whether the plant remains safe even if services such as electricity, steam, water, and compressed air for instrumentation are suddenly cut off as a result of earthquakes, storms, and so on.

EXAMPLE OF AUDIT

A characteristic feature of TPM is the practice of holding self-audits and senior-management audits at the end of each development program step. (See Chapter 4 for a discussion of audits.) Daicel Chemical Industries' Harima Plant evaluated autonomous-maintenance 5S activities by following the procedures outlined in Figure 10-4 and using evaluation criteria shown in Table 10-1. The 5S's are the foundation of zero accidents and pollution. Using this kind of evaluation checklist, some workplaces managed to raise their scores from 50 points to 90 points or more within three years.

SPECIFIC STRATEGIES FOR ELIMINATING ACCIDENTS AND POLLUTION

Although TPM initially focuses on equipment, its goal is to establish conditions that reflect an understanding that production plants are people-machine systems. Approach zero accidents and pollution from both angles. This section reviews some key strategies for preventing accidents that originate both in people's behavior and in equipment.

Preventing Accidents that Originate in Behavior — Making People Safety-Conscious

In the first autonomous maintenance step, operators hunt for disorders and abnormalities in the working environment and equipment. Many of these

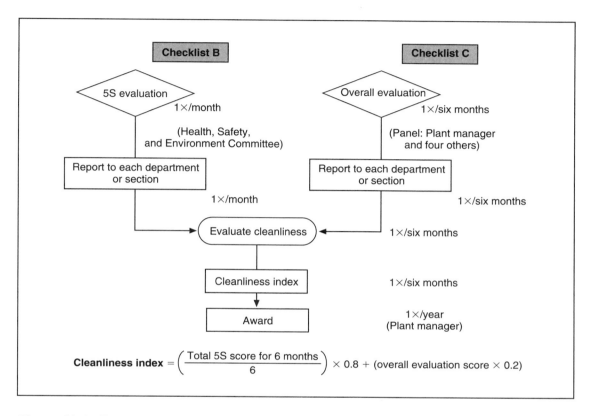

Figure 10-4. Procedure for Evaluating Cleanliness

faults compromise safety, and workers must be able to recognize them. Autonomous maintenance groups must therefore learn exactly what constitutes a safety problem. Useful training materials might include collections of safety checkpoints such as those shown in Table 10-2, and safety audit sheets such as those developed by Sekisui Chemical's Shiga Rittō Plant (Table 10-3).

In addition to potential safety problems, it is also important to detect possible sources of pollution, such as excessive vibration, noise, smells, and scattered powder. Employees correct deficiencies and disorders during Step 2 of the autonomous maintenance program, and it is best to start with those that compromise safety. Improving the safety of their own workplaces gradually sharpens operators' safety consciousness. Their behavior also changes. The number of times they slip, stumble, or get caught in machinery inevitably decreases.

Table 10-1. Overall Evaluation Checklist

Department: _PAD No.3 Workroom_   **Evaluation date:** _10/13/87_   **Evaluator:** _Rieser_

Item	5 pts	4 pts	3 pts	2 pts	1 pt	Comments
1. Has initial cleaning (Step 1) been performed thoroughly?		◯				_Work hard to maintain and improve conditions based on the 3-S maintenance criteria_
2. Have contamination sources been listed and are countermeasures being steadily implemented?	╳		╳			_Not applicable_
3. Are improvement suggestions being actively made?		◯				_Target achieved. Keep up the good work_
4. Is there enthusiasm among all team members for improving cleanliness?		◯				_Activity boards could be improved_
5. Has the room been carefully cleaned, including walls and ceiling?	◯					_Constant effort is important. Keep trying to maintain and improve present levels_
6. Have equipment, accessories, tools, etc. been overhauled; are they free of rust and peeling paint?		◯				_After cleaning, paint parts requiring rust protection in standard colors_
7. Have matchmarks been applied to important nuts and bolts to facilitate detection of looseness?			◯			_Establish fixed criteria for deciding which nuts and bolts are important, and apply matchmarks to the important ones_
8. Are control ranges clearly marked on ammeters, voltmeters, and pressure gauges, and are instruments securely fixed in readily visible locations?	╳		╳			_Not applicable_
9. Has the necessary safety equipment been correctly installed, and is it tested regularly?	╳		╳			_Not applicable_
10. Are contents and flow directions clearly displayed on pipes (color-coding contents), and are insulation and other items undamaged?	◯					_There are few pipes, and these are being well maintained. No particular comment_
11. Are passageways and work areas clearly marked, tidy and well-organized?		◯				_Passageways are difficult to mark, and work areas are clearly defined by the type of work performed in them, so the present situation is satisfactory_
12. Are required jigs, tools, and accessories provided, are their quantities marked, and are they stored in the correct places? Are any unnecessary?		◯				_Jigs, tools, and accessories are organized and stored well. More must be done to indicate monthly usage and other data_
13. Are operation checks being performed correctly on principal machinery and equipment, and are accurate records kept?		◯				_Be sure to enter required data. Initial instruction is important_
14. Are warning signs for explosives, flammables, organic solvents, radiation, pressure vessels, high voltage, etc. correctly displayed where necessary?	◯					_No comment_
15. Is protective clothing clean, tidy, and stored in the right places? Is it properly checked?	╳		╳			_Not applicable_

Table 10-2. Safety Checkpoints

Item	Checkpoints	Checked	Remarks
1. Covers, handrails, etc.	• Have covers been fitted to prevent scattering of chips, coolant, etc? • Have safety covers been fitted over dangerous mechanisms such as rotating and sliding parts? Are they in good condition? • Have platforms and walkways been installed to facilitate cleaning, checking, adjustment, and lubrication? • Are guards, handrails, stoppers, and other safety devices intact? • Are fixed ladders over 2m high equipped with back guards? • Are handrails provided around walkways and openings?		
2. Danger points	• Are inspection lights provided in pits and other dark areas? • Are work floors level and free of slippery spots? • Are transport devices such as chutes and conveyors safe and smooth-running? • Do doors of facilities such as soundproof rooms open both ways? • Is there any danger from falling objects? • Is there any risk of being burnt by touching steam pipes and other hot objects? • Are spaces such as warehouses and underground rooms properly equipped with exit signs and emergency lighting?		
3. Operability	• Are start buttons, levers, and control panels appropriately positioned? • Do all levers, handwheels, and other controls operate easily? • Are equipment weights clearly displayed?		
4. Safety equipment	• Does all fire-prevention equipment (sprinklers, smokeproof shutters, fire hydrants, gas detectors, fire extinguishers, etc.) work correctly? • Are emergency shutdown devices functioning properly? Are emergency stop buttons close at hand? • Are any operating buttons positioned so as to invite misoperation? • Do all klaxons, warning lamps, interlocks, limit switches, and similar devices operate correctly?		
5. Danger and safety signs	• Are high-pressure gases, hazardous materials, chemicals, etc. correctly indicated? • Are adequate warning signs provided for toxic gases, asphyxiatory gases, and similar dangerous substances? • Are speed limits clearly posted? • Are danger signs provided on live high-voltage cables? • Are all necessary warning signs *(No Gloves, Beware Rotating Parts, Mind Your Head, Watch Your Step, etc.)* provided?		
6. Passageway safety	• Have all temporary articles been authorized? Are any walkways unobstructed? • Are work areas, safety routes, and so on clearly marked? • Are storage areas for fuel, oxyacetylene cylinders, and so on properly enclosed and marked?		

Table 10-3. Safety Audit Sheet

Step 1 General Inspection of Danger Sources (Rotating and sliding parts)	Plant or equipment: _____ Audit date: ____/____/____ Auditor: _____ Type of audit: ☐ Self-audit ☐ Group-leader audit		
Item	**Evaluation criterion**	**Eval- uation**	**Remarks**
ROTATING AND SLIDING PARTS			
1. Are any rotating parts exposed?	Covers secure, no room to insert hand from behind		
2. Are rotating shafts free of projections (screws, couplings, etc.)?	Set bolts should be of the lost-head type		
3. Can fingers be trapped by the movement of pistons, carts, etc?	At least 3 cm between moving part and frame, etc.		
4. Must any adjustments be performed close to working machinery?	Stop machinery to perform adjust- ments (locate moving parts where they cannot be accidentally touched)		
5. Is there any possibility of straying carelessly into a danger area while a machine is running?	Isolate by means of fencing or chains		
6. Are any roller intakes exposed?	Protect with covers or bars		
7. Are important covers (ones that help prevent serious accidents) secured by interlock devices?	Equipment should stop automatically when such a cover is removed		
8. Is there any possibility of getting caught in screw mechanisms?	Display reverse rotation or rotor attachment		
9. Are blower intakes safe?	Cover with wire mesh		
10. Are pneumatic and hydraulic cylinders properly bled?	Take measures to protect against falling objects		
11. Are rotation directions clear?	Display clearly		
12. Are danger points clear?	Indicate clearly using signs or color-coding		
EMERGENCY SHUTDOWN			
1. Are emergency stop buttons positioned for easy operation?	Mark locations clearly, and position for self-operation in emergency		
2. Are emergency stop buttons appropriately shaped and colored?	Color in red, use mushroom-shaped buttons, bars, etc.		
3. Does the equipment shut down safely when an emergency stop button is pressed?	Rollers and other closing devices open (power is released)		
MANAGEMENT			
1. Are "pointing and naming" drills displayed in important locations?	Indicate clearly		
2. Are hidden danger sources being detected and corrected (including work methods)?	Display so that everyone understands		
3. Are people retrained when work or equipment is altered?	Manuals prepared and suitably revised; training results recorded		

Evaluation Example:
Use the assessment criteria (★) to indicate whether an improvement has been completed. For fairness, if it is impossible to achieve this level right away, assess as corrected (◯) if the following two conditions are satisfied:
1. An action plan list (5W1H) has been prepared for achieving this level.
2. Color codes, warning signs, and prohibitions are satisfactorily displayed.

Pass/fail Criteria:
1. **Fail** if four or more slight danger points (ones that could lead to minor accidents) have been missed
2. **Fail** if even one critical danger point (one that could lead to a serious accident) has been missed
3. **Pass** if all deficiencies have been corrected

Near-Miss Analysis

Figure 10-5 illustrates the Heinrich principle, derived from an analysis of about half a million safety-related incidents in industry.* The study showed that there were approximately 300 near misses for every serious injury or death.

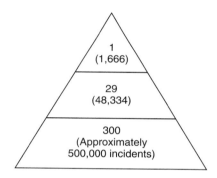

1
(1,666)

29
(48,334)

300
(Approximately
500,000 incidents)

Figure 10-5. The Heinrich Principle

Figure 10-6 shows an analysis of near misses at a certain factory in terms of the "blind spots" that led to them. Take near misses seriously. Use why-why analysis to probe their root causes, and minimize trial-and-error behavior.

Danger Anticipation

It is hard to prevent unanticipated events. The blind spots analyzed in Figure 10-6 reinforce the importance of safety routines known as danger-anticipation activities. Sumitomo Metals developed safety-routine training in 1974. Subsequently, the Central Industrial Accident Prevention Association (in Japan) adopted it as a program entitled "Round-IV Safety-Routine Training" and many Japanese businesses now practice it. The best way to minimize accidents caused by employee behavior is to establish accident-prevention training and create workplaces in which areas of potential danger are clearly visible.

---

* Considered the father of modern industrial safety, H. W. Heinrich (*Industrial Accident Prevention*, 5th Edition, McGraw-Hill, 1980) first propounded his philosophy and approach to understanding and preventing accidents in 1931.

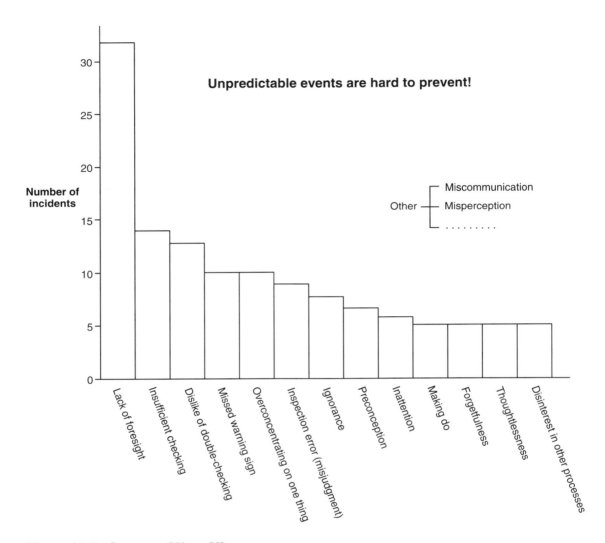

Figure 10-6. Causes of Near Misses

People's moods and the situation in the workplace constantly change. Establish "individual danger-anticipation activities" (individual safety routines) for people who work by themselves, and never stop looking for ways to make dangerous work safer.

Error-Prevention Measures

Operating skill consists of three elements:

- Accurate *perception* of the situation or information.
- *Decision* to act correctly based on this perception.
- Swift *action* based on this decision.

Misoperation occurs if an error is made at one of these points or if operating skill is insufficient. Figure 10-7 illustrates this process and lists the main causes and countermeasures. The plant in this example achieved excellent results by devising specific strategies based on this analysis. *Pointing and naming* (confirming safety points by hand and voice signals) during important operations and actions helps prevent mistakes by focusing operator attention. For it to be effective, however, the operator must have considerable knowledge and experience of the work and understand the real importance of the pointing and naming procedure. Figure 10-8 shows some experimental data on its effectiveness.

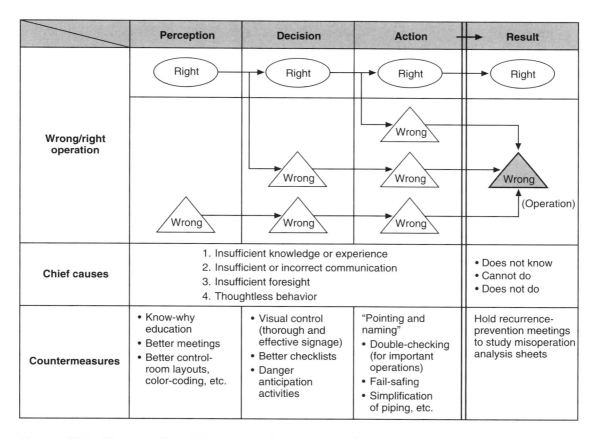

Figure 10-7. Misoperation Philosophy, Causes, and Countermeasures

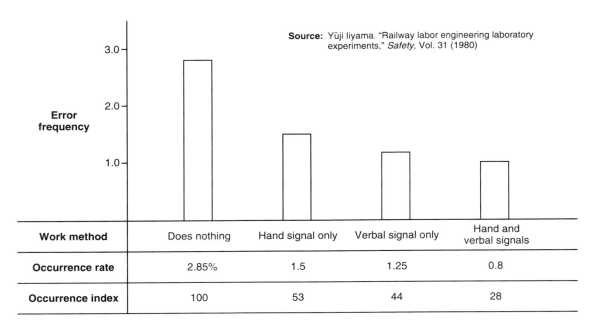

Source: Yūji Iiyama. "Railway labor engineering laboratory experiments," *Safety*, Vol. 31 (1980)

Work method	Does nothing	Hand signal only	Verbal signal only	Hand and verbal signals
Occurrence rate	2.85%	1.5	1.25	0.8
Occurrence index	100	53	44	28

Figure 10-8. Effectiveness of "Pointing and Naming"

Addressing Sources of Human Error (The Manager's Role)

Careless errors do not always lead to accidents; they only cause an accident when the error is dangerous. While it is impossible to train people never to make mistakes, they can learn to be safety-conscious. This is why different plants doing exactly the same work (with the same potential for careless errors) have very different safety records. Managers play an important part in these results, since they are responsible for the way everyone addresses safety issues (i.e. for making people safety-conscious).

Former Nihon University professor Kuniye Hashimoto classifies people's level of awareness according to the scheme shown in Table 10-4. Dozing off at the wheel and driving under the influence of alcohol correspond to phases 0 and 1 respectively. Obviously this lowers the reliability of the driving and makes an accident likely. Phase 3 — normal, clear, and active — is the most desirable state, but people cannot maintain it for long. Operators can return themselves to this state by pointing and naming when performing important actions, which decreases the risk of error.

Most work is performed in phase 2 — normal, relaxed, passive — where errors are unlikely but still possible. Fail-safe design is one way of counteracting this. Phase 4 is a hypernormal, overstressed state that arises when something out-of-the-ordinary occurs. The reliability of people's actions decreases in

Table 10-4. Awareness Levels **Source:** Kuniye Hashimoto.
Safety Engineering, Vol. 18 (1979).

	State of Consciousness	Attention	Psychological State	Reliability
Phase 0	Unconscious	Zero	• Asleep • Blackout	Zero
Phase 1	• Subnormal • Semi-conscious	Inattentive	Fatigue, monotony, drowsiness, inebriation	0.9 or less
Phase 2	normal relaxed	• Passive • Introverted	• Restful routine activity • Resting • Normal operation	0.99–0.9999
Phase 3	normal clear	• Active • Positive	Positive action	0.999999 or above
Phase 4	• Hypernormal • Overstressed	• Fixed on one point • Judgment suspended	Emotional or excited state Panic	0.9 or below

Note: Phase 3 is the optimal state for safety, but people cannot maintain this state for long. If they try to force themselves to remain in it, they become fatigued and revert to Phase 1. Remaining in Phase 2 during routine operation and deliberately switching to Phase 3 by practicing "pointing and naming" during nonroutine events is an effective way of improving safety.

this state, because their judgment is clouded. Remember that since people's psychological state affects their behavior, safety activities must take account of human characteristics such as those shown in Table 10-4. The following safety activities, for example, are integral to TPM:

Improve central control rooms. An individual can absorb and act on only so much information at any one time. Decrease the quantity and improve the quality of information presented to operators, and make instrument dials and gauges easy to read.

Use training equipment such as simulators. People's error rates shrink as their experience grows, but operators in safe plants have little opportunity to learn from experience of real problems. Simulation practice is therefore becoming more and more important.

Manage physical and mental health. Tired, impatient, bored, or angry operators are more likely to cause accidents. Rational, consistent, unstressed, safe behavior is needed. Management must create and sustain a congenial working environment.

Assuring Safety in Construction Work

Whether it is regular servicing or emergency repairs, maintenance work involves many non-routine tasks. Sometimes, maintenance personnel must work in cooperation with subcontractors, which demands excellent communication. It is vital to eliminate dangerous situations and behaviors. Table 10-5 lists some particularly hazardous types of work and their key safety points. To achieve the zero-accident goal, assess subcontractors' skills and safety awareness, provide any necessary safety training, and perform joint safety patrols of the workplace during operations.

Table 10-5. Hazardous Maintenance Work and Key Safety Points

Type of Work	Safety Point
Use of naked flames	Check for residues before working inside columns, tanks, or pipes Ensure all flames are completely extinguished after use
Opening pipes and vessels	Test for residues, residual pressures, etc. (These sometimes change with time)
Working inside columns and tanks	Check for sufficient oxygen, test ambient gases, wear protective clothing
Working in high places	Check footholds, safety nets, lifelines, etc., and take precautions against dropped tools
Collaborative work	Use verbal confirmation and other signals, especially when switching machinery on and off
Raising and lowering	Discuss work thoroughly and mark off prohibited area clearly
Moving heavy machinery	Mark work area clearly and prevent contact with other equipment

Preventing Accidents that Originate in Equipment

Designers study equipment reliability in depth, but completed equipment is never perfect. Even when nearly perfect at the outset, equipment subsequently may deteriorate, break down, or cause problems. And operators will make mistakes.

Plants have the potential to cause accidents, and accidents may occur if the staff does not deal with abnormalities correctly. This does not imply, however, that accidents are inevitable. To prevent accidents originating in equipment, implement carefully planned safety strategies.

The Path from Plant Disorder to Accident

A plant that has hitherto operated normally may become abnormal for some reason or other. If the staff does not deal with abnormality correctly, the system becomes unsafe. Figure 10-9 illustrates this qualitatively. No time scale is indicated; a plant can move almost instantaneously from an apparently stable state to a highly unstable one that leads to an accident.

Plants pass through various phases on their way from normal operation to disaster:

Phase 1: Normal operation, stable state.

Phase 2: Signs of abnormality; the system becomes more and more disordered.

Phase 3: Unsteady state, difficult to restore to normal.

Phase 4: Obvious danger as a result of failure or other abnormality, but some damage, leaks of process materials, and fires can be contained within the plant site.

Phase 5: Workers are injured from improper handling of the situation; fires, explosions, or leaks threaten the safety of surrounding community. Company and local disaster-prevention systems mobilize and make efforts to control the situation and prevent secondary effects.

Phase 6: Clearing up after the situation is under control.

As Figure 10-9 shows, various measures are taken as a plant's danger level rises on the way to an accident. General safety measures include the following:

Monitor the process and correct abnormalities. Carried out by operators, this activity corresponds to Phase 2, when an abnormality is still close to its source and the danger level is low. While it may be troublesome, operators can restore normality relatively simply.

Install and check safety equipment. When operators cannot restore normality, they take measures to prevent the abnormality from suddenly becoming a danger, such as checking existing fail-safe devices.

Act against hidden equipment abnormalities and defects. Always closely watch any parts of the equipment that give cause for concern or are exposed to severe operating conditions and liable to deteriorate rapidly. During shutdown maintenance check for hidden abnormalities that cannot be detected during operation.

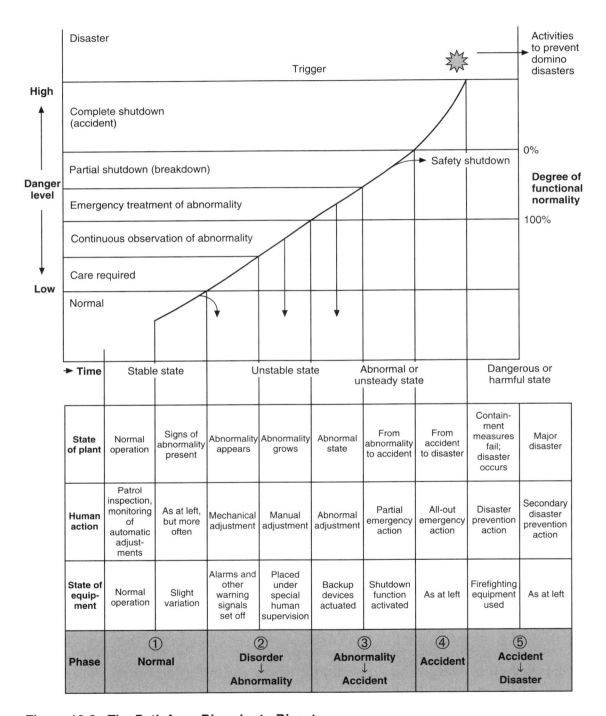

Figure 10-9. The Path from Disorder to Disaster

The following example illustrates how one plant upgraded the preceding general safety activities.

Monitoring Conditions to Detect Abnormality

Every process plant is a Pandora's box of potential abnormalities and failures. To prevent accidents and disasters, be sure to notice warning signs early and take appropriate action.

The petrochemical plant in this example, achieved excellent results by instituting a wide-ranging program of plant health management or "COMO" (condition monitoring) that consisted of routine observation and checking. They developed this program in tandem with Steps 3–5 of the plant's autonomous maintenance program. Figure 10-10 shows the relationship of condition monitoring to other activities, while Figure 10-11 shows part of the overall system.

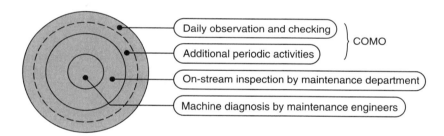

Figure 10-10. Position of COMO (Condition Monitoring Program)

Accident-Free, Pollution-Free Plant Systems

"Safety first" must mean "action first," that is, deeds before words. Assure safety through the following three principal activities:

Daily Safety Activities by Small Groups

The best guarantee of safety is small groups of high-caliber operators who know their equipment and processes well. To create an accident-free, pollution-free system, establish a program of daily activities that operators perform themselves. A safe environment becomes so only through people's own initiative; it cannot be forced. To achieve this, make safety and environmental protection integral to TPM, and make TPM everyone's job.

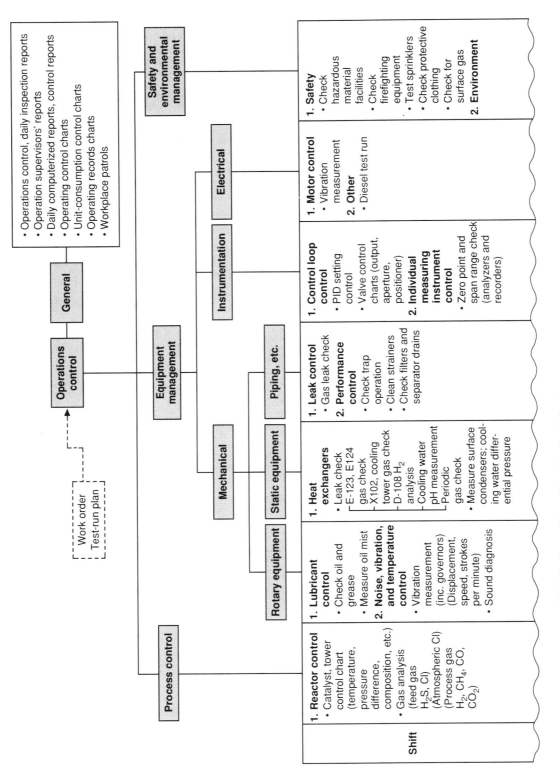

Figure 10-11. Part of the COMO (Condition Monitoring) System

Safety Activities by Engineering Staff (Including Startup Management)

Whether a plant is new or old, insufficient attention to safety engineering leads to uncorrected deficiencies, which will make it difficult to eliminate accidents. Moreover, with fewer human operators in process plants as a result of increasingly sophisticated equipment, computer control, the use of CRT displays, and so on, an important engineering task is to ensure system reliability. Treat safety activities by technical staff as the second pillar of your safety program.

Periodic Safety Audits by Senior Management

Audits and guidance by senior management have an important place in all TPM activities, including safety. Regular audits keep people and organizations on their toes and help raise technical standards. Prepare lists of audit items that relate to safety, health, and pollution; clarify evaluation standpoints and levels; and establish a system of (at least) annual on-site audits by senior managers. This is indispensable for eliminating accidents. Figure 10-12 shows a workplace safety system based on the three principal safety activities.

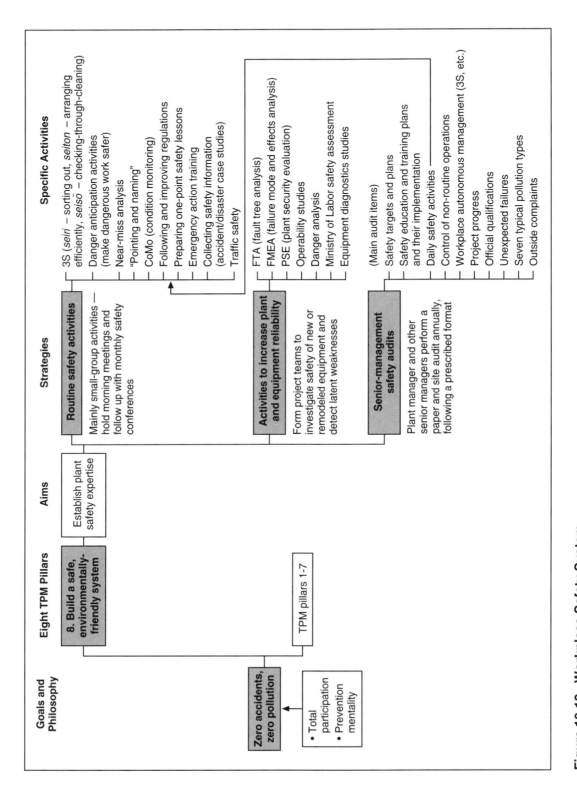

Figure 10-12. Workplace Safety System

REFERENCES

Kuniye Hashimoto. "A Proposal for Safety Ergonomics," (in Japanese). *Safety Engineering*, Vol. 18, No. 6: 306–314, 1979.

Yūji Iiyama. "The Utility and Application of Pointing and Naming," (in Japanese). *Safety*, Vol. 31, No. 12: 28–33, 1980.

Japan Institute of Plant Maintenance, ed. Proceedings. *1989 National Industrial Health and Safety Convention* (in Japanese). Tokyo: Japan Institute of Plant Maintenance, 1989.

Kōgaito Chōsa Iinkai, ed. *White Paper on the Resolution of Pollution Disputes* (in Japanese). Tokyo: Ministry of Finance Printing Bureau, 1989.

Mitsuo Nagamachi. *Behavioral Science for Safety* (in Japanese). Tokyo: Central Industrial Accident Prevention Association, 1984.

Eiji Ohshima, ed., *A Practical Dictionary of Equipment Diagnostics and Predictive Maintenance* (in Japanese). Tokyo: NTS, Fuji Technosystems, 1988.

Yoshikazu Takahashi and Takashi Osada. *TPM.* (English version) Tokyo: Asian Productivity Organization, 1990.

11
TPM Small-Group Activities

A distinctive feature of TPM is its development through companywide participation in small group activities. This chapter examines some of the distinctive features of TPM small groups, how they are organized, their roles at every level, and how they can be supported through careful planning, management, and leadership.

CHARACTERISTICS OF TPM SMALL-GROUP ACTIVITIES

TPM activities are not voluntary but part of people's daily work. This is one of the basic differences between TPM activities and QC-circle activities.

TPM Small Groups and QC Circles Compared

The original QC circles (in Japan) were small groups of front-line supervisors who met voluntarily to study QC techniques. Now, they are mainly small, temporary task forces set up to tackle specific problems as part of TQM. QC circles are always formed on employees' own initiative and consist mainly of front-line people. While encouraged and supported by management, the groups have no particular connection with the regular organizational hierarchy.

In contrast, small groups in TPM are part of the standing organization. Members direct their activities toward achieving corporate objectives by solving the problems of the organization as a whole. Although they act autonomously, they do so within the existing organizational framework. For example, TPM makes caring for equipment as part of everyone's job. To promote and support this aim, TPM small groups under the control of the permanent organization systematically develop equipment-care activities such as cleaning, checking, and lubrication. Other differences between QC circle and TPM activities are outlined in Table 11-1.

351

Table 11-1. QC Circles and TPM Small Groups

		QC Circles	TPM Small Groups
Position in organization		No relation to permanent organization (informal organization)	Built into permanent organization (formal organization)
Leader		Elected by circle members	Managers and supervisors
Time for group activities	During working hours	Not allowed	Allowed with supervisor's permission
	After work	No compensation	Compensation (overtime/holiday pay, etc.) on supervisor's approval
Topics and targets		Selected freely by circle members	Must accord with corporate/plant objectives

TPM Small Groups Implement the TPM Objectives of Top Management

TPM combines top-down management-by-objectives with bottom-up, front-line, small-group activities. Figure 11-1 illustrates the mechanism of TPM promotion based on this philosophy. The success or failure of TPM hinges on the degree of commitment from senior management. TPM is bound to succeed if senior managers truly understand and champion it.

Top management begins by incorporating TPM promotion policy and goals into the basic business policy of the company. The TPM objectives and expectations of management are thoroughly communicated to every employee at every level. Each small group must then set its own targets to satisfy those expectations. This is how the TPM small-group system works. Although TPM small groups operate autonomously within their terms of reference, they always remain under the overall direction of the formal organization.

Structure of Overlapping TPM Small Groups

TPM small-group activities are an integral part of the formal activities of the organization. TPM small groups encompass the whole of the organizational hierarchy, from top management through middle management to the front line.

This top-to-bottom integration is accomplished through overlapping small groups, as shown in Figure 11-2. Group leaders at one level are group members at the next higher level. In this way, the groups link together to form an interlocking pyramid. Figure 11-3 shows a typical example. The small group at the top of the pyramid might consist of a number of department managers headed by the CEO, a senior vice-president, or a plant manager. Under this come small groups of section managers led by their department managers, followed (in large organizations) by subsection managers led by their section managers, and supervisors led by their subsection managers. The base of the pyramid consists of front-line workers led by their supervisors or work-team leaders.

Because group leaders are leaders at one level of the organizational hierarchy and members at the next higher level, they act as linchpins, facilitating horizontal and vertical communication. This small-group structure is identical to the structure of the organization itself.

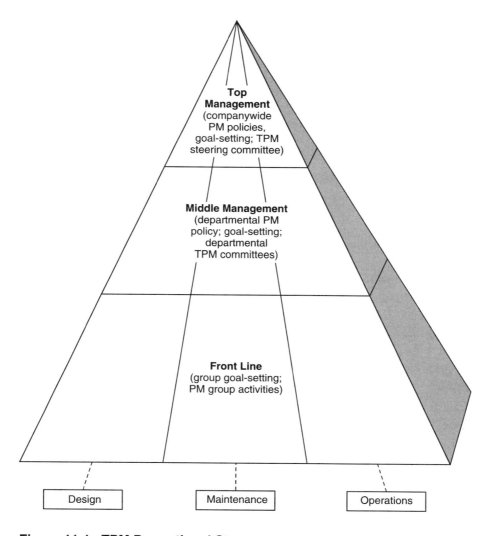

Figure 11-1. TPM Promotional Structure

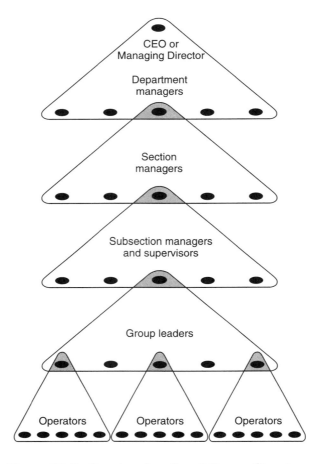

Figure 11-2. Overlapping Small Group Structure

PURPOSE AND OPERATION OF TPM SMALL GROUPS

The goal of TPM is to maximize the overall effectiveness of production systems through total participation and respect for the individual. In other words, TPM aims to develop both the company and its individual employees. Specifically, TPM aims to bring equipment to peak operating condition by eliminating the losses that hamper plant effectiveness. This brings benefits such as greater safety, 100 percent reliability in meeting production plans, quality stabilization and improvement, cost reduction, and strict observance of delivery dates. Thus, TPM boosts corporate performance and, in the process, creates lively, meaningful workplaces.

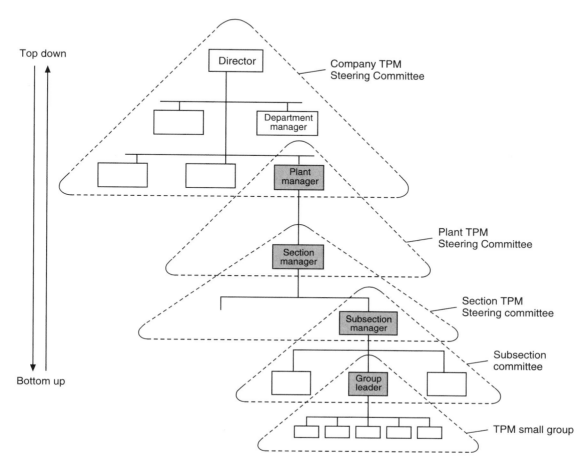

Figure 11-3. Typical Example of Overlapping TPM Small Groups

TPM promotes the mental outlook and behavior required to achieve these objectives through small-group activities. Therefore, the aims of TPM small-group activities are the aims of TPM itself (Figure 11-4).

TPM Small Groups in Action

For a small-group system to operate effectively, management and the program design team must pave the way. Preparatory steps include the following:

- Set up a promotion office
- Offer TPM introductory education to every employee.
- Form small groups
- Select group leaders

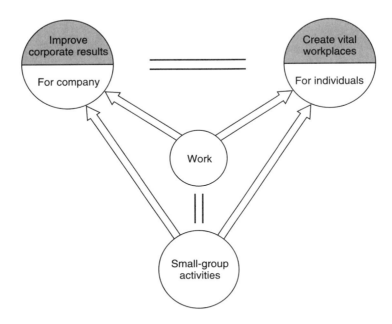

Figure 11-4. The Goals of Small-Group Activities in TPM

Preparation Phase

Set up a promotion office. To promote TPM small groups in accordance with their fundamental objectives and provide adequate support for their activities, a company needs some form of promotion organization. The role of this organization (discussed in detail below) is enormously important in ensuring the success of TPM small-group activities. The TPM promotion organization requires a full-time staff with extensive equipment experience, strong leadership qualities, and the ability to view things fairly and objectively.

Give TPM introductory education to every employee. Ensure that everyone from senior management to front-line employees (including suppliers and subcontractors) knows the background and need for TPM and fully understands why the company is introducing it. Use the education program to get everyone heading in the same direction and make them aware of their departmental and individual roles.

Form small groups. As mentioned earlier, TPM small groups are part of the formal organization, and TPM activities are part of everyone's job. The key point in forming small groups is to fit them to the existing organization. For example, a supervisor may be in charge of five operators handling ten machines. In this case, a small group of six (the five operators led by their supervisor) can deal with those ten machines. This derives from the basic autonomous-maintenance concept of having people look after their own machines. Adopt exactly the same approach when forming small groups at higher levels.

Select group leaders. Many other types of small groups elect their own leaders. Because work and TPM are the same thing, however, the appointed leader in each TPM small group is always the most senior person. For example, the plant manager is the leader of the top small group in a process plant and department managers are its members. Use the same approach when forming lower-level groups.

Implementation Phase

After small groups have been established and their leaders appointed, each group must carefully follow the *act-plan-do-check* cycle. First, each group must:

- Understand its present position and circumstances
- Identify the problems faced by its part of the organization,
- Determine the ideal conditions to aim for

This is an important step for building consensus and aligning team thinking.

On an ongoing basis, groups must also understand how this ideal is being approached — the specific objectives and numerical targets set, whether the plan is being promoted appropriately, whether groups are carrying out the necessary projects, what results they achieve, how these compare with the targets, and whether approach and progress are satisfactory. (See Figure 11-5.)

THE ROLES OF SMALL GROUPS AT EACH LEVEL

The roles of TPM small groups vary at each level of the organization, but all contribute to the overall goals of the program and support the activities of groups in levels above and below.

TPM Promotion Office

The TPM promotion office plays a central role in ensuring that small-group activities in the workplace evolve actively. In developing the TPM program, the office must monitor whether the TPM program is moving in the right direction and at the right speed, decide how to improve teamwork, keep everyone fully involved, and so on. In other words, it must keep the TPM effort on track.

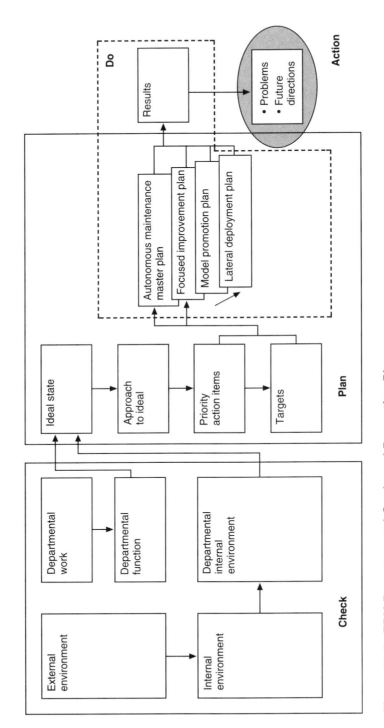

Figure 11-5. TPM Departmental Goals and Promotion Plan

In practice, promotion office staff must do more than administer and issue verbal exhortations. They must actually visit the line and listen to what people are saying, rather than nagging at them to complete the paperwork. People should be able to rely on the TPM promotion office to set a good example and provide concrete help to workplaces experiencing difficulty.

Some promotion offices issue forms without properly explaining their purpose or how to complete them. Then they add insult to injury by blaming workers when the forms return late or not at all. They present a stiff, official front and nit-pick when they find some trifling fault in the workplace. As a result, workers grow confused about their purpose, feel victimized, and become disaffected from the improvement process. To avoid this, staff in the TPM promotion office must monitor the activities of the workplace with genuine care and concern.

Senior-Management Small Groups

Senior-management small groups consist of department or section managers led by the company CEO or a plant superintendent. Such groups are equivalent to a board of directors. Their role is to establish basic TPM policy and objectives in line with plant or company business policy. They must therefore always know whether the plant or company is moving in the direction the policy mandates.

The senior-management small group must also deliberate proposals, opinions, and findings that the TPM promotion office and specialist subcommittees submit, then devolve these down through the organization. For this purpose, they should form a companywide TPM steering committee or similar body to coordinate the whole TPM effort and ensure that decisions are consistent.

Middle-Management Small Groups

Middle-management small groups are groups of section managers led by department managers, or groups of subsection managers led by section managers. Their role is to hammer out policy for their particular departments or sections in accordance with companywide TPM policy and goals. They break down the overall corporate goals into specific subgoals and hand these down to the small groups on the plant floor that are responsible for the actual autonomous maintenance work. To guide the activities, members of these middle-management groups must themselves participate directly in autonomous maintenance.

Middle-management small groups must also decide what losses to tackle through focused improvement and appoint project teams. Essentially, middle-management groups translate policy goals into action targets and often contribute directly to their achievement. For this reason they are considered the nucleus of the small-group system and are essential for good overall results.

Front-Line Small Groups

The role of front-line small groups is to develop an effective autonomous maintenance program, as detailed in Chapter 4. Their most important attributes are responsibility and accountability. In a well-established TPM environment, operators do not blame others when their equipment performs below par. Rather, they look at their own activities first for sources of a problem and take responsibility for pursuing its solution. This sense of ownership — the "I look after my equipment myself" mentality should be encouraged from the outset.

The Two Roles of Group Leaders

Small-group activities in TPM are organized and directed to reap the benefits of teamwork. They aim to capitalize on the synergy of pooling individual strengths and capabilities. Small group leaders play an important part in achieving these aims. Within the formal organization, group leaders have two roles related to "work" and "people," respectively. (See Figure 11-6.) The "work" role is to achieve group objectives by keeping activities on track. The "people" role is to build excellent teams by promoting individual responsibility and mutual respect within groups. A group leader's mission is to create a team whose members contribute fully as specialized individuals and cooperate fully with other members to achieve their assigned objectives.

Figure 11-6. Principal Roles of Group Leaders

Keys to Small-Group Success

The success of small group activities depends on three factors: motivation, ability, and opportunity. While motivation and ability are matters of individual concern, opportunity is a question of environment. Figure 11-7 divides these three requirements into "human" and "environmental" dimensions. Satisfying all three requirements is an essential task for managers and supervisors in their roles as planners and leaders.

The role of management. Highly skilled, motivated, and responsible people emerge when education fulfills individual growth needs in a group context and when training balances hard and soft skills. Such people contribute at a much higher level, both as individuals and team members. Management's first responsibility is to provide the education and training required to develop such a workforce.

Individuals and teams accomplish little, however, when the physical and psychological environment of the workplace hampers team efforts. Management can assure optimum teams performance by endorsing and participating in small group activity at every level as a companywide management strategy. Team efforts will also be enhanced when management places priority on achieving clean, safe, orderly, and visually-managed work environments through activities like the autonomous maintenance program.

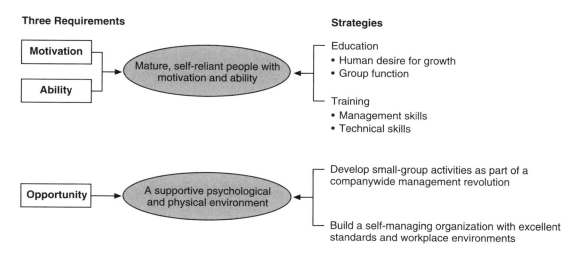

Figure 11-7. The Three Requirements for Small-Group Success

The role of group leaders. People are motivated to work for various reasons, as researchers have shown. No one works solely for financial gain, however. When considering how best to support teamwork, we must understand why we work.

No matter how often they are taken to task, group members will never be motivated if managers do not give them the opportunity to discover for themselves that work and improvement can actually be enjoyable, or that achieving management's objectives for their equipment will make work more satisfying. Moreover, no matter how highly motivated a group is, their enthusiasm will bear no fruit if individual members lack the required skills. Finally, even skilled and motivated groups become discouraged when there is no time or opportunity to exercise those skills. To guard against this, group leaders must support their members' education and at the same work with supervisors and other departments to ensure that their groups have the time and resources to pursue their activities.

12
Measuring TPM Effectiveness

TPM is widely established throughout Japanese industry, where the majority of companies that practice it have had excellent results. It now enjoys a growing reputation both in Japan and abroad. TPM is highly regarded because its benefits are both tangible and sustainable.

When people do not understand exactly how TPM is helping their company, however, the TPM drive will lose focus and direction. Gauging TPM effectiveness is essential for keeping your company's TPM efforts on track. Measure it periodically during your TPM development program, and use your findings to work out new strategies for meeting your goals.

TPM should make a major, lasting contribution to achieving your company's objectives. Systematically coordinate your company's TPM goals with its overall business goals, and regularly review the relationship between them. To establish priorities for TPM activities, break the major TPM goals down into subgoals. In addition to measuring quantitative, tangible results, be sure to evaluate intangible benefits such as improvements in skills and attitudes and the creation of cheerful, lively workplaces.

THE PHILOSOPHY OF SETTING GOALS

Step 4 of the new TPM development program consists of setting basic TPM policy and goals. The most difficult question at this stage is how high above baselines to set improvement goals. When setting goals, first decide what contribution TPM must make to the company's basic policy and to the achievement of its mid- and long-term business objectives. TPM goals must mesh with the company's business goals.

Once set, communicate TPM goals to the entire plant or department. Then, establish the approach, priorities, and strategies required to achieve those goals. Periodically evaluate how TPM goals for the whole plant or departments are being achieved through everyday TPM activities.

The TPM promotion committee plays an extremely important role in meeting TPM goals. Every three or six months, a plantwide or departmental TPM promotion committee should assess progress toward achieving the TPM goals and priorities and set higher goals when the original ones are met. When goals are not met, the committee should review the situation, identify the obstacles, issue appropriate instructions, and restart the challenge.

MEASURING TPM EFFECTIVENESS

Process industries employ a wide variety of equipment. Chemical industries, in particular, use numerous static units such as columns and tanks. Equipment units are typically very large and are connected together by complex piping and instrumentation systems to form continuous processes.

When applied to such long, continuous processes, TPM activities rarely yield instant results. Nevertheless, effectiveness indicators must accurately reflect the effort put into TPM. Be careful to take into account the following cautions on measuring TPM effectiveness.

Indicators Must Clearly Show the Results of Activities

With long, continuous processes, the results of TPM activities may not show up clearly in overall process performance. In a paper mill, for example, the pulping process consists of a continuous chain of subprocesses that extend from the chipyard to the pulping room. As well as evaluating the overall process (for example, the productivity and overall effectiveness of the pulping machines), also measure the performance of each subprocess. For example, measure the performance of the digesting process, the bleaching process, and so on. It may even be necessary to measure the performance of individual equipment units within important subprocesses (for example, the No.1 digester). In this way, you can devise measurement units that clearly show the effect of the TPM activities.

Indicators Must Evaluate TPM Efforts Fairly

TPM effectiveness indicators must be immune to fluctuations in demand or seasonal changes, and must fairly reflect the accumulated results of daily activities and countermeasures. Different departments, such as the production and sales departments, may be assessed together or independently. Whichever method you adopt, select indicators that clearly reflect each department's separate responsibilities.

Indicators Must Reveal Improvement Priorities

Devise indicators that highlight problem areas and tell what problems to solve. Indicators must facilitate timely, accurate assessments of changing situations to ensure efficient TPM progress. They must show each department what currently needs improvement, what benefits they can expect, what direction the improvements should follow, and where to focus the TPM effort.

INDICATOR TYPES

TPM effectiveness indicators can be classified into seven types: management; plant effectiveness; quality; energy-saving; maintenance; health, safety, and environment; and finally training and morale. These are now discussed together with their calculation methods and typical target values.

Management

Management indicators synthesize many individual activities. It is essential to reflect the results of TPM activities in management indicators and show how they help to improve corporate business performance.

To achieve this, work out a TPM policy based on your company's business policy, and set TPM goals consonant with its business goals. Ensure that each department clearly understands its particular responsibilities and sets targets that reflect those responsibilities. In a process plant, for example, the plant manager and other senior managers must review their departments' achievements every six months. If the original targets were met, set higher ones. If not, aim to achieve them without fail over the next six-month period.

Evaluating results and following up TPM activities at six-month intervals is the key to ensuring that your TPM program contributes to the company's business performance. However inspiring your targets, it is too late to do anything if you don't evaluate progress for three years and then discover the company never achieved the targets. Frequent, careful checking and corrective action are essential.

Table 12-1 shows some examples of common management indicators. Add to or subtract from these as necessary.

Table 12-1. Management Indicators

Indicator	Formula	Target	Interval	Remarks
Operating profit	From profit-and-loss account		Annually	Indicates overall company performance
Ratio of operating profit to gross capital	$\dfrac{\text{Operating profit}}{\text{Gross capital}} \times 100$		=	As above
Value-added productivity	$\dfrac{\text{Value added}}{\text{Number of employees}} \times 100$	1.3 - 1.5×	=	Value added per employee
Labor productivity	$\dfrac{\text{Production volume or amount}}{\text{Number of workers (or total working hours)}}$	1.4 - 2.0×	=	Output per labor unit
Cost reduction	Absolute or percentage cost reduction	In accord with annual targets	Semi-annually	Percentage reduction in cost or break-even point
Headcount reduction	Absolute or percentage reduction in number of workers	=	=	Compared with before TPM introduction
Reduction in product stock value	Absolute or percentage reduction in stock value	=	=	As above
Reduction in work-in-process value	Absolute or percentage reduction in work-in-process value	=	=	As above
Equipment investment efficiency	$\dfrac{\text{Production for period}}{\text{Book value of tangible fixed assets at end of period}}$	=	=	Indicates productivity of equipment assets
Plant/labor ratio	$\dfrac{\text{Tangible fixed assets (period end book value)}}{\text{Number of employees (period end)}}$	=	=	Process industries: $ 80,000 - 480,000/person Assembly industries: $ 24,000 - 48,000/person

Plant Effectiveness

The macro-indicator of plant effectiveness is *overall plant effectiveness* (OPE). This is made up of three sub-indicators: availability, performance rate, and quality rate.

As mentioned earlier, it is difficult to show the improvement gained through TPM activities by evaluating an overall process, especially if that process is continuous and composed of many subprocesses. In such a case, split the overall process into subprocesses and measure and evaluate the performance of each. Use the overall effectiveness of the worst subprocess as your subprocess indicator. Also, measure and evaluate the effectiveness of key equipment items in the most important subprocesses. Table 12-2 shows examples of these indicators and their methods of calculation. In addition, measure the number of plant and process failures (process problems) and use these as baselines for improvement.

Quality and Energy-Saving

Quality and energy-saving are important performance indicators. In process industries, treat them as key unit-consumption indicators that relate directly to production costs.

Three of the most important quality indicators are the number and value of customer warranty claims, and the overall yield. In addition to measures of reduced consumption (of electricity, steam, water, and so on), other key energy-saving indicators include ones that actively encourage process modifications and similar improvements. Tables 12-3 and 12-4 lists examples of quality and energy-saving indicators.

Maintenance

Evaluate two aspects of maintenance. First, assess improvements in equipment reliability and maintainability and see how these help to raise plant effectiveness and product quality. Second, evaluate the efficiency of maintenance work. In process industries, it is important to systematize and speed up shutdown maintenance and to achieve smooth, rapid startup by eliminating startup problems. To assess how effectively the maintenance budget is being utilized, find out whether the work is being carried out using the best, most economical methods. Tables 12-5 through 12-8 show examples of maintenance indicators.

Table 12-2. Plant Effectiveness Indicators

Indicator	Formula	Target	Interval	Remarks
Overall plant effectiveness	Availability × performance rate × quality rate	80-90%	Monthly	Macro-indicator of overall process effectiveness
Overall subprocess effectiveness	As above	80-90%	"	Overall effectiveness of bottleneck subprocess
Overall effectiveness of important equipment	As above	85-95%	"	Overall effectiveness of important equipment items within process
Availability	$\dfrac{\text{CT} - (\text{SD loss} + \text{stoppage loss})}{\text{CT}} \times 100$	90% or above	"	Shutdown (SD) losses: time lost through shutdown maintenance, production adjustment, and so on. Major stoppage losses: time lost due to equipment and process failures
Performance rate	$\dfrac{\text{Average actual production rate}}{\text{Standard production rate}} \times 100$	95% or above	"	Indicates plant performance
Standard production rate (t/h)	$\dfrac{\text{Standard production volume}}{\text{Time}} \times 100$	—	Review annually	Standard (nominal) plant capacity
Average actual production rate (t/h)	$\dfrac{\text{Actual production volume}}{\text{Operating time}} \times 100$	Actual value	Monthly	Actual production per unit time
Quality rate	$\dfrac{\text{Production volume} - (\text{defects} + \text{reprocessing})}{\text{Production volume}} \times 100$	99% or above	"	Straight-through rate, obtained by subtracting volume of out-of-spec and recycled product from production volume.
Number of equipment (plant) failures	Actual values for each equipment rank	Rank A: 0 Rank B: 1/10 Rank C: 1/5	"	Actual numbers (for each equipment rank) of unexpected breakdowns leading to production stoppages
Number of process failures	Actual numbers of leaks, contamination incidents, blocks, and similar phenomena	Minimize	"	Include any phenomenon that leads to process or quality abnormalities - also known as "process problems"

Table 12-3. Quality Indicators

Indicator	Formula	Target	Interval	Remarks
Process defect rate	$\dfrac{RC + OS + scrap}{Production\ volume}$	$\dfrac{1}{10}$ or less	Monthly	Rate of generation of recycled product (RC), out-of-spec product (OS), and scrap
Cost of process defects	Total cost of actual losses generated for each type of product	Minimize	"	Recycling costs, downgrading losses, and value/disposal cost of scrap
Number of defects passed on	Number of defects passed on to next process	0	"	Sampling errors, intermediate inspection errors, etc.
Number of warranty claims	Actual number of customer claims	0	"	Number: 1/10 or below. Rate: 30-100 ppm
Value of warranty claims	Actual value of claims for each type of product	Minimize	"	Total value of warranty claims actually disbursed
Overall yield	$\dfrac{Total\ product\ shipped\ (t)}{Total\ raw\ materials\ used\ (wt.)}$	Maximize	"	Overall yield for each type of product

Table 12-4. Energy-Saving Indicators

Indicator	Formula	Target	Interval	Remarks
Electricity consumption	Electricity consumption trend (kWh)	In accordance with annual targets	"	Include both purchased and self-generated power
Steam consumption	Steam consumption trend (t)	"	"	
Fuel consumption	Consumption of fuel oil, natural gas, etc.	"	"	
Water consumption	Service water consumption trend	"	"	Include fresh water, recycled water, and treated water
Lubricant/fluid consumption	Consumption of lubricants and hydraulic fluids	"	"	
Auxiliary materials consumption	Consumption of solvents, paints, etc.	"	"	

Table 12-5. Maintenance Indicators: Reliability and Maintainability

Indicator	Formula	Target	Interval	Remarks
Failure frequency	$\dfrac{\text{Total number of stops due to failure}}{\text{Loading time}} \times 100$	0.10%or less	Monthly	Count stoppages lasting 10 or more minutes
Failure severity rate	$\dfrac{\text{Total stoppage time due to failure}}{\text{Loading time}} \times 100$	0.15%or less	"	Hold total stoppage time to within 1 h/month
Emergency maintenance rate	$\dfrac{\text{Number of EM jobs}}{\text{Total number of PM and EM jobs}} \times 100$	0.5% or less	"	PM = preventive maintenance EM = emergency maintenance
Cost of stoppages due to failure	Stoppage time × cost per unit time	Minimize	"	Include lost production, energy costs, and labor-hour losses
Number of idlings and minor stops	Trend in number of idlings and minor stops	0	Monthly total (daily average)	Count number of idlings and minor stops lasting under 10 minutes
MTBF	$\dfrac{\text{Total operating time}}{\text{Number of stops}}$	2 - 10 times	Monthly	Average failure interval
MTBF	$\dfrac{\text{Total stoppage time}}{\text{Number of stops}}$	$\dfrac{1}{2} - \dfrac{1}{5}$	"	Mean repair time

Table 12-6. Maintenance Indicators: Maintenance Efficiency

Indicator	Formula	Target	Interval	Remarks
Reduction in number of shut-down maintenance days (SMD)	$\dfrac{\text{Previous SMD}}{\text{Present SMD}}$	In accord with annual targets	Annually	The goal is to extend the number of days of continuous production
Vertical startup after shutdown maintenance	Trend in number of startup problems after shutdown maintenance	Minimize	"	Prevent early failures after shutdown maintenance
PM achievement rate	$\dfrac{\text{PM tasks completed}}{\text{PM tasks planned}} \times 100$	90% or above	Monthly	Indicates level of planning of maintenance
CM trend	Trend in CM achievements	At least 10 per person per year	Annually	Level of corrective maintenance (CM) indicates technical ability of maintenance department
Maintenance head-count reduction rate	Trend in reduction in numbers of maintenance personnel	In accord with annual targets	"	

Table 12-7. Maintenance Indicators: Maintenance Cost

Indicator	Formula	Target	Interval	Remarks
Overall maintenance cost rate	$\dfrac{\text{Total maintenance cost}}{\text{Total production cost}} \times 100$	In accord with annual targets	Semi-annually	Indicates the proportion of total costs spent on maintenance
Unit maintenance costs	$\dfrac{\text{Maintenance cost}}{\text{Production volume}} \times 100$	=	=	Maintenance cost per product unit
Maintenance cost reduction rate	Trend in maintenance cost reduction	=	=	Compared with before TPM introduction
Unexpected failure repair cost	Trend in cost of repairing unexpected failures	=	=	=
Maintenance fees	Trend in maintenance fees paid to outside parties	=	=	=
Reduction in spares inventories	Trend in value of spares inventories	=	=	=
Maintenance cost rate	$\dfrac{\text{Total maintenance cost} + \text{stoppage losses}}{\text{Total production cost}} \times 100$	=	=	=

Table 12-8. Other Maintenance Indicators

Indicator	Formula	Target	Interval	Remarks
Contract maintenance rate (1)	Extent due to lack of technology and skills	=	Annually	=
Contract maintenance rate (2)	Extent needed to absorb capacity (labor) shortages	=	=	=
Renovation rate	Proportion of obsolete equipment units updated	=	=	Modernize old-fashioned equipment
In-house development	Trend in number of items of equipment developed in-house	=	=	Include remodeled items
Failure straight-through rate	Failure analysis rate × Countermeasure implementation rate × Recurrence-prevention rate	=	Monthly	To highlight weaknesses in failure countermeasures and prevent backsliding

Health, Safety, and Environment

Every plant appoints managers and supervisors to be responsible for health, safety, and environmental matters. Committee members mount plant patrols to check for problems. Nevertheless, it is still difficult to achieve long periods without accidents and pollution. Develop countermeasures to prevent past accidents and disasters from recurring, analyze the reasons for near-misses, and establish safety drills such as "pointing and naming." Table 12-9 lists some typical health, safety, and environmental indicators.

Training and Morale

Through training and hands-on practice, TPM aims to revolutionize the work force and develop highly skilled, motivated, and self-reliant people who know their equipment and processes intimately. This makes evaluating training and morale particularly important. Table 12-10 provides some typical indicators for this purpose.

EVALUATING TPM

Evaluating TPM involves assessing whether the company has achieved the policy and goals set at the introduction of TPM and realized the intended benefits. It also involves judging how effectively priority topics, action items, and quantitative targets have been pursued through improvement activities.

Naturally, it is essential to set new, higher targets in areas where the company achieved great benefits and met the original targets. In areas where the company found little benefit and missed the original targets, sort out the problems, think up fresh topics, and mount a new challenge. Table 12-11 gives examples of TPM promotion goals, while Table 12-12 illustrates TPM results and their evaluation.

MEASURING TPM BENEFITS

TPM benefits can be both tangible and intangible. While tangible benefits can be expressed quantitatively, intangible benefits, such as revolutionizing the work force and creating bright, cheerful workplaces, cannot be. Intangible benefits are nevertheless extremely important and should not be overlooked. Be sure to evaluate intangibles such as the creation of relaxed, meaningful workplaces, because these are essential requirements in the working world of the 1990s. Figure 12-1 shows both tangible and intangible benefits achieved by Nihon Butyl's Kagoshima Plant.

Table 12-9. Health/Safety/Environment Indicators

Indicator	Formula	Target	Interval	Remarks
Accident frequency	$\dfrac{\text{Number killed or injured}}{\text{Total labor-hours}} \times 10^6$	0	Annually	Number of accidents per million labor-hours
Accident severity rate	$\dfrac{\text{Days lost through accidents}}{\text{Total labor-hours}} \times 1{,}000$	"	"	Number of working days lost through accidents per 1,000 labor-hours
Number of accidents requiring time off work	Actual number	"	"	Keep below industry average
Number of accidents not requiring time off work	"	"	"	"
Number of plant accidents	"	"	"	Fires, explosions, etc.
Number of continuously accident-free days	"		Total number of days	Include accidents requiring and not requiring time off work
Number of near-misses detected	"	In accord with annual targets	Monthly	
Number of danger points spotted by safety patrols	"	"	"	By plant safety patrols
Number of improvements made to dangerous work	"	"	"	Number of safety countermeasures

Health/Safety/Environment Indicators: Environment (Pollution)

Indicator	Formula	Target	Interval	Remarks
Workplace noise level	Measure at fixed points using "noise maps"	Within statutory requirements	Periodic fixed-point measurement	Also measure light levels, dust concentrations, toxic gas levels, and other factors affecting the workplace environment
Number of external complaints	Actual number	0	Annually	Noise, dust, smells, etc.
Number of discharges to outside	"	"	"	Waste oil, sludge, etc.

Table 12-10. Training and Morale Indicators

Indicator	Formula	Target	Interval	Remarks
Number of meetings or time spent on small-group activities	Actual figures	In accord with annual targets	Monthly	Calculate total for overlapping small groups at each organizational level
Number of focused improvement topics registered	Number registered for each type of loss	"	"	Start by tackling the types of loss that will yield the greatest tangible benefits
Cost savings due to focused improvements	Total cost savings of focused improvements	"	"	Total cumulative cost savings due to focused improvements by project teams, the permanent organization, and small groups
Number of improvement suggestions	Actual number	"	"	At least 100/person/year or 8/person/month
Number of outside presentations	"	"	Annually	At learned societies, symposiums, presentation conferences, etc.
Number of one-point lesson sheets	"	"	Monthly	At least 1/person/month
Number of PM trainees	"	"	Annually	Include in-house and external (courses, etc.)
Number of official qualifications acquired	"	"	"	Include mechanical maintenance technicians

Table 12-11. Sample Promotion Goals

Control Item	FY 1983 Baseline	FY 1984		FY 1985		FY 1986		FY 1987	
		1st half	2nd half	1st half	2nd half	1st half	2nd half	1st half	2nd half
Cost reduction (compared with FY 1983)	100	92		91		79		70	
Variable production cost (compared with FY 1983)	100	93	92	93	88	71	61	57	55
Fixed production cost (compared with FY 1983)	100	100		100		97		89	
Labor productivity (compared with FY 1983)	100	⟶				120		130	
Number of failures (monthly rate at end of period)	226	216	125	100	63	38	20	10	5
Number of major failures per period	22	Aim for zero							
Number of quality claims per year	0	Hold to zero							
Number of accidents per year	Req'd time off: 0 No time off req'd: 5	Eliminate both types of accidents							

Source: Onoda Cement, Ofunato Plant

Table 12-12. Sample TPM Results and their Evaluation

◎ Excellent
○ Good

OVERALL RESULTS

Indicator	FY 1983 Baseline	FY 1986 Target		FY 1986 Result	Evaluation
Cost reduction (compared with FY 1983)	100	79	◎	77	• Failure-reduction and energy-reduction activities progressed well despite adverse effect of the appreciating yen, and targets were achieved.
Variable production cost (compared with FY 1983)	100	71 (1st half FY 1986) 61 (2nd half FY1986)	◎	70.0 (1st half FY 1986) 59.4 (2nd half FY 1986)	
Fixed production cost (compared with FY 1983)	100	97	○	96.4	• Fixed-cost increases due to rising personnel costs and prices were prevented through headcount reduction and administrative efficiency improvements. Reducing fixed costs is now our most urgent topic.
Labor productivity (compared with FY 1983)	100	120	○	120	
Number of quality claims	0	Hold to zero	◎	Keep at zero	• Labor productivity targets have been achieved, but further effort is needed.
Number of accidents per year	Req'd time off: 0 No time off req'd: 5	Aim for zero	○	Req'd time off: 0 No time off req'd: 1	

EQUIPMENT EFFECTIVENESS

Number of failures per month	226	20(87/3)	○	25(87/3)	• The PM system is becoming established and beginning to function well; the number of failures has dropped to approximately 1/10 of the baseline figure.
Number of major failures per period	22	Aim for zero	◎	7 (FY 1986 1st half) 2 (FY 1986 2nd half)	
• Failure frequency • Failure severity	0.023 (FY 1984 1st half) 0.019 (FY 1984 1st half)	0.002 (March FY 1987) 0.003 (March FY 1987)	○	0.002 (March FY 1987) 0.005 (March FY 1987)	• There have been no major failures since January 1987. • An operating rate of 100% has been maintained for all kilns since January 1987.
Kiln operating rate	99.1	Aim for 100%	◎	99.5 (FY 1986 1st half) 99.6 (FY 1986 2nd half)	

MORALE

Number of small-group improvements per year	1,142	—	◎	7,530	• Small-group activities have come alive, and the number of improvement suggestions has shot up.
Number of near-misses per year	5,863	—	◎	12,194 (FY 1986 1st half) 11,777 (FY 1986 2nd half)	• Safety consciousness has improved, and workplace safety is now well established.

Source: Onoda Cement, Ofunato Plant

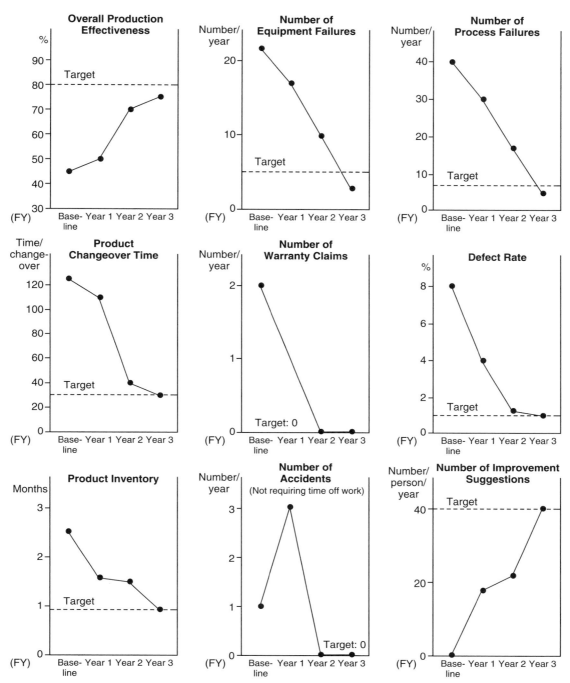

★ TPM targets have been achieved and a zero-loss workplace culture has been created
★ The idea of looking after one's own equipment has taken root and motivation to improve is growing
★ Changes in equipment and people have made everybody confident and positive

Figure 12-1. Example of TPM Benefits

REFERENCES

Seiichi Nakajima, ed. *TPM Development Program* (English edition). Portland, Ore.: Productivity Press, 1989.

Japan Institute of Plant Maintenance, ed. *TPM College: Managers' Course* (seminar text in Japanese). Tokyo: Japan Institute of Plant Maintenance, 1989.

Japan Institute of Plant Maintenance, ed. *TPM Development Programs in Process Industries* (seminar text in Japanese). Tokyo: Japan Institute of Plant Maintenance, 1988.

Appendix

TPM IMPLEMENTATION OUTSIDE JAPAN

Interest in TPM outside of Japan has been growing for a number of years. In the United States, many companies are implementing programs in both process and fabrication and assembly industries, for example, Alcoa, AT&T, Dupont, Exxon, Kodak, Ford, Harley-Davidson, Nippondenso, Procter & Gamble, Tennessee Eastman, Timken, and Yamaha Motor Manufacturing, to name just a few. Since 1990, JIPM has co-sponsored an annual TPM conference with Productivity, Inc. Each year, many companies share their experiences of TPM with many more who are interested in pursuing it. The American Institute of TPM (AITPM) offers a monthly newsletter and plant tours, seminars, and other networking activities on TPM implementation in the United States.

In Europe, TPM is practiced by Volvo Cars Europe in Belgium, the National Steel Corporation and Renault in France, as well as by various Japanese-owned companies. Italian automobile manufacturers are also taking an interest in TPM. In Northern Europe there is strong interest in TPM in Finland, Norway, and Sweden. Finland has established its own PM Prize, modeled on Japan's, and some companies have already succeeded in winning the prize. (Saab Balmet was the first winner in 1988.)

Interest is also growing in Central and South America, as evidenced by many seminars held in Brazil and the first International TPM Congress held in Monterey, Mexico (June, 1993), sponsored by Productivity de Mexico.

In Mainland China, South Korea, and various South East Asian countries, Japanese-owned as well as other companies are actively attending courses and conferences and introducing TPM.

The heightened interest outside Japan is also evidenced by a sharp increase in the number teams being sent to Japan to study TPM. Applications to visit Japanese companies and requests for TPM consultations and courses at JIPM are increasing yearly.

THE PM PRIZE

The PM Distinguished Plant Prize (PM Prize) system was established in Japan in 1964. In the 1960s, the system was used to honor plants that had achieved outstanding results through preventive and productive maintenance. Since 1971, the system has been used to examine and recognize plants that have posted excellent results through their TPM activities. The number of companies in Japan taking up the PM prize challenge has increased steadily in recent years, and winning one of these prizes is now the best way for a plant to demonstrate its manufacturing excellence. Table A-1 shows the plants that have won a PM prize since 1989.*

The Examination Process

Examination for a PM prize takes place in two stages. A preliminary examination is performed during the year before the full examination. If, at this stage, the company has little chance of success in the full examination, a one-year extension may be requested. The company receives many suggestions and comments at this stage so that management knows what must be accomplished before the full examination. Companies find this a great help with their subsequent activities.

The full examination consists of a paper audit and an on-site audit. The paper audit documents the background of the company's TPM activities (where and why it undertook the program), the nature of its activities up to the PM prize examination, and the results obtained. Once the company passes the paper audit, the on-site audit takes place. Table A-2 summarizes the items examined for a Class 1 PM prize. PM prize examiners are university professors in fields relating to equipment management.

---

* A list of winners from 1984 to 1988 can be found in Suzuki, *New Directions for TPM* (Portland, Ore.: Productivity Press, 1992). For winners from 1971 to 1982, see Nakajima, *TPM Development Program* (Portland, Ore.: Productivity Press, 1989).

The Special PM Prize

Businesses that have won a PM prize may try for a higher award, the Special PM Prize, within 3 years of receiving the first award. So far, only a few companies have won the special prize, starting with Toyoda Gosei, Aisin Seiki, Aisin AW, and Nissan for the years before 1992. Many companies have been working toward the prize, however. In 1992, Aichi Steel, Aishin Takaoka, and Osaka Gas received the award. In 1993, six companies were honored: Idemitsu Kosan (Hokkaido Refinery), Kansai NEC, Sekisui Chemical (Musashi Plant), Zexel, Dai Nippon Printing Micro Products Division, and Toyoda Machine Works.

To establish TPM firmly, companies must hold onto whatever gains they have made. Aiming for the Special PM Prize helps them do this, since it forces the company to continue and progress with TPM activities. PM prizes are awarded annually and there is no limit on the number of times a company can win it. It is extremely effective, therefore, for a company to use the PM prize or Special PM prize challenge as a means of fulfilling medium- and long-range business plans.

Table A-1. PM Prizewinning Plants (since 1989)

Fiscal Year	Prizewinners
1989	**Class 1:** Apollo Electronics Ishikawa Ironworks Idemitsu Kōsan Co. (Hokkaidō refinery) INAX (Ueno Tile Works) Osaka Gas (Izumi Kita Plant) Osaka Gas (Nishijima Works) Calsonic (Gumma Plant) Kyūshū Electronic Metals Kubota Steel (Odawara Mill) Kurashiki Chemical Industries San'yō Kokusaku Pulp (Asahikawa Mill) Sekisui Chemical (Tokyo Plant) Sekisui Chemical (Musashi Plant) Daicel Chemical Industries (Aboshi Plant) Daicel Chemical Industries (Otake Plant) Daicel Chemical Industries (Kamisaki Plant) Daicel Chemical Industries (Sakai Plant) Dai Nippon Printing (Tokyo Works, Construction Materials Division) Dai Nippon Printing (Microproducts Division) Dai Nippon Kyoto Micro Dai Nippon Kuki Micro Dai Nippon Tsuruse Micro Tōkai Dai Nippon Printing Zexel Nippon Sheet Glass (Kyoto Plant) Nippon Sheet Glass (Chiba Plant) Nippon Sheet Glass (Yokkaichi Plant) Nippon Sheet Glass (Maizuru Plant) Nihon Spindle Manufacturing Co. Yamaha Motor Rohm **Class 2:** Adeka-Argus Chemical (Mie Plant) Oxilane Chemical (Mie Plant) Kyowa Equipment Suehiro Transport Sekisui High-Polymer Chemical Industries Dai Nippon Porimā (Kashiwa Plant) Dai Nippon Porimā (Kansai Plant) Chiyoda Industries Tsuruoka Brake DGK Tokyo Foundry (Saitama Plant; Head Office) Tōa Kōgyō (Main Plant) Minami Kiso Hatzujo Nihon Denpun Kōgyō Japan Powder Alloys Hokkaidō Dai Nippon Printing Matsuda Parts Industries Musashi Chemical Industries Yoshitama Seito The Lead Co., Inc.
1990	**Class 1:** Aichi Machine Industry (Atsuta Plant Business Unit) Aichi Machine Industry (Matsuzaka Plant Business Unit) INAX (Enokido Plant) INAX (Otani Plant) INAX (Tsukuba Plant) INAX (Tokoname Plant) INAX (Handa Plant) Kayaba Industry (Gifu Kita Plant) Jyatoko

Fiscal Year	Prizewinners	
		Shinko Electric Industries Sekisui Chemical (Nara Plant) Daikin Industries (Shiga Works) Daicel Chemical Industries (Arai Plant) Higashi Atsushi INAX Tokuyama Sekisui Industries (Nan'yō Plant) Tochigi Fuji Industries Co. Toyota Automatic Loom Works Nippon Hi-Pac (Tokyo Office) Nippon Hi-Pac (Nagoya Plant) Bridgestone (Hikone Plant) Matsushita Battery Industrial (Tsujitsune Plant) Rohm Fukuoka
	Class 2:	Atom Chemical Paint Dai-Nippon Hi-Pac Suzuki Parts Manufacturing Daiko Electric Dai Nippon Machine Industries Tohoku Dai Nippon Printing Higashine Shindengen Higashine New Power Sources
1991		Nissan Motor (Tochigi Plant) (Special Prize)
	Class 1:	Volvo Cars Europe Aoyama Mfg Co. Asahi Glass (Sagami Office, Kyōhama Plant) INAX (Onomichi Plant) INAX (Tsuchiura Plant) INAX (Tokoname Higashi Plant) Onoda Cement (Tsukumi Plant) Kayaba Industry (Urawa Plant) Kayaba Industry (Gifu Minami Plant) Kayaba Industry (Sagami Plant) Kyūshū INAX Kyōwa Hakkō Kōgyō (Fuji Plant) Konica (Hino Works) Shatai Kōgyō (Auto Body industries) Shin Nikkei (Hokuriku Plant) Sekisui Chemical (Gunma Plant) Sekisui Chemical (Sakai Plant) Sekisui Chemical (Shiga Mizukuchi Plant) Sony Oita Dai Nippon Printing (Akane Plant, Commercial Printing Division) Dai Nippon Printing (Enokichō Plant, Commercial Printing Division) Dai Nippon Printing (Nara Plant, Business Form Division) Daikin Mfg. Co. (Main Plant) Nichias Corp. (Fukuroi Plant) Nissan Motor (Kyūshū Plant) Japan Hoechst Japan Butyl (Kawasaki Main Plant) Japan Butyl (Kagoshima Plant) Hitachi (Takasaki Plant) Hitachi Metals (Kyūshū Plant) Press Kōgyō (Onomichi Plant) Yazaki Shigen (Hamamatsu Plant)
	Class 2:	Nachi Industries INAX (Taku Plant) Kyūshū Saji Koga Works Daiaji Japan Sekiso Industries (Okazaki Mito Plant) Moroboshi Ink (Tokyo Plant) Yuken Kōgyō Co.

★ : Names of companies and plants are those at the time of winning a PM Prize.

★ : Category-2 Prizes are for enterprises capitalized at $4 million or less and with a work force of under 500.

Table A-2. Criteria for Awarding the PM Prize (Category 1)

Item	Key Points
1. TPM policies and goals	Relation between TPM and company policies TPM policies, goals, and their deployment
2. TPM organization and management	TPM promotion organization, its staffing and operation
3. Equipment improvements for increasing equipment effectiveness	Promotion and benefits of equipment improvements
4. Autonomous maintenance	Promotion of autonomous maintenance, audit system, implementation and 5S (industrial housekeeping) evaluation
5. Maintenance planning and management	Planning and management of maintenance work; maintenance information management; improvement maintenance; equipment diagnostics; lubrication control; and control of spare parts, dies, jigs, tools, measuring instruments, drawings, etc.
6. Education and training	Planning and practice of education and training, number of employees holding technical licenses and other qualifications, evaluation of maintenance knowledge and skills
7. Relation between TPM and management of quality, cost, production volume, and delivery schedules	TPM and quality control, cost control, maintenance costs, production volumes, delivery schedules, resource saving, and energy saving
8. Equipment investment planning and maintenance prevention (MP)	Equipment investment planning, methods of comparing the cost-effectiveness of alternative plans, equipment budgeting, equipment design standardization, MP activities, fixed-asset management
9. Management of industrial safety, hygiene, and the environment	Policy, organization, and results for industrial safety, hygiene, and environmental management
10. TPM results and evaluation	Trend in actual results achieved since TPM kickoff, evaluation of TPM benefits from overall business standpoint

Index

BOOKS FROM PRODUCTIVITY PRESS

Productivity Press publishes books that empower individuals and companies to achieve excellence in quality, productivity, and the creative involvement of all employees. Through steadfast efforts to support the vision and strategy of continuous improvement, Productivity Press delivers today's leading-edge tools and techniques gathered directly from industry leaders around the world. Call toll-free 1-800-394-6868 for our free catalog.

5 Pillars of the Visual Workplace
The Sourcebook for 5S Implementation
Hiroyuki Hirano

In this important sourcebook, JIT expert Hiroyuki Hirano provides the most vital information available on the visual workplace. He describes the 5S's: in Japanese they are seiri, seiton, seiso, seiketsu, and shitsuke (which translate as organization, orderliness, cleanliness, standardized cleanup, and discipline). Hirano discusses how the 5S theory fosters efficiency, maintenance, and continuous improvement in all areas of the company, from the plant floor to the sales office. Presented in a thorough, detailed style, *5 Pillars of the Visual Workplace* explains why the 5S's are important and the who, what, where, and how of 5S implementation. This book includes numerous case studies, hundreds of graphic illustrations, and over forty 5S user forms and training materials.
ISBN 1-56327-047-1 / 377 pages, illustrated / $85.00 / Order FIVE-B178

Becoming Lean
Inside Stories of U.S. Manufacturers
Jeffrey Liker

Most other books on lean management focus on technical methods and offer a picture of what a lean system should look like. Some provide snapshots of before and after. This is the first book to provide technical descriptions of successful solutions and performance improvements. The first book to include powerful first-hand accounts of the complete process of change, its impact on the entire organization, and the rewards and benefits of becoming lean. At the heart of this book you will find the stories of American manufacturers who have successfully implemented lean methods. Authors offer personalized accounts of their organization's lean transformation, including struggles and successes, frustrations and surprises. Now you have a unique opportunity to go inside their implementation process to see what worked, what didn't, and why. Many of these executives and managers who led the charge to becoming lean in their organizations tell their stories here for the first time!
ISBN 1-56327-173-7/ 350 pages / $35.00 / Order LEAN-B178

Productivity Press, Dept. BK, P.O. Box 13390, Portland, OR 97213-0390
Telephone: 1-800-394-6868   Fax: 1-800-394-6286

Corporate Diagnosis
Setting the Global Standard for Excellence
Thomas L. Jackson with Constance E. Dyer

All too often, strategic planning neglects an essential first step and final step-diagnosis of the organization's current state. What's required is a systematic review of the critical factors in organizational learning and growth, factors that require monitoring, measurement, and management to ensure that your company competes successfully. This executive workbook provides a step-by-step method for diagnosing an organization's strategic health and measuring its overall competitiveness against world class standards. With checklists, charts, and detailed explanations, *Corporate Diagnosis* is a practical instruction manual. The pillars of Jackson's diagnostic system are strategy, structure, and capability. Detailed diagnostic questions in each area are provided as guidelines for developing your own self-assessment survey.
ISBN 1-56327-086-2 / 115 pages / $65.00 / Order CDIAG-B178

Cycle Time Management
The Fast Track to Time-Based Productivity Improvement
Patrick Northey and Nigel Southway

As much as 90 percent of the operational activities in a traditional plant are nonessential or pure waste. This book presents a proven methodology for eliminating this waste within 24 to 30 months by measuring productivity in terms of time instead of revenue or people. CTM is a cohesive management strategy that integrates just-in-time (JIT) production, computer integrated manufacturing (CIM), and total quality control (TQC). From this succinct, highly focused book, you'll learn what CTM is, how to implement it, and how to manage it.
ISBN 1-56327-015-3 / 200 pages / $30.00 / Order CYCLE-B178

Implementing a Lean Management System
Thomas L. Jackson with Karen R. Jones

Does your company think and act ahead of technological change, ahead of the customer, and ahead of the competition? Thinking strategically requires a company to face these questions with a clear future image of itself. Implementing a Lean Management System lays out a comprehensive management system for aligning the firm's vision of the future with market realities. Based on hoshin management, the Japanese strategic planning method used by top managers for driving TQM throughout an organization, Lean Management is about deploying vision, strategy, and policy to all levels of daily activity. It is an eminently practical methodology emerging out of the implementation of continuous improvement methods and employee involvement. The key tools of this book build on multiskilling, the knowledge of the worker, and an understanding of the role of the new lean manufacturer.
ISBN 1-56327-085-4 / 182 pages / $65.00 / Order ILMS-B178

Implementing TPM
The North American Experience
Charles J. Robinson and Andrew P. Ginder

The authors document an approach to TPM planning and deployment that modifies the JIPM 12-step process to accommodate the experiences of North American plants. They include details and advice on specific deployment steps, OEE calculation methodology, and autonomous maintenance deployment. This book shows how to make TPM work in unionized plants and how to position TPM to support and complement other strategic manufacturing improvement initiatives.
ISBN 1-56327-087-0 / 224 pages / $45.00 / Order IMPTPM-B178

Productivity Press, Dept. BK, P.O. Box 13390, Portland, OR 97213-0390
Telephone: 1-800-394-6868   Fax: 1-800-394-6286

JIT Factory Revolution
A Pictorial Guide to Factory Design of the Future
Hiroyuki Hirano

The first encyclopedic picture-book of Just-In-Time, using photos and diagrams to show exactly how JIT looks and functions in production and assembly plants. Unprecedented behind-the-scenes look at multi-process handling, cell technology, quick changeovers, kanban, andon, and other visual control systems. See why a picture is worth a thousand words.
ISBN 0-915299-44-5 / 218 pages / $50.00 / Order JITFAC-B178

Kaizen for Quick Changeover
Going Beyond SMED
Kenichi Sekine and Keisuke Arai

Especially useful for manufacturing managers and engineers, this book describes exactly how to achieve faster changeover. Picking up where Shingo's SMED book left off, you'll learn how to streamline the process even further to reduce changeover time and optimize staffing at the same time.
ISBN 0-915299-38-0 / 315 pages / $75.00 / Order KAIZEN-B178

Kanban and Just-In-Time at Toyota
Management Begins at the Workplace
Japan Management Association
Translated by David J. Lu

Toyota's world-renowned success proves that with kanban, the Just-In-Time production system (JIT) makes most other manufacturing practices obsolete. This simple but powerful classic is based on seminars given by JIT creator Taiichi Ohno to introduce Toyota's own supplier companies to JIT. It shows how to implement the world's most efficient production system. A clear and complete introduction.
ISBN 0-915299-48-8 / 211 pages / $40.00 / Order KAN-B178

Manufacturing Strategy
How to Formulate and Implement a Winning Plan
John Miltenburg

This book offers a step-by-step method for creating a strategic manufacturing plan. The key tool is a multidimensional worksheet that links the competitive analysis to manufacturing outputs, the seven basic production systems, the levels of capability and the levers for moving to a higher level. The author presents each element of the worksheet and shows you how to link them to create an integrated strategy and implementation plan. By identifying the appropriate production system for your business, you can determine what output you can expect from manufacturing, how to improve outputs, and how to change to more optimal production systems as your business needs changes. This is a valuable book for general managers, operations managers, engineering managers, marketing managers, comptrollers, consultants, and corporate staff in any manufacturing company.
ISBN 1-56327-071-4 / 391 pages / $45.00 / Order MANST-B178

Productivity Press, Dept. BK, P.O. Box 13390, Portland, OR 97213-0390
Telephone: 1-800-394-6868   Fax: 1-800-394-6286

Modern Approaches to Manufacturing Improvement
The Shingo System
Alan Robinson (ed.)

Here's the quickest and most inexpensive way to learn about the pioneering work of Shigeo Shingo, co-creator (with Taiichi Ohno) of Just-In-Time. It's an introductory book containing excerpts of five of his classic books as well as an excellent introduction by Professor Robinson. Learn about quick changeover, mistake-proofing (poka-yoke), non-stock production, and how to apply Shingo's "scientific thinking mechanism."
ISBN 0-915299-64-X / 420 pages / $23.00 paper / Order READER-B178

Poka-Yoke
Improving Product Quality by Preventing Defects
Nikkan Kogyo Shimbun Ltd. and Factory Magazine (ed.)

If your goal is 100 percent zero defects, here is the book for you – a completely illustrated guide to poka-yoke (mistake-proofing) for supervisors and shop-floor workers. Many poka-yoke devices come from line workers and are implemented with the help of engineering staff. The result is better product quality – and greater participation by workers in efforts to improve your processes, your products, and your company as a whole.
ISBN 0-915299-31-3 / 295 pages / $65.00 / Order IPOKA-B178

A Revolution in Manufacturing
The SMED System
Shigeo Shingo

The heart of JIT is quick changeover methods. Dr. Shingo, inventor of the Single-Minute Exchange of Die (SMED) system for Toyota, shows you how to reduce your changeovers by an average of 98 percent! By applying Shingo's techniques, you'll see rapid improvements (lead time reduced from weeks to days, lower inventory and warehousing costs) that will improve quality, productivity, and profits.
ISBN 0-915299-03-8 / 383 pages / $75.00 / Order SMED-B178

Toyota Production System
Beyond Large-Scale Production
Taiichi Ohno

Here's the first information ever published in Japan on the Toyota production system (known as Just-In-Time manufacturing). Here Ohno, who created JIT for Toyota, reveals the origins, daring innovations, and ceaseless evolution of the Toyota system into a full management system. You'll learn how to manage JIT from the man who invented it, and to create a winning JIT environment in your own manufacturing operation.
ISBN 0-915299-14-3 / 163 pages / $45.00 / Order OTPS-B178

Productivity Press, Dept. BK, P.O. Box 13390, Portland, OR 97213-0390
Telephone: 1-800-394-6868   Fax: 1-800-394-6286

The Visual Factory
Building Participation Through Shared Information
Michel Greif

If you're aware of the tremendous improvements achieved in productivity and quality as a result of employee involvement, then you'll appreciate the great value of creating a visual factory. This book shows how visual management can make the factory a place where workers and supervisors freely communicate and take improvement action. It details how to develop meeting and communication areas, communicate work standards and instructions, use visual production controls such as kanban, and make goals and progress visible. Includes more than 200 diagrams and photos.
ISBN 0-915299-67-4 / 305 pages / $55.00 / Order VFAC-B178

Zero Quality Control
Source Inspection and the Poka-Yoke System
Shigeo Shingo

Dr. Shingo reveals his unique defect prevention system, which combines source inspection and poka-yoke (mistake-proofing) devices that provide instant feedback on errors before they can become defects. The result: 100 percent inspection that eliminates the need for SQC and produces defect-free products without fail. Includes 112 examples, most costing under $100. Two-part video program also available; call for details.
ISBN 0-915299-07-0 / 328 pages / $75.00 / Order ZQC-B178

TO ORDER: Write, phone, or fax Productivity Press, Dept. BK, P.O. Box 13390, Portland, OR 97213-0390, phone 1-800-394-6868, fax 1-800-394-6286.
Outside the U.S. phone (503) 235-0600; fax (503) 235-0909
Send check or charge to your credit card (American Express, Visa, MasterCard accepted).

U.S. ORDERS: Add $5 shipping for first book, $2 each additional for UPS surface delivery. Add $5 for each AV program containing 1 or 2 tapes; add $12 for each AV program containing 3 or more tapes. We offer attractive quantity discounts for bulk purchases of individual titles; call for more information.

ORDER BY E-MAIL: Order 24 hours a day from anywhere in the world. Use either address:
To order: service@ppress.com
To view the online catalog and/or order: http://www.ppress.com/

QUANTITY DISCOUNTS: For information on quantity discounts, please contact our sales department.

INTERNATIONAL ORDERS: Write, phone, or fax for quote and indicate shipping method desired. For international callers, telephone number is 503-235-0600 and fax number is 503-235-0909. Prepayment in U.S. dollars must accompany your order (checks must be drawn on U.S. banks). When quote is returned with payment, your order will be shipped promptly by the method requested.

NOTE: Prices are in U.S. dollars and are subject to change without notice.

Productivity Press, Dept. BK, P.O. Box 13390, Portland, OR 97213-0390
Telephone: 1-800-394-6868   Fax: 1-800-394-6286

ABOUT THE SHOPFLOOR SERIES

Put powerful and proven improvement tools in the hands of your entire workforce!

Progressive shopfloor improvement techniques are imperative for manufacturers who want to stay competitive and to achieve world class excellence. And it's the comprehensive education of all shopfloor workers that ensures full participation and success when implementing new programs. The Shopfloor Series books make practical information accessible to everyone by presenting major concepts and tools in simple, clear language and at a reading level that has been adjusted for operators by skilled instructional designers. One main idea is presented every two to four pages so that the book can be picked up and put down easily. Each chapter begins with an overview and ends with a summary section. Helpful illustrations are used throughout.

Books currently in the Shopfloor Series include:

5S for Operators
5 Pillars of the Visual Workplace
The Productivity Press Development Team
ISBN 1-56327-123-0 / incl. applic. questions / 133 pages
Order 5SOP-B178 / $25.00

Quick Changeover for Operators
The SMED System
The Productivity Press Development Team
ISBN 1-56327-125-7 / incl. applic. questions / 93 pages
Order QCOOP-B178 / $25.00

Mistake-Proofing for Operators
The Productivity Press Development Team
ISBN 1-56327-127-3 / 93 pages
Order ZQCOP-B178 / $25.00

TPM for Supervisors
The Productivity Press Development Team
ISBN 1-56327-161-3 / 96 pages
Order TPMSUP-B178 / $25.00

TPM Team Guide
Kunio Shirose
ISBN 1-56327-079-X / 175 pages
Order TGUIDE-B178 / $25.00

TPM for Every Operator
Japan Institute of Plant Maintenance
ISBN 1-56327-080-3 / 136 pages
Order TPMEO-B178 / $25.00

Autonomous Maintenance
Japan Institute of Plant Maintenance
ISBN 1-56327-082-X / 138 pages
Order AUTMOP-B178 / $25.00

Focused Equipment Improvement
Japan Institute of Plant Maintenance
ISBN 1-56327-081-1 / 138 pages
Order FEIOP-B178 / $25.00

Productivity Press, Dept. BK, P.O. Box 13390, Portland, OR 97213-0390
Telephone: 1-800-394-6868   Fax: 1-800-394-6286

Continue Your Learning with In-House Training and Consulting from the Productivity Consulting Group

The Productivity Consulting Group (PCG) offers a diverse menu of consulting services and training products based on the exciting ideas contained in the books of Productivity Press. Whether you need assistance with long term planning or focused, results-driven training, PCG's experienced professional staff can enhance your pursuit of competitive advantage.

PCG integrates a cutting edge management system with today's leading process improvement tools for rapid, measurable, lasting results. In concert with your management team, PCG will focus on implementing the principles of Value Adding Management, Total Quality Management, Just-In-Time, and Total Productive Maintenance. Each approach is supported by Productivity's wide array of team-based tools: Standardization, One-Piece Flow, Hoshin Planning, Quick Changeover, Mistake-Proofing, Kanban, Problem Solving with CEDAC, Visual Workplace, Visual Office, Autonomous Maintenance, Equipment Effectiveness, Design of Experiments, Quality Function Deployment, Ergonomics, and more. And, based on the continuing research of Productivity Press, PCG expands its offering every year.

Productivity is known for significant improvement on the shopfloor and the bottom line. Through years of repeat business, an expanding and loyal client base continues to recommend Productivity to their colleagues. Contact PCG to learn how we can tailor our services to fit your needs.

Telephone: 1-800-966-5423 (U.S. only) or 1-203-846-3777
Fax: 1-203-846-68

Productivity Press, Dept. BK, P.O. Box 13390, Portland, OR 97213-0390
Telephone: 1-800-394-6868   Fax: 1-800-394-6286